Fundamentals of Competition Management

Preparation and Organization of Design Competitions

In memory of five great friends
and colleagues who unfortunately left
much too early:

Manfredi Anello
Heinrich Burchard
Helmut Hanle
Edi Schwarz
Jafar Tukan

Fundamentals of Competition Management
Preparation and Organization of Design Competitions

Benjamin Hossbach, Christian Lehmhaus, Christine Eichelmann

INDEX – TECHNICAL CONTRIBUTIONS

INTRODUCTION		6
ELEMENTS OF A SUCCESSFUL COMPETITION		10

1	**LAUNCHING A COMPETITION**		**24**
1.1	Competition as a special way of awarding contracts		24
1.2	Competition as a special way of commissioning		24
1.3	The right moment to launch a competition		24
1.4	Concerns against competitions		25
1.5	Considering fundamental issues of a competition		25

2	**RULES FOR COMPETITIONS**		**36**
2.1	Relevant rules and regulations		36
2.2	Rules and regulations in practice		37
2.3	The most important modules of rules and regulations		38

3	**CHOICE OF THE TYPE OF PROCEDURE**		**44**
3.1	The selection of the process		44
3.2	Parameters for determining the competition type		44
3.3	The pros and cons of open competitions		47

4	**MEMBERS INVOLVED**		**54**
4.1	Sponsor		54
4.2	Participants		54
4.3	Jury		54
4.4	Technical experts		58
4.5	Preliminary evaluation team		58
4.6	Professional chambers		58
4.7	Other participants		58

5	**COMPETITION ORGANIZATION**		**60**
5.1	Who organizes competitions?		60
5.2	Compensation for competition management		60
5.3	Competition organization tasks		63
5.4	Commissioning the service of competition management		70

6	**TIME**		**80**
6.1	Total duration		80
6.2	Overall scheduling		80
6.3	Duration of procedures		80

7	**COMPETITION COSTS**		**88**
7.1	What is the total cost of a competition?		88
7.2	Total budget		88
7.3	Calculation of the competition sum		90
7.4	Honorarium for jury members		90
7.5	Further costs		90

8	**PROCEDURE DETAILS**		**92**
8.1	Required information in the competition brief		92
8.2	Admission and/or selection of participants		92
8.3	Jury criteria		94
8.4	Further commissioning		96
8.5	Competition requirements		98

9	**COMMUNICATION DURING THE COMPETITION**		**100**
9.1	Communication despite anonymity?		100
9.2	Jury colloquium		100
9.3	Significance and distribution of the competition materials		100
9.4	Written queries and colloquia		100
9.5	Personal presentations by the competitors and dialogue		103
9.6	"Virtual competition"		104

10	**COMPETITION MATERIALS**		**112**
10.1	Structure		112
10.2	Situation and planning guidelines		112
10.3	Task and program		112
10.4	Sustainability in competition		113
10.5	Illustrations		118
10.6	Plan Documents		118
10.7	Model of the surroundings		120

11	**EVENTS**	**128**
11.1	Event formats	128
11.2	Venues	130
11.3	Furnishing	130
11.4	Event planning	131
12	**PRELIMINARY EXAMINATION**	**138**
12.1	Significance of the preliminary examination	138
12.2	Tasks, team and process planning	138
12.3	Receipt and formal examination	138
12.4	Quantitative testing	140
12.5	Design concept analysis	142
12.6	Involvement of technical experts	142
12.7	Preparing the preliminary examination report	144
12.8	BIM in competitions	144
13	**JURORS' EVALUATION**	**152**
13.1	Importance of the jury meeting for the project and the competition	152
13.2	Preparation	152
13.3	Venue layout, boards for project display	154
13.4	Process	154
13.5	Completeness, chairmanship, approval of the work	155
13.6	Presentation of the designs and report of the experts	157
13.7	Decision-making process in rounds, voting methodology	157
13.8	Comments of the jury, minutes of the meeting	158
13.9	Envelope opening, notifying the prizewinners	160
14	**PUBLICITY**	**162**
14.1	Participation	162
14.2	Press	162
14.3	Project homepage	163
14.4	Exhibition	164
15	**AFTER THE COMPETITION**	**178**
15.1	Commissioning	178
15.2	Project archiving and return	179

APPENDIX		**180**
SERVICES PROVIDED BY THE COMPETITION MANAGER		182
RECOMMENDED LITERATURE		190
IMPRINT		191

Additional **TABLES OF CONTENTS** are on the cover.

EXAMPLES OF PROJECTS

QUOTATIONS

INTRODUCTION

Design competitions are an exceptional method to decide on the design of projects and select the design teams, which since decades has been recognized and proven worldwide, applying equally to disciplines such as architectural design, urban design, landscape architecture, engineering projects, exhibition design, and art in architecture. The statements in this book regard, with few exceptions, all these disciplines. Nevertheless, as architectural and urban design is encountered more frequently, the focus lies primarily on these projects.

For designers, competitions have been a familiar instrument since decades, if not longer. In the initial project phase, competitions provide the organizational framework for the necessary coordination process between the design offices involved in the design process, administrations, public and private clients, and the general public. They also stage the framework for an important contribution to building culture (Baukultur) and social development.

There are rules for conducting competitions in many places. The most important of them is the agreement –established since the beginning of regulated competitions in the 19th century– that the best design will be awarded a prize by a competent jury and the winning team will be commissioned to plan the implementation of the best design.

But how are the various processes of competition preparation and organization evaluated in detail, even by those not directly involved in design? What prejudices exist, possibly justifiably? Which opportunities and risks are known, which are not? Of course, there are no clear answers to these questions. No matter whom you ask, it quickly becomes obvious that competitions are a polarizing, fascinating, complex, and often emotional "something" about which everyone has their own opinion and experience. This is true for experts and laypeople alike. Competitions are publicly visible and sometimes controversial processes. They affect everyone's environment and are often sufficiently emblematic to spark public debate about the fundamental sense of some construction projects.

The importance of the built environment for our (well-)being is perceived very differently by individuals. Consciously or unconsciously, the personal relationship to the design and building tradition varies, as does the importance that each individual attaches to the question of the significance of the built environment. Geographical, economic, and cultural contexts have an influence on this individual consideration. Globally and regionally, the culture of architectural, urban and landscape design has always developed in a variety of ways, despite general trends. Similarly, those who work creatively in the construction industry have very different positions in society, and the design processes are established in very different ways. In some places, there is a respectful consensus about the direct connection between architecture and our well-being, while in others, the architecture and design scene is seen as a world of self-absorbed eccentrics and divas. In one place, architects are attacked as accomplices of profit-oriented investors, and in another, they are gratefully accepted actors in society within the framework of meaningfully accepted processes for the care and design of communal living spaces.

Despite all diversity of social and individual contexts, building has always been and is being done, mostly based on a concrete need, sometimes as an investment in the future or for immaterial reasons. And it is probably human nature to enjoy confronting competition.

Thus, "competing" as a method to find the best solution for construction assignments has long been known and widely used. First, the idea of competition ran parallel to the historical development of general democratic processes – it began in ancient Greece, was revived in the Renaissance, was further developed by the young democracies in the 18th and 19th centuries and was established and formalized in the period of emerging mass media; sets of rules that have remained largely unchanged in principle ever since. In the modernist era, the idea of competition made it possible to test the principle of "form follows function" and eventually became a genuine design and procurement instrument in contemporary societies – both as a driver of design excellence and as a tool for fair tendering procedures. The history of design competitions can be traced back to progressive buildings that ushered in a new era: the new dome of the Florence Cathedral in 1418, the Sydney Opera House in 1956, the Alexandria Library in 1988 or the Berlin Reichstag in 1992.

Design competitions, whether for architectural, urban design, landscape architecture, engineering structures, art in construction or for exhibition design, and whether for small, large, and more, or less prominent or complex tasks, are used today in a wide variety of projects by public and private clients as an instrument to select and optimize the design solution and for deciding on the commissioning of the most important design partners in the project. Competitions improve the quality of urban design, buildings, open spaces, and engineering solutions in a sustainable way. Without the competition discourse, the transparency in the awarding of contracts and the power of the procedure as an integrating framework for the participation of all relevant project members, innovation and building culture would not have reached the high level and wide acceptance in many places in the recent decades.

However, competitions are not only characterized by success. Ambitions and honest intentions may easily vanish into thin air, leaving a pile of unrealized designs or projects of limited quality behind. As a result, this design and tendering tool is often criticized and (rightly) questioned – sometimes on a very general and sometimes populist level, but also among the experts in the narrow circle of those who have in-depth knowledge and experience in this particular field.

It is therefore right to keep adapting the methods and qualities of these over decades developed processes to the requirements of the time: globalization, digitization, climate change, scarcity of row materials, society's desire to participate, and, finally, the experience of pandemics, all require that this proven instrument be further developed in a flexible manner so that the advantages of competitions may continue to be exploited.

In addition, there is also potential to optimize the implementation is carried out under the existing rules and regulations. The available and applied methods are highly diverse and reflect not only the differences in project content, but also the knowledge and resources of the stakeholders. In many countries, competitions are an established part in the design world, used to make decisions about projects, to promote quality and also to introduce young offices to the market. But how are they organized, what needs to be considered, who needs to be involved, what do competitions cost, and so on?

This book aims to contribute here. There are many reports and discussions about the results of competitions, and many benefits derived from them. Discussions about architectural and urban design, about design strategies and theories, about techniques and methods for presenting projects as well as about possible criteria for assessing their quality are often largely known territory in the professional world and the public. However, even in the professional circles, little is known about the preparation and organization of competitions.

Scenes from jury meetings or participant colloquia in the competitions: **1** and **7**: Wien Museum Neu, **2**: ThyssenKrupp Quarter Essen, **3**: Beirut Museum of Art, **4**: Museum for the Maidan Revolution in Kyiv, **5**: BMW Group FIZ Future Munich, **6**: Revitalization of the Old Town of Fez, **8**: University of Science and Technology Hanoi, **9**: Parliamentary Precinct Redevelopment Ottawa.

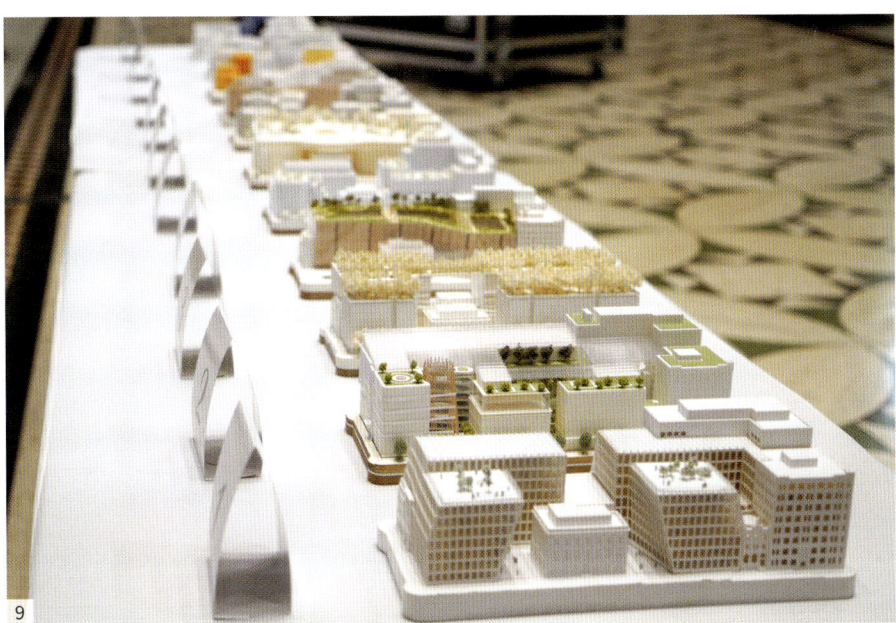

Introduction

Highlighting the main projects in the center that have been selected through competition, without claiming to be comprehensive.

Like any construction project, every competition is unique, simply because of its subject matter and the circumstances. In addition, the procedure is ideally tailored to the specific financial, scheduling, and formal framework conditions as well as the constantly changing combination of the people involved, so that the competition organizer must act within in a highly specific and flexible manner. However, there are recurring components, rules and procedures in competitions that can be solved in different ways. Based on our own experience, each of the fifteen thematic chapters deals with a part, a section of these topics. Few readers will be interested in all aspects. However, we hope that this structure will make it easier to use the book in practice as a reference work.

Between the thematic chapters, we show the applicability of competitions as a design instrument for projects of various sizes and uses in 12 typologically arranged blocks based on 60 completed competitions from all over the world that we organized. Practical tips are supplemented by quotes from prominent colleagues who were involved in competitions as participants, jury members, on behalf of the sponsor, or architectural chambers and organizations.

We would like to note that most of the observations relate to any form of task in competitions, even if some formulations initially indicate a stronger connection to architectural or urban design.

This book would not have been possible without the commitment of the colleagues who enrich competitions with their creativity and dedication as participants and jury members. Nor would it have been possible without the willingness of our clients, who for their part have put no less effort into the projects and have allowed us to publish them. Behind every competition there are many other people - our own team, the preliminary examiners, representatives of approval authorities, and all the important people in the background who take care of model making, catering, exhibition construction, printing, web and database programming. We would therefore like to thank all those who have inspired us with their commitment over the past 25 years, and who have been our conversational partners in understanding and improving processes. We would also like to thank all those who have enriched this book with their personal statements. They all share an interest in the high quality of the built environment and a desire to contribute to it with their own skills.

Benjamin Hossbach . Christian Lehmhaus . Christine Eichelmann

Benjamin Hossbach
Born in Darmstadt in 1966. He completed his training as a carpenter in 1988 and his architectural studies at the TU Berlin in 1995. After working as an online editor for Bauwelt and as a freelance architect, he founded the office [phase eins]. project consultants + design competition organizers in 1998. He is the author of numerous publications on architectural competitions and a guest lecturer at ETH Zurich, Harvard University, the Vienna Academy of Fine Arts and TU Berlin, among others.

Christian Lehmhaus
Born in 1963 in Bielefeld. He completed his architectural studies at TU Berlin in 1993. After working as an employed architect, he has been a partner at [phase eins]. project consultants + design competition organizers since 2001. In addition, he was professor for project management and project development at the University of Applied Sciences Bochum.

Christine Eichelmann
Born in Werneck in 1959. She completed her architectural studies at the TU Berlin in 1986. After working as an architect at Studio Libeskind (Berlin), OMA (London) and Karen van Lengen (New York), also as a project manager, she was a partner of [phase eins]. project consultants + design competition organizers between 2008 and 2016. She was also a research assistant at the TU Berlin and ran her own architectural practice from 1994 to 1997. Since 2016, she is working as an architect at the German Federal Foreign Office.

Elements of a successful competition

The main opportunities and risks of competitions are obvious: the participants, have the chance to win a contract and gain reputation, connections, and experience. On the other hand, the risk to fail in the competition, receiving no or too little fee, or to win the competition but still not getting a contract. There are also obvious opportunities for the competition sponsor: to obtain a solution for their project that is optimized in terms of design, function, ecology, and economy, as well as to find a potential design team. They can also initiate early coordination with the other stakeholders of the project (approval authorities, politicians, neighbors, potential users), and communicate and establish the project with positive publicity. All these issues are explored in detail in the following chapters of the book. The question of what criteria must be fulfilled for a competition to be called a successful procedure in retrospect are answered differently depending on one's point of view. But if the question is about the criteria for a fundamentally successful competition, the answer is clear:

1. the project of the competition was realized based on one of the proposed designs and the recommendation of the jury
2. one of the prizewinners was commissioned to provide the agreed design services
3. and the project was completed within a reasonable budget and timeframe

If all of the criteria were met, it can be assumed that the project also

4. contributes to design and building culture (Baukultur), as the design prevailed in the competition based on quality criteria and was obviously the most convincing proposal for the project.

However, the described path to this overall success cannot be taken for granted, and there are too many competitions that must be characterized as failures under the previously mentioned criteria. There have been competition projects, of course, that were not realized due to unforeseen events. But in the case of many projects that were stopped after the competition, one must ask whether all project fundamentals had really been taken into consideration in advance, whether the right procedure had been chosen, whether the right people were involved, or whether those involved in the competition were not just instrumentalized for the sake of an uncertain game. In each case, the reasons for the ultimate failure can certainly be explained, but are such explanations sufficient to make the effort worthwhile? And do such procedures promote the view that competitions are useful design tools?

This regards prominent projects such as the competitions for the new structures at Ground Zero in New York, for the Guggenheim Museum in Helsinki, or the extension of the City Library in Stockholm. In all these cases, chosen here only as examples, the projects were developed by hundreds of the world's best architects at enormous expense and then, only after the competitions had been completed, based on images generated during the process, did the clarification process take place on the basic question of whether and to what extent, in what form and prominence the respective projects are needed at all.

Similarly, there are numerous less prominent projects that at best end up "in the drawer" and more likely in the wastebasket. This category certainly includes procedures that are not organized as formally registered competitions and are part of attracting investors to grant a plot of land, or approve of a project. Under the label "competition", several design offices are commissioned in parallel to prepare a preliminary design to document the feasibility and attractiveness of the proposal and thus increase the value of the land.

Highlighting the main projects in the centre that have been selected through competition, without claiming to be comprehensive.

This is followed by another land sale, not a construction project. The selection of the preferred design, which could possibly be implemented in the event of a successful bid, takes place with the participation of the municipality selling the land, if necessary. This is a common practice in some Arab countries, for example, to gain the support of the rulers. There, as elsewhere, such a procedure can be quite appropriate, provided that the risky "rules of the game" are honestly communicated to all participants, that possibly none of the competition designs will be implemented at all, but all designs will remain unrealized, and therefore the risk will be compensated by appropriate expense renumeration. But it is above all the failed competitions in the countries of typical architectural competitions that raise questions. Probably every architecture firm knows several competitions across the country where the project took a completely different path after the competition than planned …

» because the formulated task was too ambitious
» because the budget was too small
» because a mentor in politics or in the sponsor's company lost their position
» because a project was initiated a long time ago and the budget was approved, developed at the working level over a long period of time, and then, although framework conditions changed in the meantime, no corrections were made before the competition because the project was approved in its original form
» because relevant technical boundary conditions were underestimated or even ignored in advance
» because the expectations of the project's sponsors were too far apart and the ability to reach a consensus drifted apart in the face of the designs – be it between several property owners jointly initiating a competition, between a private sponsor and the responsible municipality, or between a funding agency and a grant recipient
» because the sponsor only recognized the discrepancy between the ambition of their own strategic goals and the actual readiness to implement them based on the designs

» because the approvability of the project as a whole or the eligibility of the winning design was not checked carefully and with the consensus of all parties involved during preparation of the competition or during the preliminary examination and jury evaluation
» because the jury promoted a design to the rank of 1st prizewinner, although it was already clear at that point that the design would have no chance of realization but lacked the courage to bring this knowledge into the jury process

And unfortunately, there are also examples where the project was realized, but not by one of the prize-winning offices, but by another design office that was commissioned with organizing the implementation of the project.

Therefore, there are many reasons why competitions and competition projects fail, and many cases may be justifiable. In brief, however, they represent a waste of resources and lead to a loss of trust. Trust in the competition system in general, but also in individual municipalities or private sponsors, especially if this a recurring phenomenon. The risk here is that in the long run the trust of the design offices and their willingness to participate in further competitions of these sponsors will diminish – their reputation will be permanently damaged.

Dr. techn. Heinz Priebernig
Architect Dipl.-Ing.,
Chairman of the Federal Competition Committee of the Austrian Chambers of Civil Engineers

" The search for the best project is documented in Homer's Iliad and in the agōn, the competition of the Greeks in the 5th century BC. Since the early Renaissance, concurs has been a model for exploring and responding to issues of architectural culture. Architects and engineers offer multi-dimensional solutions in anonymous competitions, a jury of architects and engineers ranks the submitted projects according to a technical discourse in which the urban, functional, ecological, economic, and architectural qualities of the submitted competition projects are examined comparatively.
Without this thorough analysis of the design task set by many, the client has only one answer for his design project, and often a wrong one. Why do some clients shy away from architectural competitions and commission lawyers to formulate workarounds? Allegations against architectural competitions are that they are too complicated to organize, that it is impossible to assess the large number of entries, and that the risk of objections under public procurement law is too high. Empirical data does not support these assumptions.

1. In negotiated procedures as defined by the European procurement rules for services and design, a team of designers or the general planner is selected on the basis of suitability and selection criteria such as references, operational turnover and the like. In this way, the client forgets that the search for architectural answers is first and foremost about the best project.
2. n architectural competitions, an expert jury selects the best project from many possible solutions. After the architectural competition – in the negotiation procedure – the client can negotiate with the competition winner the content of the contract, the composition of the project team and the schedule.
3. The decision of the expert jury legitimizes the social compatibility of the one – and best – architectural response and facilitates the rapid implementation of the winning project in the 1:1 model. Empirical data confirm that objections under public procurement law against the ranking of the competition projects and oppositions of the residents against a building project, which was preceded by an architectural competition, are less frequent than in the case of a project, which was based on a single design.

Unlike construction services, which are precisely defined by plans and specifications, the tendering of services/design services requires a different procurement practice to find the most suitable design professionals, since the design and planning of a prototype is the subject of the contract award. The assumption by clients and their legal advisors that eligibility and pre-qualification criteria are better used to select the group of suitable service providers is incorrect. There are many examples of references and turnover that do not attract the most suitable designers; it is not uncommon for an innovative project to be awarded to design firms that have never participated in an architectural competition. I recall the 1417(18) competition for the vaulting of the octagonal tambour of Florence Cathedral, announced by the Arte della Lana (Wool Weavers Guild), won by Brunelleschi; Alvar Aalto, who won the 1927 architectural competition for the sanatorium in Paimio, Finland, without references; the sanatorium was built from 1927 to 1933 and is now an architectural monument.
Diversity of thought and criticism are the maxims for clients, architects, and engineers when addressing construction and design challenges. Open anonymous architectural competitions are a proven contribution to finding the best solution. Even for small building tasks, anonymous architectural competitions are better suited than negotiated procedures with upstream application processes. In the search for the most suitable architects and engineers, the risks of objections under public procurement law are low when the planners are selected through upstream anonymous, one- and two-stage architectural competitions, and the construction results are higher than in non-open procedures. The competition among the participants brings to light answers that the client had not previously considered. It is this diversity of solutions that is the great treasure of anonymous competitions.

"What should be considered when organizing a competition?"
4. Contact a competition organizer who will advise and support you during the process: competition rules, announcement, examination and compilation of the design material, evaluation criteria, composition of the jury, examination, and electronic communication.
5. Competition organizers ensure that an architectural competition brings advantages for you as the client – different approaches to solutions – from which the expert jury competently selects the best project, the second best, the third best … according to the evaluation criteria formulated in the competition brief. You gain procedural and legal certainty when advising competition organizers, e.g., against objections to the procedure.
6. Should you have any questions about an architectural competition, you can contact the respective professional association of architects and engineers. Architects and engineers are glad to take part and submit their designs for competitions that are endorsed by a chamber of architects and engineers. In Austria, the Chambers of Civil Engineers offer their advice to interested developers – free of charge for you – and conduct cooperation negotiations on your competition based on your proposal. In case of cooperation with the professional association of architects and engineers, your competition will be advertised on WEBSITES. Architects and engineers will gladly take part in competitions cooperating with a chamber of civil engineers and offer a competition design.

The positive essence of the architectural competition is the variety of solution approaches (competition entries) that the client receives, the increased procedural security for clients, architects and engineers, the research contributions to the further development of building culture and the design of a sustainable living environment.

Hanna Bondar
Architect and politician, member of the Ukrainian Parliament

❙❙ Despite the challenges of the war waged by the Russian aggressor on the territory of Ukraine, design competitions are currently experiencing a new round of prosperity. This is due to the changes that have taken place in Ukrainian society – the need for more transparent selection procedures, the demand for quality, and the overall democratization of society. Over the past 10 years, the annual number of competitions initiated by city administrations has tripled.

The decentralization reform has influenced the development of competitions, and municipalities have begun to develop on a competitive basis. Despite the prospects, the level of competition culture is not very high, the market of professional competition organizers is still being formed, and clients, participants, and jury members have insufficient knowledge and skills.

When signing the EU-Ukraine Association Agreement, the Ukrainian government committed itself to implement the requirements of the European Directive on Public Procurement, including the use of competitions as the main means of implementing large-scale projects. This year, this issue has finally moved forward, and the relevant ministry is preparing the necessary draft law. We wish a successful passage in the Verkhovna Rada of Ukraine.

The Competition Commission of the National Union of Architects of Ukraine has started its activity, advising the parties involved in the competitions to improve their quality and professionalism. All this inspires further steps towards high quality modern Ukrainian architecture.

It is my hope that this book will contribute to the improvement of the quality of competitions in Ukraine and elsewhere.

PhD Ihor Poshyvailo
PhD in History, cultural anthropologist, General Director of the National Memorial to the Heavenly Hundred Heroes and Revolution of Dignity Museum, Co-founder of the Heritage Emergency Response Initiative (HERI), Kyiv

❙❙ A design competition for open spaces or architecture is the most effective, professional, and democratic way to achieve the best outcome and reach the competition's final goal – the successful implementation of the project idea. In Ukraine, a few architectural competitions for historic or cultural venues have been organized since the regaining of independence in 1991. After the Maidan revolutions in 2004 and 2013–2014, it was a huge request from civil society to develop urban and cultural infrastructure in a democratic and transparent manner.

Thus, the Ukrainian government launched the design competition for the National Memorial to the Heavenly Hundred Heroes and Revolution of Dignity Museum (Maidan Museum) in 2017. It was such an important and challenging task that foreign experience and expertise were needed. That's how [phase eins]. was engaged in organizing the international competition in Kyiv. The biggest challenge was a short historical distance between the dramatic events when over a hundred protesters were killed and thousands were wounded in clashes with riot police and the corrupted pro-Russian government and the social and political request for memorialization. The competition lasted almost a year and was completed with two winners selected by a representative international jury in two nominations – projects for a Memorial and a Museum in the very heart of Ukraine's capital city. It was quite a complicated and emotional process engaging public and private actors, and a wide range of stakeholders including families of the killed people, wounded activists, authorities, expert groups, local communities and politicians.

Currently, at the beginning of 2023, the projects are in the status of different implementation phases – the Memorial is ready to be constructed but postponed because of a still ongoing investigation on crimes against the protesters. The Museum is in a state of project design and estimates documentation development. This competition and its implementation look like a battle for memory and identity, for a new commemoration and cultural space in the most important site in Ukraine. The lessons learned in this battle include a need for change in Ukraine's laws on international competitions and their implementation, activating open architectural and design markets, effective involvement of all stakeholders in dialogue and cooperation, need for social agreement and political leadership in disputed issues on presentation of contested history and preservation of traumatic memory. The important issues include deliberate planning of the design competition brief, which should include all aspects of the site's social, historical, architectural, cultural, and urban planning details, assessment of risks and solutions, and engagement of cultural heritage protection officials and activists.

The fruitful partnership with a competition manager like [phase eins]. was crucial for Ukraine's design competition, architectural, museum, and memorial fields as it brought into the discussion so many important issues and practices to change on the way of successful implementation of international design competition outcomes. It happened to be an important step for Ukraine towards European best practices and world standards in memorialization our past for the future, making our memory active and relevant for the present.

So, what are the most important aspects of a successful, or even sustainable, competition? We see the following eight elements of a successful competition:

1. Choosing the right type of procedure
2. Agreeing on fair and clearly formulated procedural conditions, especially with regard to the admission and selection of participants and promise of a contract after the competition
3. Clarifying, coordinating, and formulating precisely the competition task
4. Composing a competent jury with a quorum and authorized to make decisions
5. Conducting a thorough preliminary examination of the submitted designs with the aim to present the relevant information to the jury in a compact and comprehensible manner
6. Designing an organizational framework for the participants' colloquia and jury meetings, allowing an intensive communication in sufficient time
7. Appointing an experienced competition manager
8. Cultivating a positive atmosphere among all involved parties

All these actions require a fundamental approach as well as considerable effort and high level of commitment. The careful preparation and organization of competitions require attention to key issues and numerous necessary details. This effort is well invested, as it is well known that the decisions that are essential to the overall success of a project are made in its early stages.

The effort is also well invested because in this phase the almost magical moment when a project transforms from theoretical reflection and mere intention into concrete form, which is not only magical but also essential for project communication. After a sometimes very long preparation and abstract consideration of the task, images hang on the wall for the first time on the day of the jury meeting. Shortly afterwards, they are presented to the public. In the minds of those involved, these images must fulfill the expectations that have been built up beforehand, ideally surprising them in a positive way, triggering emotions and inspiring confidence, in order to be robust enough in the design process that then begins to hold their quality until realization. Experience shows that the staging of this moment is therefore of great importance in determining the motivation with which the participants carry the project into the design and realization phase that follows the competition.

In this respect, we encourage every potential sponsor to recognize the importance of this phase of their project for its overall success and to plan competitions with special attention. We hope that this book will provide those responsible for the management of competitions with suggestions and assistance in the above-mentioned eight essential components and other challenges when preparing and conducting competitions, ensure better comprehensibility of the necessary processes for participants and the public, and thus contribute to successful competition procedures.

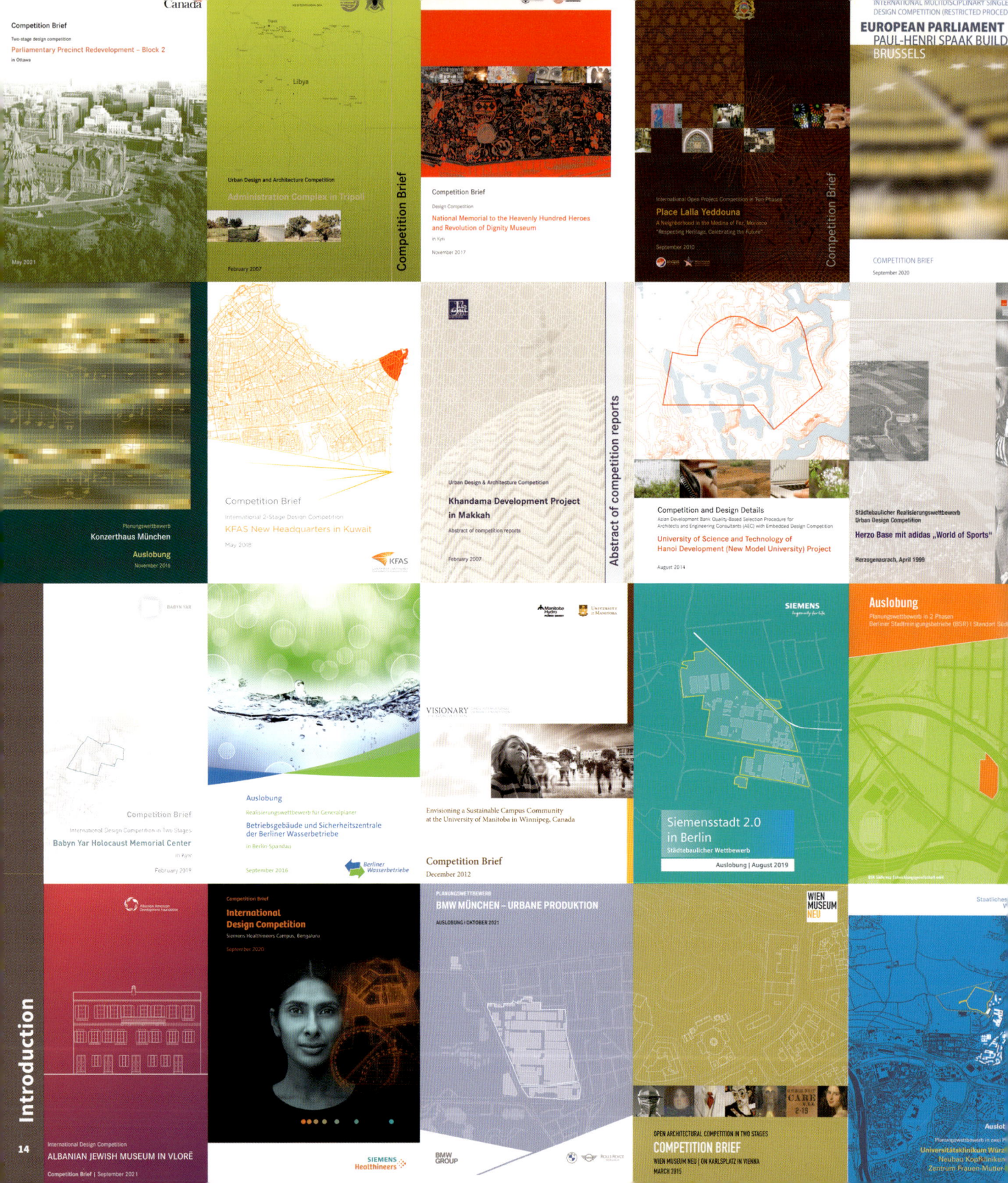

Prof. PhD Jean-Pierre Chupin

MOAQ architect, MRAIC, Professor at the Université de Montréal and holder of the Canada Research Chair in Architecture, Competitions and Mediations of Excellence (www.crc.umontreal.ca)

▌▌ A good "competition question" addresses the complexity of a situation to be transformed. Let me specify from the outset that my take on competitions is not so much a personal opinion as it is supported by two decades of research on competitions and documentation in the Canadian Competitions Catalogue (CCC) (www.ccc.umontreal.ca). I have been contributing to the international network of researchers on competitions first at the Université de Montréal Research Chair on Competitions (2011 to 2017) and, from then on, as the Canada Research Chair in Architecture, Competitions and mediations of Excellence (www.crc.umontreal.ca).

When asked to choose a few essential ways of considering architecture competitions, I would certainly point out the role of "competition questions" in the face of complexity. Whenever the situation to be transformed is complex enough, i.e., whenever more than three sources of expectations compete, the competition organizers need to invite the teams of architects, landscape architects and urbanists on the basis of a good, stimulating, challenging and puzzling "competition question."

Complexity, by definition, lies at the core of most projects in the built environment. Now, how can one represent such a complexity in a competition brief? Is it even possible, needless to say, logical, to summarize the complexity of a situation to be transformed, of a project to be built? There are no easy answers, of course, but there is a strong and safe device which should be seriously considered by any competition organizer and I would call it the "competition question." Such a question should be both clear and deep. It should be open while it clearly frames what is needed to answer the expectations of a specific situation. It should be socially meaningful and at the same time culturally open, particularly when considering an international competition format.

A competition question can never be substituted for by the summary of a brief and even less so by the brief itself. It should also be noted that a competition question can paradoxically be weakened by the type of competition chosen by the organizers. Research tends to demonstrate that an anonymous two-stage type of competition can better address potential controversies which are often related to the complexity of the situation rather than to the competition process itself. Competitions are far more transparent than calls for tenders, hence they might appear more controversial precisely because of their democratic openness. It is logical that the debates are less lively around calls for tenders precisely because one never really knows what is going on behind the closed doors of calls for projects. On the contrary, a competition process can be debated, including in its budgetary aspects, because the competition is by definition a place for public debate, a forum. This also explains the increasing importance of public presentations, public defense and public voting in competitions in the last ten years or so.

The question of what is often wrongly called "two-stage selection" seems to me to be all the more worrying since it is not precisely a question of two project stages, but more often of a preselection stage followed by a project stage. When the judgment is not made on two series of projects, one should speak of a one-stage competition preceded by a preselection. From the point of view of the jury's skills, it should be noted that in the case of a competition with a selection based on the candidate's portfolio of projects, the jury must operate in stages which correspond to two different evaluation operations:

1. select a team from among others on the basis of portfolios which, in reality, are rarely comparable, then
2. compare and judge projects on common and comparable deliverables clearly stated in the competition rules.

In contrast, in a two-stage competition, especially when the first stage is anonymous, projects are judged only for what they represent in the brief and commission defined in the program. As it stands, the rule of anonymity remains a much healthier rule than a portfolio-based preselection.

There is currently a worrying gray area in these preselection phases, since it is very rare that all the members of the competition juries have a real knowledge of the professional milieu - even less so of the next generation. It is probable that an architect who has realized several library projects is in some way better prepared. But by following this logic systematically, one locks the production into repetition, or worse, one encourages the repetition of conventional solution and indirectly stimulates conformism in so many ways that contradict the very idea of the competition and the openness to new ideas in architectural history. Regardless of the advisers who intend to supervise the jury with experts in construction, budgetary and environmental matters, all our observations and analyses of the juries show that each member is a self-proclaimed expert (of architecture, of the users, of citizens, of financial aspects, on special interests, etc.).[I]

There is little room for debate in first-stage portfolio flipping, unless the comparative criteria are explicitly formulated to lead to a true objective comparison of competencies. Why proceed by competition if not to open the problematic at stake to the greatest possible emulation and to the most innovative points of view, that is, by definition, the least repetitive? Since all registered architects have received a professional training, validated by professional association or strict accreditation bodies, it is abnormal to add a procedure claiming to protect the public from a hypothetical lack of professionalism that would potentially come from younger firms. If this were the case, remarkable buildings such as the Pompidou Center, the Parc de la Villette or the famous Vietnam War Veterans Memorial would never have been built.[II]

All procedures aimed at complicating the participation of offices that do not (yet) have a portfolio of so-called comparable achievements are potentially discriminatory and have no other purpose than to tighten the competition on a few offices in an advantageous situation. A good competition question – carried by a good professional adviser in a good competition brief – remains both the Trojan Horse to architectural quality and the best way of protecting the complexity of public good.

[I] On the question of the noisy concert of expertise in competition juries see the study by Professor Carmela Cucuzzella in: Architecture Competitions and the Production of Culture, Quality and Knowledge (An International Inquiry), edited by Jean-Pierre Chupin, Carmela Cucuzzella and Bechara Helal, Montreal, Potential Architecture Books, 2015, pp. 144–161.

[II] See our book in open access: Chupin, Jean-Pierre, G. Stanley Collyer, Young Architects in Competitions (When Competitions and a New Generation of Ideas Elevate Architectural Quality), Montreal, Potential Architecture Books, 2020, 158 pages. https://crc.umontreal.ca/en/sdm_downloads/chupin-jean-pierre-g-stanley-collyer-young-architects-in-competitions-when-competitions-and-a-new-generation-of-ideas-elevate-architectural-quality-2/.

CULTURAL BUILDINGS

Cultural buildings have always been considered by architects as the highest discipline. Historically, they were probably the first buildings in which architecture sought expression, being the subject of the first design competitions in Ancient Greece and Renaissance Italy. They often served rulers and churches as expressions of power, splendor, generosity, and connection to the divine, often leaving their mark on cultural history. In this respect, it is not surprising that architects are still strongly interested in the exterior and interior design of cultural buildings, and that in these projects the interaction of the basic elements of space, light, function, and structure is constantly tested.

Cultural buildings are usually public buildings and therefore of general interest that often serve the purpose of creating identity in and for their place. The high expectations of such buildings place special demands on the professional competence of the competition organizer in the preparation and conduct of a competition. On the one hand, it is necessary to control the design of a building with highly complex functional requirements, such as internal development and circulation, light and sound design, security, logistics, and flexibility to ensure the adaptability required for changing exhibitions, concerts, and various events. At the same time, often extremely precise specifications, for example, artworks, concerts, and archival objects, as well as educational concepts and inclusion goals must be formulated and examined during the process. The extensive but usually little-known behind-the-scenes program for depots, workshops, artists' dressing rooms, rehearsal rooms, delivery areas and administration must be explained, as must the requirements for cafés, shops, ticketing, and visitors' dressing rooms. On the other hand, this design task requires a special kind of framework for the creative excellence of the disciplines involved. This often requires a high degree of moderation skills on the part of the competition organizer in order to mediate between the committed interest groups with persuasiveness, motivation, innovative spirit, and openness.

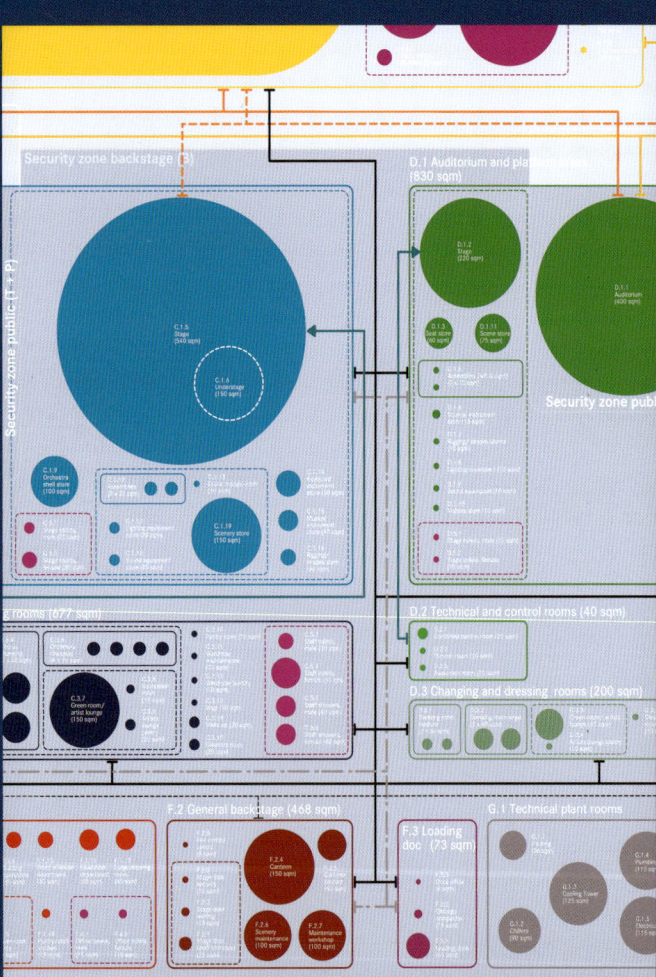

Spatial and functional diagram of the "Concert and Theater House Amman" competition

Munich Concert Hall

MUNICH, THE CITY OF MUSIC Munich is a world-class musical metropolis. It was home to composers such as Richard Wagner, Richard Strauss and Orlando di Lasso. Works by Mozart were premiered here. The Bavarian Staatsoper is among the leading opera houses worldwide. High-class orchestras such as the Bayerisches Staatsorchester, the Symphonieorchester des Bayerischen Rundfunks and the Münchner Philharmoniker are based in Munich. Outstanding soloists give regular guest performances. For many years the citizens, the general public and, last but not least, international performers have been calling for the establishment of an adequate concert hall. This project plays a most important role in setting the course of the Bavarian State Governments cultural policy.

THE PROJECT The concert hall will contain two concert chambers, a Large Hall seating 1,800 and a Small Hall seating 600 persons, plus a "Workshop" seating 200. With this variety the Munich Concert Hall is to provide venues with high-class acoustics for both symphony concerts and soloists or smaller ensembles while at the same time creating an inviting ambiance able to inspire new audiences for musical culture. Educational projects will be launched that address children, adolescents and adults and seek to integrate audiences from diverse societal backgrounds. Thus, music can be experienced in a novel quality and with 21st century performance formats.

THE SITE After an investigation into a number of alternative sites for the construction of the concert hall, the Werksviertel neighborhood had been identified as the most appropriate and feasible choice. The Werksviertel is located southeast of Munich's Ostbahnhof within an area that for more than a century had been a major industrial and commercial zone that has been undergoing a process of transformation since the mid-1990s.

Ort: Munich **Client:** The Free State of Bavaria **Year:** 2016 – 2017 **Project size:** approx. 9,500 sqm UFA **Type of competition:** Restricted design competition **Participants:** 31 **Competition budget:** EUR 500,000 (prizes and honorable mentions)

PRIZEWINNERS:
(01) **1st prize** Cukrowicz Nachbaur Architekten ZT GmbH, Bregenz (A); **2nd prize** PFP Planungs GmbH, Hamburg (D); **3rd prize** David Chipperfield Architects Gesellschaft von Architekten mbH, Berlin (D); **4th prize** 3XN AS, Copenhagen (DK); **5th prize** Staab Architekten GmbH, Berlin (D)

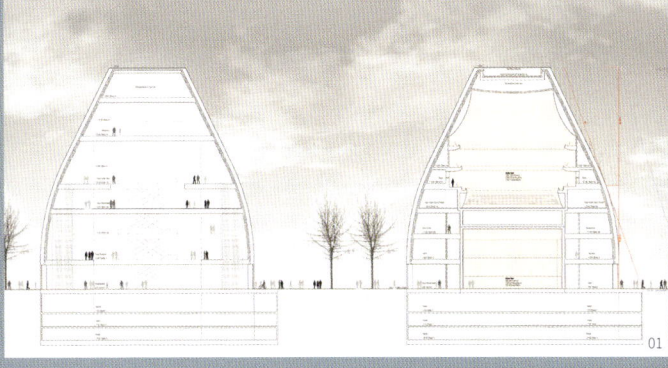

Munich Concert Hall

Location: Kyiv, Ukraine **Client:** Ministry of Culture of Ukraine **Year:** 2017 – 2018 **Project size:** approx. 27,500 sqm GFA museum, approx. 15,000 sqm open spaces **Type of competition:** International design competition **Participants:** Museum, Stage 1: 12; Stage 2: 6; Memorial: 9 **Competition budget:** EUR 190,000 (prizes: EUR 85,000; Compensation Stage 1: EUR 15,000)

PRIZEWINNERS:
(01) **1st prize** Kleihues + Kleihues Gesellschaft von Architekten mbH, Berlin (D); **2nd prize** Burø architects, Kyiv (UA); **3rd prize** Lina Ghotmeh – Architecture, Paris (F)

Maidan Revolution of Dignity Museum, Kyiv

REVOLUTION OF DIGNITY The Euromaidan was a Ukrainian nationwide protest movement that lasted from November 2013 to February 2014. These historic events were triggered by the abrupt rejection of its foreign policy towards Europe and the refusal to sign the EU Association Agreement by Ukraine's former leadership. Following the brutal beating of young people by the government special forces, the protest movement developed into a continuing civil disobedience campaign against unchecked state power, corruption, and human rights abuses. The Revolution was an incisive moment in history for Ukraine. It resulted in the deaths of 107 protesters (known as the Heavenly Hundred), the disposal of the corrupted President and his government, Russia's annexation of Crimea and the start of a war in the Donbas region. It also led to the consolidation of a democratic society in the Ukraine.

MAIDAN MEMORIAL AND MAIDAN MUSEUM
With two connected sub-tasks, the objective of the project focuses on the very center of Kyiv. The task for the memorial was to create a permanent place for individual and official commemoration, symbolizing the ideas of Maidan and carrying the memory to future generations. The task was open to monuments and landscape designs that could be located within the area of the Maidan and the adjacent street where most of the victims are to be mourned. The Revolution of Dignity Museum will be a state institution of scientific research as well as a place for cultural, educational, and methodological activities. Located on an authentic site of the shootings on the hill above the Maidan, it will be both an active center and a symbol for civic sense, democracy, and tolerant societies within the European family.

PROCEDURE The competition was organized as two parallel processes with unified multidisciplinary jury and participants selected separately in open procedures.

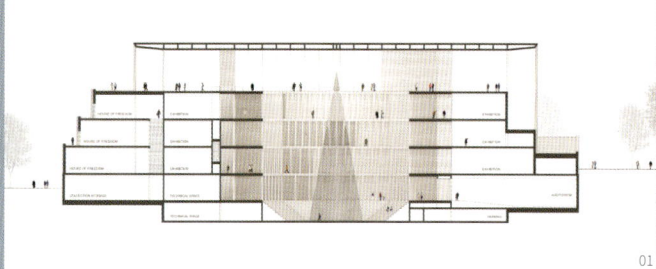
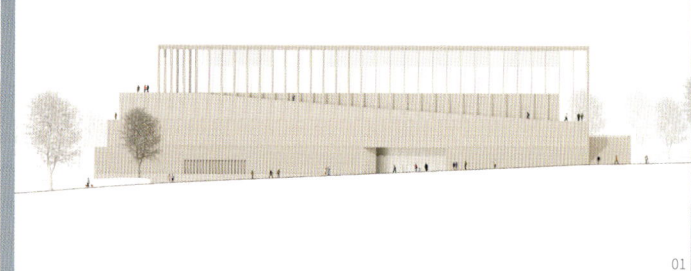

Swiss Pavilion on the EXPO 2010, Shanghai

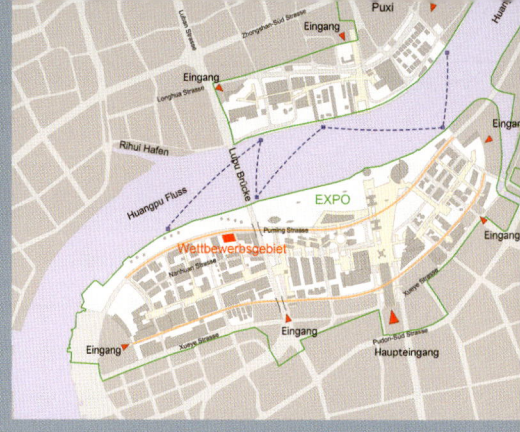

EXPO 2010 SHANGHAI EXPO 2010, the World Fair, was held in Shanghai from May to October that year. Its theme was "A Better City, A Better Life". A pavilion built by Switzerland was part of the show. The EXPO 2010 fair grounds were on both banks of the Huangpu River, to the south of the inner city of Shanghai. Until that time, docks and industry were the defining features of the area. The Swiss Pavilion was at a 4,000 sqm site on the river's south bank in "Zone C", where there were also pavilions from other European countries, the Americas and Africa. The competition task was to come up with an overall concept that would integrate the pavilion itself, seen as building or object, with the exhibition on display. To elaborate on this idea, a cinema capable of screening a large-format, fully conceptualized film was to be included. The Pavilion, no more than 4,000 sqm, should provide space for receptions, events and include places to pass the time, a restaurant, retail, and office areas, as well as the exhibition area.

PROCEDURE The competition was held as an open two-stage procedure, open to architects, exposition designers, interior architects, communication experts, visual artists, and theater-set designers. At least one member of the design team had to be a Swiss citizen or resident. Only teams consisting of at least one architect, a mechanical and a structural engineer, plus a participant qualified in one of the five disciplines mentioned above, were admitted to the second phase.

COMMUNICATING SWISS IDENTITY Like other invitees in such situations, Switzerland faced the challenge of presenting its own cultural identity and societal perspectives to a wider, mainly Asian public. Thus, it was of prime importance that Chinese visitors were able to identify with the exhibition and make associations with their own history and culture. On the other hand, it was important that Switzerland, Swiss citizens, and Swiss companies were able to relate to the Exhibition within the context of their own culture.

Location: Shanghai, China **Client:** Swiss Confederation represented by Präsenz Schweiz **Year:** 2006 – 2007 **Project size:** approx. 4,000 sqm **Type of competition:** Open, interdisciplinary, two-stage project competition **Participants:** Stage 1: 104; Stage 2: 12

PRIZEWINNERS:
(01) **1st prize** Buchner Bründler AG Architekten BSA, Basel (CH); (02) **2nd prize** group8, architects associés, Geneve (CH); (03) **3rd prize** lee + mundwiler architects, Buus (CH); (04) **4th prize** lehmann fidanza & associés, Zurich (CH)

01

02

03

04

Albanian Jewish Museum, Vlorë

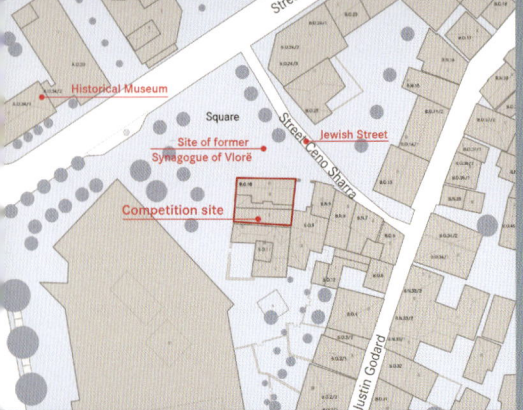

Location: Vlorë, Albania **Client:** Albanian-American Development Foundation (AADF) **Year:** 2021 – 2022 **Project size:** approx. 800 sqm NFA **Type of competition:** International design competition **Participants:** 4 **Competition budget:** USD 11,000 (prizes)

PRIZEWINNERS:
(01) **1st prize** Kimmel Eshkolot Architects Ltd., Tel Aviv (IL); **2nd prize** Winkler+Ruck Architekten ZT GmbH, Klagenfurt (A); **3rd prize** Wandel Lorch Götze Wach, Frankfurt a. M. (D); **3rd prize** Studio Terragni Architetti, Como (I)

JEWISH LEGACY IN ALBANIA The 2,000-year history of Albania's Jewish community is closely linked to the city of Vlorë in the South of the country. The harbor city on the Adriatic Sea was home to the country's largest Jewish community until the early 1990s. In the second half of the 20th century, however, the vast majority of the Jewish community emigrated to Israel and the United States. Nevertheless, today there is still a strong Jewish influence on the social and economic life of the city, or it is gradually re-emerging. The museum will reflect on this and on the unique and gratifying story of the protection of all Albanian and many other European Jewish people by the local population during the Holocaust. The building, financed by the AADF together with the Albanian Ministry of Culture, is to become part of a future museum district in the old city.

SITE An old historic 3-story residential building from the 19th century in the historical center of the city of Vlorë was chosen as the new home of the museum. Right next to the museum, where a large public plaza is now located, was the synagogue of the city until the beginning of the 20th century. The facade of the historic building has been renovated within the framework of a master plan for the "Restoration and urban enhancement of the historic center of the city of Vlorë", as well as dozens of other buildings from the late 19th and early 20th centuries in the neighborhood.

TASK The subject of the competition was the design of a new museum with a floor space of almost 800 sqm, which significantly exceeds the capacity of the historic building, so that an extension was necessary. Its main structure and the renovated facade were to be integrated; for the necessary enlargement there were options for an extension and a floor addition as well as a part of the public plaza. The program included spaces for permanent exhibition, temporary exhibitions, public events and educational programs, a library, an archive, a museum store, and administrative offices.

State Archives Kitzingen, Würzburg

STATE ARCHIVES OF BAVARIA The State Archives of Bavaria have preserved the written tradition of Bavaria since the early Middle Ages – back through the kingdom and the electorate to the Duchy of Bavaria. The State Archives in Würzburg hold (as of the end of 2017) around 8,500,000 archive units with a total volume of around 25,600 linear meters at its locations in Würzburg Residenz and Marienberg Fortress. The total volume grows annually by 300–400 linear meters due to levies from the state authorities. For the district of the Bamberg Higher Regional Court (administrative districts of Upper and Lower Franconia), the Würzburg State Archives are the notarial archives, currently holding about 6 million notarial deeds from 1862 to the present day.

LOCATION Kitzingen has a population of around 22,000 and is a large county seat with ten districts in the county of the same name in Mainfranken with the seat of the district administration office. The approx. 2 ha large "Deusterareal" is a currently vacant area at the northern edge of the Kitzingen city center, on the western slope above the Main riverbank. The competition area is characterized by the strong topography with an incline of 23 m and is bordered in the north by the state road no. 2272 and the Mainstockheimer street. The design had to take into consideration the underground cellars under parts of the competition area, which are protected as historical monuments and attest to an early phase of industrial beer production.

TASK The subject of the competition was the design of a new magazine and administration building, as well as its outdoor facilities, on a state-owned 8,500 sqm part of the so-called "Deusterareal", which covers a total area of 21,000 sqm. For the design of the remaining areas, outdoor space design concepts were to be developed for the city of Kitzingen as a part of the idea. The design had to be harmonious with the townscape. The program with approx. 8,000 sqm net floor area included not only conventional archive spaces but also spaces for public use, which should attract a higher number of visitors.

Location: Wurzburg, Germany **Client:** Würzburg State Building Authority **Year:** 2019 **Project size:** approx. 8,000 sqm UFA realization area, approx. 600 sqm GFA ideas area **Type of competition:** Design competition **Participants:** 22 **Competition budget:** EUR 204,000 (prizes)

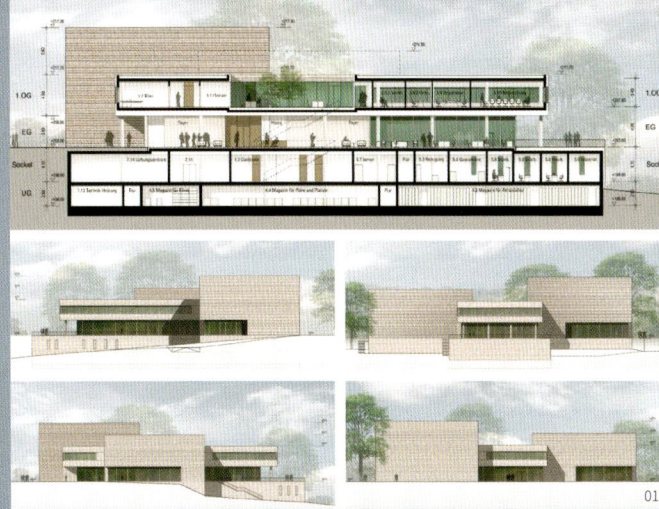

PRIZEWINNERS:
(01) **1st prize** gmp · Architekten von Gerkan, Marg und Partner, Hamburg, (D), with Capatti Staubach urbane Landschaften PartGmbH, Berlin (D); **2nd prize** Brückner & Brückner Architekten, Würzburg (D), with Realgrün Landschaftsarchitekten Gesellschaft von Landschaftsarchitekten und Stadtplanern mbH, Munich (D); **3rd prize** Bruno Fioretti Marquez Architekten GbR, Berlin (D), with Atelier Loidl Landschaftsarchitekten, Berlin (D); **4th prize** Heinle, Wischer und Partner, Dresden (D), with UKL Ulrich Krüger Landschaftsarchitekten, Dresden (D); **Mention** Staab Architekten GmbH, Berlin (D), with arc.grün Landschaftsarchitekten Stadtplaner GmbH, Kitzingen (D); **Mention** Scheidt Kasprusch Gesellschaft von Architekten mbH, Berlin (D) with Henningsen Landschaftsarchitekten Part GmbH, Berlin (D)

Darat King Abdullah II for Culture and Arts, Amman

Location: Amman, Jordan **Client:** Greater Amman Municipality (GAM) **Year:** 2007 – 2008 **Project size:** 12,000 sqm **Type of competition:** Restricted project competition preceded by an application procedure **Participants:** 6 **Competition budget:** EUR 110,000

PRIZEWINNERS:
(01) **1st prize** Zaha Hadid Architects, London (UK); (02) **1st prize** Delugan Meissl Associated Architects, Vienna (A); (03) **3rd prize** Snøhetta, Oslo (N)

AMMAN With a population of over 2 million, Amman is one of the most vibrant and modern cities in the Middle East. An influx of refugees since the 1970s from Palestine, Lebanon, and Iraq has resulted in an increase both in population and in social tensions. Still, the cosmopolitan character of its residents, the political stability and relative openness of the kingdom itself, has enabled Amman to secure its position at the same time as a cultural focus of the Middle East. Art institutions and their appreciative fans are steadily on the rise. Indeed, Amman's creative artists are getting bolder all the time in their use of new media, and choice of subjects.

GAM STRIP The task set for this competition was a design for Amman's new culture and art center, the "Darat King Abdullah II". The project's principal, the Greater Amman Municipality, or GAM, envisioned the center as the hot spot of the regional art scene. It was to be accommodate the performing art center and host events like concerts, music, and theatre performed by foreign and Jordanian artists, among them the Amman Symphony Orchestra, the State Music Conservatory, and various other sources. The "Darat King Abdullah II" was one of several projects meant to liven up the city center and bridge social barriers separating its residents. To this end, a number of public buildings was to be constructed in what is called the "GAM Strip", a site at the heart of the city, and a point of contact between two hugely different neighborhoods. The "Darat King Abdullah II" aside, the city administration building, the Hussein Culture Center, and the National Museum (opened in 2008) were already sited along a stretch of valley at the foot of Jabal Al Akhdar. Ample, open, and emphatically a public space, the "GAM Strip" (and the "Darat King Abdullah II" in particular) was to make everyone in Amman feel welcome there.

PROJECT The 19,000 sqm site of the new culture and art center was at the western end of the strip. The spatial program comprised 12,000 sqm of ancillary usable area, a concert theater with 1,600 seats, a smaller theater with 400 seats, rehearsal rooms and lecture halls, top end stage equipment, a sweeping foyer, a restaurant, a café, and club combination, as well as administrative offices.

Folkwang Museum, Essen

CITY OF ESSEN AND FOLKWANG In 2010, Essen and the Ruhr area would be the designated European Capital of Culture. The new extension to the Folkwang Museum was one of a small number of newly built projects within the framework of this event, the motto of which, "Change through culture, culture through change", was coined by Karl Ernst Osthaus, the museum's founder. Originally located in Hagen and opened in 1902, the Folkwang Museum was the first in Europe to acquire works by van Gogh and Matisse. It was among the first institutions to dedicate exhibitions to Nolde, Hodler and Munch, and the first museum to show objects from Africa and the Pacific Rim within the context of European art. After the early death of Osthaus, the collection was transferred to Essen and merged with the Essen Museum of Art to form the new Folkwang Museum.

PROJECT Conceived as a complement to a heritage-protected wing dating from 1960, the new project was to have a usable area of approx. 12,000 sqm and was to replace a section built in 1983 which was being abandoned due its lack of economic viability. While the extant building was to be reserved chiefly for the main works of the 19th century collection and classical modernity, the new building was to house post-World War II and contemporary art. The project also included a new entrance zone, spaces for changing exhibitions, educational facilities, offices, workshops, depots, and halls for the presentation of those parts of the collection that, due to lack of space, were hitherto inaccessible to the public. In addition, the collection of the German Poster Museum was to be given a home here for the first time.

CHALLENGES Principally the project task required integration with the residential neighborhood, the orientation of the building and its main entrance towards the city center, and a response to the high-level noise generated on the adjacent through road. The aim was to create an architectural and conceptual urban landmark while integrating the museum and its new wing within the existing urban context. To this end, the redesigned museum was to form a common campus with the Institute of Cultural Sciences bordering it in the south.

Location: Essen, Germany **Client:** City of Essen, represented by Geschäftsbereich 6A **Year:** 2006 – 2007 **Project size:** 19.000 sqm **Type of competition:** Restricted cooperative project competition preceded by an application procedure **Participants:** 12 **Competition budget:** EUR 530,000

PRIZEWINNERS:
(01) **1st prize** David Chipperfield Architects, London/Berlin (UK/D); **2nd prize** Adjaye Associates, London (UK); **3rd prize** Gigon Guyer Architekten, Zurich (CH); **Honorable mention** Staab Architekten, Berlin (D); **Honorable mention** Zaha Hadid Architects, London (UK)

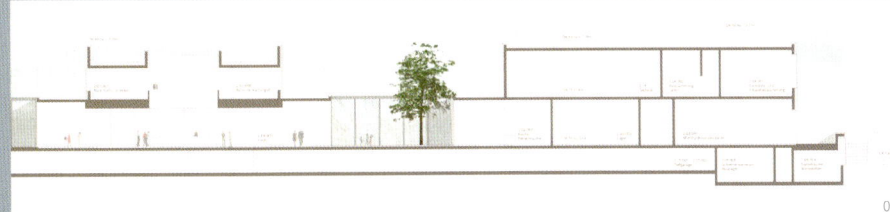

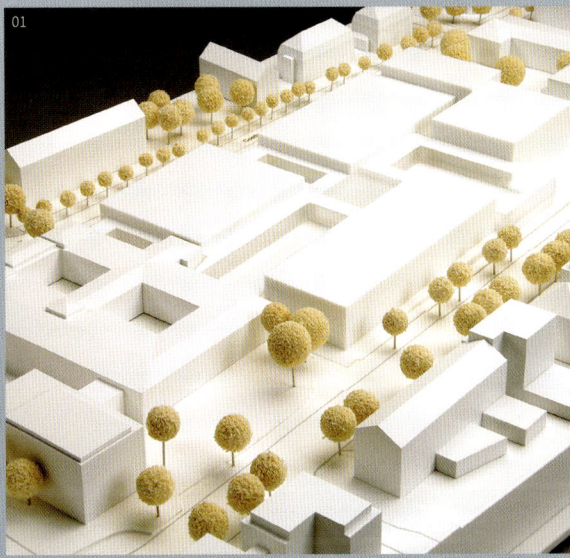

1 LAUNCHING A COMPETITION

1.1 Subject of competition

Design competitions are used as an instrument for selecting and optimizing the design solution and for preparing the commissioning of the most important project partners in a wide variety of projects in the construction industry. They are useful for almost any project to make decisions based on quality criteria. The subject of a competition can thus be:

› **regarding the scope of services:** architectural design, urban design, landscape architecture, engineering projects, and art in architecture, or exhibition design
› **in terms of size:** small, large, and more, or less prominent, or complex tasks
› **in relation to the client:** projects by public, private, and institutional clients

1.2 Competition as a special way of commissioning

Competitions play a special role in public procurement law. As a rule, a contract cannot be awarded without an evaluation according to clear criteria. The design tasks cannot be described conclusively, and the –often– complex requirements require interdependent evaluation criteria.
Thus, preparing of decisions on the awarding of design contracts on basis of a consultation by a committee with mostly independent experts (jury) is regarded as a proper and acceptable method. However, this special approach in public procurement law must be explained again and again and, if necessary, enforced. At the same time, this special position of competitions in the context of public procurement law repeatedly requires adaptation of established tendering systems developed for classic forms of awarding (e.g., official journals and awarding platforms).

1.3 The right moment to launch a competition

The initial idea and decision to organize a design competition takes place in the earliest phase of a project, for very different reasons and through the initiative of various parties involved in the project:

› Out of a natural routine and positive prior experience with the tool of competition
› Hoping to inspire new solution approaches
› Convinced to obtain a better solution through the competition
› Due to contractual obligations, e.g., between a municipality and a private project developer
› By public pressure or to avoid it
› After objective consideration of the options of public procurement law or in-house tendering principles
› On the initiative of individuals within the developer's organization, or on the recommendation of an external designer trusted by the developer
› Knowing that in this way a decision will be reached by consensus of many stakeholders
› In the hope of winning prominent planning offices for the project in this way

Sometimes it is a combination of these motives, maybe combined with a dose of curiosity. Often enough, not everyone involved in the project is convinced at the beginning of the use of this method or there is a lack of experience with competitions and the options they offer. In many cases, there are still uncertainties regarding –more or less– relevant requirements for the task, so that it is uncertain when exactly to start a competition: possibly the program has not yet been finally defined or approved, essential expert opinions are still missing (e.g., on the property), a political approval of the project or the financing has not yet been finally clarified or confirmed.

Jury meeting in the "BMW Group FIZ Future Munich" competition, 2014

A generally valid rule for the right moment to launch the competition cannot be formulated, but the following can be said with certainty:

Advice 1: It is never too early to seek professional advice.

Advice 2: Professional advice is best given by independent persons or companies with expertise both in the relevant discipline (architecture, urban design, etc.) and experience in organizing competitions and guiding the client through this design phase.

Advice 3: Open questions can be also clarified in or throughout the competition. It may not be necessary to have specified all boundary conditions before the competition. On the contrary, it is often advisable to leave questions open and allow the competition process to generate creative solutions.

A schedule and plan of action should then be developed jointly to clarify fundamental questions about the procedure, including the question of what type of competition should be held or whether a competition is the most appropriate planning tool in this case.

1.4 Concerns against competitions

The idea of conducting a competition is often accompanied by concerns, some more and some less justified and presented with varying degrees of vehemence, mostly on the topics:
› Competitions are expensive
› Competitions consume too much time
› In competitions, I lose control over the decision
› The task of my project is too specific and can only be solved by a design office that is already familiar to me or with the topic – but not by offices that I do not have access to at this stage of the design process

These concerns are understandable. Reservation and critical questions are important in the initial discussions about projects and their implementation, as is an open discussion about expectations and concerns, especially regarding the aspects mentioned above. Thus, at the beginning of a project and at the question whether to run a competition, there is often a mixture of optimism and pessimism at the same time, which at best can be clarified very quickly in a positive mood prevailing in the process altogether. Some concerns are only dispelled in retrospect, after the competition has been completed.

1.5 Considering fundamental issues of a competition

However, the above-mentioned concerns are not valid reasons for rejecting the idea of a competition per se but should motivate a thorough discussion and decision on the question of the best possible procedure, an open-minded attitude, a realistic assessment of opportunities and risks, and then to careful prepare and conduct the competition or – if necessary – a justified decision against its implementation. At the beginning of the procedure, decisions must be made on key questions that have a decisive impact on potential, costs, and the process. This is followed by an overview of the strategic aspects. Further details on all topics are presented in the next chapters of the book.

1.5.1 Planning the planning of a design competition – selecting the procedure type

The most important strategic decision is to choose the type of procedure. While there is the overarching concept of a design competition that encompasses all types of competitions, there is still no "one single" process for all competitions. Choosing the type of procedure means a multitude of options as regards the process, which allow (and require) adapting to the respective project

and have a considerable influence on the result and thus the project as a whole (for further details please refer to Chapter 3):
› Project competition or ideas competition
› Open or restricted competition
› Single-stage or two-stage competition
› Number of participants
› Disciplines entitled to participate
› Regional or international competition
› Single or multi-stage procedure
› Anonymous or non-anonymous (cooperative)
› Competition or parallel multiple commissioning

1.5.2 Selecting the project partners: competition organization

At the earliest possible stage, it should be clarified who will be responsible for the organization (preparation and execution) of the competition and whether, or to what extent, external support should be brought in for this purpose. Depending on the competence and capacity of the sponsor as well as the complexity of the construction task and the planned procedure, the total effort and thus also the services to be provided by external support can vary greatly. Also, the position of external partners as competition organizers can be very different. The role of external consulting in the project follows worldwide and even regionally different traditions:

› **Competition advisor:** A single experienced external person (widespread e.g., in North America) who advises the sponsor on strategic issues, but the major workload is covered by the sponsor's team itself or by another external firm not necessarily experienced in competition support.
› **Competition consultant:** An external consulting firm supports the competent sponsor as an "extended workbench" through capacities and selective expert advice, thus rather with the character of a "competition secretary", in which the sponsor continues to be responsible for selected central administrative parts of the procedure.
› **Competition manager:** In this scenario, the external company specializing in this service offers a complete service, and the promoter can concentrate on their tasks as the sponsor, that is defining the planned use and deciding on strategic issues prepared by the competition manager.

Peter Ortved
Architect, Canada

❧❧ What is important to me as a Professional Advisor, when organizing a competition, is that the Professional Advisor recognizes the three main responsibilities essential to success.
Firstly, the PA should be fully involved with the drafting of the Competition Brief and advise the Sponsor on the rules, documentation, program, conditions, and honorariums. These must be appropriately formatted to address both the design expectations and the capabilities of current architectural practices. In other words, act as a surrogate client.
Secondly, the PA should act on behalf of all the competitors during the competition process to ensure the requirements are reasonable, that the process is consistent throughout and that all teams are presented with equal opportunities at all times. The PA acts essentially as the agent of the competitor teams and they are dependent on the PA to represent their interests to the Sponsor.
Thirdly, the PA should oversee and maintain the integrity of the procedures, in overseeing the fairness and equity of the process for all participants. The PA must be, and be seen by all parties to be, the honest broker. If these three criteria are met, then a competition will be regarded as professionally well organized, responsible, and hopefully, successful.

1.5.3 Selecting the project partners: jury and experts

The technical jury assumes the most important advisory role for the sponsor within the framework of the final decision on the competition result. At the same time, the jury advises on the formulation of the terms of reference and ensures a fair, objective process towards the offices interested in participating and those taking part in the competition, as well as towards the public.

Accordingly, the selection of the jury members must be made with much care. Recommended, and in many countries established or regulated as standard, is a composition of an independent technical jury and a general jury, which represents the interests and expertise of the sponsor but also other relevant project participants: e.g., user interests, neighboring interests, interests of the approving authorities and, if applicable, the funding agencies.

The selection of the jury members signals to the outside world the attitude of the sponsor, depending on how the committee is staffed, for example, in terms of number of members, origin, internationality, interdisciplinarity, but also as regards gender and age representation and diversity in basic architectural attitudes.

1.5.4 Cost planning

The competition costs vary greatly depending on the task, the chosen procedure, and the size of the jury. The items listed below affect the competition costs:

› Prize money and expense allowance (= competition sum) for the participants
› Honoraria for external technical jurors and technical experts
› Event costs for room rental, catering, display boards, transportation, etc.
› Process costs for document printing, model construction, model photography, etc.
› Communication costs for exhibition and website
› Travel expenses
› Competition management (fee for preparation and organization of a competition)

In addition, the costs for the personnel employed by the sponsor themselves should not be underestimated.

1.5.5 Schedule

The process of competitions is usually divided into four stages:

› **Preparation** (approximately 3 months to 3 years): The time required for this stage varies greatly and depends especially on the extent of existing preliminary work (e.g., whether a requirements program and necessary expert opinions and measurements are already available) and on the required extent of coordination of the specifications or other important parameters of the competition process, e.g., with (political) committees, the public, or design partners. In the case of restricted competitions, the selection of the offices participating in the competition can take place in parallel.
› **Competition/working period** (2 to 3 months): Depending on the complexity of the task and the position of the working period in the vacation calendar, an appropriate period should be provided for the design offices. In the case of two-stage competitions, there are two of these periods, whereby the working period can be reduced to 4 to 6 weeks, depending on the required services.
› **Decision** (1 to 1.5 months): Prior to the jury meeting, a preliminary evaluation takes place, in which the submitted materials for the presentation to the jury are reviewed, analyzed, and prepared in a report. The jury meeting itself usually lasts 1 to 2 days.
› **Communication and commissioning** (approx. 2 months): After the actual competition is completed, on the one hand the commission is to be negotiated and on the other hand the result is to be presented to the public in the form of an exhibition (possibly with a public vernissage), online presentation and, if necessary, printed documentation formats as well as via a press conference or press release.

Scenes from jury meetings in the following competitions **1:** Babyn Yar Holocaust Memorial Center in Kiyv (Rainer Mahlamäki, János Kárász, and Kjetil Thorsen), **2:** Technical City Hall Düsseldorf (Elke Delugan-Meissl) **3:** Administrative building for the European Commission in Brussels (Co front: Brian Cody, Dominique Lyon, and Monica von Schmalensee), **4:** City Hall Dallgow-Döberitz (Regine Leibinger)

Kjetil Thorsen
Architect, Oslo

❝ Architectural practice is all about portraying the inherent contextual specifics of a place into shapes and programs. Architectural competitions enlighten people in a jury on the different possible approaches and ways of thinking within a limited timeframe of design. Thus, some few observations on the art of competing from my side. As program and competition parameters are laid out by different stakeholders, the first thing to do is to decipher the task. Look for less obvious information and combine the pragmatic with inspired associations. Stay true to your concept, don't design for the jury, but for the place. What does this mean for the organization of competitions? The more clearly the task and potential conflicts of interest or contradictions are formulated in the competition brief and communicated in colloquia, the less likely misunderstandings will lead to incorrect design proposals – the more open the attitude of the client, the more innovative and surprising solutions can be.

Elke Delugan-Meissl
Architect, Vienna

❝ As a juror as well as a participant in numerous competitions, I consider a detailed, precise task definition with a creative scope for individual solutions to be the basis for an innovative, future-oriented result of a competition meeting diverse expectations.

Dominique Lyon
Architect, Paris

❝ Among the jury members, at least one third will be architects.
In the prequalification, the jury will select a variety of architectural profiles: established/new, local/foreigner, wise/speculative, calm/communicative.
The first design stage is about conceptual design. Limit the size and number of documents requested for presentation. An A1 and an A4 sheet are enough.
During the final stage, the jury will consider, above all, architecture as a cultural field that put ideas into forms. The jury will address the following questions: how architecture enhances our awareness, how it stimulates our mind, when the global tendency is to install dullness? The jury will shun clichés: architecture is always a surprise.

Regine Leibinger
Architect, Berlin

❝ What is important for us as participants when organizing a competition? The decisive factor for us is the quality, or more precisely: the precision of the competition texts and the preparation of all the basic information for the task. This is a translation service between clients and planners, which a competition manager like [phase eins]. masters. It certainly has a positive effect in terms of good solutions if one listens to the architectural jury early in the competition. Because in architecture, too, the answers can only be fitting if the question is well posed.

1.5.6 Quality of the competition brief

As many colleagues quoted in the book confirm, the quality of the brief is the most important guarantor of project success.

As confirmed by numerous colleagues quoted in the book, the quality of the description of the task is the most important guarantor of project success. The more complete, better coordinated and clear the brief, the greater the likelihood that design teams will understand the objective and be able to develop appropriate designs on that understanding. As each project is unique, the competition brief must be created anew for each project; an effort that is worthwhile and cannot be reduced to copying together existing text modules.

The structuring of the competition brief documents is a particular challenge because the design tasks are usually characterized by a high degree of complexity. The central topics must be highlighted as such in order to be comprehensible in the multitude of information required. In the case of detailed information, it must be considered whether it is necessary for the next planning step and can therefore be omitted (at this point), if needed.

The complexity of the construction tasks can be explained more easily and precisely in many points with the help of plans, photos, and other graphics, which is why a proper competition brief is also characterized by the quality of the illustrations.

Title page, table of contents, and excerpts from the competition brochure for the 'Wien Museum Neu' competition in 2014.

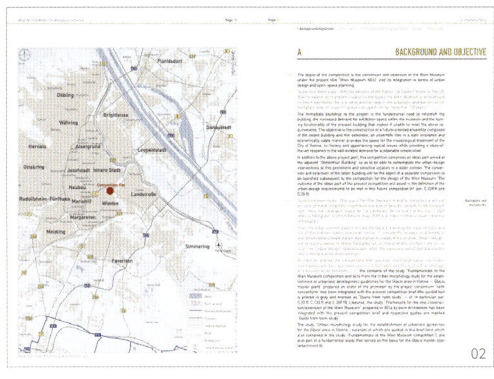
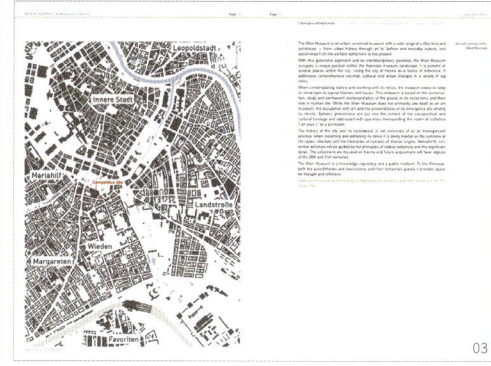

A: Background and Objectives

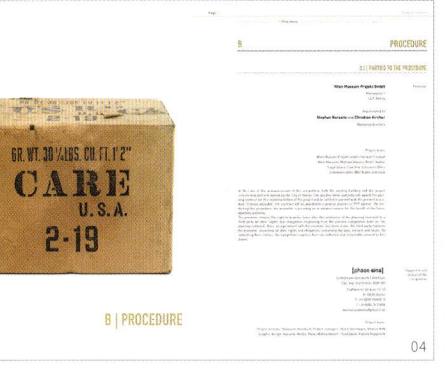
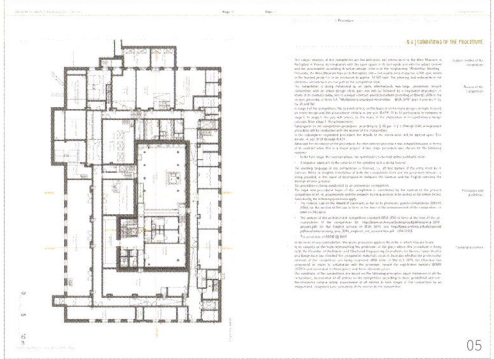

B: The Procedure

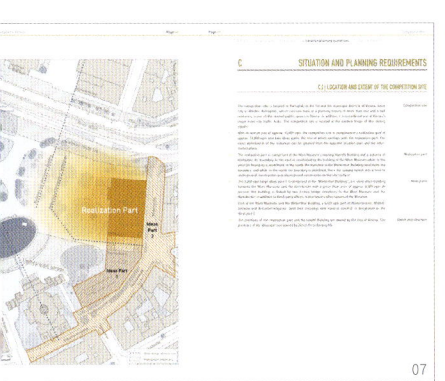
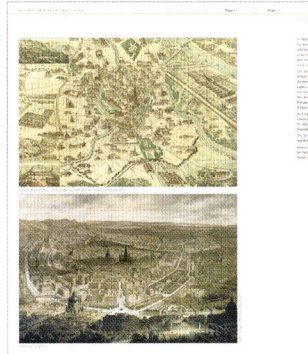
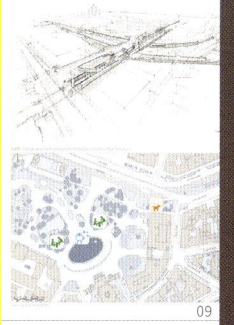

C: Situation and Planning Guidelines
D: The Task

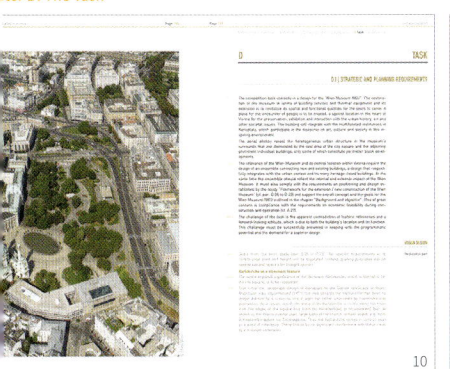
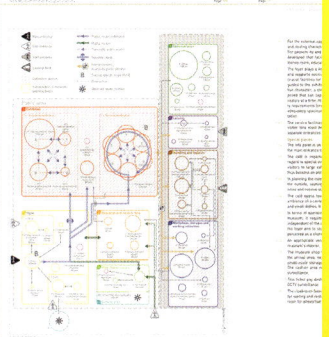
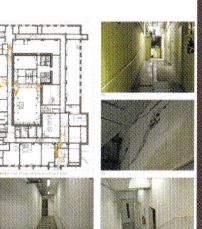

Nezar AlSayyad

Ph.D, Distinguished Professor Emeritus Architecture, Planning and Urban Design, University of California, Berkeley

" As someone who helped organize competitions, I think one of the most important things is to insist with the client at the beginning to get them to identify what do you really care for and want in a building, and to remind them that they will be held accountable to it.
As a juror who served on many international competitions, I think the most important issue for me is the clarity and eligibility of the competition rules which I will adhere to and will also insist that competitors are measured by and held accountable to them. While I am open to competitors who propose minor changes to site and program, I do not think they should ever be awarded for violating the competition rules.

1 Launching a competition

II GOVERNMENT BUILDINGS

In our experience, government buildings are among the most coordination-intensive projects in the competition preparation phase. The required effort and time should not be underestimated by the competition organizer. Usually, the projects already have a history of several years in clarifying and approving the demands, so many issues have already been resolved. Nevertheless, the requirements for coordinating the content of the competition task are very complex due to of the numerous and varied requirements of these buildings, which are usually owner-occupied. Government buildings have a strong public profile, so the design must meet high standards. They should be exemplary and at the same time avoid an inappropriate use of taxpayers' money. Increased demands on public relations must be also considered when organizing the competition. Often complicated design aims increase the effort in formulating the task and organizing the preliminary examination. Even the requirements of comparatively simple administrative buildings (e.g., ministries and large central services) are significantly more complex than those of conventional office buildings. For example, areas for special purposes, increased security requirements and representational functions must be taken into consideration.

Designing parliamentary buildings is even more complex, as is organizing a competition for these special buildings. In addition to the numerous meeting and conference areas with advanced technical equipment, one of the major challenges is the security requirements with separate access to the different areas for parliamentarians, other staff, the press, and the public – usually with different room occupancy and security options during the session periods, depending on the presence of e.g., state guests and in between sessions. In addition, parliament buildings must meet the requirements of visibility and participation in democratic processes and express this in their architecture. All these aspects, as well as the seating arrangement in the plenum and the great symbolic significance the building, should be considered in the competition brief and during preliminary examination.

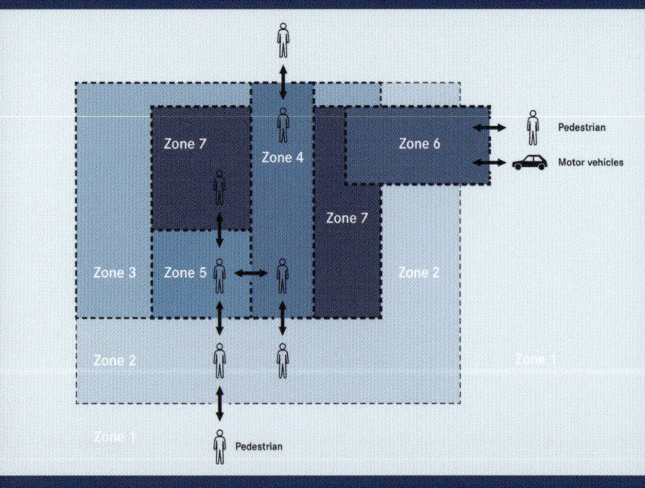

Diagram explaining the security zones in the competition "European Parliament in Brussels"

European Parliament – Paul-Henri SPAAK Building, Brussels

EUROPEAN PARLIAMENT The European Parliament (EP) is the only directly democratically elected European institution, central to the continent's modern history. The EP, through its directly elected Members, represents nearly 450 million European citizens. Its built heritage is significant not only for the European legislators, but also for citizens, providing important public spaces for dialogue and for experiencing European democracy and values. It is also a venue for European commemorations and celebrations. In addition to Strasbourg and Luxemburg, Brussels is one of the three locations of the European Parliament. The EP is open to citizens, meetings can be followed live or by web streaming, it engages with them and provides them with an extraordinary experience when visited.

PAUL-HENRI SPAAK BUILDING In Brussels, the EP is housed in a significant complex of buildings in the European Quarter, within which the SPAAK building is the main EP building. It houses the Chamber, a number of committee meeting rooms as well as the main welcoming functions for citizens, media and official visitors. Completed in 1995, the building is located between Place Luxembourg and Parc Léopold and above the underground railway line with Luxembourg railway station.

TASK During the past years, the number of member states has grown, and with it the Parliament, the quantity of committees and the need of facilities. In addition, studies have shown that the general condition of the building, especially its building services, require at least a radical renovation. One of the main components of the competition was to identify the right approach to this question, defining that the notion of "renewal" includes a wide gamut of approaches, ranging from "renovation" to "reconstructing" the building. The new building should meet the requirements of a transparent organization and fulfill the complex functional requirements and necessities of security.

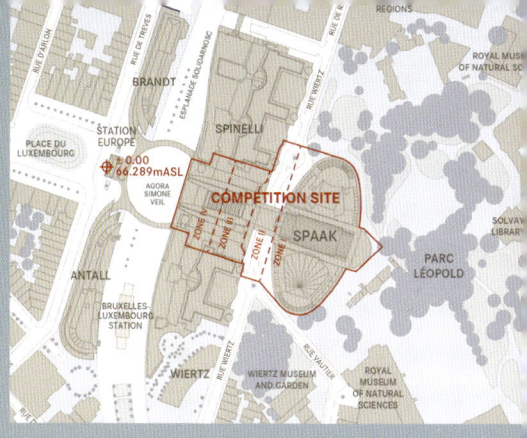

Location: Brussels, Belgium **Client:** European Parliament **Year:** 2020 – 2021 **Project size:** approx. 180,000 sqm GFA (buildable volume); expressed needs approx. 90,000 sqm GFA (program) **Type of competition:** International design competition for interdisciplinary teams **Participants:** 15 **Competition budget:** EUR 1,525,000 (prizes: EUR 400,000; remuneration per participant: EUR 75,000)

PRIZEWINNERS:
(01) **1st prize** JDS Architects, Copenhagen (DK), with Coldefy, Lille (F), NL Architects, Amsterdam (NL), Carlo Ratti Associati, Torino (I), ENSAMBLE STUDIO, Madrid (E), UTIL cvba, Schaerbeek (B), Ramboll, Copenhagen (DK); (02) **2nd prize** Jabornegg & Palffy Generalplaner ZT GmbH, Vienna (A), with KUEHN MALVEZZI, Berlin (D), AXIS Ingenieurleistungen ZT GmbH, Vienna (A); **3rd prize** Moreau Kusunoki, Paris (F), with Dethier Architectures, Liège (B); **4th prize** Belvedere Architecture, Paris (F), with Ove Arup & Partners International Ltd (UK); **5th prize** A2M, Brussels (B) with VK ENGINEERING (B), C.F. Møller Architects, Århus (DK)

European Parliament – Paul-Henri SPAAK Building, Brussels

Parliamentary Precinct Redevelopment, Ottawa – Block 2

Project title: Parliamentary Precinct Redevelopment Ottawa – Block 2 **Location:** Ottawa, Canada **Client:** Government of Canada **Year:** 2020 – 2022 **Project size:** approx. 30,000 sqm UFA **Type of competition:** Architectural design competition in two stages **Participants:** Stage 1: 11; Stage 2: 6 **Competition budget:** CAD 2,935,000 (prizes: CAD 505,000; Compensation per participant Stage 1: CAD 120,000; Compensation per participant Stage 2: CAD 165,000)

PRIZEWINNERS:
(01) **1st prize** Zeidler Architecture Inc., Toronto (CDN), in association with David Chipperfield Architects, London (UK); (02) **2nd prize** NEUF Architects, Ottawa (CDN), in joint venture with Renzo Piano Building Workshop, Paris (F); (03) **3rd prize** Watson MacEwen Teramura Architects, Ottawa (CDN), in joint venture with Behnisch Architekten, Boston

PARLIAMENT HILL Ottawa is the center of Canada's parliamentary democracy. At its core is the Parliamentary Precinct, the symbolic centerpiece of the city and country, and host to Canada's legislatures – the House of Commons and the Senate of Canada – as well as the Library of Parliament. This triad of historic Parliament Buildings, now referred to as Centre Block, sits upon a dramatic escarpment, a high cliff edge overlooking the broad and turbulent Ottawa River with the rapids and falls considered sacred to Indigenous peoples within view.

BLOCK 2 Wellington Avenue marks the edge between the area of the parliament buildings and the orthogonal grid of the city. In this first row, Block 2 forms a complete city block whose historic buildings once housed the first U.S. Embassy and branches of Canada's major banks. Once redeveloped, Block 2 will effectively form the fourth facade of the great Parliamentary Lawn, framing this public space of national importance.

OBJECTIVE As an important part of an overarching master plan, the entire Block 2 will be transformed into a government quarter for parliamentarians in Ottawa including offices and conference rooms. In addition to the task of designing contemporary workplaces, integrating a balanced relationship between developing a conservation approach and establishing an appropriate setting for the parliamentary buildings, a particular challenge was the respectful consideration of the Indigenous Peoples' Space (IPS) situated in the center of the block. In 2017, Canada donated two buildings in Block 2 to the Indigenous Peoples of Canada, so that in the future they will have a location directly on the symbolic Parliamentary Lawn. In addition to the development of a symbolic-visual and spatial solution, the IPS signifies a division between West Block and East Block, which had to be connected architecturally.

Real Estate Complex "Loi 130" for the European Commission, Brussels

EUROPEAN COMMISSION The European Commission was established in 1958 and is the politically independent executive arm of the European Union. Political leadership of the Commission is provided by a team of Commissioners (one from each EU Member State). The day-to-day running of European Commission business is performed by its staff organized into departments, better known as Directorates-General, each responsible for a specific policy area. A total of around 33,000 people are employed by the Commission, of which 24,000 are based in Brussels.

PROJECT The task was the design for the redevelopment of an entire city block, located at the Rue de la Loi in the midst of the so-called "European Quarter" in Brussels, into an efficient building complex for the European Commission. With up to 190,000 sqm GFA above ground, the mixed-use complex should provide office space for more than 5,250 employees as well as meeting facilities, two childcare centres, the European Commission's Visitor Centre, retail facilities and a car park. In addition, the design should comprise a new entrance to the Maelbeek metro station. Urban planning regulations, defined by the masterplan at the time, allowed for two high-rise buildings of respectively 165 m and 114 m high to be constructed on the site.

COMPETITION AND PROJECT STATUS At the time of the competition, the "Project Loi 130" the biggest and most important real estate project for the European Commission in Brussels. To receive forward-looking, innovative and cost-efficient constructions, aiming at the highest sustainability targets, the European Commission launched the design competition in two phases for interdisciplinary teams in close collaboration with the UIA. After the decision and the announcement and public exhibition of the result, the region changed the masterplan for the area and the COVID pandemic changed strategic plans of the Commission, which unfortunately led to the termination of the project.

Location: Brussels, Belgium **Client:** European Commission **Year:** 2018 – 2019 **Project size:** 190,000 sqm GFA **Type of competition:** Architectural competition **Participants:** Stage 1: 28; Stage 2: 9 **Competition budget:** EUR 900,000 (prizes: EUR 300,000; Compensation Stage 1: EUR 300,000; Compensation stage 2: EUR 300,000)

PRIZEWINNERS:
(01) **1st prize** Rafael De La-Hoz Arquitectos (E), Perkins+Will UK Limited (UK), Latz + Partner Landscape Architecture Urban Planning (D), MC2 with Tecnica Y Protectos S.A. (E); **2nd prize** 2portzamparc (F), Florence Mercier Paysagiste (F), Artelia Batiment & Industrie (F); **3rd prize** Buro II & Archi+I (B), C. F. Møller Danmark A/S (DK), Delva Landscape Architects (NL), vk Engineering (B), Transsolar Energietechnik GmbH (D)

Real Estate Complex "Loi 130" for the European Commission, Brussels

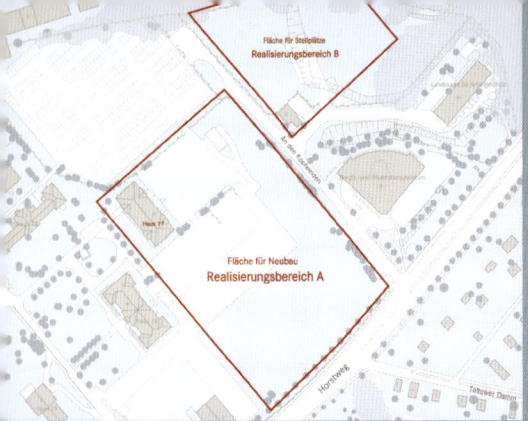

Location: Potsdam, Germany **Client:** Bundesamt für Immobilienaufgaben (BImA) represented by the Brandenburgischer Landesbetrieb für Liegenschaften und Bauen (BLB) **Year:** 2013 – 2014 **Project size:** 16,250 sqm UFA **Type of competition:** Project competition preceded by an open application procedure **Participants:** 23 **Competition budget:** EUR 275,000 (prizes: EUR 140,000; honorable mentions: 35,000 EUR; fee per participant: EUR 4,000)

Federal Police Headquarters, Potsdam

BACKGROUND INFORMATION The Bundespolizeipräsidium was established in its current form as an oversight and coordinative organization of the federal police force in 2008. At the time of the competition the newly formed organization was provisionally housed in three different locations in Potsdam. The command and control center unit of the federal police is the central point of contact for domestic and international security organizations. The federal police also operate its command post for specific assignments, both domestic and international, from their headquarters.

LOCATION OF SITE The new building for the Federal Police Headquarters is on a parcel of land on Heinrich-Mann-Allee 103 in Potsdam where other state authorities are also located. The current urban situation dates back to construction of the Wilhelmstift, a church-funded institution from the second half of the 19th century and the buildings' brightly plastered facades and red brick plinths dominate the character of the site even today. The competition included two parcels of land: one for a new building integrating an existing building; and another for the construction of a parking facility. The street "An den Kopfweiden" runs between the two lots.

COMPETITION SITE The task placed particularly high demands on planning quality for the various security areas in the command and control center. The objective was to design a representative building ensemble with approximately 15,000 sqm UFA for almost 1,000 employees. The building should set design standards for future building projects for state authorities on and around the property. Emphasis was placed on the quality of internal organization – particularly in the command and control center area – and the design of optimal conditions for the future office spaces.

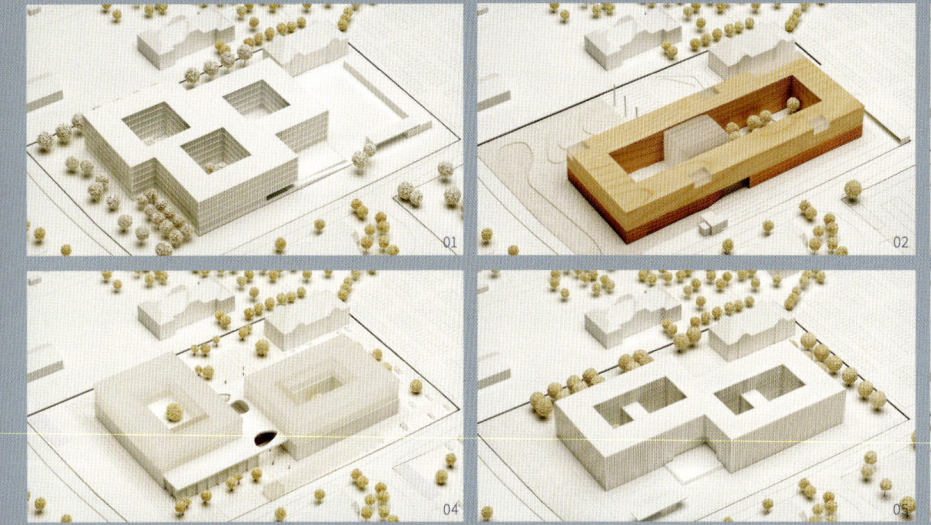

PRIZEWINNERS:
(01) **1st prize** CODE UNIQUE, Dresden (D), with herrburg Landschaftsarchitekten, Berlin (D); (02) **2nd prize** gmp International with Man Made Land, Berlin (D); (03) **3rd prize** Bodamer Faber Architekten with Plankontor S1 Landschaftsarchitekten, Stuttgart (D); (04) **Honorable mention** hks Hestermann Rommel Architekten with plandrei Landschaftsarchitektur, Erfurt (D); (05) **Honorable mention** h4a Gessert + Randecker + Legner Architekten, Stuttgart (D), with Planstatt Senner, Überlingen (D) (06) **Finalist** Weinmiller Architekten with LA.BAR Landschaftsarchitekten, Berlin (D)

State Parliament of Lower Saxony, Hanover

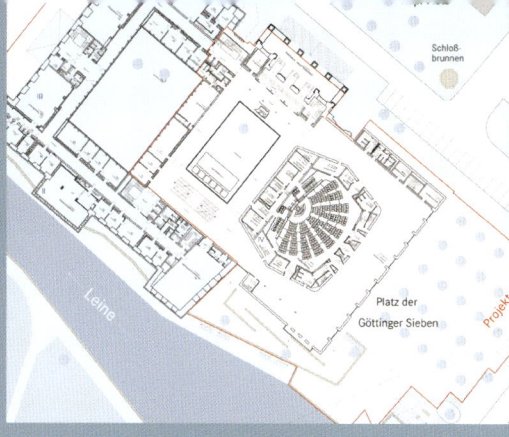

STATE PARLIAMENT IN THE LEINE CASTLE The State Parliament of Lower Saxony has been seated in Hanover's Leine Castle since 1962. The origins of the oldest sections of the castle trace back to a Franciscan (Minorite) monastery built in 1291. The building had subsequently undergone numerous changes and renovations and was almost completely destroyed in an air raid in 1943. The architect Dieter Oesterlen reconstructed it as the State Parliament building based on a competition design from 1954. The parliamentary chamber in particular reflected characteristics that translate a specific idea of activity into built and spatial form: parliament members had to work in a concentrated atmosphere without the distractions of external influences. The building's exterior juxtaposed the historical facade of the castle with the cubic plenary hall representing a connection of historicity and modernity.

IMPULSE BEHIND THE PROJECT The existing plenary area no longer met the functional requirements of State Parliament and its ambition of making parliamentary work transparent. Furthermore, construction deficits existed, and barrier-free access is lacking in some parts of the chamber areas. For these reasons, it was decided to initiate the conversion or renovation of the plenary area including the entrance situation, meeting, office, visitor, and media areas as well as the restaurant.

THE NEW STATE PARLIAMENT BUILDING The task was to design a plenary area whose appearance should have an identity-forming character and emphasize the building's function. The parliament building is an architectural monument, necessitating a careful approach to adapting the form of the listed building's substance. Part of the competition task required a response to conflicting goals: elimination of functional deficiencies; implementation of spatial and functional programs; and preservation of the monument or significant parts of the monument.

Location: Hanover, Germany **Client:** Federal State of Lower Saxony represented by the State Construction Management Hanover **Year:** 2009 – 2010 **Project size:** 8,500 sqm UFA **Type of competition:** Open two-stage design competition **Participants:** Stage 1: 57, Stage 2: 16 **Competition budget:** EUR 171,000 (prizes: EUR 137,000; honorable mentions: EUR 34,000)

PRIZEWINNERS:
(01) **1st prize** YI ARCHITECTS, Cologne (D); (02) **2nd prize** Walter Gebhardt Architekt, Hamburg (D); (03) **3rd prize** mm architekten, Hanover (D)

II Government buildings

2 RULES FOR COMPETITIONS

2.1 Relevant rules and regulations

A wide range of national and international experience, methods and rules have been used since around 150 years to define the formal framework for design competitions.

International rules and regulations

› **UIA Guidelines:** In 1956, the General Conference of UNESCO adopted rules for international competitions in architecture and urban design (revised in 1978) and entrusted the Union Internationale des Architectes (UIA) with the task of implementing them and assisting clients. To this end, the UIA has developed the "UIA Competition Guide – Guidelines for design competitions in architecture and related fields" (last updated in 2020), which describes detailed conditions for international competitions that form the basis for the monitoring of international competitions by the UIA (https://www.uia-architectes.org/wp-content/uploads/2022/02/2_UIA_competition_guide_2020.pdf).
› **World Bank:** The World Bank's "Consulting Services Manual" describes the formal requirements for the (very rare) use of "design contests" in the context of World Bank projects (https://openknowledge.worldbank.org/handle/10986/7047).
› **ACE:** The Architects' Council of Europe (ACE) has formulated "Recommendations for Design Contests" (latest version 2016) (https://www.ace-cae.eu/uploads/tx_jidocumentsview/6.1.1_GA2_17_Compet-Rules.pdf).

National guidelines

Rules and regulations have existed in several European countries (including Germany, the UK and Austria) since the 1860s. There are now similar regulations in several countries around the world, including:

› **Australia:** Australian Institute of Architects (RAIA, www.architecture.com.au): Guidelines for the Conduct of Architectural Competitions, 2016, and Architectural Competitions Policy, 2015.
› **Austria:** Federal Chamber of Architects and Chartered Engineering Consultants (www.architekturwettbewerb.at): Wettbewerbsstandard Architektur (WSA), 2010
› **Canada:** Royal Architectural Institute of Canada (RAIC, raic.org): Regulations for Competitions in Canada
› **Finland:** Finnish Association of Architects (SAFA, www.safa.fi): Kilpailusäännöt, 2021
› **France:** Interministerial Mission for Quality in Public Construction (MIQCP, www.miqcp.gouv.fr): Le concours de maîtrise d'œuvre: dispositions réglementaires et modalités pratiques d'organisation, 2020
› **Germany:** The Guidelines for Planning Competitions ("Richtlinien für Planungswettbewerbe", currently the RPW 2013) replaced in 2008 the "Principles and Guidelines for Competitions in the Fields of Spatial Planning, Urban Design and Construction – GRW 1995" ("Grundsätze und Richtlinien für Wettbewerbe im Bereich Raumplanung, Städtebau und Bauwesen – GRW 1995"), which had been revised several times since the 19th century, as well as the "Rules for the Awarding of Competitions (RAW)" ("Regeln für die Vergabe von Wettbewerben (RAW)"), which had been developed in parallel in the individual federal states. It was introduced in all federal states as a binding basis for design competitions by public and private sponsors and is an integral part of the Public Procurement Act (www.bmi.bund.de) for public clients. A new update of the RPW is currently being prepared. The Association of German Architects (BDA) has formulated a commentary and recommendations for the application of the RPW (www.bda-bund.de)
› **India:** Council of Architecture (CoA, www.coa.gov.in): Architectural competition guidelines
› **Italy:** National Council of Architecture (CNA PPC, www.awn.it): Regolamento per l'organizzazione e lo svolgimento dei Concorsi di Architettura, 2017
› **Japan:** Japan Society of Civil Engineers (JSCE, jsce-int.org): Guidelines for Civil Engineering Design Competitions
› **Sweden:** Swedish Association of Architects (Sveriges Arkitekter, www.arkitekt.se): Sveriges Arkitekter informerar om Arkitekttävlingar och Sveriges Arkitekters tävlingsservice, 2016
› **Switzerland:** Swiss Society of Engineers and Architects (SIA, www.sia.ch): sia Ordnung 142 für Architektur- und Ingenieurwettbewerbe, sia Ordnung für Architektur- und Ingenieurstudienaufträge, 2009
› **Turkey:** Public Procurement Authority (Kamu Ihale Kurumu-KHK, www.ihale.gov.tr): Mimarlik, Peyzaj Mimarliği, Mühendislik, Kentsel Tasarim Projeleri, Şehir ve Bölge Planlama ve Güzel Sanat Eserleri Yarişmalari Yönetmeliği
› **Ukraine:** Cabinet of Ministers of Ukraine (www.kmu.gov.ua): Про затвердження Порядку проведенняархітектурних та містобудівних конкурсів, 2013
› **United Kingdom:** Royal Institute of British Architects (RIBA, ribacompetitions.com): RIBA Guidance for Clients and RIBA Guidance for Competition Entrants
› **USA:** American Institute of Architects (AIA, www.aia.org): The Handbook of Architectural Design Competitions, 2019

Draft of the first competition regulations in Germany from 1867

Title pages of the rules and regulations for competitions in France, Japan, Germany and Austria, as well as the UIA

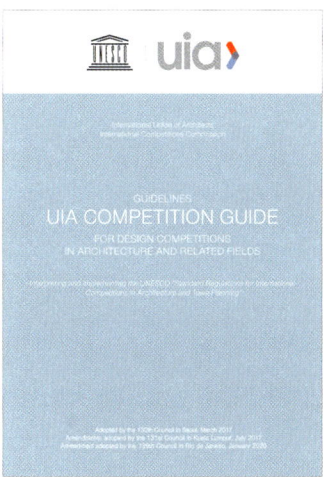
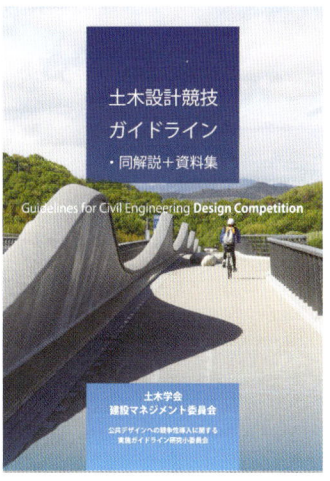

Basic principles

The basic principles of all the rules are almost identical:
› Equal treatment of all competitors
› Precise and comprehensive brief
› Evaluation of all entries solely based on clear, predefined, and non-discriminatory criteria
› Evaluation of all entries by an independent and professional jury
› Anonymity of entries
› Reasonable price-performance ratio
› Clear declaration of intent and obligations of the client to subsequently commission the winner with further design services ("obligation to commission")
› Publication of the results

The differences between the sets of rules lie in the scope of the rules on the one hand, and in details on the other, e.g., in the specifications for the composition of the jury, the recommended method for calculating the prize money, or the question of whether or to what extent anonymity in the competition may be lifted as an exception.

2.2 Rules and regulations in practice

In practice, the main differences are not in the content of the regulations, but in their enforcement. Internationally, there are several major differences, influenced by the economic, political, and cultural situation in the countries and the status of architecture in the societies, as well as a diversity of practice in the concrete application of rules that are similar in principle. Even within some countries there are differences in the application of national competition rules and in the advice/monitoring of compliance with the rules by the respective chambers of architects, for example in federally structured countries such as Germany or Canada, where there are different practices and sometimes relevant differences in the application of the rules in the various federal states or provinces on partial aspects, partly explained by different economic conditions and the associated possibilities for enforcing principles, partly by the views of the respective responsible actors.

The main difference in the application of the rules, however, concerns the basic establishment of competition as an instrument. In some countries there are rules, but they are far from being applied regularly. At best, they are used for individual (prestige) projects. In other countries, competitions and their rules are well established in society, accepted, and therefore protected. As a result, the rules are applied more frequently. Ultimately, when applying rules and regulations, the question must always be clarified as to how the rules can serve to achieve the overriding goals of the procedures: finding a high-quality solution for the project and selecting the design partners in a fair process. It is likely that a large number, perhaps the majority, of competing procedures are not carried out 100 % in accordance with the applicable rules and regulations but based on an interpreted application of the rules. This sounds sobering, but it is only due to the individuality of each task and the need to adapt to the respective constellation, e.g., the persons involved. The procedural rules also need to be flexible enough to deal with both issues.

However, the diversity in the application of rules and regulations must be divided into two groups. On the one hand, there are the procedures in which the rules and regulations are interpreted on a project-specific basis and within the given scope - while respecting the basic principles mentioned above.

On the other hand, there are procedures in which one must talk about bending or disregarding the rules beyond a given scope. In this case, one or more of the above-mentioned basic principles may be disregarded to the detriment of the offices participating in the competition, which makes it necessary to draw clear boundaries. At worst, such procedures are an expression of a susceptibility to power games and corruption, rather than a genuine interest in well-planned projects and fair dealings between those involved in design. But it's not just about the extreme cases. Many clients feel that they are the "masters" of the process and put the principle "the one who pays, decides" over an appropriate application of the rules and regulations. This leads to procedures that are usually carried out at the expense of the designers, with partly unfair conditions: too low fees for the competition participants, possibly combined with exaggerated performance requirements and too short working periods in the competition, unclear contract promises for the winners selected by the jury, breach of copyrights, imprecisely prepared tasks, juries with mostly insufficiently qualified jurors, etc.

The aspects mentioned here as examples and examined in more detail below show that the question of a fair and "correct" application of the rules and regulations is not easy to answer and that it is not possible to distinguish between clearly "good" and clearly "bad" competitions. There are always many "adjusting screws" that can be used to make a procedure more appropriate and fairer, especially since many aspects are not "either/or", but rather precise gradations within the possibilities of applying the rules. However, a certain ambiguity remains as to how "good and fair" a procedure is, even where the obligation to register competitions (usually with architectural associations) is intended to guarantee compliance with the rules. In short, proper application of the rules is the basis for a successful competition and, ultimately, for a good relationship between the future design partners.

2.3 The most important modules of rules and regulations

In the competition brief and, if necessary, beforehand in the public announcement, the following aspects are to be defined as the contractual basis of the procedure. They are briefly mentioned here and will be considered in detail in further chapters of the book.

Parties of the procedure
The "contracting parties" must be named, i.e., the sponsor, who initiates the procedure and who will normally subsequently act as the client in the design contract with the successful office (with the address and names of the persons representing it), as well as the members of the jury, any technical experts involved in the process on behalf of the sponsor, and the competition organizer. In the case of invited competitions. The extent to which the offices participating in the competition are mentioned in the competition brief is handled differently in view of the anonymity of the procedure.

Type of procedure
The procedure selected in accordance with the rules and regulations applied must be precisely stated (see separate chapter on "Choice of procedure"), as well as the rules and regulations on which the procedure is based.

Registration note
The endorsement of the procedure by the responsible Chamber of Architects or similar institution and, if applicable, the registration number must be stated.

Eligibility
The qualification required for participation in the competition must be defined. For example, for competitions in Germany, it is specified that only individuals are eligible to participate who, on the day of the announcement of the competition and pursuant to the legal provisions of their country of residence, are entitled to use the occupational title "architect".
Individuals from countries where the occupational title "architect" is not subject to statutory regulations are eligible, provided that they hold a degree or submit any other evidence of formal qualification that is recognized in the EU under 2013/55/EU (EU Directive on the recognition of professional qualifications) or provided that they hold a degree or submit any other evidence of qualification or practice permitting them to exercise as architect in their country of residence. It is also necessary to determine whether there are any geographical limitations on eligibility with respect to the origin of the individuals and whether consortia of several individuals and legal entities are permitted and what conditions they must fulfil.

Multiple participation
Multiple participation by individuals in the same competition must be prohibited.

Obstacles to participation and conflicts of interest
Reasons must be given why individuals cannot participate in the procedure, e.g., because they would be favored by their participation in the preparation or organization of the competition or in the preparation of studies prior to the contest, or because they could influence the decision of the jury.

Evaluation criteria
The criteria by which the designs submitted to the competition will be judged must be specified. For detailed information, please refer to Chapter 8.3.

Franz-Josef Höing
Chief Planning Director of the Free and Hanseatic City of Hamburg

❝ There are no strict requirements for design competitions, except that they be carefully prepared and always appropriate to the task and place. The necessary sense of proportion is important, and that everyone is engaged and sufficiently involved. It is also important to accurately select the participants and the jury members. The following still applies: the designers must be given the necessary appreciation, and the procedure should always leave enough space for surprising and enriching contributions.

Prize money and allowances
The competition sum, i.e., the sum of all prizes and fees, must be specified, as well as the planned number prizes and their distribution.

Project Commissioning (contract promise)
In the case of project competitions, a clear statement must be made as to what further design services are to be commissioned through the competition if the project is carried out. The scope of the promised services is intended to ensure that the quality of the winning design is implemented, which is why services up to and including detailed design are usually agreed. Depending on the rules and regulations, the commitment is made that the winner or one of the prize-winners, usually the winner, will be commissioned. This is subject to conditions, usually that the contract will be awarded based on the jury's recommendation and only if there is no good reason not to award the contract. In the case of interdisciplinary competitions, it should be clarified to which disciplines the commission relates.

Copyrights and ownership of submitted documents
It must be made clear that, in principle, copyrights remain with the authors of the designs. The framework for the transfer of the rights of use of the designs as well as the ownership of the submitted plans and models must be defined. Particularly in the case of ideas competitions where no contract is promised, the intention and framework for the use of the winning ideas must be specified.

Confidentiality
It should be noted that announcements of any kind about the content and procedure before or during the competition, including the first publication of the competition entries and results, may only be made, for example, by the sponsor. Furthermore, the documents provided for carrying out the competition task may only be used in connection with the competition. For any other use, in whole or in part, or the disclosure to third parties requires the express consent of the sponsor and the competition supervisor, among other things, to protect copyright.

Documents
To ensure that all participants use the same materials, the documents provided must be listed: competition brief, plan documents, forms, studies; minutes of the Q&A and any colloquia, etc.

Required services
The deliverables required in the competition (plans, models, forms, reports, digital files, etc.) must be defined. In order to ensure fair competition and comparability, the number and format of the sheets to be submitted as well as the scale and subject matter of the representations should be specified as precisely as possible. It must be ensured that the required scope, thus the effort, is in reasonable relation to the amount of the competition sum and the promised contract and that only the services required for the decision in the jury are requested.

Additional services
In order to ensure a fair competition, the submission of additional documents and material by competitors or their presentation to the jury must be prohibited.

Dates
The event dates as well as submission deadlines and locations must be specified.

Oleksandr Baranovskyi
National Association of Architects of Ukraine, Kyiv

" In the summer of 2022, a competition for the design of the reconstruction of destroyed residential buildings was announced in Ukraine. Architects were called to prepare proposals for three typical buildings of different sizes. The announcement includes the statement that the winning designs will be implemented many times as standardized projects. Unfortunately, the procedure was characterized by numerous questionable relevant details. The conditions of the competition did not provide for any prizes for the winners or any guarantees of preservation of authors' rights. There was also no information about the jury members. Further on, the working period from the moment of announcing the competition to the deadline for submission of works, the organizers of the competition have planned only about 20 days.

The National Association of Architects of Ukraine was informed about the competition through an official letter only a week before the completion of the competition. In an official response, the Association of Architects pointed out that the competition does not correspond to the legislation of Ukraine. As far as I know, the competition gathered dozens of projects, but its results were not implemented in any way in the reconstruction of Ukraine.

Regardless of this particular case, it is important to note that competitions, even in special cases such as the current situation, must adhere to essential standards in order to ensure fairness among participants and to achieve sustainable quality results.

Friedrich Passler
Architect, Vienna

" The competition brief must not only clearly describe the task and the schedule, but also the conditions for the participants. Important: A clear commissioning intention, an appropriate fee for all competitors instead of high prize money and … that negotiations will be held with the winner of the competition. Only if these negotiations fail for good reason, one should negotiate with further prize winners.

Tillman Prinz
Director, German Federal Chamber of Architects

" The intellectual and creative achievements of the competition participants make it possible to find the best planning solution for both the clients and society. The great value of these achievements must be protected by transparent and fair procedures. This is what the qualified competition managers stand for.

III MEMORIALS AND ART IN PUBLIC SPACE

Memorials – be they monuments to historical events or places of remembrance for individuals or groups – are certainly the competition task requiring the greatest emotionality and individuality in the design and its evaluation. Depending on the respective task, feelings of sadness, joy or controversy are touched on sensitive terrain. Quite rightly, these competitions are often openly advertised in terms of the composition of the design team. If the memorial is also a building, the competition is primarily addressed to architects, possibly in collaboration with landscape architects. It is also advisable to include artists from a wide range of disciplines and, if necessary, other disciplines such as philosophy, literature, history – depending on the content and focus of the task. The jury should also be interdisciplinary. Pure art competitions, whether concerning art in buildings or art in public spaces, are more open thematically and may be more "playful". Here, the task is usually defined only by location, function, and budget, and is rarely characterized by guidelines for content.

In both cases, the formulation of the task seems rather simple compared to, for example, complex building competitions, since the task can simply be designed very openly. However, it is even more difficult to put the expectations of the project initiators into words or graphics to communicate them to the participants. In the case of a task for a building with the usual specifications, it is generally expected that they will be fulfilled, and the sponsor and jury members have corresponding evaluation standards.

In a task very open to solutions and their emotional quality, these standards are often clarified only when the submitted proposals are compared. During the jury meeting, it usually becomes quickly clear that certain choices are not considered appropriate, so the question may ask why such approaches were not excluded from the start. The answer is simple: recognizing that specific conceptual proposals are out of the question presupposes the existence of alternatives, and these can often be difficult to identify and describe in advance by means of an abstract discussion, and rarely by a consensus of all participants. This is precisely why, competitions are the best planning tool for such tasks, and the events they involve are the best possible discussion forum.

Impressions of the location of the planned projects commemorating the Maidan Revolution in Kyiv, the Babyn Yar Massacre in Kyiv, and the Luther Memorial in Berlin

Babyn Yar Holocaust Memorial Center, Kyiv

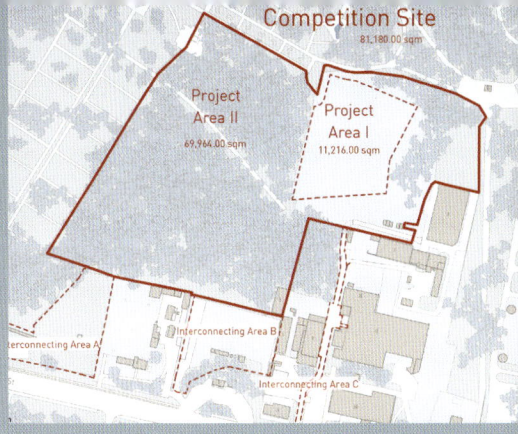

BABYN YAR In 1941, for the very first time in history, a metropolitan city in Europe lost virtually all of its remaining Jewish inhabitants to premeditated murder. On the edge of Kyiv, in and near the ravine called Babyn Yar, more Jews were slaughtered in two days during World War II than in any other single German massacre. During only two days, on September 29 and 30, 1941, 33,771 Jews were shot at Babyn Yar. Recent estimates by historians are that 37,000 to 38,000 Jews were murdered in autumn 1941, followed by at least 2,000 more Jews thereafter. In addition, 20,000 prisoners of war were killed and at least 6,000 non-Jewish civilians. The other victims were Roma, people with mental disabilities from a psychiatric hospital, Ukrainian nationalists, Soviet prisoners of war, members of the Communist underground, as well as other categories of citizens.

BABYN YAR HOLOCAUST MEMORIAL CENTER
Along with several existing memorials, the Center was intended to become part of a broader discourse on commemorating the victims, honoring those who came to their rescue, and recognizing the survivors. Located on the authentic site, the Center was meant to become a place of memory and a multifunctional museum that connects various narrative threads of history in modern and up-to-date exhibitions. With innovative and internationally oriented places of learning and examining a future for history, it was intended to become an institution of scholarly research and a place for educational and methodological activities.

INITIATIVE In close collaboration with the city administration and state government, the project was initiated by a charity fund of private donors. After the competition and due to changes in leadership of the fund and its strategies, the concept of a Center was not continued until today, remaining a valid proposal for the future. Instead, until the beginning of the war, the foundation initially initiated and realized a number of art projects on site, aiming for an even broader understanding of the site and its tragic history.

Location: Kyiv, Ukraine **Client:** Charity Fund "Babyn Yar Holocaust Memorial" (BYHMC) **Year:** 2018 – 2019 **Project size:** approx. 12,400 sqm UFA **Type of competition:** International design competition in two stages **Participants:** Stage 1: 11; Stage 2: 5 **Competition budget:** EUR 165,000 (prizes: EUR 45,000; Compensation per participant stage 1: EUR 10,000; Compensation per participant Stage 2: EUR 10,000)

PRIZEWINNERS:
(01) **1st prize** querkraft architekten zt gmbh, Vienna (A), with Kieran Fraser landscape Design e.U., Vienna (A); **2nd prize** Dorte Mandrup A/S, Copenhagen (DK), with Martha Schwartz Partners, New York (USA); **3rd prize** merz merz gmbh & co. kg, Berlin (D), with Topotek 1 Gesellschaft von Landschaftsarchitekten mbH, Berlin (D)

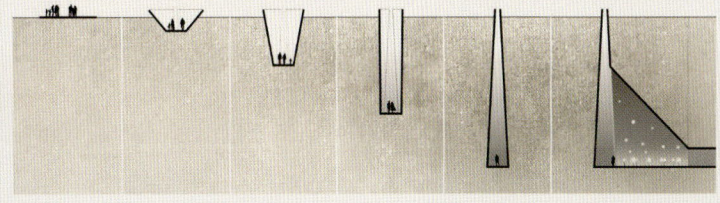

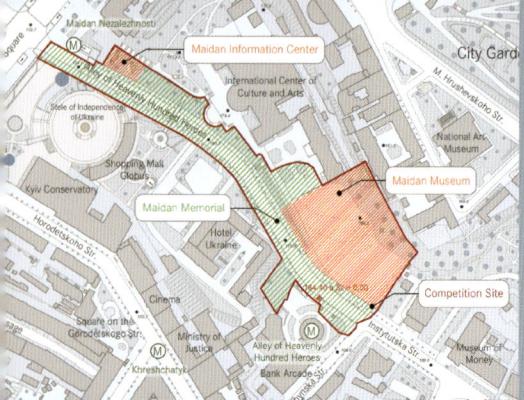

Location: Kyiv, Ukraine **Client:** Ministry of Culture of Ukraine **Year:** 2017 – 2018 **Project size:** open area of up to approx. 15,000 sqm **Type of competition:** International design competition **Participants:** 9 **Competition budget:** EUR 42,500 (prizes)

PRIZEWINNERS:
(01) **1st prize** MIstudio, Lviv (UA), and Rotterdam (NL); **2nd prize** blauraum Architekten, Hamburg (D); **3rd prize** Atelier Schmelzer Weber, Dresden (D), with Prof. Andreas Theurer, Mittenwalde (D)

National Memorial to the Heavenly Hundred Heroes, Kyiv

REVOLUTION OF DIGNITY The Euromaidan was a Ukrainian nationwide protest movement lasting from November 2013 to February 2014. These historic events were triggered by the abrupt rejection of its foreign policy towards Europe and the refusal to sign the EU Association Agreement by Ukraine's former leadership. Following the brutal beating of young people by the government special forces, the protest movement developed into a continuing civil disobedience campaign against unchecked state power, corruption, and human rights abuses. The Revolution was an incisive moment in history for Ukraine. It resulted in the deaths of 107 protesters (known as the Heavenly Hundred), the disposal of the corrupted President and his government, Russia's annexation of Crimea and the start of a war in the Donbas region. It also led to the consolidation of a democratic society in the Ukraine.

MAIDAN MUSEUM The task for the memorial was to create a permanent place for individual and official commemoration, symbolizing the ideas of Maidan and carrying the memory to future generations. The task was open to monuments and landscape designs that could be located within the area of the Maidan and the adjacent street where most of the heroes are to be mourned.

PROCEDURE The competition was held in parallel with the competition for a museum – with a joint multidisciplinary jury, but for each nomination participants were selected separately in open procedures. As part of the process, several events with the public and the press were held, including a public exhibition of the designs on the Maidan the day before the jury meeting, inaugurated by the President of Ukraine.

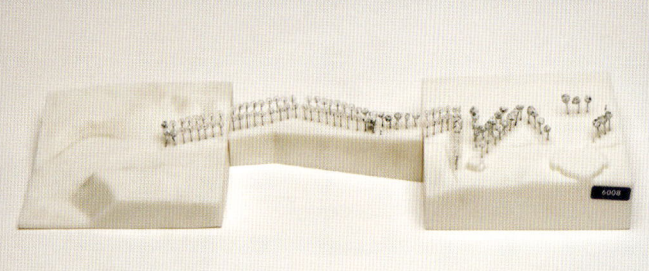
01

01

01

Luther Memorial Berlin 2017

SITUATION The Luther Decade of the Protestant Church for the Reformation anniversary in 2017 was the occasion to return the Berlin Luther Memorial at St. Mary's Church in Berlin Mitte to its original location. The former memorial to Martin Luther, also known as the Reformation Memorial, was one of the largest monument projects of the Second German Empire in Berlin. The location was programmatically in front of the main portal of St. Mary's Church, which had been stripped of its medieval alterations since 1886 and functioned as a kind of spatial hinge between the old market square, the exposed St. Mary's Church and the axis to the city palace on the newly laid out wide street leading to the palace. The current location of the bronze figure of Luther directly next to the church building is to be understood as a provisional measure and a result of the destruction of the historical monument in World War II, the securing of the old Luther figure outside the city and the installation at the current location during GDR times.

TASK The subject of the open competition was the design for a new memorial on the site of the historical memorial, incorporating the preserved elements of the historical memorial. A reconstruction of the memorial from 1895 was not intended. With the return, the preserved bronze figure with the original plinth is to be placed in a representative and newly designed context in the cityscape that can be experienced by the public today.

CHALLENGE The goal was to use the artistic design of the site to create a variety of approaches to the intellectual and emotional examination of the Reformation and Luther's work, and to preserve these for future generations to experience. In the context of dealing with the significance of Luther and the Reformation as well as with the history of their reception in the different epochs, it had to be decided to what extent and in which form the other personalities of the historical monument or others should be represented together with the Martin Luther figure (Simulacrum vs. Figura).

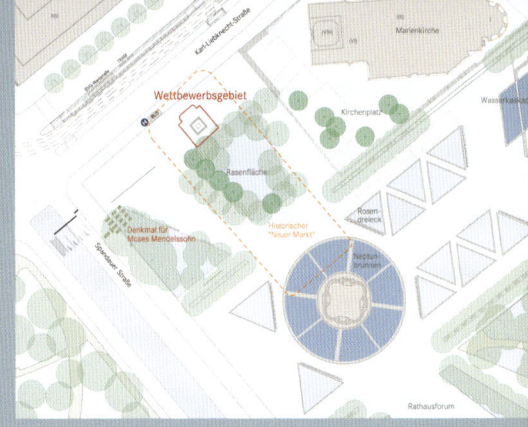

Location: Berlin, Germany **Client:** Evangelischer Kirchenkreis Berlin Stadtmitte **Year:** 2016 **Project size:** n/a **Type of competition:** Open ideas competition in two stages **Participants:** Stage 1: 52; Stage 2: 6 **Competition budget:** EUR 27,400 (prizes: EUR 13,000; compensation per participant Stage 2: EUR 2,400)

PRIZEWINNERS:
(01) **1st prize** Atelier Albert Weis with Zeller & Moye, Berlin (D), Mexico City (MX); **2nd prize** Werner Mally with Kunze Seeholzer Architektur & Stadtplanung, Munich (D); **3rd prize** Studio Katrin Wegemann with ew architects, Berlin (D), Recklinghausen (D); **4th prize** MONOBLOQUE with Häfner Ingenieure GmbH, Berlin (D)

3 CHOICE OF THE TYPE OF PROCEDURE

3.1 The selection of the process

To the outside world, a competition is a competition, and the public rarely asks how exactly a design competition was organized. Nevertheless, the choice of the competition type has a considerable influence on the result, possibly even the greatest impact of all factors when preparing and conducting a competition. Depending on the importance, scope, and complexity of the project, as well as the procurement or competition law situation, the chosen procedure should be adapted to the requirements. Especially since there are many variants of competition types, and these lead to significantly different conditions, results and effort, the decision on the type of procedure must be made with great care in the interest of all parties involved. Advice on this is one of the first and most important services that the competition consultants can provide at this stage. In addition, the respective professional chamber or, for example, in the case of international competitions, the UIA (Union International des Architectes) is usually available for advice.

There are many different types of competitions. Architectural competitions are representative of all types of competitions for architecture, landscape architecture, urban design, engineering, and art. It is necessary to decide whether and how to publicize the competition, to decide how many participants are admitted and what qualifications they must have. For example, the participation of consortia of several professional groups may be recommended or even required. Furthermore, there is the possibility to divide the process into phases, which can enable a more intensive dialogue within during the competition. Finally, in the case of complex projects, it can be helpful to refrain from anonymity in favor of a direct dialogue with the participants. It is important to make full use of the legal framework that applies to the competition in the respective country, in the interests of the project and all participants.

The task of the competition organizer is thus also to formulate the conditions of the procedure in a way that is binding for all participants, to provide a binding framework for the cooperation of all those involved in the competition and to stipulate the mutual obligations of the sponsor and the participants in the competition. Formally, they form the contractual basis of the competition.

The following is a summary of the essential parameters for defining the type of procedure, mentioned, and specified in this or a similar form in most of the standard rule sets used worldwide.

3.2 Parameters for determining the competition type

PROMISE OF CONTRACT	**Project competition** The project competition is the classic competition where designs are requested for a specific task and, at the end of which a team is commissioned to further develop the winning concept and a binding contract is formulated for this purpose. Of course, "ideas" are also expected in the project competition, which is why project competitions are more often confused with ideas competitions.	**Ideas competition** In an idea competition, the task is not conclusively clarified in advance, or the competition is often launched to collect "ideas," for example, for the development of an urban district. Since there is no immediate intention to realize the project, there is no promise of a contract in an idea competition, in contrast to a project competition. Therefore, a higher competition sum (prizes and potentially expense allowances) must be offered to compensate for the lack of a contract opportunity. Ideas competitions can provide the planning basis for a subsequent project competition.
ACCESS TO PARTICIPATION	**Open competition** If all offices with appropriate professional qualification, e.g., architects, are allowed to participate, the competition is considered "open". In addition to qualifications, eligibility may be limited to a geographically defined area. In some cases, a minimum size of office or proof of completed projects may be required, but this contradicts the idea of open competition and creates additional formal and organizational work.	**Restricted competition** If the number of teams participating in the competition is limited in advance by a pre-selection process, this is referred to as a restricted or invited competition. In the case of a restricted competition, the selection is organized by an open pre-qualification procedure (pre-qualification) preceding the competition, in which all qualified and interested offices can apply with reference projects and their office profile, and the participants are then selected from this pool. There is no open access prior to an invited competition. In this case, a list of eligible offices is usually first prepared, often with the advice of the competition organizer, and these offices are asked whether they are interested. Subsequently, shortlisted offices are selected from these candidates. In the case of a restricted competition, the first participants are sometimes selected in advance. In this way, but also by creating a list of candidates, the sponsor declares their claim to the outcome of the competition, so that this issue is often subject to coordination between the project partners (e.g., a private sponsor and the responsible municipality) and has a project-political dimension.

NUMBER OF PARTICIPANTS	**Open competition**	**Restricted competition** During the preparation of restricted competitions and at the second phase of two-phase competitions, the number of invited participants or those qualified for the second stage must be precisely determined. A larger number of "starting positions" simplified means: › greater variety of ideas and thus higher probability of finding a suitable winning project, › more opportunities for the desired offices to participate, › more effort in the process – for processing fees, preliminary review and time spent in jury meetings, › increased competition among the participants and thus a less attractive procedure to participate in. The decision has a considerable influence on the character of the competition and must be made according to the situation. In invitational competitions, the number of participants is usually between 3 and 10, in public restricted competitions between 3 and 30. In two-stage competitions, the following combinations are common: Stage 1: open Stage 2: 10 – 25 Stage 1: 25 Stage 2: 7 – 10 Stage 1: 12 Stage 2: 5 – 7 Stage 1: 8 Stage 2: 3 – 5
PROJECT OBJECT	**Single discipline tender** If the task and the subsequent contract relate to only one discipline, e.g., architecture, urban design, or landscape architecture, this is a single discipline tender. Accordingly, the procedures are often named "architectural competition", "urban design competition" or similar.	**Interdisciplinary competition** In interdisciplinary competitions, several disciplines are invited to work jointly on the competition task with the intention of subsequently receiving a contract as a team, possibly for a general design service. Accordingly, the task is formulated and the preliminary examination is carried out in a more complex way. In addition, the jury must be interdisciplinary (corresponding to the disciplines admitted to the competition). The competition sum is higher because its calculation must take into account the effort of all disciplines involved.
NUMBER OF COMPETITION STAGES	**Single-stage competition** Competitions are usually held in one stage, i.e., there is a working period, at the end of which participants submit their designs, and a jury meeting takes place for the selection of the winning projects.	**Two-stage competition** In a two-stage competition, at the end of the first stage, in a first meeting, the jury selects from a larger number of designs those projects that have the greatest potential for further development in the second stage of the competition. The then reduced number of participants in the second stage revises the designs based on the jury's recommendations and then the jury selects the winning projects in its second meeting at the end of the second stage. The effort of the procedure is higher, especially because two preliminary examinations and two jury meetings must be organized and held. However, the staggering into two stages can also contribute to efficiency if, for example, the first stage is designed to be open and/or with only very reduced requirements for the depth of processing and the preliminary examination. More intensive processing and examination only take place in the second stage. As a rule, the jury must be identical in both stages of the competition.

COMBINING SEVERAL COMPETITIONS	**Single-stage competition** As a rule, competitions are single stage, i.e., self-contained procedures with only one final decision by a jury.	**Multilevel procedure** In contrast to the two-stage competition, the multilevel competition is the combination of two competitions carried out in succession by the same sponsor and formally self-contained, each with its own call for entries, but which in principle have the same task as their subject. The formal connection is made through continuity in the composition of the jury and, if necessary, the promise of participation in the second stage by the offices awarded prizes in the first competition stage. This procedure is used, for example, to carry out an urban design investigation in the first stage with regard to use and/or planned density (possibly as an ideas competition), with the aim of deriving findings and decision-making bases from this first stage for the more detailed task in the subsequent second stage competition, in which a now more concrete task is then dealt with in a project competition.
COMMUNICATION	**Anonymous competition** One of the basic principles of design competitions has always been the anonymity of the procedure. If necessary, the names of the participating offices can be revealed to the jury, and in the rules of some countries it is also permitted for members of the jury to meet people from the participating offices in person at the participants' colloquium. The decisive factor for anonymity, is that the designs are submitted anonymously, i.e., only provided with an identification code or password. The designs are presented anonymously to the jury and then evaluated without knowledge of the authorship.	**Cooperative competition** The possibility of removing anonymity is handled and accepted differently around the globe in registered competitions. The aim of lifting anonymity is to enable direct dialogue between the jury and the participants (e.g., in the context of a colloquium with an intermediate presentation by the participants) to achieve a deeper understanding of the task or the approaches to the solution before the designs are finally elaborated and submitted. With the knowledge of the authorship, the responsibility of the jury increases not to be influenced by the personal knowledge and possibly the personal appearance of the participants in the presentation or in the intermediate colloquium, but to decide exclusively based on the quality of the presented solutions.
ADMISSION AREA	**Regionally limited** In open competitions, and in proqualification procedures, the area of eligibility may be limited geographically to control the number of participants. In the case of public sponsors, however, the possibilities are limited, at least in theory, due to international agreements against restricting competitions (EU procurement law, GATT). Therefore, they should only be used for very small projects and art competitions – in practice, however, they are often used outside the EU, even by public sponsors.	**Open and internationally open** In contrast to the regionally restricted open competitions, open procedures allow the participation of all qualified persons worldwide or at least of those who are resident in the member states of the GATT agreement. If the procedure has an explicit multinational or international orientation, the procedure must be correspondingly more complex and, if necessary, organized in several languages. The title "international competition" is generally reserved for procedures registered by the Union Internationale des Architectes (UIA). An essential requirement here is that the jury must also be international.

FORMAL FRAMEWORK

Competition

The term "competition" is usually reserved for those procedures that have been formally registered by the relevant organization (usually the national or regional architectural association), which is intended to ensure compliance with the regulations in force in the respective country. One of the central basic principles of the competition is the promise of a contract, whereby the competition represents an opportunity for the participants to gain a contract, and it is therefore accepted in return that many participating offices have ultimately submitted a design without a fee or with a fee that is significantly too low. This aspect is also accepted by the architectural community because, for example, young offices are thus given the opportunity to enter the market and because the competition system contributes to discourse within the profession and to the further development of building culture (Baukultur).

Parallel multiple commissioning

For various reasons, sponsors conduct competition procedures in which not all the rules of a registered competition are applied, or in which registration is shied away from for other reasons. These procedures are referred to, for example, as expert meetings or workshops, or may be part of procurement procedures beyond competition (e.g., negotiated procedures with a solution approach, competitive dialogue, PPP awards for design-and-build contracts). In these cases, all participants in the procedure are formally commissioned in parallel to provide the services in the procedure. Nevertheless, for pragmatic reasons and to build trust, the rules and regulations of such procedures are often based in organizational components on the established rules of registered competitions, e.g., by convening an evaluation panel with independent jurors.

3.3 The pros and cons of open competitions

Open competitions are the classic competitions in many places and are considered the best option for promoting innovation and market access for young or smaller offices.

Beyond the concerns mentioned in Chapter 1.4, there are additional reservations among potential competition sponsors prior to choosing this procedure. In addition to uncertainty about the number of projects submitted and concerns that the most qualified offices are less likely to participate in open competitions, there is a particular concern about being confronted after the competition with a winning team with too little practical experience: lack of experience in designing projects of comparable size and complexity, and possibly lack of experience with the local building code in case of a foreign prizewinner. These concerns are understandable but can be addressed by including a clause in the rules and regulations that in such a case, a joint venture with a suitably qualified partner office will be formed after the competition and the lack of suitability will be compensated by a so-called "suitability loan".

A higher number of competition entries is also an advantage in the first place. To recognize the high workload of the participants, appropriate logistical arrangements must be made for the competition, for example, with regard to the handling of larger quantities of plans and models, the size of the required premises and the duration of the meetings.

Taking these precautions into account, an open competition may be the most suitable procedure despite the greater effort involved - also because it does not require a prequalification procedure that is questionable in terms of procedural law and professional policy. In the case of medium-sized and large projects, a two-stage competition may be preferred, in which the effort for the participants in Stage 1 can be reduced to conceptual representations, and in Stage 2 a focused processing and evaluation can take place.

Along with the perspective of the sponsor, it is also important to consider the perspective of the designers, among whom the issue of open competitions is a subject of intense and controversial debate. On the one hand, the participants make an enormous economic and intellectual investment, which ends without successful results for almost everyone involved. Could this effort be justified? Probably only if one considers the possibility of new colleagues entering the market and the high goal of innovation inherent in open competitions. Moreover, open competitions can be morally justified more easily if either the project receives special democratic recognition through the competition, or a lower number of participants is to be expected due to the comparatively low importance of the project.

Matthias Sauerbruch
Architect, Berlin

❙❙ What is important in competition organization for me as a participant? Design competitions are a democratic method of deciding on the Gestalt of the built environment. The advantage of such a procedure is the openness of the process, which can really lead a client to the best ideas. Often, the client could not even imagine before the procedure what would actually be realized in the end. The disadvantage of a voting process of this kind, however, is the fact that a compromise must always result from the comparison of different opinions. Whether at the end of such a process a strong work is nevertheless ready for realization, convincing for everyone, depends quite decisively on the mediation and the discussion within the jury. It is therefore important to have a brilliant, creatively thinking, and assertive jury that can really lead the competition of the best to its intended result.

IV ADMINISTRATION BUILDINGS

Public administration buildings, together with hotels and other private or commercial office buildings, are the projects with the greatest repetition of usage units. This should also be reflected in the design competition when formulating the requirements: e.g., how many standard floors should be depicted to understand the building, and at what scale? Should expansion options be shown? As opposed to commercial office buildings, the users of administration buildings are known, being public or private institutions. In this way, the spatial and functional program can be precisely formulated and analyzed at a later stage, especially with regard to the overall expectations in terms of design, sustainability aspects, security, etc. The complexity of the functional requirements lies in the organization of the central functions such as foyer, conference area, storage, delivery, catering, but above all in the implementation of the demands for the office areas. These must meet the technical requirements for lighting, use and fire compartments and barrier-free accessibility, as well as fulfilling the allocation requirements for central and decentralized special functions (meeting rooms, copy rooms, kitchenettes, etc.). In particular, the workplace model must be clarified in advance and explained in the competition brief. The workplace model ("working environment") is an essential part of the building's character and has a significant influence on the building's depth and internal accessibility. Public administrations are often still characterized by fixed hierarchies and/or guidelines, which may be expressed in rigid specifications for room sizes, layouts and even furnishings. Even if the current need is based on a concrete spatial requirement and current structures, the competition and subsequent design must ensure that the building is also suitable for other structures and changing requirements in the long term and that an appropriate degree of long-term flexibility is guaranteed.

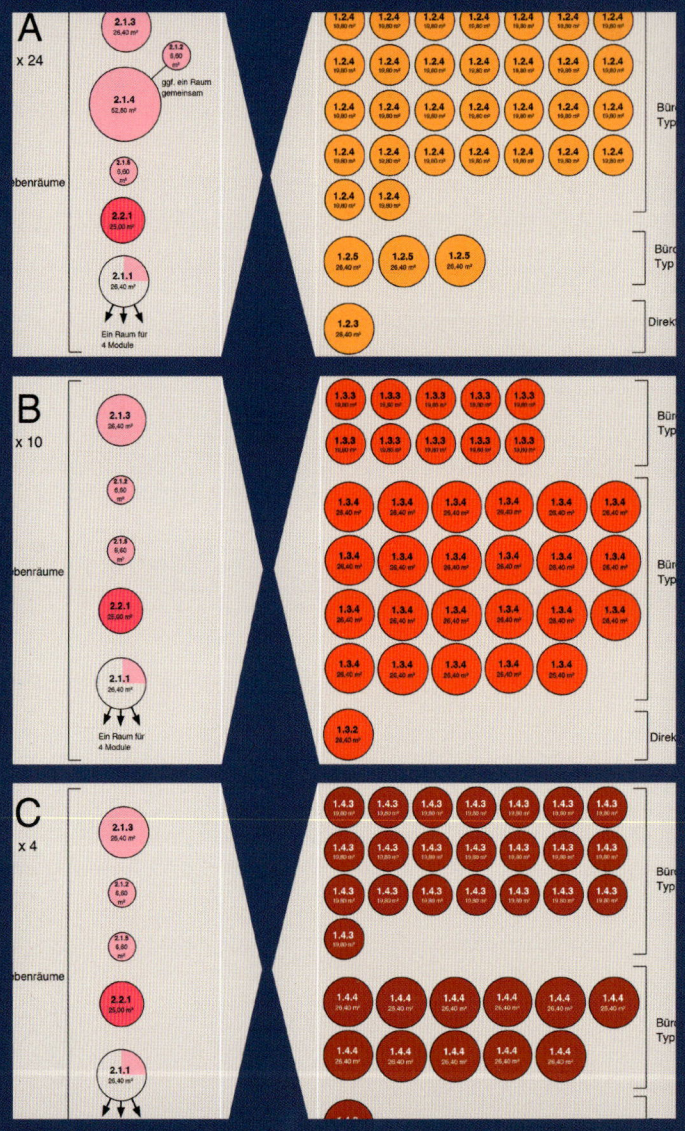

Diagram explaining the required division of the same office space unit in the competition "European Patent Office in the Hague"

Administrative City Hall, Düsseldorf

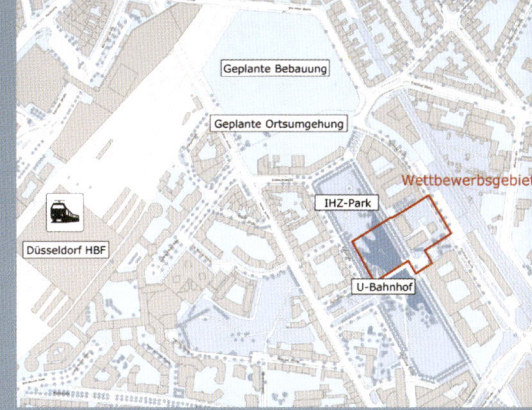

CITY ADMINISTRATION OF DÜSSELDORF The capital of state Düsseldorf employs more than 11,000 people in the city administration, who are assigned to nine departments with a total of 45 offices and institutes. This makes it one of the largest employers in the region. Contemporary demands on office concepts as well as urban planning and energy standards would make it uneconomical to renovate the five existing buildings currently in use.

TASK The new site was chosen primarily due to its central location near the main train station and for its direct connection to the public transportation network, although the property requires planning as a high-rise building. Approx. 3,000 workplaces and conference and training rooms for the administration as well as a citizens' office and citizens' service center will be created on approx. 70,000 sqm of above-ground GFA. In addition to the quality of the working environments, ecological and economic sustainability were particularly relevant for the client, which was expressed, regarding the realization of concepts for recyclability, building greening and production of regenerative energy on site. In this sense, the competition was already an interdisciplinary design service.

PARTICIPATION In order to ensure a successful change in working methods, the employees and offices were actively and very closely involved in the procedure prior to the competition so that their knowledge and ideas could be incorporated into the task and so that the employees could be prepared for the new working environment in the form of a change process. Citizens were involved in the process before, during and after the competition, and the competition was organized in two phases in order to make optimal use of the opportunities for dialogue with the designers in the anonymous competition.

Location: Düsseldorf, Germany **Client:** IPM Immobilien Projekt Management Dusseldorf GmbH **Year:** 2021 – 2022 **Project size:** approx. 45,000 sqm UFA **Type of competition:** Restricted design competition in two stages **Participants:** Stage 1: 21; Stage 2: 9 **Competition budget:** EUR 1,600,000 (prizes: EUR 480,000; Compensation Stage 1: EUR 560,000; Compensation Stage 2: EUR 560,000)

PRIZEWINNERS:
(01) 1st prize AllesWirdGut Architektur ZT GmbH, Vienna (A), Hertl.Architekten ZT GmbH, Steyr (A), ZFG-Project GmbH, Baden (A), FCP Fritsch, Chiari & Partner ZT GmbH, Vienna (A); **(02) 2nd prize** HDR GmbH, Dusseldorf (D), WINTER Gebäudetechnik, Engineering & Services GmbH, Dusseldorf (D), KREBS+KIEFER Ingenieure GmbH, Berlin (D); **(03) 3rd prize** ingenhoven associates GmbH, Dusseldorf (D), ASSMANN Beraten + Planen, Hamburg (D), Werner Sobek AG, Stuttgart (D); **(04) 4th prize** caspar.schmitzmorkramer gmbh, Cologne (D), Drees & Sommer SE, Stuttgart (D), Werner Sobek AG, Berlin (D)

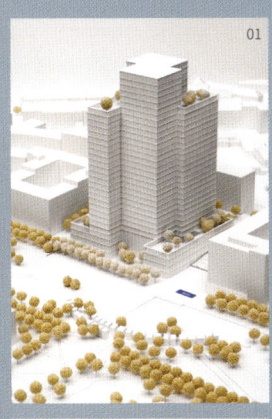

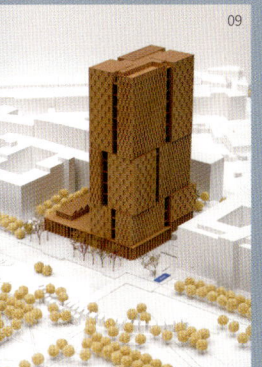

MENTIONS:
(05) KSP Engel GmbH, Frankfurt a. M. (D), Buro Happold GmbH, Munich (D), Weiske und Partner GmbH Beratende Ingenieure VBI, Stuttgart (D); **(06)** Müller Reimann Generalplaner Gesellschaft von Architekten mbH, Berlin (D), Ebert Ingenieure GmbH, Berlin (D), GSE Ingenieur-Gesellschaft mbH Saar, Enseleit und Partner, Berlin (D); **(07)** Barcode Architects B.V., Rotterdam (NL), Ramboll Danmark A/S, Copenhagen (DK); **(08)** Eller + Eller Architekten GmbH, Düsseldorf (D), ZWP Ingenieur AG, Dresden (D), Kempen Krause Ingenieure GmbH, Aachen (D); **(09)** Baumschlager Eberle Architekten (BE Berlin GmbH), Berlin (D), Buro Happold GmbH, Berlin (D)

Headquarters Waste Management, Berlin

BERLIN CITY SANITATION (BSR) BSR is a service company owned by the state of Berlin and is responsible for waste collection, street cleaning and waste treatment for the state of Berlin. With nearly 6,000 employees, the company is one of the largest employers in Berlin and the largest municipal waste disposal company in Germany. Beyond this, BSR operates, among other things, the Berlin waste-to-energy plant, a biogas plant and 15 recycling centers spread across the city of Berlin.

LOCATION The competition site is located at Südkreuz station in the Tempelhof-Schöneberg district, which is linked to both the Berlin S-Bahn ring and the north-south line. It is also one of four intercity rail stations in Berlin, making it an important transportation hub for the city. The area at the so-called "Schöneberger Linse" is currently developing into an urban and multifunctional urban quarter.

TASK The new BSR site is to house approx. 6,000 workplaces for BSR employees who are currently based at other buildings that are no longer fully up to date. Situated centrally in terms of transportation, the site is to become a meeting point both for all employees as well as for citizens (customers) and guests. BSR will use the northern part of the project area. Part of the task was to design the maximum possible capacity of approx. 55,000 sqm GFA (above ground) in an urban planning compatible and concise manner and to design additional office spaces in the southern section for lease. Due to the vicinity of the railroad line, special requirements for noise and vibration protection had to be taken into account in the design.

Location: Berlin, Germany **Client:** BSR Südkreuz Entwicklungsgesellschaft mbH & Co. Immobilien KG **Year:** 2021 – 2022 **Project size:** approx. 55,000 sqm GFA **Type of competition:** Design competition in two stages **Participants:** Stage 1: 19; Stage 2: 9 **Competition budget:** EUR 475,000 EUR (prizes: EUR 250,000; Compensation Stage 1: EUR 120,000; Compensation Stage 2: EUR 105,000)

PRIZEWINNERS:
(01) **2nd prize** ZRS Architekten GVA mbH, Berlin (D); **2nd prize** Burckhardt + Partner Generalplaner GmbH, Berlin (D); **2nd prize** Franz und Sue ZT GmbH, Vienna (A), with Schenker Salvi Weber ZT GmbH, Vienna (A); **Mention** Ortner & Ortner Baukunst Gesellschaft von Architekten mbH, Berlin (D)

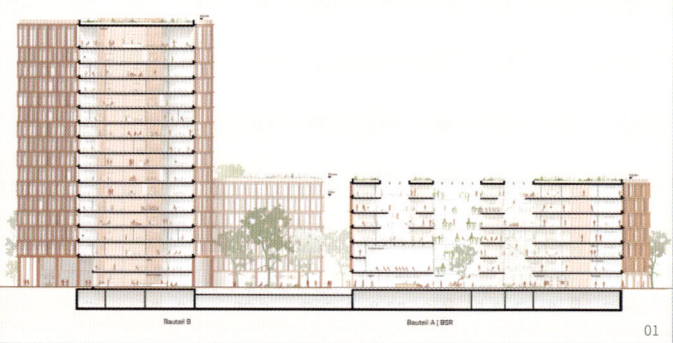

KFAS Headquarters and Convention Center, Kuwait

KFAS The Kuwait Foundation for the Advancement of Sciences (KFAS) is the leading organization for funding, promoting, and advancing science, innovation and technology, as well as research and development in the State of Kuwait for 40 years. The main objective of the non-profit organization KFAS is to stimulate creative initiatives and build a solid scientific and technological base while at the same time creating an environment that encourages innovation.

SITE Due to the expansion of the Foundation's programs and initiatives, and the subsequent increase for the grow in staff, the Foundation has long outgrown the maximum capacity of its current headquarters in the heart of Kuwait City's business and financial district. Hence, KFAS has been allocated two new sites from the Kuwait Municipality, to house a new Headquarters and Conference Center. The competition site is located in Block 1 in the District of Salmiya and is referred as "Ras Al-Ard," which literally means the "Head of Earth". Salmiya is located approx. 12 km southeast of Kuwait City center in the west coast of the Hawalli province. The district is bordered by the Arabian Gulf on the east and Highway 30 on the west.

PROJECT Each building, Headquarters and Conference Center, shall have an approximate net utilization area of 12,000 sqm. The program for the headquarters includes workplaces for approx. 250 employees and a large public section. The program of the conference center includes exhibition areas, library, multimedia theater (500 seats), conference and meeting facilities and guest apartments. The task was not limited to the buildings itself, rather it has included the development of the entire area into a science-oriented district integrating adjacent science and technology functions that are currently in the area: the existing Scientific Center of Kuwait, the Kuwait Institute for Scientific Research, the Environment Public Authority, and the Public Authority for Agricultural Affairs. The master plan for the area shall establish strong spatial connections between the new buildings and open spaces with quality. Further, the task has included traffic planning and definition of design guidelines. Following the competition, the design of the 1st prize winning architects was further developed, nevertheless the commencement of the construction site has not been initiated yet.

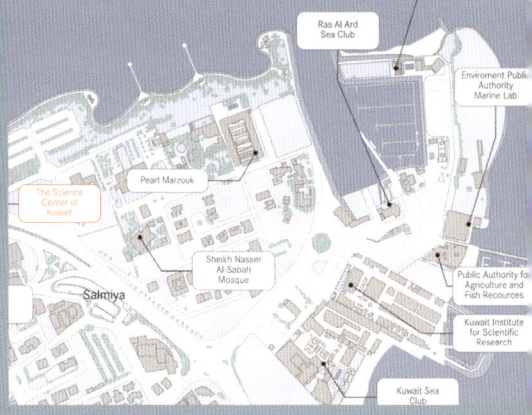

Location: Kuwait City, Kuwait **Client:** Kuwait Foundation for the Advancement of Science (KFAS) **Year:** 2018 – 2019 **Project size:** approx. 12,500 sqm UFA headquarters, approx. 12,300 sqm UFA convention center **Type of competition:** International design competition in two stages **Participants:** Stage 1: 43; Stage 2: 10 **Competition budget:** USD 530,000 (prizes: USD 130,000; Compensation stage 1: USD 400,000)

PRIZEWINNERS:
(01) **1st prize** Topotek 1 Architektur GmbH, Zurich (CH); **2nd prize** Metaform architects with Sideshore Architecture + Urbanism, Luxemburg (L); **3rd prize** querkraft architekten zt gmbh, Vienna (A); **4th prize** Nasrine Seraji Architect with Petitdidierprioux Architects, Paris (F), VS-A Hong Kong and Djao-Rakitine LTD, London (UK)

City Hall, Dallgow-Döberitz

DALLGOW-DÖBERITZ The municipality of Dallgow-Döberitz, together with the town of Falkensee, marks the eastern edge of the Brandenburg district of Havelland in transition to the Berlin city limits. It is located on the federal highway 5, the historical connection between Berlin and Hamburg. Due to its attractive location and residential quality as well as the good educational opportunities, the community has grown considerably since the 1990s. Since 1990, the population has risen from about 2,900 to about 9,200 in 2015 – a further increase is forecast.

PROJECT The growth of the municipality also results in increased space requirements for the administration, which was the reason for the project. In addition, the situation at the three locations used at the time was inadequate, both in terms of the spatial-structural situation of the existing buildings and the excessive distance between the locations. The aim was to bring the municipal administration together in a new city hall building, to create there approx. 40 workplaces of appropriate quality and an administration that is attractive for the citizens, and thus to form a new central location in the municipality. A large meeting room for internal and external events will be integrated.

TASK For the project an area in the heart of the municipality is intended, in which today among other things the existing city hall is located, but which is otherwise little developed as a functional neighborhood center but is primarily a little maintained green area with unused remains of a water tower blown up in World War II. In accordance with the importance of the project and in the sense of an orderly urban development, the new development should fulfill the functions of an administrative headquarters and, with an independent and sustainable design, support the identification of the citizens with the city hall and thus also with their administration. At the same time, appropriately structured and organized spaces were to create improved working conditions and thus meet the dynamics of the municipality with a contemporary, close administration.

Location: Dallgow-Döberitz, Germany **Client:** Municipality of Dallgow-Döberitz **Year:** 2014 – 2015 **Project size:** approx. 1,400 sqm GFA **Type of procedure:** Negotiation procedure in accordance with the Regulation on the Awarding of Contracts for Freelance Services (VOF) **Participants:** 6 **Compensation:** EUR 66,000 (Compensation per participant: EUR 11,000)

COMMISSIONED:
(01) Lieb+Lieb Architekten BDA, Freudenstadt (D)

Forschungszentrum Jülich Office Building 16.17

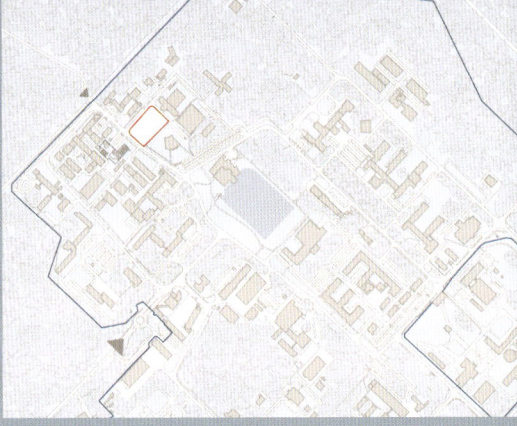

FORSCHUNGSZENTRUM JÜLICH With its competencies in materials research and simulation and its expertise in physics, nano- and information technology as well as life sciences and brain research, the research center develops the foundations for future key technologies through interdisciplinary cutting-edge research. In this way, the research center contributes to solving major societal challenges in the fields of energy and the environment as well as information and the brain. Forschungszentrum Jülich is breaking new ground in strategic partnerships with universities, research institutions and industry in Germany and abroad. With almost 6,000 employees, it is one of Europe's major interdisciplinary research centers as a member of the Helmholtz Association (Helmholtz-Gemeinschaft).

LOCATION The site, which covers an area of approximately 2.2 square kilometers, is in the southwest of North Rhine-Westphalia, outside the city of Jülich. The center uses more than 200 buildings and has nine research institutes with more than 50 institute areas in the fields of energy and climate research, bio- and geosciences, medicine and neurosciences, complex systems, simulation sciences and nanotechnology.

PROJECT The building 16.17 will offer space for approx. 300 workplaces in a transparent, open, light structure, which will serve the teams of several departments in different sized modules. The aim is to repeatedly occupy the rooms in new and variable ways with possibly very different requirements to provide temporary space within the overall campus for departments whose actual areas are either still lacking or are being refurbished. Accordingly, the development of a flexible spatial and technical structure was required, which also included centrally shared areas.

Location: Forschungszentrum Jülich, Deutschland **Client:** Forschungszentrum Jülich GmbH **Year:** 2017 – 2018 **Project size:** approx. 6,000 sqm GFA **Type of competition:** Restricted competition for general planners **Participants:** 8 **Competition budget:** EUR 106,000 EUR (prizes: EUR 36,000; Compensation: EUR 70,000)

PRIZEWINNERS:
(01) **1st prize** hks | Architekten GmbH, Aachen (D); (02) **2nd prize** pbr Planungsbüro Rohling AG, Düsseldorf (D); (03) **3rd prize** Itten+Brechbühl GmbH, Berlin (D); (04) **4th prize** kadawittfeldarchitektur GmbH, Aachen (D)

4 MEMBERS INVOLVED

4.1 Sponsor

The sponsor of a competition is the public or private institution or the person who conducts the competition. They are usually the subsequent client of the design services and developer of the project. They are the contractual partner of the participants in the competition procedure, responsible for the subsequent commissioning of the design services and thus responsible for the contract promise.

The sponsor bears the costs of the procedure and is organizationally, legally, and ethically responsible for all essential decisions in the procedure as well as for the fairness of the process. Depending on their own experience and capacity, they may commission an external competition consultancy for their own advice and support (see Chapter 5) and delegate some of the tasks to the competition consultancy. The sponsor determines the type of procedure, appoints the jury, and defines the task, if necessary, coordinating with other parties involved (approving authorities, professional associations, technical experts) and obtaining advice from them.

The most important tasks are:
There have been rules and regulations in several European countries (such as Germany, Great Britain and Austria) since the 1860s.
There are now corresponding regulations in a large numeber of countries around the world, for example:

› **Appointing an internal project team:** Even if an external competition consultancy is commissioned to provide comprehensive services, the sponsor is left with important and possibly intensive tasks, which may require the creation of a trained team with decision-making authority, possibly across multiple hierarchical levels.
› **Selecting and commissioning those involved in the process:**
Appointing exernal technical jurors, competition consultants, and technical experts.
› **Securing and managing the procedure budget:** estimating the funding requirements (see Chapter 7) and securing the budget as well as, if necessary, setting up an escrow account in which the funds for the allowances and prizes are made available.
› **Commissioning third parties:** handling the commissioning of competition consultants, jury members, technical experts, service providers (catering, printing, model making and photography, event technology, exhibition construction, etc.) and legal advice, if necessary.
› **Deciding on the terms of reference:** The sponsor makes key decisions in the formulation of the task by specifying the global project objectives, outlining detailed requirements, or formulating them themselves, and coordinating the requirements and specifications with the relevant authorities and, if necessary, technical experts.
› **Convening and/or participating in project teams/committees:** Depending on the task and project composition, the sponsor participates in committees of the process before and, if necessary, also during and after the competition, and also initiates them if necessary. Depending on the situation, they can have very different formats. These can be relevant, for example, internally for the clarification of requirements or with external participation for the coordination of framing conditions of the project with, for example, the responsible authorities, the citizens, or political committees. If relevant, these bodies often send representation to the jury as voting members, technical experts and/or guests.
› **Organizing events:** Depending on the service profile of the competition consultancy, the sponsor themselves participates in the organization of events: venue search and rental, catering, event technology, agenda, etc. (see Chapter 13.2).
› **Participating in the jury:** Since the jury makes the most important decisions in the competition, it goes without saying that the sponsor should be represented on the jury panel (see Chapter 13).
› **Drafting the contract:** The sponsor formulates thebterms and conditions of the draft contract (contract for the design services to be provided later), which may be published in full or in substantial parts at the beginning of the process and is later negotiated with the prize-winning team(s).

4.2 Participants

The persons (including legal entities) entitled to participate in the competition form the group of "participants" (see "Eligibility", Chapter 2.3).

4.3 Jury

Tasks
The original task of the jury is to evaluate the competition entries with the aim to select, after discussion, those designs that best meet the requirements of the competition brief and to make recommendations to the sponsor for further development of the task. The jury members perform their duties personally and independently and solely according to technical aspects and based on the criteria stated in the competition brief. In addition, the jury has formal tasks during the competition process. For example, it should advise the sponsor on the formulation of the terms of reference before the competition begins, for which purpose it is advisable to hold a jury colloquium. And at the beginning of the jury meeting(s), it has the task of deciding on the formal admission of the competition submissions. Afterwards, members of the jury are often involved in communicating the results, whether by participating in press events and, as part of public relations, the opening of a public exhibition of the competition projects or participation events.

Significance in terms of external impact

The jury exercises an overarching function through the collective reputation of its members. To the participants and the public, the reputation of a properly composed jury signals the fair evaluation of the submitted designs in terms of quality and content, as well as a respectful treatment of the enormous intellectual achievement of the participants. With this reputation, publicity can go a long way in attracting the most qualified and talented candidates to participate and engaging in the process with strong competition entries. The professional competence and independence of the jury ensure that the promise made is kept.

Composition of the jury

The composition of the jury is one of the delicate tasks in the preparation of a competition. First, formal requirements must be met. According to most rules, the jury is composed of an odd number of technical and general jury members, with the technical jury members having the majority and being mostly independent from the sponsor. However, there are also regions with a practice in which the jury consists exclusively of technical jurors and the sponsor attends the jury panel only as a guest, only to deal with the decision afterwards. We would not recommend this approach, as it does not exploit the potential of an integrative decision in competitions.

Of course, all members of the jury must be independent of all competition participants and must not have any personal interests the implementation of the project. In the case of interdisciplinary competitions, all relevant disciplines should be represented on the jury with voting rights.

In addition to the formal aspects of jury composition, it is important to assemble a committee that has the professional competence to evaluate the designs. Equally helpful is practical knowledge of the jury from preparing and conducting comparable projects, as well as experience in academic teaching, in which critical evaluation and explanation of designs and concepts takes place on a regular basis. It is important to have a genuine interest in professional discourse as well as openness to solution approaches that may not correspond to one's own "school".

Jury meeting for the Concert Hall Munich, 2017

Exemplary composition of a jury

Other aspects in the composition of a jury are an appropriate mix of regional and supra-regional experience as well as consideration of gender balance and diversity. Involving multiple generations makes sense in the evaluation process and at the same time serves to pass on evaluation experience to younger colleagues.

A position in the jury is often filled, if available and if the project is of relative importance, by the individuals politically responsible for architecture and design in the city – city architect, head of the responsible building or planning service, etc. If the persons in question have the appropriate professional qualifications, they can participate as members of the technical jury following many sets of rules. Usually, however, they are part of the general jury, which is also composed, for example, of user representatives. In some cities, it is common for the political groups of the city council to be represented with voting rights in the general jury. This leads to a large increase in the size of the jury, but sometimes promotes the subsequent acceptance and political support of the project. In addition, in international competitions conducted under UNESCO or UIA regulations, the jury must be in its majority composed of members of different nationalities, where at least one person is appointed by the UIA to represent them.

Qualification

Technical jurors must meet the professional requirements to serve in an outstanding manner based on their professional qualifications. Many rules require that they have the professional qualifications that would entitle them to participate in the competition – in other words, that they act "on a professional level" with the competitors. This practice has proven itself in general as well as in individual cases, where the question of professional qualifications has been interpreted more openly, e.g., when the construction task has a special symbolic significance, in which case the inclusion of experts, for example, from the fields of history, philosophy, or art in the technical jury is justified and appropriate. General jurors should be particularly familiar with the content of the competition task and the local conditions. They usually represent the sponsor and, if it is not the sponsor, the political body of the municipality.

Number

As a rule, a number of seven to eleven members with voting rights is a recommended size of the jury, which on the one hand ensures a sufficient diversity of knowledge and points of view, and on the other hand a good working capacity of the panel. Especially if many stakeholders (possibly representation of political parties) or many disciplines are to be represented in the panel, the panel can also be significantly larger, so that we have also experienced jury panels with 23 voting members. Moderating the panel, time management, and logistical issues are correspondingly challenging.

Jury chair

According to many rules, the jury chair, also referred to as jury president, is elected by the jury at the first meeting among the technical jury members. Nevertheless, the necessary experience moderating jury meetings had been already taken into consideration when the jury was composed, so that the nomination is often made by the sponsor. The chair should be independent of the sponsor and represent the main professional discipline corresponding to the competition task. The chair presides over the meetings of the jury and ensures that the competition rules are observed – both in close coordination and often also role sharing with the project management of the competition management or consultant. Further tasks of the jury chair are the release and signing of minutes of the response to queries, the colloquia, and the meetings of the jury and, if required, the representation of the jury after the conclusion of the competition. Especially in the case of two-phase competitions and larger panels, it is advisable to appoint a deputy chair.

Mike Brennan
Royal Architectural Institute of Canada

" When organizing a design competition, one of the most important aspects is the jury. The group of individuals are to represent the values of the community in which the project is taking place and ensure design excellence. This allows for a project that is innovative, that strives for social and spatial equity, embraces and respects inclusivity and fosters diversity. Thoughtful change is created in the built environment and ultimately creates a better world for all.

Prof. Dr. (Univ. Firenze) Elisabeth Merk
Planning Director of Munich

" Competitions for urban design, landscape architecture and architecture are important elements of our building culture (Baukultur). They thrive on dialogue and discourse and are thus an expression of living democracy. They set important impulses and open doors for those who sponsor and for all who participate. From my many years of experience, I can say that special attention should be paid to the transdisciplinarity of the jury, and I always advocate that local and young offices be invited along renowned ones.

Substitution

If one or more regular voting members of the jury are unable to perform their duties due to illness or unavoidable absence during the discussion, the sponsor should appoint several deputy jury members for both the technical and the general jury. The deputy jury members should attend all meetings to be prepared in terms of content for the case that they assume voting rights. In some sets of rules it is stipulated that members of the technical jury, in the event of their absence, even temporarily, are to be replaced for the entire further duration of the jury session, in the case of multi-phase competitions for the duration of all jury sessions, by one of the deputy technical jury members who was permanently present during the previous session of the jury, whereas members of the general jury may be temporarily replaced by their deputies if they remain involved in the opinion-forming process.

Stefan Kögl
Architect, Siemens AG, Berlin

❞ For more than 125 years, Siemensstadt in Berlin has stood for a globally unique mix of uses, combining production, science, living, and leisure in one place. Now the Siemensstadt Square project is transforming part of it – the previously closed production site covering more than 70 hectares – into a hybrid urban concept of the future. This includes numerous dimensions, because the city of the future is productive and livable, technical and natural; in it, history and the future, hardware and software, digital and real worlds blend into a harmonious whole. Such a complex task also places great demands on competition management. Coupled with the very high-quality standards on the part of the competition project initiator and promoter, the Senate of Berlin and the district administration must also be involved at an early stage. Only intensive discussions and close coordination can ensure that the master plan works at all levels. This also includes an intact mix of uses and an adequate mix of functions, where internal user preferences must be known and incorporated into the task. The very important sustainability issues must also be named exactly, be sustainable and feasible. At the same time, a qualifying procedure cannot lead to the desired success without a clear economic objective. All planning is based on a clear idea of the architectural design with the help of previously developed design guidelines. It is also crucial for the success and public acceptance of a hybrid, sustainable and innovative urban quarter. For an innovative future project like Siemensstadt Square, digital planning is essential, here with the use of a digital twin and the BIM method. Only through it and with it can a real urban district be created that is built and operated sustainably and efficiently, while being highly integrative and livable. That is why digitization must and will be requested as "state-of-the-art" from all participants in the competition process.

Dorte Mandrup
Architect, Copenhagen

❞ What is important to me as a participant in a competition … There should always be a clear, unequivocal brief containing all necessary instructions for the participants to understand the context, intent, constraints, and opportunities. The brief provides the foundation for a successful design proposal, and it should leave enough leeway to allow experiments and creative freedom. A competition is an opportunity to challenge the status quo and explore angles and ideas that would have otherwise gone unnoticed. If the conditions and demands of the brief are too excessive it can become suffocating for the creative process, and you risk never discovering the full potential. One of the first things I look at when receiving the brief, is the composition of the jury. Are the members competent? Ambitious? Are they likely to see the value in experiments and bold enough to select designs that challenge conformity? Be thorough when selecting your jury and pick professionals with the right experience. Then of course, you should always remember that the budget should match your aspirations and offer the architects a basis to explore and create high-quality, ambitious designs.

Jury meetings **1**: Jewish Museum in Albania (left: Rainer Mahlamäki, Elva Margariti and Martin Mata), **2**: Government Quarter Tripoli (right: Peter Zlonicky), **3**: University of Manitoba in Winnipeg (Marc Angelil and Tobias Micke), **4**: Concert Hall Munich (Arno Lederer and Markus Allmann), **5**: Parliamentary Precinct Redevelopment Ottawa (center: Bruce Haden), **6**: BMW FIZ Future Munich (Kaspar Kraemer), **7**: European Parliament Brussels (Dorte Mandrup, Marilyne Andersen, Manuelle Gautrand and Lisa de Visscher)

4.4 Technical experts

For the preparation of the competition as well as for the preliminary examination and to support the jury without voting rights, the sponsor may invite technical experts for advice. They are recognized experts in their field, usually external specialists for partial aspects of the task (traffic, structural design, planning of technical equipment, ecological-technical sustainability and energy planning, fire protection, acoustics, history, costs), representatives of the responsible authorities (urban planning, building approving authorities, traffic, landscape, monument protection) or have special knowledge of the intended functions and uses. The participation of technical experts in the preparation of the competition takes place e.g., through the contribution to the process of developing and defining the framing conditions of the project, together with the authorities or by the preparation of text modules for the competition brief. To be able to provide quick and well-founded advice during the jury meeting, it is also very important to involve the technical experts in the preliminary examination (see Chapter 12.6).

Prof. Dr.-Ing. e.h. Klaus Daniels
Munich

❝ Due to the finite nature of resources (building materials) and energy (as well as CO_2 emissions), it is becoming increasingly important to develop overall concepts that are ACTUALLY capable of fulfilling the "cradle-to-cradle principle" and minimizing and managing energy use through renewable energies. These requirements must be evaluated much more in the future – and as a result, competitions must be more comprehensively launched and more honestly evaluated in the future (architecture + landscape architecture + construction + technology: from a single source).

4.5 Preliminary evaluation team

The preliminary examination team is either a part of the project team of the sponsor or of the competition managers. In order to be able to carry out the technical and content-related analysis carefully, the preliminary examiners should have the technical qualifications of the participants. At the same time, these persons usually must present the projects neutrally in the jury, so that a corresponding communicative competence is required. They are supported by an internal team of assistants, who take over further tasks of the preliminary examination, e.g. quantitative examinations and logistic tasks. The preliminary examination team works closely with the technical experts during the preliminary examination.

4.6 Professional chambers

In many places, chambers of architects and engineers or other professional associations play an advisory role before, during, and after competitions. In some countries (e.g., Germany and Austria), this involvement is anchored in the regulations. Here, their involvement includes the registration of the competition, which formally confirms that the conditions of participation and competition have been complied with. In the case of interdisciplinary competitions, the involvement of several professional chambers or associations is desired or required, e.g., not only the architects' chambers but also the engineers' chambers), and in the case of art competitions that of the corresponding professional organizations. Elsewhere, the participation of professional associations is less formalized, but nevertheless practiced. In international competitions, the UIA assumes the task of consultation and registration.

4.7 Other participants

Without voting rights, other persons can be part of the jury as guests, usually to observe the jury on behalf of other groups involved in the project. Usually these are the representatives of the architectural chambers, political parties, the users of the planned project or the citizens. In some places, the sponsor only participates in the procedure as an observing guest. In individual cases, representatives of the trade press are also admitted (see Chapter 2.14). If persons with special significance for the project are to be involved in the procedure, they can also be invited as "honorary guests" to assume a form of patronage and to signal this in the communication of the project.

Technical experts: **1:** Prof. Dr. Klaus Daniels (Preliminary Examination Revitalization of the Old Town of Fez), **2:** Karlheinz Karas (Participation Event BMW FIZ Future Munich), **3:** Prof. Brian Cody (Parliament Quarter Ottawa). Pre-examiners at the presentation in the jury: **4:** Friedhelm Gülink (KFAS Kuwait), **5:** Christine Eichelmann (USTH Hanoi), **6:** Helmuth Hanle (Museum for the Maidan Revolution Kyiv), **7:** Georg Dux (Wien Museum Neu), **8:** Brigitte Kochta (Technical City Hall Düsseldorf), **9:** Marc Dufour (KFA Kuwait), **10:** Richard Ollig (Urban Drainage and Environmental Analysis Nuremberg)

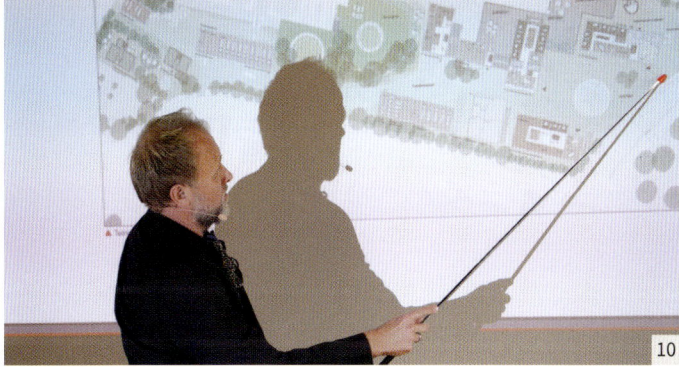

4 Members involved

5 COMPETITION ORGANIZATION

5.1 Who organizes competitions?

Internal or external management

Competitions are organized either by the sponsor's own staff or by external offices, or the work is shared between the two. The external partner is usually an architectural or urban design firm or a project management company. In countries with a well-established competition system, a niche has developed for this area of activity and many of these offices regularly undertake this task or are fully dedicated to consultancy and management in this area.

Qualification requirements

Some of the relevant guidelines for the conduct of competitions include statements on the minimum qualification of the competition managers to the effect that they should be at least as qualified as the competitors. (Quote from the UIA Guide, Art. 9: "… preferably an architect …", quote from the RPW 2018 § 2 para. 5: "… They have the professional qualification of the participants. Sponsors with expertise may also undertake the competition management themselves.").

Position of the competition organization in the overall project

The competition organizers operate on the same hierarchical level as the decision-makers on the part of the sponsor and the architectural and design offices participating in the competition. This does not only mean that the professional and personal qualifications of the competition organizers and managers must enable them to fully understand all aspects of the subject under consideration and of the motives on the part of the sponsor. It also means that the competition managers must be able to already show the sponsor the choices to be made and to advise them on possible strategies and the consequences of individual decisions. At this point, the terms competition management and competition coordination may be too restrictive and thus misleading: Instead, it is often also a matter of strategic advice that leads to –but is by no means limited to – the preparation and coordination of complex processes.

Prerequisites

Education and previous experience as an architect or urban designer are undoubtedly the best basis on which to build up the skills needed to perform these specific consulting services and technical procedures, since most project competitions are conducted in this field. However, the requirements go far beyond the usual profile for architecture and design: the consultancy content requires applicable business and legal knowledge, as well as all technical and organizational skills that can be applied in this context.

An important prerequisite for exercising this activity is, first of all, familiarity with all technical issues in the fields of architecture and urban design. It is also important to have experience in moderating between the parties involved in the project – a typical role for architects. In competition management, however, this takes place in a variety of formats, including the moderation of more, or less, public events with large numbers of participants, the moderation of meetings between experts, politicians, and laypeople, and so on. Experience is also required in areas such as construction and public procurement law, commercial and legal project development, graphic design, press and public relations, and IT logistics. Personal skills such as negotiation skills and thinking in complex technical, economic, and political contexts are also required. In this respect, the activity is not structurally very different from other consulting activities; in some respects, it is more like these than to engineering in the conventional sense, ultimately a combination of both.

5.2 Compensation for competition management

The activity of a competition manager is structurally closer to that of a management consultant than to that of a design architect. Therefore, it is not possible to calculate the fee for this activity (in case of commissioning an external office) using the same procedure as for architectural and urban design offices. In Germany, for example, according to the Fee Structure for Architects and Engineers (HOAI), the fee is determined by the complexity of the project type and a percentage of the expected construction costs or the size of the project area.

Instead, it is common practice in competition management to base the fee on the actual effort and the expected complexity of the project, usually through a flat fee. The appendix to the UIA Guide for International Competitions in Architecture and Town-Planning (2017) explains that "the fees of the professional and technical advisors as well as for any other advisors (e.g., for the definition of the spatial and function program), varies according to the complexity of the competition program and regulations and the country in which the competition is being run (…) Their transport and additional expenses will also be met by the sponsor."

Performance profile and standards

Nevertheless, there is no list of minimum standards in the field of competition management in the sense of a binding detailed catalog of services. The catalogs developed by some professional associations or public sponsors are not sufficiently precise to solicit comparable bids for these services and to establish an assignment that is clear to both contracting parties. A sample catalog prepared by the authors is included in the appendix. It has proven to be a reliable basis for describing the required services and thus for a fair calculation of the costs. It includes the following service groups:

01. Basic elements of the project in terms of organization and content
02. Definition of the competition task
03. Coordination with authorities and other external parties
04. Preparation of the competition materials
05. Selection of participants or, in case of open competitions, registration
06. Events of the competition procedure
07. Preliminary examination
08. Jury meetings
09. Final documentation of the competition
10. Public presentation
11. Conclusion of the competition procedure

1: Jury meeting "Babyn Yar Holocaust Memorial Center in Kiyv", **2:** Documentation "BMW Welt Munich", **3:** Display boards "Wien Museum Neu", **4:** Transport "Museum for the Maidan Revolution Kyiv", **5:** Preliminary report app "Wien Museum Neu", **6:** University and State Library Darmstadt

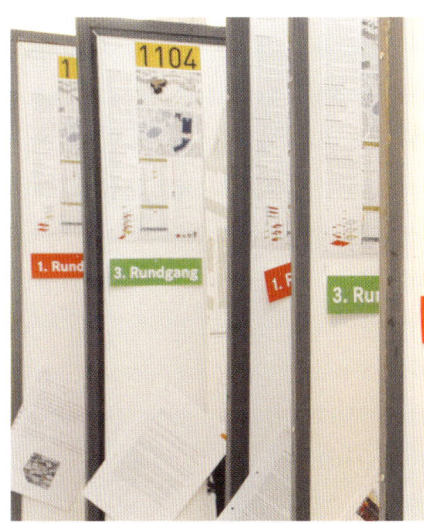

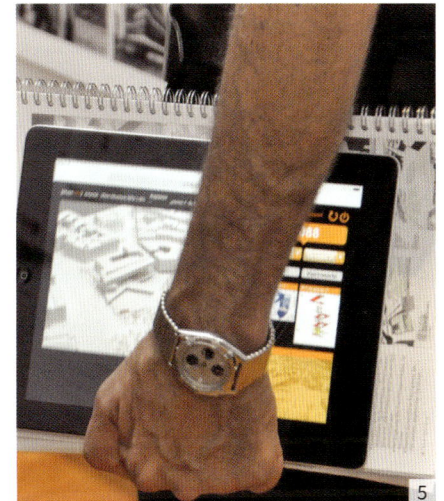

5 Competition organization

Estimation of effort

Estimating the required effort is also important for the sponsor if they intend to manage part or the entire competition themselves. In principle, it is easy to assess the effort and calculate a flat fee, if necessary supplemented by quantity scales or sliding-scale clauses for certain items, such as the number of meetings required or the number of applications or drafts to be examined in the preliminary examination. However, this requires a precise and comprehensible description of the scope of services.

The actual fee is therefore based primarily on the experience of the competition managers and an estimate of the effort to be expected according to the complexity of the project and the parties involved as well as due to the selected procedure. Accordingly, the fee amount, as well as the scope and quality of the services provided, can vary according to the requiremen

Given all the project and situational contingencies, it is not possible to establish a general rule for the specific fee for external competition management (see Chapter 7).

In any case, four key questions need to be considered when estimating the fee:

› Role allocation of sponsor/competition managers: what proportion of the required services will be outsourced?
› Which procedure will be chosen?
› How complex is the project?
› How complex is the structure of the stakeholders to be involved, including the sponsor?

Additional and third-party costs

It should be clarified in the contract to what extent costs for travel and accommodation of the competition organizer are to be included in the fee or reimbursed upon proof, which is usually more transparent for both sides. Furthermore, it can be agreed that third party services (e.g., printing, model construction, model photography, etc.) are not procured directly by the sponsor, but are commissioned by the external competition organizer and are usually provided by subcontractors.

Fee level

Depending on the subject of the project, the type of procedure, extra services, and the complexity of the sponsor as well as the concrete agreement on the division of tasks between the sponsor and the competition manager, the competition manager's fee is between 40,000 euros (net) and 250,000 euros (net without incidental and travel expenses); in exceptional cases, even higher. The scope of services of the competition organizer is to be planned accordingly in the procurement of these services.

Thierry Montpetit
Senior Director, Public Services and Procurement Canada, Government of Canada

❝ Faced with a major urban renewal project that would affect the seat of Canada's Parliament in Ottawa, Public Services and Procurement Canada initiated an international design competition. We quickly entrusted this major national city building initiative to [phase eins]. as competition manager. Their involvement, expertise, and ability to work with the Government of Canada and the houses of Parliament, concluded in the best possible result. This result could not have been remotely achieved without [phase eins]. To put it in other words, the selection of the competition manager is an essential building block on the way to the overall success of the project.

Simone Raskob
Executive Board Division 6 of the city of Essen

❝ Thanks to the vast experience of the offices that have been organizing competitions and their numerous contacts to architectural offices, they could give us as municipality helpful and valuable ideas and advice for our planned projects, to achieve an (even) better result in the end. This is also shown by the awarding of the "Promoter prize 2022" of the Chamber of Architects of North Rhine-Westphalia to the city of Essen.

Martin Hahm
formerly employed architect at BMW Group

❝ I had the great fortune to have been involved in the last three major international design competitions for BMW AG, all of which were managed and supervised by [phase eins]. While in the competition for the central building at the BMW plant in Leipzig I was initially "only" an employee who witnessed the procedure and the result of the competition management, I was responsible for the last competition in Munich. What was important in selecting the right and essential partner and necessary to convince internal procurement of the required "single sourcing"?

› Knowing the language of the different parties involved.
› Diplomatic skills and experience to unite diverging interests into a target-oriented product.
› Knowledge of the fundamentals for a proper and appropriate competition system.
› Understanding that the need to know and select the right architects is fundamental for an appropriate outcome, but also for the subsequent collaboration.
› Competence to prepare a professional competition brief and result analysis that can convince even professional skeptics.
› A good and trusting interaction on a personal level.

5.3 Competition organization tasks

Depending on the extent to which the project has already been developed and coordinated when the external competition managers step in, its scope of services initially includes strategic consulting to clarify fundamental issues:

- **Project goals:** meeting demands, financial objectives
- **Boundary conditions:** technical, political, and planning conditions
- **Procurement process:** which services are to be procured, how and in what timeframe
- **Communication:** involvement of political and broader public as well as selected stakeholders.

More concrete and detailed services follow then for the implementation of the procedure. Here, the competition manager is are not only the organizer, but also the moderator of content-related coordination processes, especially in the context of the creation of spatial and functional programs, and, if necessary, also initiators and implementers of these processes:

1. Clarifying and describing the site situation and planning guidelines
2. Defining the competition task
3. Preparing the competition documents (brief brochure, plans, model of surroundings)
4. Advising on the selection of jury members and experts
5. Consulting on the type of procedure to be chosen
6. Formulating and agreeing on the formal conditions of the procedure
7. Launching, if applicable, a pre-qualification procedure for the selection of participants
8. Communicating with participants by means of written questions and colloquia
9. Preparing, moderating, and documenting all events
10. Conducting a preliminary examination of the submitted projects
11. Participating in the jury meeting(s)
12. Organizing exhibitions and being responsible for public relations
13. If necessary, preparing and conducting a procurement procedure for the negotiation of the respective contract
14. Creating the project website for the exchange of information and data
15. Monitoring costs and deadlines during the competition procedure

1. Clarification and description of the situation and planning basis

The occasion for commissioning a competition manager is (more or less already clarified) need to construct, extend, or convert a building to serve a purpose that is already defined but perhaps not yet be described in detail. This can also be an urban design need, include a dimension of open space design or engineering, concern the design of a product or an exhibition design, or even the creation of a work of art.

Thus, depending on the task, the preparation of a competition also includes the collection of existing documents and preliminary studies for the project, as well as the research of all conditions of the site, the land, its condition, and buildability (subsoil, topography, existing buildings, existing pipelines), the traffic development, climatic conditions, as well as the historical development of the site.

Construction projects usually require approval – whether by the administration, the government, or other stakeholders whose consent, or at least goodwill, is required for the project. It is necessary to promote the ability to obtain legal or general approval by involving the relevant persons or institutions in the process described at an early stage. Thus, the preparation phase is also a discussion platform, a "round table." The result of this early involvement is usually a significant simplification of the subsequent design and approval process – and thus directly becomes a measurable success factor.

Part of this service of the competition management is also, if necessary, to question the specifications already made in advance by the sponsor in the interest of specifying the task more precisely. In any case, the task of the competition managers is to check the completeness and validity of the information and, if necessary, to obtain missing details.

2. Definition of the competition task

Besides clarifying the existing situation, the service of the competition managers includes defining and describing the goals of the project. These are usually strategic, urbanistic, economic, and functional goals. To describe the latter, it is necessary to clarify the concrete requirements that are to be met by the project – be it the improvement of a design situation, the creation of spaces, traffic engineering solutions, and so on. The competition managers then create a requirements' program.

From the requirements' program, the competition manager prepares the spatial program for the competition, or a spatial and functional program. It shows in an appropriately detailed form the requirements in areas (square meters), any technical requirements (e.g., desired room heights, building physics requirements and lighting conditions), and describes the desired relationships that individual spaces and space groups should have to each other. The process of creating these programs requires extensive coordination with, for example, the users, special designers (e.g., hospital consultants, theater consultants) and, if necessary, research into reference projects as well as standards and guidelines. If necessary, conflicting interests must be reconciled in a moderation process. Ultimately, the competition managers should formulate the task in a way that is comprehensible and consistent, achieving consensus among all parties involved.

The final stage of the coordination process is the jury colloquium, in which all members of the jury meet for the first time to discuss the content of the competition brief and decide on it as a consensus document. The preparation, moderation, and documentation of this event and, if necessary, of the accompanying program (site visit) is a task of the competition managers.

3. Preparation of the competition documents

The general conditions and objectives of the project should be formulated and prepared in such a way that the intention of the project is clear to everyone involved in the competition and the design offices participating in the competition have the necessary documents at their disposal to work on the task. The documents are made available to all participants in the competition, if necessary, as a download from the competition homepage.

Competition brief

The competition brief is the primary medium for communicating the terms and objectives of the project. It summarizes all the key messages in text, tables, and graphics, and if necessary, in multiple languages. Since participants are often unfamiliar with the location of the project, they should understand the brief as quickly as possible. It has been proven helpful to present the content as clearly as possible, in many cases graphically. A well-designed brief signals the importance and ambition of the project.

Plan materials

An important part of the brief is the plan material which will be used by the competition participants to prepare their designs. The existing material must be sifted through, supplemented, and prepared into a coherent, reasonably structured plan file (basic file). Ultimately, this also serves to ensure that the decision in the competition is made on the basis of coherent and coordinated fundamentals. The contradictions that often exist between plans from different sources must be resolved before the documents are distributed to the participants. For example, it is the responsibility of the competition managers to arrange in case of doubt for a land survey to be commissioned and to provide correct specifications.

Model of surroundings

Organizing the construction of the model of surroundings is another task that the competition manager undertakes. The following partial services required:

› Advising the sponsor on the size and scale of the model, considering the expected costs for construction and potential transport
› Preparing the digital plans for the model-maker
› Inviting model-makers to tender and commissioning the suitable bidder
› Controlling the model's production and delivery

4. Advice on selecting jury members and experts

The experience of the competition managers helps to find the right parties to the procedure – jury members, technical experts and, if necessary, participants, and assembling a group of people suitable for each activity. Neutral consultation – as opposed to taking sides or even competing in the same market – creates the necessary opportunities for contact and communication. The competition manager should not be in a competitive relationship with other project members but see themselves as a partner - for the benefit of the sponsor and the design process with the aim to optimize the project.

5. Advice on choosing the type of competition

There are many different types of competitions – architectural competitions stand here for of all types of competitions in the fields of architecture, landscape architecture, urban design, and engineering. Depending on the importance, scope, complexity, and legal situation regarding procurement law or competition regulations, the chosen procedure can be adapted to the project.

Left page: Model packaging in the "Wien Museum Neu" competition
Right page: Models in the "KFAS Kuwait" competition

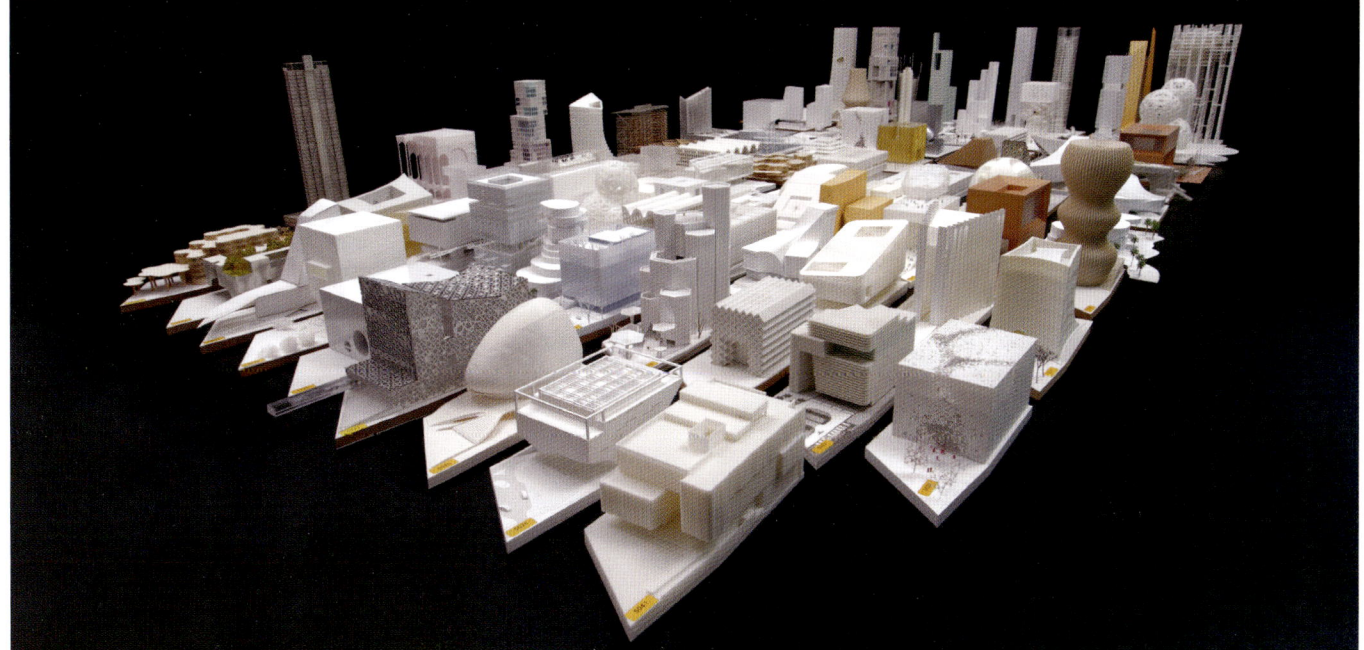

The relevant professional association of architects is available for advice; in Germany, this is usually the Chamber of Architects.

Decisions should be made on whether and how to announce the competition, how many participants to admit, and what qualifications to request – e.g., the formation of interdisciplinary working groups of several professions may be recommended, if not required. The process could also be divided into phases, to enable a more intensive dialogue during process of learning and coordination. Finally, in complex projects, it may be helpful to lift anonymity in favor of a direct dialogue with the participants. During the consultation and selection process, it is important to make sensible use of the legal framework for competitions in the respective country, in the interest of the project and all participants (for more details see Chapter 3).

6. Formulation and coordination of the formal conditions of the procedure

Formulating the conditions of the procedure binding for all participants and thus creating the contractual basis for conducting the competition is also a task of the competition managers. This includes:

› Identifying the participants
› Explaining the conditions of the procedure (type of competition, endorsement of the Chamber, eligibility to participate, selection criteria, exclusion criteria, prize money, promise of contract, copyright, and so on).
› Compiling a list of competition documents
› Providing details of the services required
› Defining of dates and deadlines

7. Announcement and, if necessary, conduction of a prequalification procedure for the selection of participants

Restricted competition

In the context of selecting participants for design competitions, it is necessary to find answers to the questions of which designers are suitable for solving the task at hand, which criteria can be applied, and which committee, if any, makes the selection of participants. It is easy to imagine that at this phase, crucial positive decisions can be made for the further course of the project, or crucial mistakes can be made. For this reason, and to ensure that the process is neither formally nor politically vulnerable, careful consultation is essential at this point. Finally, it is important to find a sufficiently large, competent, and at the same time heterogeneous pool of participants for each project.

In the case of public sponsors, consideration must be given to the applicable public procurement law, which generally requires publication of the opportunity to participate, but similar compliance rules often apply to businesses. Selection is then made either on the basis of pre-defined criteria or by lottery. In the case of private sponsors, the selection can also be made without applying the procurement law binding on the public sector, but it should not be subject to lower requirements in terms of the transparency and comprehensibility of the selection process and the care taken in defining the selection criteria. In order to keep the effort of such procedures reasonable for all parties involved, it is advisable to set clear requirements for the application and to keep the requested services as part of the application within reasonable limits.

The task of the competition managers is to control the entire process, starting with advice on how to proceed, defining the selection criteria, setting up forms, receiving and processing the applications, moderating the selection process and its documentation.

Open competition

A special case is the open competition, in which any person with appropriate professional qualifications can participate. In this case, there is no selection of participants in the competition before the competition task is processed; the winner is selected in a single step solely based on the quality of the submitted design. The open competition thus represents the "pure form" of design competitions. In Europe, these procedures sometimes reach such a high number of submitted designs that they can only be justified under special circumstances due to the high effort for all project members. The task of the competition managers in open competitions is limited at the moment of the competition launch to organizing the registration of those who are interested in participating, among other things to be able to communicate with them – e.g., by answering questions or issuing additional documents.

8. **Dialogue with the participants via written questions and in colloquia**

Competitors have the opportunity to submit questions and aspects of the project for discussion. The background to this process is twofold. On the one hand, the aim is to give all participants a maximum understanding of the project and its framework; on the other hand, it is clear at this point that the competition also serves to tap the experience and creativity of all people involved in the project at this early stage: The questions and suggestions are intended to open up the possibility of reflecting on, reconsidering and, if necessary, modifying individual aspects. This dialogical situation is usually established in the context of a participants' colloquium at the project site.

In addition, participants can anonymously submit questions in writing. For this purpose, an online forum has proven to be useful, where participants can ask questions and receive answers over a defined period of time. This has the advantage that questions arising during the work process may also be clarified. It is important that all participants have the same level of information. Therefore, all answers and clarifications are recorded and made available to all participants as a further working basis. The documentation of all questions and answers then becomes part of the task itself. In the case of cooperative competition, the participants' colloquium can also be used for an interim presentation by the participants to the jury and a discussion of the solutions with the aim to further clarify the task.

9. **Preparation, moderation, and documentation of all events**

It is part of the competition managers' services to prepare, moderate and document all events in the process. In particular, this includes preparing the agenda, organizing the meeting rooms with their furnishings and seating arrangements, preparing handouts and presentations, moderating and taking minutes.

10. **Preliminary examination of the submitted designs**

The preliminary examination and the tasks of the competition organization in this context are explained in detail in Chapter 12.

Formal examination	› Receipt of submissions, checking that deadlines have been met › If necessary, ensuring anonymity with camouflage numbers or similar › Controlling completeness
Quantitative check	› Checking the fulfillment of the program required in the competition brief (areas, volumes, etc.)
Technical examination	› Checking the formal requirements formulated in the competition brief (e.g., planning law requirements, allocation of use, development, preservation of protected building components or tree population) › Checking compliance with building regulations (e.g., fire protection, accessibility) › Checking the plausibility of information on costs or economic viability
Report	› Preparation of a clear preliminary examination report

11. **Participation in the jury meeting (decision making body)**

In this context, the process of the jury meeting and the tasks of the competition organizers are explained in detail in Chapter 13.

Organization	› Preparation (scheduling, invitations, agenda) › Organizational framework of the event (selection of rooms, sound and lighting equipment, furniture, movable walls, transportation) › Presentation of the competition projects (display of the plans, model exhibition) › Follow-up (taking minutes, dismantling the project exhibition, informing participants of the results)
Participation	› Co-moderation with the chairperson of the jury › Presentation of the projects during an informational round › Advice on the formal procedure and the voting process
Overall tasks	› Working to ensure that all parties important for strategic reasons are involved into the process › Ensuring that the competition entries are evaluated with fairness and respect

1: Voting in the jury meeting "Concert Hall Munich", **2:** Models in the competition "Urban drainage and environmental analysis Nuremberg", **3:** Preliminary report "Babyn Yar Holocaust Memorial Center in Kyiv", **4:** Display boards in the open competition "Revitalization of the old town of Fez"

5 Competition organization

12. Exhibition and publicity

The public exhibition of all designs submitted to the competition and the publication of the jury's decision, first of all, expresses respect for the commitment and achievement of all participants by showing that not only the prize-winners, but all participants have contributed to the development of the project and to the discussion in the jury. It also promotes public acceptance of the project. The exhibition is usually accompanied by publications in professional journals and a presentation of the results on the project's homepage.

The competition managers are also responsible for the organization of the exhibition, including the labeling of the designs with the names of the authors as well as the compilation of the documents for the press and the support of the sponsor at the press conference that may be held. In order to provide the desired comprehensive information at the exhibition, it is helpful to include information posters about the reason and purpose of the competition, the course of the procedure, and so on. In the case of extensive exhibitions, for example, the plans of the participants are reprinted to achieve uniform printing and paper quality, or screens are set up with pictures and films of the events of the procedure, which are in turn created by the competition manager.

13. Tender procedure/contract negotiations

After a competition, negotiations for the commissioning of further planning services take place either with the authors of the 1st prize-winning design only or with the authors of all prize-winning designs. In the case of public sponsors, these negotiations take place, for example in Germany, on the basis of the Public Procurement Ordinance (VgV).

The competition managers participate in the negotiations, if necessary, in cooperation with the sponsor's purchasing/contracting/procurement department:

› Preparing, coordinating, and designing forms
› Preparing the components of the bidding documents, including participation in the formulation of the contract specifications
› Sending out the invitation to bid
› Receiving questions from bidders as well as drafting, coordinating, and sending responses
› Carrying out preliminary evaluation of bids according to formal requirements
› Preparing negotiation meetings including scheduling, invitations
› Moderating and recording negotiations
› Preparing and letters of acceptance and rejection
› Preparing contract award recommendation
› Documenting of the tender procedure and, if necessary, drafting the contract

Daniel F. Ulrich
Chief officer for planning and construction of the city of Nuremberg

" In Nuremberg, we are happy to support all kinds of competitions for urban design and architectural projects, both for our own and for private projects, because we are convinced that these can make an important contribution to building culture (Baukultur) and thus to the positive urban development of the city. Competitions also create a certain transparency in the decision-making process.

Above all, by bindingly defining the spatial program ("competition task"), they secure a project in many respects at an early stage. If we look at project competitions from different perspectives, we notice: The promoter of the project gains security in planning and can create acceptance through a transparent, fair procedure.

It is often only through intensive preparation in advance that a developer recognizes the potential of the site. The variety of results also enables the developer to choose from different approaches. This then serves as a means of communication to the outside world. The competition participants have the opportunity to contribute their ideas and possibly acquire a contract for which they would not have been able to apply without the competition.

They can use successful competition entries as a reference to present themselves to the market. In the end, through competitions, architects can, above all, advance the building culture and create something new. Especially the preparatory phase of competitions is, to my view, an important goal-setting process that plays a fundamental role for all participants. In almost all types of competition, different actors from the administration (including public agencies), politicians and locally active interest groups can be involved in the process. These involved parties can help to control functionally and quantitatively the contents of the competition and present needs as well as critical points, thus contributing significantly to the success of the competition or to a positive result. The expectations of the future planning of our cities are high. We see the city as an organism that is constantly adapting to new conditions. All competition types are part of this adaptation strategy. They involve an examination of the future and further development of the urban design/architectural context on a wide variety of levels. Every competition deals with the question of how the city will develop: Continue building as before or address current issues? Competition managers bear a great responsibility here. They can show the client how the competition gives the chance to gear project to the future. Especially when the municipality is involved in a competition, the decision-making processes of the administration often differ from those that the client is used to. Good competition managers know both sides, the view and interests of the client and the requirements and processes in the administration and can coordinate them.

They can mediate between involved partiers or clearly point out where the differences lie and where solutions should be found. As a result, a well-structured and clearly formulated competition brief is the key to solving a design task.

Competitive procedures do not have to follow the strict framework of the RPW (German guidelines for project competitions) alone. The number of possibilities is large, and public procurement law sets a broad framework here that must be used wisely. A completely open procedure is not always the right approach; other models often suggest themselves for many reasons. Competitions in the broader sense are an instrument that offers many more possibilities than one might think at first glance. To show the client the options with which a procedure can be optimally adapted to the task is a task that cannot be overestimated. The sometimes technically inexperienced clients are accompanied and advised by the supervisor during the procedure. They must deal with situations that do not correspond to their professional orientation and can rely on the expertise of a qualified competition supervisor.

14. Creation of a project website for the exchange of information and data

The project website, coordinated by the competition organizers, serves with several modules for the communication between the project members:

› Publicizing the process and attract professionals to participate in it
› Providing information about the project with plans and images
› Handling of the competition with online forms for entering information about the applicants (if relevant)
› For open competitions, providing the opportunity to register
› Allowing applicants and participants to submit questions and then presenting them the responses
› Providing files
› Presenting an online exhibition with the result of the competition
› In case of negotiated procedures: Receiving offers by upload

15. Cost and schedule control

Deadlines
For the duration of their assignment, the competition manager is responsible to coordinate the deadlines. This requires, first of all, the creation of an outline schedule, which can be integrated into the overall project schedule, in which, in turn, the timeline up to the realization of the project is designed and tracked. Once the jury members have been selected, coordinating the dates of the events is the most important task of the competition managers. In case of delays in the project, updating the schedule belongs also to their tasks.

Costs
Cost control first requires the preparation of a total cost estimate for the procedure (Chapter 7 for details), including the following items:

› Competition sum (prizes and honoraria)
› Honoraria for external jurors and experts
› Events (rent, catering, technical equipment, etc.)
› Printing and model making
› Travel and accommodation

As this is the largest single item in medium and large projects, the calculation of the competition sum is the most important part of the tasks of the competition managers in the context of cost control. During the process, the continuation of the total cost estimate based on the real costs as well as the invoice verification are then further tasks of the competition managers.

Andrea Gebhard
Landscape Architect and Urbanist, President of the German Federal Chamber of Architects

❞ The composition of a jury contributes significantly to the success of a competition. The architectural jurors are familiar with the current competition rules and procurement laws and deal intensively with the task. They ensure that the best ideas emerge from a competition task. Recognizing quality beyond one's own attitude is a challenging task. Some architectural chambers keep lists of members of architectural juries. This enables public and private clients to check the composition of the jury in a targeted manner.

Ethan Kimmel
Architect, Tel Aviv

❞ What is important for me as a competition participant, when organizing a competition, is to be sure that the client is as serious as I intend to be if I decide to participate, and I must be impressed by the quality of the materials and the brief of the project sent to me as well as to be sure the competition will be reviewed by a professional jury.

Prof. Rainer Mahlamäki
Professor and Co-Founder of Lahdelma & Mahlamäki Architects, Helsinki

❞ During my career, I have served on the jury of dozens of architectural competitions; including a few organized by [phase eins]. As juror, it is a pleasure to start the evaluation of the proposals on base of a profound professional technical analysis and a general preview by the expert examination. As a result, the evaluation processes can be efficient. The members of the international juries will be able to quickly get to the heart of the proposals: the architecture. With their attitude and methodology, [phase eins]. has made a significant contribution to the European competition system over the years. I can only say that these competitions have been among the best organized.

5.4 Commissioning the service of competition management

Basic considerations
If the sponsor wishes to commission external support for activities related to the preparation and execution of a competition, it is necessary to organize the tendering of these services.
Depending on whether public procurement law or the internal procurement guidelines of a private sponsor are to be considered, the appropriate rules for tendering these freelance services must be applied.
First, the usual steps must be taken to determine the type of contract:

› Determine the scope of services
› Estimate the contract amount (see Section 5.2)
› Define the commissioning criteria

Selection procedure
The selection process of the competition managers is usually carried out by means of a restricted invitation to tender. As a first step, the bidders should meet at least the following eligibility criteria: appropriate professional qualifications, capacity (average office size/turnover in the past three years, proof of professional liability insurance).
In addition to the fee, the proposal should include information about the project team, references, and the planned approach to the project (see "Selection criteria"). It is advisable to hold a presentation meeting with the short list of bidders, in which the concept is explained in person for a better evaluation.

Scope of services and fees
Regardless of whether competition consulting, competition support, or the entire competition management is to be outsourced in accordance with Chapter 1.5.2, the necessary tasks are always divided between the sponsor's project team and the contractor (external competition managers) during the project. In this respect, it is advisable to describe precisely not only the scope of services, but also the interface between the external services and the sponsor's own services.

› **Competition advisor:** In this case, the services usually include advice on strategic issues related to the preparation of the procedure, in particular the selection of the type of competition and the selection of the jury members, as well as the support for colloquia and jury meetings. Accordingly, the services are highly dependent on the need for advice, for example, the number of committees in which advice is required and the number of meetings of these committees. In this respect, an assignment with invoicing according to time spent in hours or daily rates is expected and fair for both sides. In the case of smaller projects, even a few days of consulting can be of significant help; in the case of complex projects, this service alone can require several dozen days of consulting. In special cases, competition consulting can be helpful in parallel with external competition management, especially if, for example, competition consulting can complement specific local expertise.

› **Competition consultant:** Particularly in this scenario, the planned interface and the part of externally commissioned services must be described precisely. On this basis, commissioning via a flat fee is common. Services that can be separated from the overall catalog of activities required within the framework of competition management include the preparation of selected components of the competition brief (e.g., description of the development of the competition site, the planning situation and boundary conditions of the competition area) or the preliminary review of the submitted designs.

› **Competition manager:** Even in the case of commissioning an external party with the entire portfolio of competition organization, a precise examination of the concrete requirements is advisable before the services are put out to tender. A look at the detailed service catalog (see Appendix) shows that, depending on the type of the selected procedure, various parameters of the procedure and the need for support in other areas (press relations, event organization, auditing, etc.), clarification of the concrete division of tasks is necessary. As soon as the services have been sufficiently described, it is also usual to place an order for a flat-sum fee, especially if the partial services are priced by item and can thus be ordered by module, if necessary.

Tender procedure
The persons and offices invited to bid should be provided with as complete information and documentation as possible about the planned project and the procedure, but at least the following should be provided.
In addition, it should be explained as precisely as possible to what extent individual tasks are to be understood as already completed and boundary conditions as decided, or only represent an advanced project basis or only starting points.

› General description of the project (aim and objective, site plan, project members), current planning situation.
› Key data on the spatial or area program (total NUF or estimated GFA, main functions) or, in the case of urban design competitions, the planned utilization program (residential units or similar).
› Cost estimate, if applicable, cost framework for the construction project.
› Scheduled timeframe for the competition and the realization of the project.
› The regulations, laws, and ordinances to be considered when organizing the competition.
› If already determined, the planned type of competition. If the type of procedure has not yet been determined, it is helpful to indicate whether the offer is to be based on one type of procedure and the order will be revised in the corresponding positions if another type of procedure is to be carried out, or whether alternative procedures are to be presented and offered in the offer.
› The expected language of the competition or whether bilingual implementation is foreseen or will be offered as an option.
› The location of the competition events (city, country).
› It should be stated whether the competition manager is to undertake all requested services themselves or through subcontractors or whether certain services are to be provided by third parties within the scope of the competition, whose services the competition manager is only to control.
For example, the competition manager will request offers for these services, make recommendations for the commission of these service providers and other third parties, supervise and accept the services and check the invoices. This refers, among other things, to the service groups of printing or copying work, model construction, model photography, web programming, renting of venues, catering, stand rentals, transportation, and so on.

In addition, it is helpful to mediate the following aspects:
› Whether the preliminary examination and any related expert meetings should/can take place on the premises of the competition managers or whether these must necessarily take place on the premises of the sponsor.
› The competition fundamentals will be developed in an integrative process in which, in addition to the competition managers and the sponsor, other external consultants may participate.
› Only in the case of a public sponsor: Which online based tender platform is to be used for handling the steps relevant under public procurement law (announcement, queries, etc.) – whether the competition management may/should provide this or whether it is mandatory to use another specific platform.

› The competition manager should set up and manage a project homepage, which is also to be used for the registration of competition participants or the participation's pre-selection process (for more details, please refer to the service description).
› In the case of open pre-qualification procedures and open competitions, the specification of a planned/estimated number of participants (if applicable, in both stages of the competition) as well as an estimate of the number of participation applications, which is to serve as a basis for calculation.
› An estimate of the expected number of jury members and whether the panel should have non-local (international) members.

Two to three weeks should be given for the preparation of the proposal with an opportunity to clarify questions at the beginning.

Selection criteria

Depending on the size and complexity of the project, the level of effort required to manage the competition may vary. However, even for smaller projects, it makes sense to consider the experience and approach of the bidder, especially since the formulation of the terms of reference varies widely and it must be ensured that the concept is appropriate for the project in question. The following criteria are recommended for the evaluation of bids when tendering competition management services (or partial services in the sense of competition consultation), on which information should be requested and evaluated:

› **Project team:** Professional qualifications and personal references of the project leader and other team members, as well as the plausibility of their organization and task assignment.
› **References:** Information on managing competitions comparable in terms of procedure type and project size. Ideally, the candidate should present several references comparable in both respects. For complex tasks, it is worth asking for letters of recommendations from former clients. If an open competition is forseen, experience in managing such open competitions should be highly valued. If the scope of services includes the organization of a public tender in accordance with public procurement law, experience with the supervision of such public procedures should be greatlty appreciated.
› **Concept:** The concept for the structure of the competition documents should be requested, supported by at least one reference (competition brief, information plans for the participants), the structure of the preliminary examination report, supported by at least one references (preliminary examination report, matrix of expert criteria) and the methodology for the graphic presentation of the spatial program also with the help of at least one reference.
› **Fee:** A flat fee should be considered, the incidental costs rate and potentially a flat rate for travel expenses, whereby the latter is usually reimbursed upon proof and should not be included in the evaluation.

It is advisable to hold a presentation meeting with the companies requested to organize the competition to get to know and evaluate their project team and concept. In such an appointment, the opportunity can be created to involve other project members on the part of the sponsor, to get to know the people who will take over the most important consultation in the upcoming phase. The competition manager assumes a central role in the coordination of the project in this phase, and the trust of all project members in this important tender is important.

We recommend the following key for weighting to tendering criteria (contract criteria):

PROJECT TEAM	20 %
REFERENCES	30 %
CONCEPT	30 %
FEE	20 %

Dipl.-Ing. Torsten Schröder
Technical Authorized Representative, IPM – Immobilien Projekt Management Düsseldorf GmbH

❝ The basis for the large number of strong and requirements-oriented designs in the general planning competition for the new TVG Düsseldorf Building was a thorough background research and a detailed, but at the same time realistic requirements profile. In addition to determining the technical boundary conditions of the building site, one had to identify, scrutinize critically, analyze in detail und finally concretize the requirements of the future building users. Close cooperation with the administration of the state capital of Düsseldorf to incorporate the above-mentioned improvements and the wealth of experience of the competition management in the comprehensive and detailed preparation of the competition brief were essential for success. For this to succeed, sponsor, users and competition management worked intensively and trustingly hand in hand, ensuring a constant flow of information. The goals set at an early stage were persistently pursued and fully achieved to the satisfaction of all involved.

V OFFICE BUILDINGS FOR PRIVATE DEVELOPERS AND USERS

Design competitions for private office buildings differ from those for public administration buildings primarily in the nature of the sponsor. The decision to hold a competition is usually made by private stakeholders for other reasons, with different expectations of the process and outcome, as well as personal responsibility. Both are expressed in the design of the procedure, the selection of participants, the organization of events, etc. In many respects there is more freedom, although large companies are often structured like large public administrations.

The motivation to hold a design competition may be driven by the requirements of the approving authorities or by planning law, but it can also come from the desire to achieve better solutions through the competition or to generate added value through higher quality architecture. The sponsors have often a strong construction background and are able to answer a wide range of questions, often based on experience gained from previous projects or market observations. This experience is then incorporated into the competition. As a result, there is often a keen desire for a process that allows for direct dialogue with the design teams and the ability to influence the design before the final decision. At the same time, there is a widespread concern that involving independent experts as well as public authorities could lead to the jury losing control and thus decision-making authority. Regarding design specifications, a distinction should be made between projects with previously known users and those for an unknown tenant structure that may be also change after design. Common to both is the need for flexibility to be redesigned according to the wishes of the users/tenants and the interest in having the outcome of the design competition agreed with the authorities as a basis for subsequent approval procedures.

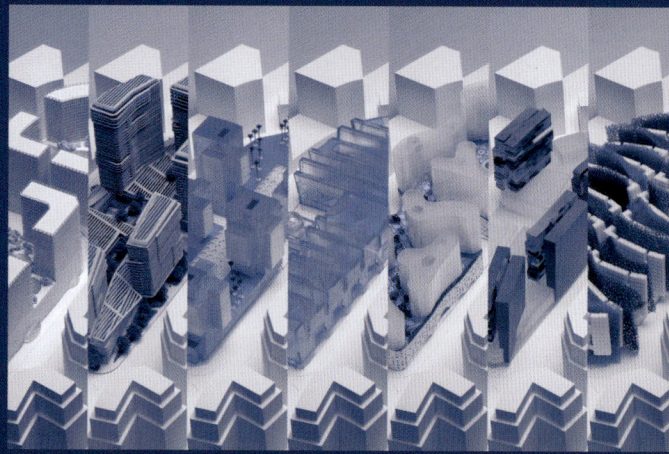

Models in the competition "Eco Bay Project in Abu Dhabi"

Stephan Kahl
Architect, R&S Immobilienmanagement GmbH, Munich

" For us at R&S Immobilienmanagement GmbH, the quality of a design has the highest priority, especially since the projects will remain in the portfolio for a long time after completion. The competition brief should reflect this quality requirement in every phase, from the serious organization of the procedure to the evaluation, to the consultation, and final jury meeting. Especially a project as demanding as the "iCampus im Werksviertel" neighborhood development, in which urban planning requirements are just as important as increased public interest, requires well thought-out, innovative designs that can only see the light of day in a suitable process.

Plot 4 Tower at Europaplatz, Berlin

HEIDE STREET / EUROPACITY URBAN DISTRICT The urban district is developed based on the "Heide Street Master Plan", which was approved by the Senate of Berlin in 2009. As a large-scale railroad site from the 19th century, the area had been abandoned for decades since World War II, forming an inner-city "edge" and urban border. With the reunification of Berlin, the interest in the approx. 40 ha large area changed. "Europacity" will be the urban link between the north Berlin district Wedding, the vicinity of the central station and the government quarter in south Berlin. Europacity will be developed on a large scale as a typical Berlin mix of residential and commercial uses, shopping, culture and leisure.

PLOT 4 The approx. 2,500 sqm site is located at Europaplatz, on the northern part of Berlin's central station. According to the master plan, the third highest building (84 m) is to be constructed here, to form a triad next to already constructed buildings the "Tour Total" (69 m) and the "50hertz Netzquartier" (43.5 m). For the latter, [phase eins]. had also organized a competition between 2012 and 2013.

PROGRAM The auditing company KPMG will be the single user of the new building. Workplaces are designed with the capacity to serve around 1,100 employees, who will be brought relocating to the new building from company's other locations to a more central and easily accessible Europaplatz. Part of the task was to design a structural connection to the immediate neighbor plot 3, on which an office building for the same user at the time of the competition was already in construction designed by KSP Jürgen Engel Architects.

Location: Berlin, Germany **Client:** CA Immo Deutschland GmbH **Year:** 2016 – 2017 **Project size:** approx. 2,400 sqm UFA **Type of competition:** Invited design competition with subsequent revision stage **Participants:** 9 **Competition budget:** EUR 230,000 (prizes and mentions: EUR 110,000; compensation per participant: EUR 12,000)

PRIZEWINNERS:
(01) **2nd prize/1st rank revision stage** Allmann Sattler Wappner Architekten GmbH, Munich (D); **2nd prize/2nd rank revision stage** Thomas Müller Ivan Reimann Gesellschaft von Architekten mbH, Berlin (D); **2nd prize/3rd rank revision stage** UNStudio van Berkel en Bos U. N. Studio BV, Amsterdam (NL); **Mention** Ortner & Ortner Baukunst Gesellschaft von Architekten mbH, Berlin (D); **Mention** Kleihues + Kleihues Gesellschaft von Architekten mbH, Berlin (D)

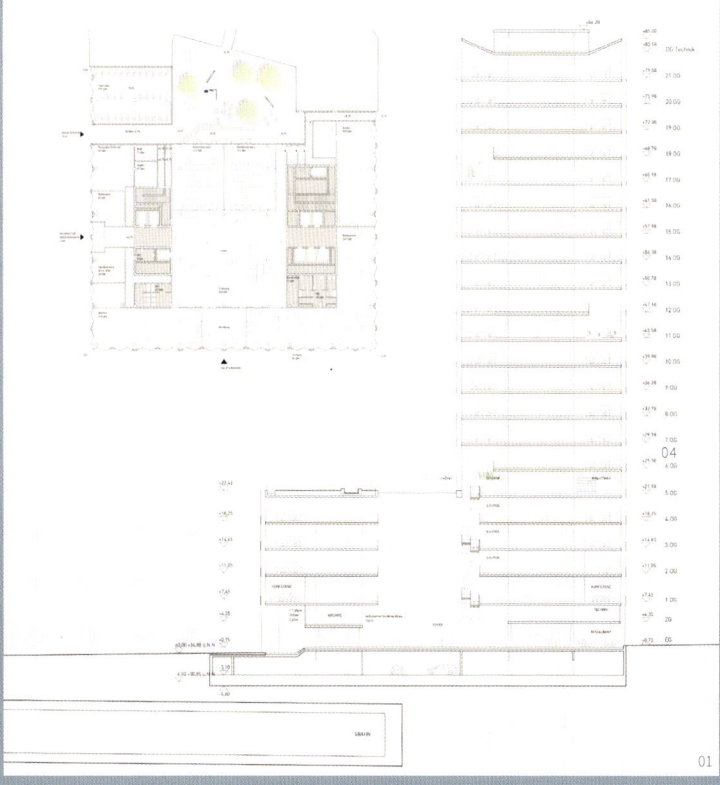

Siemens Healthineers Campus, Bengaluru

Location: Bengaluru, India **Client:** Siemens Healthcare Private Limited **Year:** 2020 **Project size:** approx. 170,000 sqm GFA **Type of competition:** Design competition **Participants:** 6 **Competition budget:** EUR 490,000 (prizes: EUR 70,000; Compensation per participant: EUR 70,000)

PRIZEWINNERS:
(01) **1st prize** Eller + Eller Architekten GmbH, Dusseldorf (D);
(02) **2nd prize** Henning Larsen Architects A/S, Copenhagen (DK);
(03) **3rd prize** DP Architects Pte Lte Ltd, Singapore (SG) **Other participants:** (04) Serie Architects, London (UK); (05) Vastu Shilpa Consultants, Ahmedabad (IN); (06) Gensler Design India Pvt. Ltd., Bengaluru (IN)

SIEMENS HEALTHINEERS As a leading medical technology company headquartered in Erlangen, Germany, Siemens Healthineers enables healthcare providers worldwide through its regional companies to increase value by empowering them towards expanding precision medicine, transforming care delivery, improving the patient experience, and digitalizing healthcare. Siemens Healthineers also provides a range of services and solutions to enhance healthcare providers' ability to provide high-quality, efficient care to patients. In 2019, Siemens Healthineers had approximately 52,000 employees worldwide.

BENGALURU CAMPUS The new campus in the south of Bengaluru is expected to become the central site for research and development for the Indian subsidiary of Siemens Healthineers and will include spaces for administration, laboratories, and manufacturing. Approx. 160,000 sqm gross floor area (including parking) is to be organized on up to 18 floors: with strict planning regulations on the required distances and stacked floors. The possibility of implementation in multiple construction phases had to be considered. The core of the task was to create a working environment that would meet the expectations of an international corporation as well as the local cultural and climatic requirements. Overall, the serious objective was to realize in the shortest possible time a project that exemplifies sustainability and respect.

COMPETITION PROCESS The competition was organized in cooperation between [phase eins]. and the Indian consulting firm MACE (Haryana) on behalf of the Indian subsidiary of Siemens Healthineers and with the involvement of the company headquarters in Erlangen. A special challenge was the execution of the procedure during the Corona pandemic. All workshops, the preliminary examination, the expert evaluation and also the meeting of the jury were organized as virtual events via video conferences or specific online platforms as a consequence of the worldwide travel restrictions and quarantine measures.

iCampus Office Building, Munich

WERKSVIERTEL The site is located on Friedenstrasse in the Werksviertel district, southeast of Munich's Ostbahnhof station. For over 100 years, the Werksviertel was an important location for industry and commerce in Munich. After the abandonment of the manufacturing sites, a variety of event and art facilities were established since the mid-1990s, making the area known far beyond munich as "Kunstpark Ost" and "Kultfabrik". Currently, this approx. 40-hectare, well-developed area is one of the largest contiguous development sites in the Munich urban area, which has been transformed for years since the abandonment of the various industrial manufacturing facilities.

iCAMPUS With a development area of 110,000 sqm, the iCampus forms the northern section of the Werksviertel and extends from Friedenstrasse in the west to Ampfingstrasse in the east. Seven sub-projects are being developed here by the competition organizer. The project iCampus Rhenania is one of them, for another [phase eins]. was allowed to organize another competition.

PROJECT The new building with up to 6 floors and a floor area of approx. 18,000 sqm is going to provide flexible leasable office spaces, which should be suitable for one or multiple tenants. High standards of economic efficiency, the design of a large underground parking and the desire to create an identity for the iCampus at this prominent location had to be taken into account. The particular challenge but also opportunity was the integration of the listed neoclassical building, the Rhenania Villa in the project, for which a fitting use with a public focus had to be found.

Location: Munich, Germany **Client:** R&S Realty I GmbH & Co. KG **Year:** 2017 – 2018 **Project size:** approx. 19,000 sqm UFA **Type of competition:** Design competition **Participants:** 6 **Competition budget:** EUR 202,000 (prizes: EUR 99,000; Compensation per participant: EUR 15,000)

PRIZEWINNERS:
(01) **1st prize** HENN, Munich (D); **2nd prize** Kleihues + Kleihues Gesellschaft von Architekten mbH, Berlin (D); **3rd prize** Henning Larsen, Munich/Landau Kindelbacher, Munich (D)

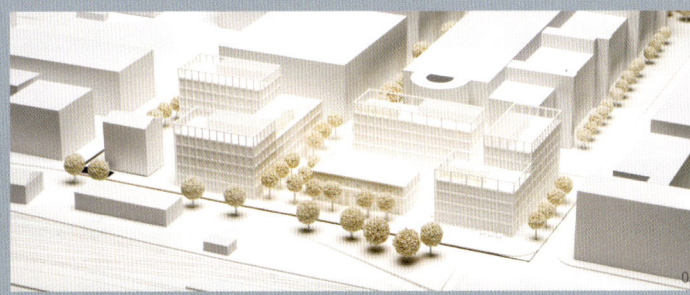

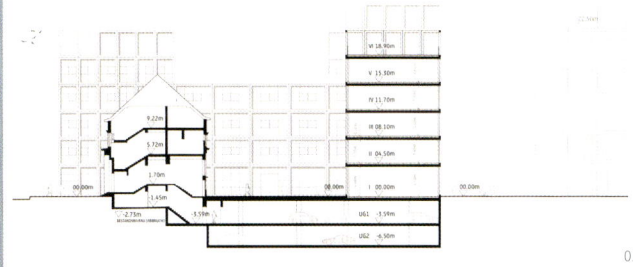

D3 Tower at Alexanderplatz, Berlin

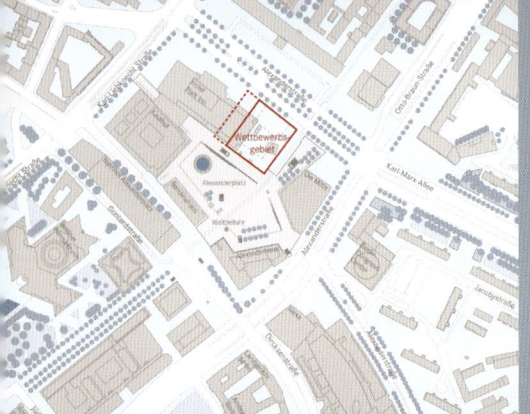

Location: Berlin, Germany **Client:** Foncière des Régions **Year:** 2017 – 2018 **Project size:** up to 70,000 sqm FA **Type of competition:** Design competition **Participants:** 9 **Competition budget:** EUR 400,000 (Prizes: EUR 120,000; Compensation: EUR 180,000)

PRIZEWINNERS:
2nd prize Diener & Diener Architekten AG, Basel (CH); (01) **2nd prize** Sauerbruch Hutton Gesellschaft von Architekten mbH, Berlin (D); **3rd prize** Jean-Paul Viguier et Associés, Paris (F)

ALEXANDERPLATZ Alexanderplatz was built at the end of the 18th century on the northeastern edge of the old town of Berlin. In the 1920s, an urban planning competition was held to transform the square into a "metropolitan square" and to connect the city's business centers in a traffic-friendly manner. The two buildings designed by Peter Behrens, Berolinahaus and Alexanderhaus, were built and still exist today. A large portion of the buildings were demolished during World War II. The East Berlin administration considered the area as the center of the GDR capital, with the exception of the two Behrens buildings, the square largely cleared and enlarged into a pedestrian zone of approximately 8 hectares. By 1970, the Interhotel Stadt Berlin and the HO-Centrum department store had been built, among others, which continue to exist today as Park Inn and Galeria Kaufhof.

MASTERPLAN Based on the design by Hans Kollhoff and Helga Timmermann, which were the winners of an urban planning competition in 1993, the new development plan was established in 2000. It provides for seven- to eight-story base buildings and ten 150-meter-high towers along the ring of streets surrounding Alexanderplatz from the east, consisting of Karl-Liebknecht-Strasse, Alexanderstrasse and Grunerstrasse. They are intended to make Alexanderplatz an distinctive place and, together with the television tower, to create the image of a new city crown for the eastern part of the city from afar.

TASK The promoter, representing the owners of three building sites on the square, intends to develop these sites D1 to D3 while retaining the Park Inn Hotel. The subject of the competition was the design of the building on construction site D3 (base building and high-rise building) with the main uses of retail, residential and office. The floor area (above ground) is approx. 70,000 sqm, of which approx. 41,000 sqm in the high-rise building.

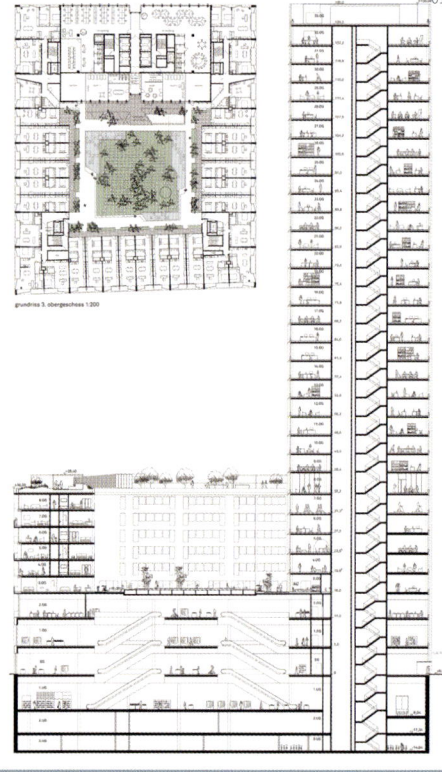

Hypoport SE Headquarters, Lübeck

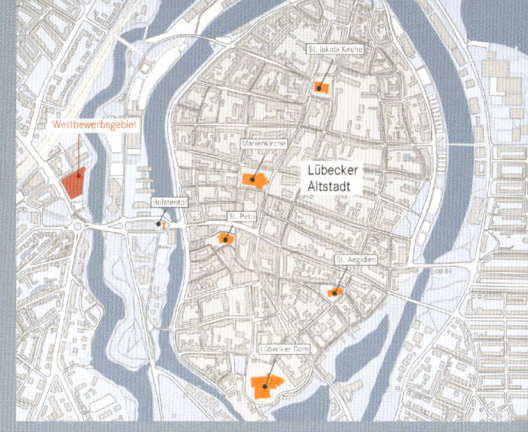

HYPOPORT With more than 2,000 employees, the Hypoport Group is a network of technology companies for the credit, real estate, and insurance industries.

LÜBECK AND THE PROJECT AREA The Hanseatic city of Lübeck was founded in 1143 and developed into a leading trading power in the North and Baltic Sea region with the rise of the Hanseatic League, a community of Baltic and North Sea merchants founded in the 12th century, which helped the city achieve great prosperity and political power and influence. Large parts of the medieval old town have been preserved and even today, in the former "Gateway to the North", over 1,000 listed buildings bear witness to Lübeck's importance since the Middle Ages. St. Mary in Lübeck is considered one of the main works and the "mother church" of the northern German Brick Gothic. Today, with its 217,000 inhabitants, Lübeck is the second largest city in Schleswig-Holstein after Kiel and an important university city.

PROJECT AREA The project area is located close to the city center, west of the listed Lübeck Old Town and the historic city moat, and close to the Holsten Gate and Lübeck's main train station.

PROJECT In addition to office space for 800 employees as the main use, the new building is to provide a variety of meeting rooms and areas for gatherings and events. Additionally, public or semi-public uses such as a café and a daycare center will be integrated to the complex. The challenge was to create a design that would meet the demands for a contemporary working environment and company presentation, as well as the requirements of historic preservation at one of the most prominent and visible locations near the Old Town.

Location: Lübeck, Germany **Client:** Hypoport SE **Year:** 2022 **Project size:** approx. 15,000 sqm GFA **Type of competition:** Invited design competition with subsequent revision stage **Participants:** 11 **Competition budget:** EUR 295,000 (prizes and mentions: EUR 125,000; compensation competition: EUR 110,000; compensation revision stage: EUR 60,000)

PRIZEWINNERS:
(01) **1st prize** Haascookzemmrich STUDIO2050 with Ramboll Atelier Dreiseitl, Stuttgart and Überlingen (D); **2nd prize** C.F. Møller Deutschland GmbH, Berlin (D); **Mention** HENN GmbH with Capatti Staubach Urbane Landschaften Landschaftsarchitekt und Architekt PartGmbB, Berlin (D)

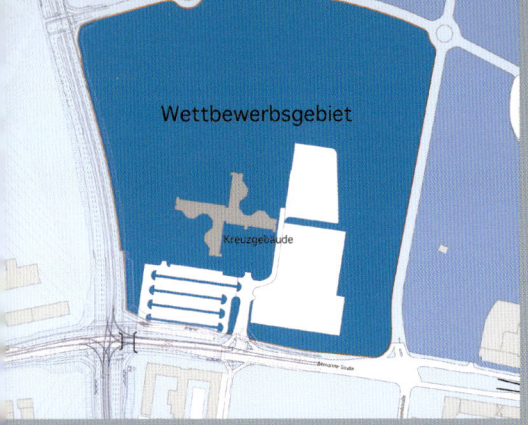

ThyssenKrupp Quarter, Essen

Location: Essen, Germany **Client:** ThyssenKrupp AG, represented through ThyssenKrupp Real Estate GmbH **Year:** 2006 **Project size:** 40,000 sqm **Type of competition:** Open two-stage project competition with cooperative second stage **Participants:** 1st stage: 106; 2nd stage: 11 **Competition budget:** 260,000 EUR

PRIZEWINNERS:
(01) **1st prize** Chaix & Morel et Associés, Paris/JSWD Architekten und Planer, Cologne (D); **2nd prize** Architekten Brüning Klapp Rein, Essen; (D) **3rd prize** Zaha Hadid Architects, London (UK); **3rd prize** Manfred Nagel with DHBT, Kiel (D); **5th prize** KSP Engel und Zimmermann Architekten, Frankfurt a. M. (D)

THE CORPORATION ThyssenKrupp AG planned to reorganize and focus its administrative offices (currently scattered across North Rhine-Westphalia) in one place, signaling the start of a new era for the corporation formed some years back by the merger of two firms, Krupp and Thyssen.

A key element in this context was the construction in the coming years of the "ThyssenKrupp Quarter" in Essen. It was to house ThyssenKrupp's headquarters for worldwide activities, reflect the corporation's self-image and establish its public brand. This administrative center had to reflect ThyssenKrupp's international and historic significance and besides improving staff flexibility, performance, and motivation, it had also to constitute a paradigm of corporate architecture. The site for Krupp's headquarters was approx. 16 ha and located in the west of Essen, part of an area that for many decades Krupp put to industrial use, but after World War II gradually declined. The result was an inner-city wasteland which was then to be revived and enhanced in value, within the framework of a broader program of revitalization, by working closely with the city administration. So, as well as signifying the corporation's roots and now its international reach, the Quarter was to contribute to a sense of spatial and cultural convergence on a site rich with symbolic and historical value. The expansive area in Essen's inner city was to accommodate administration buildings with a gross floor area of 175,000 sqm. Apart from the headquarters for the corporation's top management and other office blocks, it was also to house its conference center (to be used for holding events of various kinds), a hotel and ancillary service facilities. Another challenge posed to the planners was the urbanistic and architectural integration into the new Quarter of an extant structure, the so-called "Cruciform Building". With its procedural choice of an open competition, ThyssenKrupp lived up to its ambition of taking on societal responsibility for sustainability and openness, for which it was "rewarded" with an outstanding design.

New Headquarters 50Hertz, Berlin

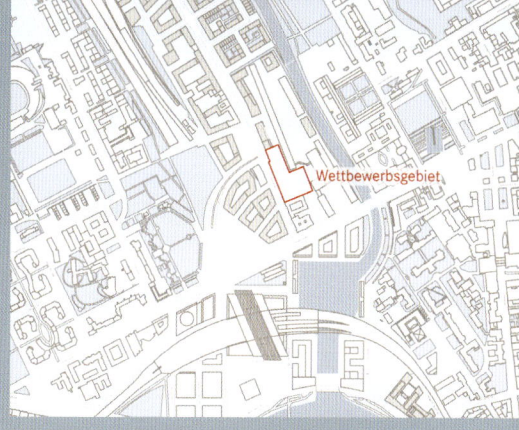

50HERTZ The network operator 50Hertz is responsible for electricity supply networks, electricity transport and secure energy supply for businesses and approximately 18 million people throughout northern and eastern Germany. With around 800 employees, 50Hertz is a mid-sized corporation regulated by Germany's Federal Network Agency. The competition for the "50Hertz Netzquartier" should find a solution that is both innovative and economical and which is in line with the corporate culture of transparency, interaction, and communication. To facilitate an open and dialogue-oriented attitude, an appropriate spatial environment for employees should be created.

EUROPACITY The 8,145-sqm property is part of the new Heidestrasse-Europa City development stretching over a total of 40 ha along the Berlin-Spandau shipping canal north of Berlin's Hauptbahnhof (Central Station). The new development will link the district of Wedding in the north, Hauptbahnhof and the government district in the south. For the development the Berlin Senate together with the Berlin-Mitte district office decided on the Heidestrasse masterplan. The masterplan sets the framework for the establishment of a city district with typical Berlin mixed-use spaces incorporating business and residential, shopping, culture and leisure in the various building types addressing different target groups and user needs.

COMPETITION TASK The focus of the project is construction of a building with approximately 18,000 sqm GFA with the possibility of expanding to approximately 25,000 sqm GFA for up to 580 people. In addition to office space, a conference center and daycare center, the alternative Transmission Control Center (TCC) is at the heart of the building. The TCC is a highly secure control room for monitoring and managing the electricity transmission network.

Location: Berlin, Germany **Client:** 50Hertz Transmission GmbH **Year:** 2012 – 2013 **Project size:** approx. 18,000–25,000 sqm GFA **Type of competition:** Project competition preceded by an open application procedure **Participants:** 18 **Competition budget:** EUR 220,000 (prizes: EUR 101,000; honorable mentions: EUR 11,000; fees per participant: EUR 6,000)

PRIZEWINNERS:
(01) **1st prize** LOVE architecture and urbanism, Graz (A); **2nd prize** Henning Larsen Architects, Copenhagen (DK); **3rd prize** alexa zahn architekten with swap architekten, Vienna (A); **4th prize** Thomas Müller Ivan Reimann Architekten, Berlin (D); **Honorable mention** KSP Jürgen Engel Architekten, Frankfurt a. M. (D); **Honorable mention** wwa – wöhr heugenhauser architekten, Vienna (A)

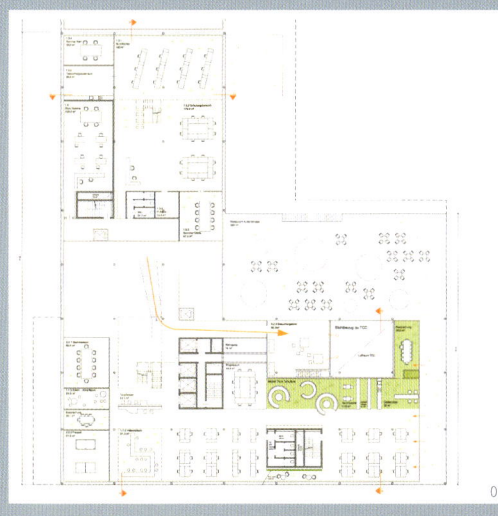

01

01

01

01

6 TIME

6.1 Total duration

When it comes to the amount of time required for a design competition, concerns and prejudices are not uncommon. For this reason, clients often find it difficult to decide whether to hold a competition (see Chapter 1.4). Discussion and, if necessary, a comprehensive evaluation and presentation of this topic must often take place before the decision to hold a design competition is made. Detailed scheduling is one of the first tasks of the competition organizers immediately after the decision to conduct the procedure. The course of a design competition is divided into three phases (see diagram): preparation, execution, and conclusion. While the time required for execution and conclusion is almost standardized and therefore predictable, the time required for preparation depends largely on the type of project, the status of the discussions and coordination already made in advance, research and studies already carried out, and the complexity of the individual persons and institutions involved. Thus, a careful preparation of a design competition, starting from the first moment the competition organizer is involved, can ideally be completed in 6 months, if necessary, even earlier, but it can also require one or two years.

Required time compared to design processes without competitions
Organizing a design competition is undoubtedly time consuming. However, the time required to prepare and conduct a design competition can be compared to the time required for noncompetitive design, which requires the same amount of time to research the basics, clarify the requirements, and coordinate the boundary conditions with all stakeholders (basic research), as well as time to develop alternative design approaches (preliminary design).
Even if the time required to collaborate with only one team is potentially accelerated through direct, intensive dialogue and efficient coordination, compared to the execution phase of a design competition, there is always the risk that the selected design variant meets with criticism by third parties involved (authorities, general public, etc.), and the design phase has to be repeated (possibly several times) and the anticipated time gain is not achieved. For public projects, the alternative to design competition is usually a negotiated public procurement process, which also takes several months to select design partners – to the point where the design team is under contract but the design itself has not even begun. Comparing the various options, it is therefore important to consider not only the time at which the contract is concluded as the completion of this stage, but also the time at which the initial design (preliminary design) is completed. In this respect, it can be said that the time required for a design competition compared to a direct tender or a negotiated procedure is not an argument against a design competition, but rather an argument in favor of it. By interlinking the tender process, design development and optimization, and coordination with the project members, in particular the planning and building authorities, the design competition offers a schedulable process and time frame, the use of which, if managed wisely, tends to accelerate rather than delay the process.

6.2 Overall scheduling

The following factors are relevant to the development of the overall schedule and must be clarified and considered early:

› Choice of competition type
› Need of confirmationl or formal decision of intermediate steps by a higher approving authority (e.g., choice of the type of competition, jury composition, content of the competition brief)
› Fixing the meeting dates with the members of the jury, considering their availability and possibly the availability of premises for the meetings
› Vacation time, public holidays as well as lead times for committee decisions

6.3 Duration of procedures

Preparation phase
As explained above, the time required for this phase, both in terms of total duration and the need for coordination meetings during this time, is highly project-dependent and varies from about 3 to up to 24 months.

Working period
Few rules and regulations for competitions provide concrete specifications for the duration of the working period given to the competitors. The UIA recommends "sufficient" time, the Austrian Competition Standard for Architecture (WSA) recommends 10 weeks for the invited competition and 11 weeks for the open competition – time periods that have also been tried and tested elsewhere for single-phase competitions, so that a duration of 9 to 12 weeks can be recommended as a rule, depending on the complexity of the task.
In the case of two-stage competitions, Stage 1 can be reduced to 4 or 5 weeks if the requirements are limited to the development of a concept with correspondingly reduced representations (Stage 2 then approx. 8 to 10 weeks).

Additional time for model construction and free style presentations
Since participants can only begin with model building and the creation of free style graphics (such as renderings) after the design is completed, allowing additional time of one to two weeks and thus determining a second, later deadline for these components of the required competition entry is reasonable.

Time for questions and answers
Following the distribution of the competition documents to the participants, a certain period should be allowed for questions to be submitted. Depending on the duration of the working period, this should be approx. two or three weeks. It is important to ensure that the minutes of all questions and answers are sent out immediately after the end of the questions and answers period, so that there is enough time for the competitors to implement corresponding changes to the design. The requirements for this differ in the various regulations. It is recommended that the questions and answers period be limited to the first third of the working period.
The duration of the period for inquiries also depends on the timing of the participants' colloquium, during which questions can also be asked. It is recommended that the written question period continue for several days beyond the day of the colloquium.

Duration of colloquia

Experience has shown that a participants' colloquium requires sufficient time for a tour on the competition site plus two to four hours for a joint session, i.e., the colloquium itself. In the case of colloquia in elaborate invited design competitions, especially when international offices are participating, the side program may require additional time. In the case of colloquia with intermediate presentations, these require one to three days, depending on the number of participants, since each individual session should not be less than 45 minutes, including discussion rather 60 to 90 minutes, so as to exploit the potential of such a dialogue and justify the effort involved.

Duration of jury meetings

In general, a full day of meetings is appropriate, considering the effort and requirements (see Chapter 13). In the case of many entries or non-anonymous competitions with personal presentations by the competitors, a meeting lasting several days, usually 2 days, is advisable. Particularly in open competitions, the concept for the implementation of the event must be carefully planned to ensure that all the submissions are adequately evaluated and discussed, and a careful selection can take place – in such rare cases, meetings lasting three or more days are not impossible.

Exhibition

To give as many people as possible the opportunity to visit the exhibition of the competition projects, the place and time of the exhibition should be announced as early as possible, and if possible, the period should include two weekends, taking thus into account the non-local competition participants. Moreover, experience shows that it is often the coverage of the opening or the exhibition itself that generates interest. In Art. 42 of its Guidelines, the UIA recommends a duration of at least two weeks.

Manuelle Gautrand
Architect, Paris

❚❚ WHAT IS IMPORTANT FOR ME AS A JUROR …: The first advice that I always give to a developer who wants to choose an architect through a design competition is that this competition will be of crucial importance to him. A competition is a huge chance to challenge architects and engineers, and in consequence, to have at the end the very best design for his future building. But some conditions have of course to be fulfilled: to be fruitful, a competition must be very well organized, otherwise all this potential benefit can be ruined.

As a juror I can really claim that a competition is never a waste of time, it is a magnificent opportunity for a client to go beyond his hopes and goals. For that they need to dedicate enough time: to expect architects (and engineers) to invent a project in two weeks is not serious, nor thinking that a whole competition (establishing a list of teams, asking them to answer and create an amazing design, waiting for their proposals and keeping the right time to analyse their proposals properly) could be wrapped in one month. A competition always needs several months: but this period is so crucial, it is the key factor to get the best project, to create an architecture that will last in time, that will be a landmark over time. At the whole scale of time, a competition duration is minuscule. And the benefit can be wonderful, very much beyond the anticipated success.

When I'm a jury member, I know that a good organisation of a competition is fundamental. Without this good organisation and a clever and complete analysis, the client, helped by the jury members, cannot make a good choice. The quality of the analysis is delicate and requires a good balance, as it needs from the panel who analyses a lot of skills: in one hand they need to analyse and detail everything, scanning all possible problems while revealing all qualities, but in the other hand they have to integrate the fact that every project can be improved, and that some defects can be solved at a later date. First and foremost, an excellent project is the one who translates a functional program and an urban context in a powerful and clever response, able to go through the time with perennity and ability to be adaptable. A good management implicates to analyse all the projects with both a critical and a well-meaning eye, so that the jury members feel free to choose the best one, sometimes despite some small defects that can be easily solved.

A competition is such a chance for clients, that they can be confident: if the duration of it is around 3–4 months or even sometimes more, at the end of the day, it helps them saving years: they will be able to find the most clever and beautiful architecture, something that will "put them on the map", and be built for decades an decades … in comparison, 3–4 months are so small. By the range of different proposals, it is a huge opportunity for the client to choose the most unique project, fitting in the best way with his own character and objectives. I'm always impressed by the inventiveness of architects/engineers, able to propose solutions and projects that are so different, while the program was exactly the same for all the teams. And in this case, how to compare such different projects? The analysis becomes a crucial stage, where comparisons must be balanced, sensitive and in a way "positive". And the analysis has to cover so many disciplines: from the urban qualities to the technical qualities, going through the cost-efficiency, the flexibility, the ability to express the client DNA, his symbolic goals, the potential to give meaning to his programme and approach.

I also remember that the most successful juries I have participated in were those able to devote enough time: we need time to discover the other participants, to deeply understand the client's goals and hopes, and then to debate in a productive, respectful, and rewarding way. In a jury session, there is a time for listening, accumulating a wide range of information and data, then there is a time to lengthily debate and share your thoughts in an open-minded way, and then finally a last time to make your own choices before voting. What is important for me as a juror is the fact that none of these steps can be rushed: Most of the time, the experts in the pre-evaluation have so hardly worked to analyse all projects in all aspects, that this time spent with the jury members and the experts together is fundamental. It is also respectful, towards all the work and investment made by all the architect's teams.

Kees Kaan
Architect, Rotterdam

" An architectural design is a joined effort of many people, it takes a lot of energy, and it has a delicate and complex character. Presentations on panels is a one-way communication method which may be too 'flat' and limited to expose the true intelligence of a well worked design. Therefore, a plea for personal presentations, if possible, even a scheduled dialogue.

When participating in a competition, one of the starting points is the understanding of the brief and the deliverables: what is wanted, in which appearance and by what rules. Absolute clarity in formal process and descriptions is key, as ambiguous descriptions, even to a small extent, tend to be discovered in close proximity of the unforgiving deadline.

Organizing one's architectural practice has many aspects, one of them is planning related to the workforce. Competitions usually tend to be won or lost, with subsequent implications. However, many competition briefs don't express any date on publication of results. It is much appreciated to include this in order to have a better judgement of what to know when and have the best team available for your project.

3 to 18 months

Preparation phase

PROCEDURE
Discussion and concretization of:
- Type of competition
- Participants' eligibility
- Details on further commission of winner
- Competition budget
- Competition duration and schedule

Approval:
- Endoorsement / registration by Chamber of Architects

PARTICIPANTS' SELECTION
In invited competitions:
- Candidate selection (long list)
- Request candidates to participate
- Participant selection (short list)

With open pre-qualifications:
- Definition of selection criteria
- Defining the eligibility criteria (minimum requirements)
- Competition announcement

Application period
1 month

- Completeness check
- Evaluation according to criteria
- Selection

Selection committee
Selection

JURY SELECTION
Definition of:
- Committee composition
- Candidate selection
- Request candidates to participate
- Clarification of the honorarium

Coordination of:
- Event dates

Compiling the competition materials
Discussion and concretization of:
- Competition brief
- Plans
- Spatial and functional program
- Illustrations
- Model of surroundings

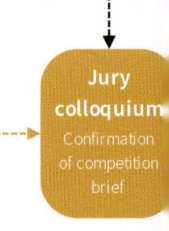

Jury colloquium
Confirmation of competition brief

Flowchart of the process and time periods of competitions,
above: with one stage of preparation,
below: with two stages of preparation

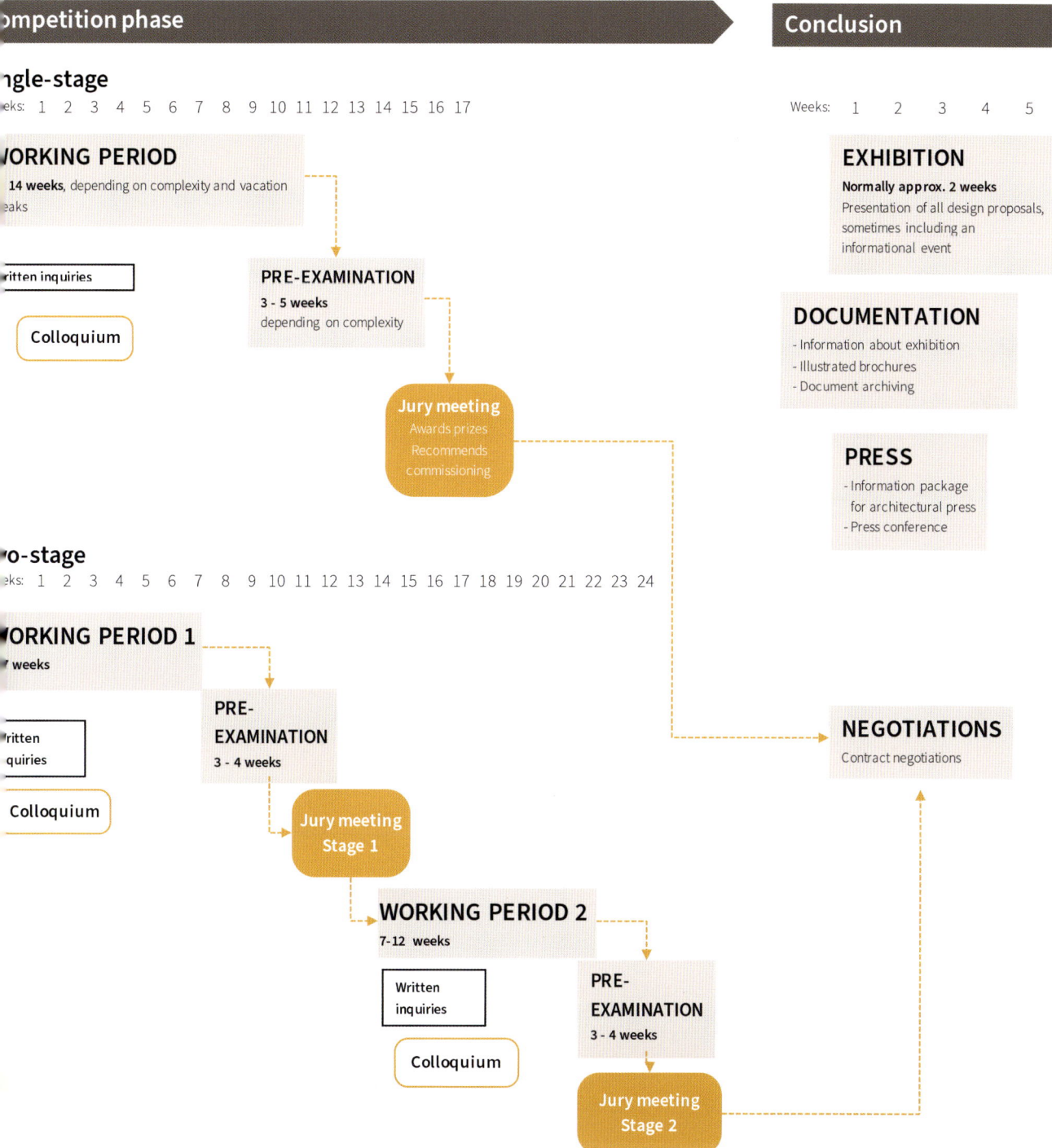

VI | LANDSCAPE AND SQUARE DESIGN

Public squares combine complex requirements. Often located in an urban context, they must meet diverse demands for traffic flow, technical infrastructure, robust surfaces, lighting, and planting, as well as develop an identity-creating character, create amenity qualities, contribute to climate resilience, and counteract microclimate warming – all ideally with a reasonable maintenance effort. These and other requirements must be reflected in the design competition in the selection of experts and the involvement of the responsible administrations, in the formulation of the task, and in the focus of the preliminary examination. Other outdoor public spaces, parks, and gardens, which are also the subject of design competitions, have very similar requirements. Comparable to urban design tasks, they are directly in the public interest, which is why public participation in such competition tasks has a long tradition and undoubted justification that should be considered when designing such competitions.

Diagram explaining the technical specifications in the competition "Entrance area of Siemensstadt Square in Berlin", © ST raum a. and [phase eins].

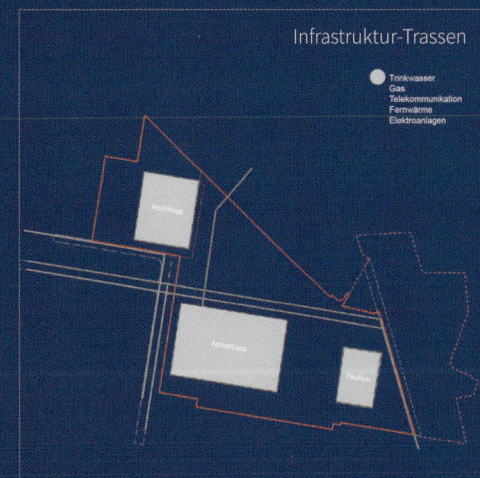

Leuphana University Campus Landscape Design, Lüneburg

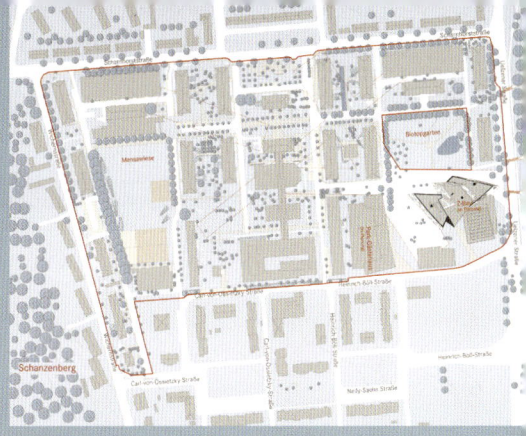

LEUPHANA UNIVERSITY With the development of Leuphana University into a Model University, Lüneburg was to establish itself as a hub of science and scholarship of supra-regional importance and as a motor of regional economic development. In 2010, the Leuphana is dispersed over three different locations. The central campus (approx. 16 ha) was located on property that used to house the Scharnhorst military barracks from the late 1930s. With its ample green spaces and tree-lined alleys, the site was situated between the urban landscaping of the Kurpark (spa park), Ilmenau Valley and the Lüneburger Switzerland. The existing architecture is characterized by traditional, brick barrack buildings arranged on a strictly defined axial grid.

DANIEL LIBESKIND'S CAMPUS STRATEGY

Daniel Libeskind's strategy for campus development and the design of the central building was to place a deliberate counterpoint to the existing schematic architecture.

THE COMPETITION TASK The core of the design task was to design a masterplan for the approximately 16 ha of outdoor facilities around the Leuphana campus. Competition participants were asked to prepare a masterplan that defines a long-term, flexible, timeless, and thus "robust" development concept that can be implemented in several construction stages. The challenge presented to the landscape architects was to make visible the differences between the grid of historic construction and tree-lined alleys on the one hand and Libeskind's design strategy on the other, and to connect both via new axes. Altogether, the outdoor facilities were to be given a new contemporary appearance and have reduced motorized traffic. The campus design should also measure up to the character of Leuphana and its main research areas in sustainability, culture, education, as well as meet the university's standards of management and business operations.

Location: Lüneburg, Germany **Client:** Stiftung Universität Lüneburg **Year:** 2010 **Project size:** approx. 15 ha **Type of competition:** Design competition preceded by an open application procedure **Participants:** 6 **Competition budget:** 48,000 EUR (prizes: EUR 18,000, fees per participant: EUR 5,000)

PRIZEWINNERS:
(01) **1st prize** Karres en Brands Landschapsarchitecten, Hilversum (NL); **2nd prize** Weidinger Landschaftsarchitekten, Berlin (D); **3rd prize** Breimann & Bruun Landschaftsarchitekten, Hamburg (D)

Burchardplatz Hamburg

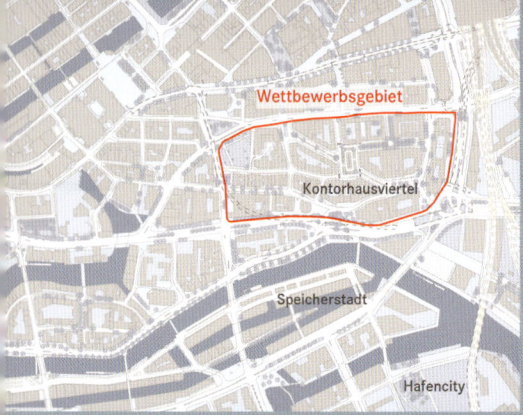

Location: Hamburg, Germany **Client:** State of Hamburg **Year:** 2021 **Project size:** 18,200 sqm design area, 48,500 sqm ideas area **Type of competition:** Urban design and ideas competition **Participants:** 9 **Competition budget:** EUR 99,000 (prizes: EUR 39,000; Compensation: EUR 60,000)

PRIZEWINNERS:
(01) **1st prize** WES GmbH LandschaftsArchitektur, Hamburg (D);
(02) **2nd prize** Vogt Landschaftsarchitekten AG, Zurich (CH);
(03) **3rd prize** POLA Landschaftsarchitekten GmbH, Berlin (D)

KONTORHAUSVIERTEL The project area is located in the Kontorhausviertel, one of the most impressive urban quarters of the 1920s Germany and a landmark of the city of Hamburg. It is located close to the city center and HafenCity district and was designed as the first office-only district in Europe. It gained international recognition for its distinctive office buildings, which were used, among other things, to trade goods that were stored in the adjacent Speicherstadt warehouse district. The buildings in the densely built-up central area are characterized by their in-part expressionist and in part functional forms and striking brick facades. The Kontorhausviertel district and many of the individual buildings are listed monuments. In addition, the "Speicherstadt and Kontorhausviertel with Chilehaus" was added to the UNESCO World Heritage List in 2015.

BURCHARDPLATZ Burchardplatz is located in the center of the district. As a central public square and as an open space directly adjacent to three of the iconic buildings in the neighborhood, namely the Chilehaus on the southern edge of the square, the Mohlenhof to the west and the Sprinkenhof on the eastern long side, Burchardplatz takes on a new meaning that its current design and function as a large inner-city square does not do justice to.

TASK For Burchardplatz, the five owners of the adjacent buildings agreed within the framework of a BID initiative to upgrade the design and use of the square and to initiate a joint process with the City of Hamburg in this regard. The task included, on the one hand, the concrete planning of the future design of the Burcharplatz and directly adjacent square areas in the center and, going beyond this, a concept for the further network of public street spaces in the Kontorhausviertel.

Entrance Area of Siemensstadt Square, Berlin

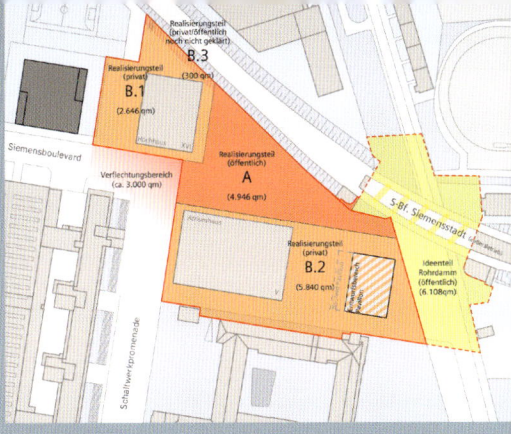

SIEMENSSTADT 2.0 Already with the first concept for the Siemensstadt in 1897, the Siemens founders combined modern, company-owned housing with the on-site working environment. Cultural and social institutions such as churches, schools, recreational facilities, and parks were also included. This more than 100-year-old tradition is now to be continued and further developed! A lively part of the urban fabric is to be created through the development of the previously inaccessible industrial area, considering the existing uses and workplaces, as well as through a sustainable approach to the existing listed structures that shape the character of the site. The aim is to create a 76-ha urban quarter with international appeal and quality of life and neighborhood, with a mixture and immediate proximity of production, research, and housing. An urban planning competition was initially announced for the development of the site, on the results of which was created a master plan.

FIRST CONSTRUCTION PHASE For the design of the first construction phase, a competition for two high-rise buildings and a landscape design competition followed. The second determined the landscape design in this first construction phase, especially the entrance square, that forms the most important new access to the quarter, where an S-Bahn station is also located.

ENTRANCE PACE Siemensstadt Square will in future be accessed via a new east-west axis, the Siemens Boulevard. This has its starting point at the new entrance to Siemensstadt and runs westward through the quarter. The subject of the competition was the planning for a climate-friendly and qualitatively appealing design of the open spaces in the 1st construction phase as well as the adjacent traffic areas in the transition from the future Siemensstadt S-Bahn station via Rohrdamm to Siemens Boulevard. The entrance plaza forms the representative entrance to the neighborhood, is an intensively used traffic location, forecourt of the new high-rise building, place to stay and takes on a signal function for the attitude of the entire neighborhood through its climate-friendly design.

Location: Berlin, Germany **Client:** Siemens AG **Year:** 2022 – 2023 **Project size:** approx. 20,000 sqm **Type of competition:** Invited design competition **Participants:** 9 **Competition budget:** EUR 120,000 (prizes: EUR 30,000; Compensation: EUR 90,000)

PRIZEWINNERS:
(01) **1st prize** GREENBOX Landschaftsarchitekten Hubertus Schäfer + Markus Pieper, Cologne (D); **2nd prize** POLA Landschaftsarchitekten, Berlin (D); **3rd prize** GM013 Landschaftsarchitektur, Berlin (D)

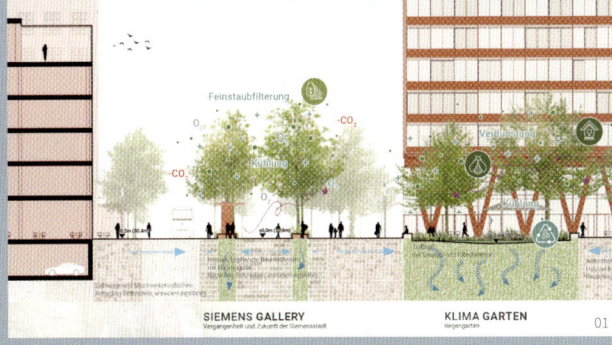

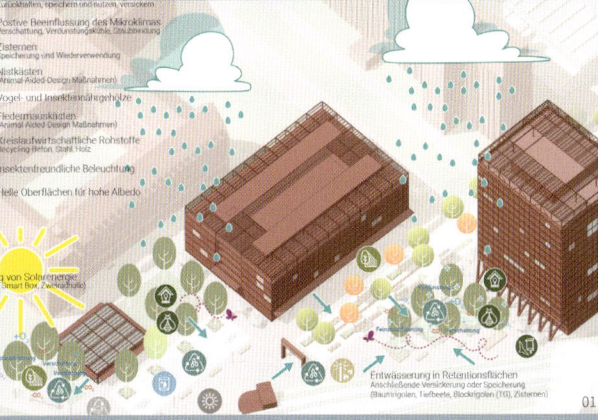

7 COMPETITION COSTS

7.1 What is the total cost of a competition?

The appropriateness of the costs of a competition has probably been a topic of discussion since the beginning of design competitions. It is not without reason that the question of the amount of prize money was addressed in the earliest competition rules and regulations.

An obvious argument to justify the expense of a competition is its contribution to building culture (Baukultur), the architectural discourse and thus the further development of architecture.

This contribution undoubtedly exists, but it cannot be quantified and will convince only a few potential sponsors of the significance of holding a design competition. More widespread is the concern of the clients that they will lose control over the decision in a design competition. Prizes could be awarded to overpriced designs that "the jury fell in love with, but no one looked at the costs". While such incidents have certainly occurred and continue to occur, they are usually attributed to poor organization and communication.

Instead, the assumption that design competitions – namely, competitive design processes – lead to more cost-effective solutions has already been statistically tested many times and essentially confirmed. In this respect, it is certainly not unfair to claim that the procedure costs, or at least the additional costs compared to the design costs incurred anyway, are counterbalanced by the improved economic efficiency of the winning project in terms of construction and/or operating costs.

There is then the added value of the completed building, which, because of its advanced design, is more sustainable in its use, potential reuse, or possible resale, or because architectural quality adds value. But what does a design competition cost? In our experience, the various attempts to generalize the total cost of a competition or to reduce it to a simple formula (x % of the construction cost or similar) are not reputable. Too many factors influence the cost. For the same project, a simple competition could be designed and one with multiplied costs. Therefore, the pros and cons of cost effectiveness must be calculated and weighted.

7.2 Total budget

Irrespective of the size and subject of the project as well as the type of competition, the costs listed in the adjacent table are always nearly identical. The differences in the level of these costs are therefore even more significant. Of course, the total costs are also related to the construction costs and the complexity of the project. However, this relationship is not linear: there are additional factors that lead to a wide range in the individual costs, as shown in the adjacent table:

› **Competition type/number of participants:** An open competition typically has significantly more participants than a restricted competition. However, even in restricted competitions, the number of participants can vary greatly. The number of participants affects the time and effort required for the preliminary examination, the duration of the meetings and consequently the venue rental, catering, and meeting fees. Additional costs for model photography, exhibition, printing, etc. also arise.

› **Competition type/number of stages:** The difference in cost between a single-stage and two-stage competition also depends on the number of selected participants. The two-stage competition is more expensive if participants are required to provide extensive services already in Stage 1, which then must be evaluated by examiners and experts at a corresponding cost. Additionally, the duration of the jury meeting extends with the number of designs to be evaluated. If Stage 1 of a competition is designed more as a concept phase with a limited scope of services, a two-stage competition can be carried out cost-neutrally compared to a single-stage competition in which the same number of participants provide extensive services in one stage, which then need to be evaluated.

› **Size of the jury:** A larger jury leads not only to higher fees for meetings but also to additional costs for venue rental, catering, printing costs and, if necessary, costs for travel and accommodation.

› **International aspiration:** The inclusion of international participants usually resulting in additional costs, especially in the case of invited competitions, where prestigious offices are attracted to participate and expect higher compensation. Moreover, due to the multilingual nature of the procedure and additional travel costs, as in such competitions the jury is usually also composed of international members.

Jakob Dunkl
Architect, Vienna

❚❚ What is important for me as a participant in the organization of a competition?

1. **Appreciation:** Competitions represent an enormous added value for sponsors and society. The juries must be excellently composed, and the competition requirements must be formulated in a particularly dignified manner. The greatest possible appreciation for the work of the participants is indispensable.

2. **Surprise:** Competitions must allow for an unexpected result. Therefore, a preamble makes sense that all ideas that do not comply with the competition specifications are admitted, are judged by the jury, and are not already eliminated in the preliminary examination.

3. **Contract:** Competitions are a contract between sponsor and participant. We therefore demand an unambiguous promise for further commission of the winning team covering all service phases as well as the obligatory promise of adequate compensation for all participants if the project is not implemented. Thus, serious procedures are guaranteed.

4. **Prize money:** Competitions are the biggest lever for the quality of a project. The winning project is sure to be at least 1 % better than the average of the submitted projects. Therefore, the winner must receive an amount equal to 1 % of the construction sum. This high amount can be deducted in stages from project development phase 2 onwards. Thus, there are no additional costs for the client. It is as simple as that.

5. **Expenses compensation:** Competitions are becoming more and more elaborate and complex in their requirements. For this reason, compensation for expenses must be increased substantially in general.

6. **Efficiency:** Competitions must become more efficient – for everyone involved, i.e., jury and participants. The incredible waste of intellectual effort must be minimized again. Therefore, it is necessary to have pre-selection procedures, first competition stages with low effort. Then very few participants should give their best in the actual competition.

7. **Young talent:** Competitions should enable unknown winners. A system where young, inexperienced participants can be selected is important. The required reference projects must be checked very strongly for their meaningfulness.

No.	Position	Remarks	
Pos. 1	**Participants**		20,000 - 2,000,000 Euro
Pos. 1.1	Prize money		
Pos. 1.2	Compensation fee		
Pos. 2	**Jury**		20,000 - 300,000 Euro
Pos. 2.1	Technical jurors	usually daily rates per meeting and extra fee for chairmanship	
Pos. 2.2	Technical experts entitled a honorarium	usually daily rates per meeting and per day of participation in the preliminary examination	
Pos. 2.3	General jurors	sponsor's persons and the administration in the jury usually do not receive any fee. In individual cases, lump sums are granted for meetings	
Pos. 2.4	Expenses of jury members		
Pos. 2.5	Additional fees	e.g. for feasibility studies or other reports	
Pos. 3	**Events**		10,000 - 100,000 Euro
Pos. 3.1	Venue costs		
Pos. 3.2	Catering		
Pos. 3.3	Presentation boards for the jury meeting	Rental or purchase cost	
Pos. 3.4	Technical and event equipment	Rental and set-up/technical support for projection, sound and lighting equipment as well as purchase of name badges, pens, etc.	
Pos. 3.5	Transport		
Pos. 3.6	Interpreters		
Pos. 3.7	Customs fees		
Pos. 4	**Procedure**		20,000 - 100,000 Euro
Pos. 4.1	Copying/Printing costs	Production of brochures, posters, table templates, etc.	
Pos. 4.2	Materials, packaging materials		
Pos. 4.3	Plan materials / photos	Purchase of images for the competition brief and potentially the costs for the copyright	
Pos. 4.4	Announcements, official journal fees	Costs for the announcement of open procedures	
Pos. 4.5	Homepage and data banks	Costs for programming or available existing systems	
Pos. 4.6	Model making	Construction of model of surroundings and insert plates as well as repaint of participants' models	
Pos. 4.7	Model photos		
Pos. 4.8	Postage/courier services	Shipping of brochures and models	
Pos. 4.9	Translation costs	In case of multilingual procedures for translation of competition brief, minutes etc.	
Pos. 5	**Excibition costs**		0 - 100,000 Euro
Pos. 5.1	Security		
Pos. 5.2	Set-up		
Pos. 5.3	Exhibition system		
Pos. 5.4	Technology		
Pos. 5.5	Transport		
Pos. 5.6	Venue costs		
Pos. 6	**Travel and accommodation costs**		0 - 200,000 Euro
Pos. 6.1	For participants	especially in international invited competitions cost are reimbursed or a lump sum is paid	
Pos. 6.2	Jury and technical experts	Reimbursement of costs upon proof	
Pos. 6.3	Competition management team	Reimbursement of costs upon proof	
Pos. 6.4	Visa costs	Reimbursement of costs upon proof	
Pos. 7	**Competition management**		40,000 - 350,000 Euro
Pos. 7.1	Fee		
Pos. 7.2	Additional costs lump sum		

Typical items of a budget for a competition procedure and range of costs

7.3 Calculation of the competition sum

There are very different international guidelines and approaches for calculating and determining the competition sum, i.e., the total amount of money paid to the participants in the form of prizes and remunerations:

› **UIA:** The recommendations do not include a specific calculation methodology but emphasize the importance of distributing a total ammount that corresponds to the complexity of the project and the services required in the competition. Recommendations are made regarding the number of prizes and mentions.
› **Germany:** In the RPW 2013 it is determined that the competition sum corresponds with the fee that would be due for the preliminary design of the same project according to the German Schedule of Services and Fees (HOAI), in the case of direct commission. This "competition sum", which is then distributed in full in the competition – either in its entirety as prize money or divided into equal payment for each participant and prize money in a ratio of 60:40, for example. This special case of undercutting the fee payable to each participant for the service provided ("one fee for x designs") is justified by the fact that it is promised that one of the prize winners of the competition will receive the subsequent design contract ("contract promise") and thus, for example, new offices gain access to the market. In ideas competitions, the competition sum is to be increased "appropriately"; this unclear formulation of the RPW 2013 with regard to ideas competitions often leads to uncertainty in practice.
› **Austria:** The Competition Standard for Architecture (WSA) provides the most precise calculation method in an international comparison. Similar to the German system, it refers to the fee that a design team would be entitled to for comparable services. However, various surcharges lead to higher competition sums for an essentially identical task. According to the WSA, the competition fee should be doubled for idea competitions.
› **Switzerland:** sia regulation 142 also specifies a method for calculating the competition sum that is based on the usual fee for the same services. Unlike the current German RPW 2013, a concrete statement is made regarding ideas competitions, according to which the competition sum must be tripled.

Benjamin Schneider
Professional City Councilor and City Building Official,
Head of the Nuremberg Building Department

" A targeted competition is closely coordinated in advance with the building authorities, since in addition to the concerns of local building law, other local concerns important for the urban community and for future urban development issues can be considered in the description of the competition task. This automatically increases the chances of achieving a result that is close to implementation and is widely accepted by the public.

Dominique Jakob
Architect, Paris

" Developing a competition proposal is hard work that involves several members of an architectural team. This work must be remunerated. However, we continue to see competitions where 3–4 prizes and 2 recognitions are given for a total of 10–25 competing teams.
This means that a significant number of participating teams will not be remunerated for their time and intellectual effort invested in developing the proposal. Instead, we would suggest an approach practiced in Switzerland, France, and Belgium, where the number of selected teams is coordinated with the prize fund, so that the work of each competing team is compensated. Teams are always motivated to win, the difference between first and fifth place in terms of participation would not change the involvement of the selected teams. The requirement to present a specialist team (structural and MEP engineers, landscape designer, sometimes other specialists) at the pre-qualification stage puts unnecessary workload on the architects – because this happens too early!
We believe that the key criteria to be qualified for a competition is the architect's capacity to respond with an original and relevant design idea. The best way to demonstrate this ability is to present references. At the same time, the fact that the reference projects were built proves that the architect is capable of assembling a team that implements the concept. In the competition process, presenting the specialist team can be required later, at the proposal development stage, which is when cooperation with other specialists is needed.

7.4 Honorarium for jury members

The recommendations for the compensation of the external jury members differ, as also happens with the calculation of the competition sum. The usual daily rates in Germany are rather low in comparison with other European countries. As provided in the tables of various federal institutions, federal states and/or chambers of architects, there is an unnecessary variety of specifications, some with only minor differences, compliance with which is sometimes pursued with great bureaucratic effort. The daily rates are currently between 1,000 and 1,200 euros, whereby only participation in meetings (colloquia, jury meetings) is taken into account. In contrast, members of the technical jury in Austria can also charge for their time and effort in preparing the content and for travel time, for example. In the case of international competitions with long-distance travel, session honoraria of 4,500–6,000 euros are appropriate due to the long travel times.

7.5 Further costs

In addition to the direct costs for the procedure shown in the overview table, the sponsor must take into consideration their own costs for their own project team, the provision of available resources (venues, catering, technical equipment) and, if necessary, insurance.

Total and breakdown of prizes and compensation for various types of competitions

Project	Country	Year	Function	Services	Construction costs / Size	Total budget	Prize budget	1. prize	2. prize	3. prize	4. prize	5. prize	6. prize	Mention	Total compensation budget *
L130	B	2018	Administration	Architecture	190.000 euros	EUR 900.000	EUR 300.000	EUR 120.000	EUR 100.000	EUR 80.000					EUR 600.000
ZRM	D	2019	Administration	Architecture	130M euros	EUR 625.000	EUR 210.000	EUR 84.000	EUR 63.000	EUR 42.000	EUR 21.000				EUR 415.000
MBB	CHN	2013	Museum	Architecture	35.000 sqm GFA	EUR 600.000	EUR 150.000	EUR 75.000	EUR 50.000	EUR 25.000					EUR 450.000
KFAS	KWT	2018	Office and conference center	Architecture	60 ha / 25.000 sqm UA	EUR 530.000	EUR 130.000	EUR 50.000	EUR 35.000	EUR 25.000	EUR 20.000				EUR 400.000
KOM	D	2016	Theatre	Architecture	350M euros	EUR 500.000	EUR 500.000	EUR 125.000	EUR 100.000	EUR 75.000	EUR 60.000	EUR 40.000		EUR 100.000	
BSR	D	2021	Office	Architecture	2.100 Euro/sqm GFA	EUR 475.000	EUR 250.000	EUR 125.000	EUR 75.000	EUR 50.000					EUR 225.000
ECN	D	2019	Education	Architecture	70M euros	EUR 470.000	EUR 140.000	EUR 56.000	EUR 35.000	EUR 21.000				EUR 28.000	EUR 330.000
BAE	D	2022	Masterplan	Architecture	4M euros	EUR 420.000	EUR 210.000	EUR 85.000	EUR 53.000	EUR 32.000				EUR 40.000	EUR 210.000
AMM	HKJ	2007	Theatre	Architecture	60M euros	EUR 400.000	EUR 100.000	EUR 45.000	EUR 35.000	EUR 20.000					EUR 300.000
UKE	D	2014	Healthcare	Architecture	80M euros	EUR 340.000	EUR 156.000	EUR 70.000	EUR 41.000	EUR 30.000	EUR 15.000				EUR 184.000
ICV	A	2013	Hotel	Architecture	750-1.950 euros/sqm	EUR 324.000	EUR 90.000	EUR 40.000	EUR 30.000	EUR 20.000					EUR 234.000
HEI	D	2016	Residential	Architecture	200M euros	EUR 300.000	EUR 60.000	EUR 35.000	EUR 21.000	EUR 4.000					EUR 240.000
AD3	D	2018	Hotel	Architecture	0,6 ha	EUR 300.000	EUR 120.000	EUR 60.000	EUR 36.000	EUR 24.000					EUR 180.000
S21	D	2020	Office	Architecture	85M euros	EUR 257.000	EUR 77.000	EUR 34.000	EUR 26.000	EUR 17.000					EUR 180.000
HPL	D	2021	Office	Architecture	40M euros	EUR 235.000	EUR 125.000	EUR 60.000	EUR 40.000	EUR 25.000					EUR 110.000
BF4	D	2016	Office	Architecture	54M euros	EUR 230.000	EUR 110.000	EUR 50.000	EUR 30.000	EUR 20.000				EUR 10.000	EUR 120.000
50H	D	2012	Office	Architecture	1.550 euros/sqm	EUR 220.000	EUR 112.000	EUR 38.000	EUR 27.000	EUR 20.000	EUR 16.000			EUR 11.000	EUR 108.000
DBE	D	2020	Office	Architecture	2.000 euros/sqm GFA	EUR 220.000	EUR 107.500	EUR 53.000	EUR 33.000	EUR 21.500					EUR 112.500
ICR	D	2017	Office	Architecture	1.800 euros/sqm	EUR 202.000	EUR 97.000	EUR 47.000	EUR 31.000	EUR 19.000					EUR 105.000
HPQ	D	2010	Hotel	Architecture	60M euros	EUR 200.000	EUR 100.000	EUR 50.000	EUR 30.000	EUR 20.000					EUR 100.000
GE3	D	2020	Office	Architecture	2.300 euros/sqm GFA	EUR 200.000	EUR 40.000	EUR 18.000	EUR 13.000	EUR 9.000					EUR 160.000
MRD	UA	2017	Museum	Architecture	2,6 ha / 25.000 sqm UA	EUR 190.000	EUR 85.000	EUR 42.000	EUR 26.000	EUR 17.000					EUR 105.000
FBS	D	2022	Office	Architecture	25M euros	EUR 176.000	EUR 60.000	EUR 30.000	EUR 18.000	EUR 12.000					EUR 116.000
HIRI	D	2018	Technology and Research	Architecture	22M euros	EUR 155.000	EUR 62.000	EUR 25.000	EUR 19.000	EUR 12.000	EUR 6.000				EUR 93.000
TKH	D	2011	Office	Architecture	2.800 sqm UA	EUR 154.000	EUR 42.000	EUR 17.000	EUR 13.000	EUR 8.000	EUR 4.000				EUR 112.000
SEE	D	2015	Mixed Use	Architecture	2 ha / 100 sqm GFA	EUR 150.000	EUR 45.000	EUR 20.000	EUR 15.000	EUR 10.000					EUR 105.000
BioC	D	2014	Technology and Research	Architecture	12M euros	EUR 142.000	EUR 58.000	EUR 23.000	EUR 17.000	EUR 12.000	EUR 6.000				EUR 84.000
WMN	A	2015	Museum	Architecture	60M euros	EUR 138.000	EUR 42.000	EUR 15.000	EUR 10.000	EUR 8.000				EUR 9.000	EUR 96.000
EGW	D	2022	Residential	Architecture	10M euros	EUR 95.000	EUR 55.000	EUR 27.500	EUR 16.500	EUR 11.000					EUR 40.000
CIF	D	2020	Technology and Research	Architecture	8M euros	EUR 86.000	EUR 86.000	EUR 43.000	EUR 26.000	EUR 17.000					
GAR	D	2015	Residential	Architecture	1.500 euros/sqm	EUR 27.000	EUR 6.000	EUR 3.000	EUR 2.000	EUR 1.000					EUR 21.000
MAR	D	2005	Education	Architecture	1M euros	EUR 21.700	EUR 10.700	EUR 5.400	EUR 3.200	EUR 2.100					EUR 11.000
AJM	AL	2021	Museum	Architecture	170 ha	EUR 19.889	EUR 19.889	EUR 9.471	EUR 6.156	EUR 4.262					-
MIM	LAR	2016	Museum	Architecture	36M euros	EUR 0	EUR 0								
KWGA	D	2023	Museum and memorial	Architecture and Exhibition design	20M euros	EUR 120.000	EUR 40.000	EUR 18.000	EUR 13.000	EUR 9.000					EUR 80.000
SPL	D	2014	Sports	Architecture and Structural design	3M euros	EUR 60.000	EUR 60.000	EUR 24.000	EUR 18.000	EUR 12.000	EUR 6.000				
SHI	RI	2020	Office and research	Architecture and Landscape design	90M euros	EUR 560.000	EUR 70.000	EUR 29.000	EUR 24.000	EUR 17.000					EUR 490.000
HBS	D	2022	Office	Architecture and Landscape design	175M euros	EUR 400.135	EUR 135	EUR 60	EUR 45	EUR 30					EUR 400.000
BImA	D	2023	Administration	Architecture and Landscape design	43M euros	EUR 283.000	EUR 103.000	EUR 41.000	EUR 31.000	EUR 21.000	EUR 10.000				EUR 180.000
SAK	D	2019	Administration	Architecture and Landscape design	40M euros	EUR 204.000	EUR 204.000	EUR 75.000	EUR 55.000	EUR 35.000	EUR 15.000			EUR 24.000	-
EUS	D	2021	Education	Architecture and Landscape design	20M euros	EUR 190.000	EUR 100.000	EUR 50.000	EUR 30.000	EUR 20.000					EUR 90.000
BWB	D	2016	Office and Industrial	Architecture and Landscape design	3 ha	EUR 166.000	EUR 91.000	EUR 37.000	EUR 27.000	EUR 18.000	EUR 9.000				EUR 75.000
BYHMC	UA	2019	Memorial	Architecture and Landscape design	7,2 ha	EUR 165.000	EUR 45.000	EUR 20.000	EUR 15.000	EUR 10.000					EUR 120.000
VReG	D	2022	Office	Architecture and Landscape design	14M euros	EUR 93.000	EUR 37.000	EUR 16.000	EUR 12.000	EUR 9.000					EUR 56.000
FDM	D	2023	Visitor center	Architecture and Landscape design	5M euros	EUR 53.000	EUR 17.000	EUR 6.800	EUR 4.250	EUR 2.550				EUR 3.400	EUR 36.000
KPI	D	2014	Education	Architecture and Landscape design	3M euros	EUR 22.000	EUR 22.000	EUR 10.000	EUR 7.000	EUR 5.000					
HZB	D	2020	Office	Architecture and Techn. Ausrüstung	45M euros	EUR 460.000	EUR 115.000	EUR 45.000	EUR 35.000	EUR 23.000	EUR 12.000				EUR 345.000
ELB	D	2022	Museum	Exhibition design	4M euros	EUR 150.000	EUR 48.000	EUR 25.000	EUR 15.000	EUR 8.000					EUR 102.000
BHA	D	2020	Museum	Exhibition design	2,9 M.	EUR 35.000	EUR 0								EUR 35.000
UKW	D	2021	Healthcare	Generalplanung	360M euros	EUR 2.249.000	EUR 2.124.000	EUR 849.600	EUR 637.200	EUR 424.800	EUR 212.400				EUR 125.000
TVG	D	2022	Administration	Generalplanung	330M euros	EUR 1.600.000	EUR 480.000	EUR 160.000	EUR 105.000	EUR 70.000	EUR 50.000			EUR 95.000	EUR 1.120.000
EPB	B	2020	Administration	Generalplanung	320M euros	EUR 1.525.000	EUR 400.000	EUR 120.000	EUR 100.000	EUR 80.000	EUR 60.000	EUR 40.000			EUR 1.125.000
PPR	CDN	2021	Administration	Generalplanung	250M euros	EUR 539.560	EUR 344.910	EUR 150.260	EUR 112.690	EUR 81.960					EUR 194.650
1617	D	2017	Office	Generalplanung	10M euros	EUR 68.000	EUR 38.000	EUR 13.000	EUR 12.000	EUR 8.000	EUR 5.000				EUR 68.000
S2E	D	2022	Open space	Landscape design	20 ha	EUR 120.000	EUR 30.000	EUR 13.000	EUR 10.000	EUR 7.000					EUR 90.000
BUR	D	2021	Open space	Landscape design	6,7 ha	EUR 99.000	EUR 39.000	EUR 17.000	EUR 13.000	EUR 9.000					EUR 60.000
LEU	D	2010	Education	Landscape design	16 ha	EUR 54.000	EUR 18.000	EUR 8.000	EUR 6.000	EUR 4.000					EUR 36.000
DSO_K	D	2015	Percent for Art	Arts	320.000 Euro	EUR 29.000	EUR 11.000	EUR 5.000	EUR 4.000	EUR 2.000				EUR 1.000	EUR 18.000
LUT	D	2016	Memorial	Arts	900.000 euro	EUR 27.400	EUR 13.000	EUR 5.000	EUR 4.000	EUR 2.600	EUR 1.400				EUR 14.400
BPoL_K	D	2020	Percent for Art	Arts	465.000 Euro	EUR 18.500	EUR 16.000	EUR 8.000	EUR 5.000	EUR 3.000					EUR 2.500
DOM	D	2019	Percent for Art	Arts	100.000 Euro	EUR 10.000	EUR 0								EUR 10.000
UOM	CDN	2012	Education	Urban design	8 ha	EUR 184.418	EUR 40.982	EUR 16.393	EUR 12.295	EUR 8.196	EUR 4.098				EUR 143.436
RNM	D	2013	Masterplan	Urban design	4 ha	EUR 80.000	EUR 80.000	EUR 32.000	EUR 24.000	EUR 14.000				EUR 10.000	-
HEN	D	2018	Residential	Urban design	8,5 ha	EUR 75.000	EUR 0								EUR 75.000
S20	D	2019	Masterplan	Urban design	70 ha	EUR 650.000	EUR 200.000	EUR 80.000	EUR 60.000	EUR 40.000	EUR 20.000				EUR 450.000
W1	D	2021	Industrial	Urban design	45 ha	EUR 420.000	EUR 90.000	EUR 40.000	EUR 30.000	EUR 20.000					EUR 330.000
HSU	D	2022	Education	Urban design	30 ha	EUR 180.066	EUR 66	EUR 29	EUR 22	EUR 15					EUR 180.000
BTS	D	2015	Residential	Urban design	2,1 ha	EUR 31.500	EUR 7.500	EUR 3.400	EUR 2.400	EUR 1.700					EUR 24.000
FIZ	D	2014	Industrial	Urban design and Architecture	177 ha	EUR 498.000	EUR 60.000	EUR 30.000	EUR 20.000	EUR 10.000					EUR 438.000
FES	MA	2010	Masterplan	Urban design and Architecture	7,3 ha	EUR 440.000	EUR 120.000	EUR 55.000	EUR 40.000	EUR 25.000					EUR 320.000
USTH	VN	2014	Education	Urban design and Architecture	65 ha	EUR 150.000	EUR 150.000	EUR 45.000	EUR 35.000	EUR 25.000	EUR 20.000	EUR 15.000	EUR 10.000		-
LUE	D	2018	Technology and Research	Urban design and Architecture	13 ha / 10.000 sqm UA	EUR 140.000	EUR 40.000	EUR 18.000	EUR 13.000	EUR 9.000					EUR 100.000
FAL	D	2014	Residential	Urban design and Architecture	1.500 euros/sqm	EUR 83.000	EUR 31.000	EUR 14.000	EUR 10.000	EUR 7.000					EUR 52.000

* for two-stage competitions, only for participants in the 2nd stage if applicable

8 PROCEDURE DETAILS

8.1 Required information in the competition brief

Besides formulating the competition task, the competition brief also forms the basis of the contract between the participants and the sponsor and, in case of public tenders, is usually part of the tender documents. Accordingly, the wording must be chosen carefully, especially since it provides the basis for subsequent cooperation and defines mutual claims during and after the competition. In restricted competitions and in case of competitions with open pre-qualification procedures, but also in open competitions, public sponsors must declare many of the procedural conditions mentioned in the brief already already in the announcement (usually EU announcement).

In any case, the competition brief should contain statements on the following topics (see also 2.3):

› Sponsor and competition organizer
› Parties involved (jury members, experts)
› Type of procedure
› Endorsement note (Chamber of Architects or similar)
› Declaration of agreement on the part of all participants with the conditions mentioned in the brief
› Eligibility (required professional qualification)
› Evaluation criteria of the jury
› Prizes and remunerations ("competition sum")
› Commissioning following the competition ("contract promise")
› Explanation of the procedural conditions regarding obstacles to participation, exclusion criteria, confidentiality, rights of ownership and copyrights, liability issues and jurisdiction
› Competition materials provided
› Submission documents requested from competitors
› Procedural process: Detailed description of the events of the procedure (date, venue, and, if already known, time), communication channels and rules as well as duration of the questions and answers period, deadlines, and location for the submission of the competition entries, announcement of project exhibition (location, time) as well as an overview of all relevant deadlines

8.2 Admission and/or selection of participants

Open competitions

Compared to a restricted competition, the open competition offers the advantage that admission to it does not require a formally complex and possibly legally challengeable procedure. In the case of open project competitions, which serve a basis for subsequent design contracts, many sponsors are concerned in advance whether the team that wins the competition indeed has the necessary experience and capacity to undertake and successfully complete the design task. However, to address this concern and the risk of a possible lack of experience or capacity, it is not very advisable to increase the eligibility requirements only before the open competition, such as allowing participation if a reference project of a certain size has already been designed or realized. This would mean converting the open competition into a restricted competition with all its disadvantages. Instead, the criteria for participation in open competitions should be initially designed to be as open as possible to attract a wide range of potential competitors. In both ideas and project competitions, proof of the required professional qualification should be sufficient.

For example: "Eligible to participate are individuals residing in the EEA and in the countries that are parties to the WTO Agreement on Government Procurement (GPA) who, on the day of the announcement of the competition and pursuant to the legal provisions of their country of residence, are entitled to use the professional title 'Architect' and work independently as freelancers. Individuals from countries where the professional title 'Architect' is not regulated by law are eligible, provided that they hold a degree or submit any other evidence of formal qualification that is recognized in the EU under 2013/55/EU (EU Directive on the recognition of professional qualifications)."

The initial confidence in the competence of a design team that has won in an open competition against possibly strong competitors should therefore be based first on the fact that this team has proven its capabilities. It is also possible and advisable to state in the competition announcement that certain predefined and specified evidence of design experience and capacity will be required after the competition as part of the contracting process. This allows for the possibility that these credentials may be provided by design partners added later for reinforcement ("suitability loan").

Restricted competitions

In the case of public sponsors, the selection of participants for restricted competitions is usually a formalized process in compliance with the applicable public procurement law. However, even in the case of private sponsors, there are usually compliance regulations or standards for the implementation of fair and comprehensible selection processes, which entail certain procedural steps. When the competition is announced, interested parties are given time to form teams and submit the application documents. The selection is then made by first checking the formal criteria of all applications for participation (adherence to deadlines, completeness of documents, sufficient proof of eligibility, etc.) and then on the basis of evidence of design competence acquired in the past. This can be demonstrated by providing information on references, supported by letters of reference where appropriate. Another criterion may be financial capacity (size of the office and information on turnover to demonstrate sufficient financial stability). In addition, there may be certain project-specific requirements, such as technical requirements for international projects, experience in managing projects abroad.

The methodology for obtaining/requesting and verifying this information (forms, application specifications, etc.) should be selected depending on the requirements of the applicable procurement law and whether the effort is reasonable for all parties involved.

When evaluating references, their comparability with the subject of the project must be relevant. References that are more comparable to the project in terms of complexity and size should be evaluated positively. References of recent and, if applicable, completed projects should also be evaluated more highly. The extent to which only partial services were provided in the reference projects should be taken into account.

In addition to the assessment of comparability in a technical dimension, the design competence documented by the references should also be evaluated. For this evaluation, it is advisable to convene a specialist committee (selection committee) in which independent experts are involved to make the evaluation comprehensible internally and, if necessary, to third parties.

Competitors

B.06 Architects, Urban Designers/Planners, or Landscape Architects are eligible to participate in the competition. One of these disciplines must be the prime consultant either independently or in joint venture. Architects, Urban Designers/Planners and Landscape Architects are only permitted to participate in the competition with one project team (for more information on the conditions of the procedure and eligibility see B.14).

B.07 In Phase 2, the involvement of transportation planners is expected; the consultation by engineers and other experts, such as environmental and social specialists is recommended. Approximately seven competitors from Phase 1 shall be chosen by the jury to participate in Phase 2.

B.II | Conditions of the Procedure

Competition Type

B.08 The competition is organized as an international open design competition in two phases. The procedure will maintain the competitors' anonymity until all work is exhibited after the competition.

Principles and Guidelines

B.09 Unless otherwise specified the competition rules are based on the UNESCO Standard Regulations for International Competitions in Architecture and Town Planning, as well as the UIA Guide for International Competitions in Architecture and Town Planning published by the Union Internationale des Architectes (UIA) and the RAIC regulations for competitions in Canada, published by the Royal Architectural Institute of Canada (RAIC) on www.raic.org.

B.10 The Competition Rules are governed by the following basic principles: equal opportunities for all candidates; assessment of applications exclusively in accordance with clear, pre-defined and non-discriminatory selection criteria; assessment of the submitted concepts in both phases by an independent jury; and anonymity of candidates in both phases.

Consent

B.11 By virtue of their participation in or contribution to the competition, all parties including the promoter, participants, jurors, technical experts, examiners and guests declare their consent to the present conditions set forth in the competition brief.

B.12 By virtue of their participation in or contribution to the competition, all the above parties further agree to their personal data being stored, within the framework of the competition, in the [phase eins]. data bank. The data stored are: name, address, phone number, position within the competition procedure, and, in the case of the competito banking details. On conclusion of the procedure, this data will be deleted upon reques

B.13 The admission area is unrestricted in terms of countries and regions.

B.14 Eligible for participation are individuals who, through recognition by the professio body in their country of residence, on the day of the announcement of the competiti were entitled to use the occupational title "Architect" and/or "Urban Designer/Plann and/or "Landscape Architect" in their country of residence. Individuals from countr where the occupational title "Architect", "Urban Designer/Planner" or "Landsca Architect" is not subject to statutory regulation are eligible, provided they hold accredited degree or similar certificate of professional qualification.

B.15 Also eligible for participation are consortia formed of individuals and legal entities tl include at least one person eligible according to paragraph B.14. Legal entities are o eligible in such consortia if their statutory objectives include planning activities relev. to the competition task. Legal entities and architect consortia must name a sin authorized representative who will be responsible for the fulfilling of the competiti requirements according to paragraph B.14. The authorized representative as well as authors of competition entries must meet the eligibility criteria applying to competitors. Notwithstanding the designation of a single authorized representative, each member of any consortium shall be jointly and severally liable for any submission from its consortium.

B.16 The statements made in the Declarations of Authorship forms in both phases are considered legally binding. Competitors are required to individually certify their eligibility for participation with the Declaration of Authorship in Phase 1.

B.17 Subsequent to both jury meetings, the authors' eligibility for participation will be rechecked.

Impediments to Participation

B.18 Ineligible for participation are those who, due to their collaboration in the preparation or running of the competition, might be in a favoured position or able to influence the jury's decision, including, without limitation, members of the jury and the promoters staff, employees and other permanent collaborators of participants as well as those who were involved with it in any way, as well as their spouses, first- and second-degree relatives or in-laws, their permanent business or project partners, and the immediate superiors and staff of ineligible persons.

B.19 Ineligible for participation are also associates and members of representative or supervisory bodies of companies or partnerships participating in the competition.

B.20 Ineligible for participation through a separate entry are also a competitor's non-permanent collaborators involved with the preparation of a competition entry as well as members of consortia.

B.21 Ineligible for participation are also those having a business interest in the object of the competition beyond the scope of the competition's planning services, if this is likely to influence bidding processes for services required for the physical implementation of the competition object.

B.22 Participants economically linked with a building contractor may qualify for participation by securing that contractor's commitment to not bid for any construction work contract related to the object of the competition.

B.23 The eligibility principles outlined in this brief shall apply to each member of any consortium.

VISIONARY OPEN INTERNATIONAL DESIGN COMPETITION
THE GENERATION

Envisioning a Sustainable Campus Community
at the University of Manitoba in Winnipeg, Canada

Competition Brief
December 2012

Invited competitions

The selection of participants in an invited competition is also a decisive step in the entire process. Usually, the sponsors in invited competitions are private and free to select the participants, but this step should be carried out carefully and with the involvement of a competent competition organization and with the participation of the authorities and/or architectural associations, if necessary, analogous to the selection by a selection committee in the formalized selection process of the restricted competition.

The usual procedure is to compile a long list of suitable candidates, for which either references are first researched, or which are directly approached regarding their interest in participating in the competition. The offices to be invited to participate are then selected from this list. Even in such procedures, it is advisable to keep the circle of invited offices wide in terms of experience, design approach and office size to obtain a variety of solutions. Relying solely on large and possibly prominent offices unnecessarily reduces the potential of such competitions.

8.3 Jury criteria

The evaluation criteria of the jury stated by the sponsor in the competition brief (and, if applicable, in the public announcement) form the basis for the evaluation of the designs submitted in the competition and should be discussed with the jury during the jury colloquium. It is a special feature of design tasks that the criteria for assessing the designs cannot be formulated in a conclusive manner that differentiates them from one another. Thus, no clear or even definitive weighting of individual criteria is possible. Instead, the fact that the quality of a solution for a design task is determined by a multitude of formative and interdependent individual features is the decisive reason why it is recognized that the designation of this quality can only take place through the assessment by an expert committee (jury), which carries out the necessary weighing and final evaluation of the overall solution. This principle, which in a certain sense represents a unique selling point of design competitions and the decision-making processes in competitions, is the basis for the interlinking of public procurement law and design competitions. The jury's evaluation criteria catalog must be complete and sufficiently unambiguous on the one hand, and sufficiently open to a variety of solution approaches on the other.

Guido Hager
Landscape Architect Zurich/Berlin/Genf/Munich/Stuttgart

❙❙ When architects approach us to enter in an architectural competition, there are always three questions that we must first answer YES to consider participating:
1. Is there a landscape architect in the jury who could appreciate our contribution?
2. Is there a prospect of further commission for the winning team?
3. Does the copyright remain with the project authors?

Then, if we have the capacity for the desired period, we gladly say yes!

Example 1: For example, the criteria for architectural project could be worded as follows: The jury's criteria for the assessment of the entries are listed below, together referring to the projects' overall sustainability.
However, the listing order does not reflect any priority or ranking.

› Design idea
› Urban design references and integration into the context
› Subdivision of the building massing
› Design of the building structures and open spaces
› Interior design proposals
› Interior and exterior accessibility
› Compliance with the spatial program
› Distribution and assignment of uses and their functional organization
› Flexibility of the building structure
› Ecological quality and efficiency of energy use
› Economic efficiency and feasibility
› Compliance with planning and building regulations and permission processes

Example 2: Should the task include special challenges, or should the sponsor wish to assign a special status to a topic, this should be underlined by the addition of further criteria or the breakdown of above criteria, e.g.:

› Integration into the listed context
› Integration of ground monuments
› Comfort of use
› Ecology and new technologies
› Safety concept

Example 3: It is also conceivable that the individual criteria formulated in general terms in Example 1 could be explained in more detail by means of a short specification. Here is an example from a landscape design competition, with the specification in brackets: The competition entries will be evaluated on the basis of the following criteria, which as a whole relate to the sustainability of the design (explained here in brackets in each case). However, the listing order does not reflect any priority or ranking.

› Design idea (including conceptual development of a mission statement, considering the specifications of the design manual)
› Open space quality (i.a., structuring of spaces as well as spatial and functional linkage with the neighborhood, innovative and sustainable urban development)
› Climate-friendly design (i.a., water-sensitive design or decentralized rain water management and precautions against heavy rainfall, as well as consideration of the water supply of the urban green)
› Design (including materiality, surfaces, and color scheme; lighting; vegetation; furniture)
› Functionality (i.a., distribution of use, security concept)
› Accessibility concept (i.a., route network for motorized traffic, public transport, bicycle and pedestrian traffic, emergency routes and delivery)
› Approvability (i.a., protection of historical monuments, accessibility – design for all, road traffic regulations)
› Ecological quality (i.a., nature and species conservation, climate, near-natural water balance)
› Economic efficiency in implementation and operation of the outdoor facilities

Example 4: In the case of two-stage competitions, the criteria catalog can be structured, for example, to initially focus on the conceptual aspects in Stage 1 and then supplement the feasibility check with the criteria of functionality, economic viability, and approvability in Stage 2.

Anton Oliynyk
Architect, Kyiv

" Looking back, I must say that we owe a lot to architectural competitions. Just before the second Maidan unfolded, we had founded our company BURØ, and we were lucky to have some work, rather an exception for a young architectural office at the time. After the victory of the Revolution of Dignity in Ukraine, several competitions related to the commemoration of the events and heroes of the revolution were organized. Furthermore, as a response to new requests from the society, competitions for public squares took place. During this time, we took part in competitions for the first time. In two of them we won the first prizes – Terra Dignitas and Kontraktova square in Kyiv. Immediately after that, our office turned from a small office with some work to a small one with a lot of work. The company began to grow and, accordingly, we gained new clients.

Participating in competitions is always interesting. Working on the competition resembles working with a tuning fork: the architects check the relevance of their ideas by comparing them with the ideas of other participants. Given that all participants work simultaneously, these ideas shape an architectural image of the era. Furthermore, it turns out that the competition is also a process of team training for us, where we expand our knowledge in certain areas and improve our skills.

For these advantages to unfold, quality in the organization of the competition is extremely important. The participating architects must be provided with the most objective (clearest) task. This means that the clients itself and with the organizers must deal intensively with the task before the start of the competition in order to develop an attitude for difficult specifications in the project. Only with this preliminary work the framework can be unveiled for the main task for architects, which since ages lies in the materialization of an idea.

New times require acceleration of all processes. This also applies to architectural design, but competitions tend to slow down project development. But on the other hand, who needs an irrelevant and ineffective solution with a little added value? Therefore, competitions are again like a tuning fork, allowing the client to find a better solution and select the qualified architects. I have no doubts that competitive practice will expand, especially in Ukraine.

Presentation of procedural details in the competition "University of Manitoba in Winnipeg": Assessment criteria

Competition Brief
B Procedure — Page 31

B.24 The main criteria to be applied by the jury in the assessment of entries, responding to the competition requirements (B.IV), the Goals + Guiding Principles (D.II), the General Design Objectives (D.III), and the four urban design components (D.IV to D.VII); these criteria may be refined during the discussion of the submitted entries:

Assessment Procedure during the Competition

B.25 For Phase 1 and Phase 2, the following requirements: Design detail shall be in accordance with the required drawing list and drawing scales listed in B.80 and B.102:

- Basic concept and overall vision (conceptual translation of the strategic objectives; inspirational potential towards higher standards in sustainable urban planning and regional architecture; originality, creativity and innovation of the concept);
- Sensitivity towards the site and the university context, especially the existing vegetation, topography, and habitat as well as environmental, social, cultural, historic and architectural qualities of the existing campus;
- Overall urban design (subdivision of built volumes, building height distribution);
- Compliance with functional requirements (distribution and assignment of land uses, accessibility, flexibility in terms of changing utilization);
- Relationship between enclosed volumes and open spaces;
- Transportation concept, accessibility and exterior circulations for: active transportation, bus rapid Transit (BRT), vehicular network, and parking, including road safety, equity and accessibility;
- Architectural and landscape design and impact of spatial ensemble, in particular the conceptual design of the demonstration project sited in the Southwood Phase One Plan;
- Design of Open Areas;
- Campus Entrances; consideration for threshold conditions, indicating a sense of arrival that is expressive of the region's distinct identity;
- Edge Conditions; treatment of transitional areas between the site boundary and the surrounding urban context.
- Potential social, environmental and economic opportunities;

B.26 All of the items from B.25 developed in more detail, and the following additional items for Phase 2:

- Feasibility (phasing concept, economy, planning regulations);
- Sustainability concept describing the ecological relationship between urban design (the built environment), natural and human made systems, and nature;
- District Energy Strategy.

B.27 Technical Experts may be called upon to assist in the jurors' assessment.

Johannes Hoffmann
Architect, Director Zaha Hadid Architects, London

‖ At Zaha Hadid Architects, we operate globally. Competitions are at the core of our practice's existence. On an annual average, we participate in about 50 competitions worldwide, with our competition successes accounting for about 65 % of our annual new commissions. This gives us a very good overview to compare how competitions are organized on an international level.

In competitions, we first look at the brief, the scope of the promised commission, the client and/or jury, and the aspiration (including budget). Then we determine our chances compared to the effort. If the overall picture is positive, we participate.

We participate in competitions in Germany again and again, but we find it increasingly difficult to justify the effort, because effort and chances are often in an unhealthy ratio here. From our point of view, it should be a goal for the client or organizer to concentrate the scope of the required deliverables to the most necessary or important.

To explain this a bit more: The task is often interesting, often urban and inner-city, and the clients are often public or legal entities. In themselves, therefore, good construction or planning tasks. However, the number of participants in the competition is very high in Germany in comparison with international competitions, usually 20–30 participants. At the same time, the performance expectations are also among the highest; but the remuneration or fees are often very low.

Often performance is required here, which goes beyond the architectural vision and idea. Among other things, competence is tested that should already have been clarified in the pre-qualification process. In addition, services that belong to HOAI service phase 2 (pre-design) are often already requested. Often, the deliverables are then examined and evaluated in detail by experts to support the jury in its decision - although in most cases jury decisions are made based on the architectural idea, the general spatial organization, and the visual design - which is quite correct and reasonable. However, this means a lot of wear and tear and effort on the part of those involved to collect information, which in most cases is of no consequence at all.

A suggestion could be to hold more two-stage competitions, whereby it must be ensured that the submissions of the first stage are only based on sketches. The number of competition participants could then be reduced to a handful for the second round, so that the effort required then can be realistic and fairly rewarded.

Ascan Mergenthaler
Architect, Herzog & de Meuron, Basel

‖ From the participants' perspective, two factors play an important role in a competition: the clarity and consistency of the competition requirements, and the scope of materials to be submitted. Often the requirements for the requested materials are too many; limiting them to the essentials helps both participants and sponsors.

8.4 Further commissioning

In every design competition, regardless of whether it is an ideas competition or a project competition, there should be a clear statement in the competition brief and, if applicable, already in the announcement as to what the sponsor intends to do with the results of the competition once it has been completed. In the case of project competitions, as explained in Chapter 2, this statement must include a promise to award a contract to one of the prizewinners, effective if and as soon as the project is realized. The commitment to a minimum scope of services, the relevant contract conditions and the procedure for negotiating the contract, if necessary, with all prizewinners, must be explained in a transparent and comprehensible manner.

Depending on the procurement law situation and the applicable rules and regulations of the competition, the following text modules are applicable:

Standard wording
"Acknowledging the recommendation issued by the jury, the sponsor of the competition will commission one of the prize winners, preferably the winner, with the rendering of further design services up to construction design (execution design), provided that the project be implemented and the prize winner can guarantee the proper execution of the requirements pertaining to further commissioning, and, in the jury's opinion, the execution of this prize winner's competition entry stays within a reasonable cost framework. The sponsor has the option of commissioning additional services."

Implementation as a general or total contractor project or as PPP project
The following clause may be added if implementation by a general or total contractor or, for example, in a PPP contract is foreseen: "If, due to the commissioning of a general contractor or investor with the implementation of the project, or the implementation is foreseen in a PPP contract, the prizewinner needs not render the complete design of construction drawings for the tendering of the construction services, it is to be assured, by commissioning the prizewinner adequately (with services such as standard details, plan release, statement of work, assessment of tenders, quality control), that at least the competition design's architectural quality is being realized."

Interdisciplinary competitions
If design teams of several disciplines, for example, architecture and landscape architecture, were involved in the competition or if general design services are to be commissioned, their services must also be adequately described as part of the promise for further commission.

Fees and Prizes	B.28 The promoter will provide the net amount of approximately 270,000 Canadian Dollars (CAD) for fees and prizes for services rendered. The total amount of prizes was determined in relation to the size of the project and competition requirements. The final total depends on the number of participants at Phase 2; the figure above is based on the assumption of a number of seven finalists.
	B.29 Every participant who advances to Phase 2 and submits a detailed design concept conforming to the requirements laid down in the competition brief will receive a flat-rate fee of 30,000 CAD irrespective of expenses incurred, inclusive of any applicable taxes.
	B.30 In addition to this, the following prizes shall be awarded:
- 1st prize: 24,000 CAD
- 2nd prize: 18,000 CAD
- 3rd prize: 12,000 CAD
- 4th prize: 6,000 CAD
	B.31 The jury is entitled to unanimously decide to allocate the prize money differently as long as the total remains 60,000 CAD.
	B.32 No other expenses will be paid or reimbursed. Prize amounts and fees will be paid to the competitors within one month following presentation of an invoice after the announcement of results.
Jurisdiction	B.33 It is agreed by all parties that in case of litigation related to this competition, appeal will be made to an international board of arbitrators. The arbitrators' decision will be final and binding.
Project Commissioning	B.34 The jury will submit a recommendation for further commissioning pertaining to the competition. Acknowledging the jury's recommendations, the promoter will then commission one of the prize winners to further develop his or her campus plan design at least from preliminary design to final design, and parts of further stages for the assurance of the implementation of the Fort Garry Campus Plan and a site plan for the Southwood Precinct, provided that the project is implemented and that, in the promoter's opinion, the costs of this prize winner's competition entry stays within a reasonable limit, and the prizewinner can guarantee the proper execution of the requirements pertaining to further commissioning. The commission may be divided in stages.
	B.35 Further on, again acknowledging the jury's recommendations, the promoter may then either directly or through a third party commission one or several of the prize winners to further develop his or her demonstration project design from preliminary to final design and parts of further stages for the assurance of the competition design's quality: e.g. standardized details, collaboration in plan approval, formulation of specifications, assessment of offers, quality control, provided that the project is implemented and that, in the promoter's opinion, the costs of this prize winner's competition entry stays within a reasonable limit, and the prizewinner can guarantee the proper execution of the requirements pertaining to further commissioning.
	B.36 By submitting their entry the competitor agrees to enter, if being commissioned with the further elaboration of the design, a contract (RAIC document 6 with University of Manitoba amendments or equivalent), which is governed by Canadian law and Manitoba law where applicable and which includes provisions concerning ownership of copyright and the rights of use and modification of the design submitted by the competitor.
	B.37 The promoter's qualified in-house expertise and resources will be involved in the technical, financial and legal aspects of the planning process. Such involvement by the promoter will not result in a reduced scope of services awarded to the winning team as specified in B.35.
	B.38 If, in the case of further commissioning, essential parts of the unmodified competition entry serve as the basis for further design development, work already performed as part of the competition requirements will only be paid for, if the amount payable is not fully covered by the amount of the prize money or flat-rate fee.
	B.39 If, within twenty-four months after announcing the jury's award, no contract for carrying out the project is signed with the authors of the first prize, a compensation of 24,000 CAD shall be paid to the author(s) of the first prize. In so compensating the first prizewinner the promoter does not acquire the right to carry out the project except with the collaboration of its author(s).
	B.40 Where the promoter is in agreement with the jury's recommendation, but where the author of the recommended design does not have sufficient professional capacities/experience to plan and develop the project in Canada with respect to the scale and magnitude of the competition project, the promoter may ask that author to form a design team with a design practice contributing the additional resources and local professional designation that the author may be lacking. The promoter will participate in the selection of the design team partner. It is required that both the promoter and the prizewinner agree upon the design team partner. In the contract governing the design team's activities it must be stipulated that, as between the prize winner and design team partner, the prizewinner whose design is being implemented has the final say as to the planning process and architectural intent together with the promoter.
	B.41 In order to facilitate data exchange during further project development and/or archiving, …ments prepared in the commissioned work stage must also be …es in a format to be agreed upon.
Ownership and Copyright	…ents and the model submitted in Phase 2 along with the copyright …e the property of the promoter.
…orship and the right to publication of the design remain with each …notwithstanding, the promoter holds the right of first publication and …ocument and exhibit the competition entries subsequent to the …procedure and to have them published by third parties all this while …he authors and their collaborators, but without obligation to pay any …tion.
…hree months after the jury's decision, the promoter has not published …competition designs, the competitors, having obtained the sponsor's …ission, may on their own, publish their entries.
…ntitled to use for the intended purpose the competition entry whose …sioned with further planning services. The authors and their assignees …w deviations from the submitted design for exterior spaces and future …h. To the extent that the promoter or owner may reasonably be …so, they must consult the prize winner prior to making major …he executed work. Proposals submitted by the competitors are to be …t unless, in the opinion of the promoter or owner, they are judged to …impracticable on economic, functional or design-related grounds, …ould be stated.
…collect entries to Phase 1 two weeks after termination of the exhibition, …On request within six weeks after termination of the exhibition, …s will be returned to their authors post-free.

8.5 Competition requirements

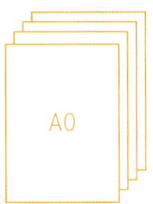  

Presentation boards
- Site plans
- Floor plans, Elevations, Sections
- Detail drawings
- 3D Renderings
- Conceptual diagrams

Explanatory texts
- Design idea
- Technical aspects
- Sustainability concept

Formsheets
- Building parameters
- Construction details
- Compliance with the program

Design model
- Insert model

Digital submission
- digital submission of all of the physically submitted materials

Scope and content of the requested documents

To ensure a fair procedure with equal conditions for all participants and to enable the jury to compare the designs, the scope, format, and content of the documents to be submitted by the participants must be specified precisely. The specifications are to be developed depending on the task and should leave sufficient freedom of presentation to enable the explanation of different design approaches. The graphic shows an overview of the required deliverables from two competitions. In addition to this overview, it is advisable to provide a sufficiently precise description of what is expected for each item.

Here is an example of a description for a site plan and a detailed section:

Example 1: Site plan
at a scale of 1 : 1,000 serves to present the following information:
› Overall design concept
› Integration with urban and landscaping patterns
› Top view of built volumes, with indication of number of floors and building heights, referred to the reference height
› Traffic areas/accessibility (roads and paths, parking spaces, main entrances)
› Open spaces with indication of trees
› Distribution of the uses according to the task
› Indication of proposed construction stages
› Indication of location of sections
› Indication of the fire department driving and parking areas
› Contour lines

Example 2: Facade detail
at a scale of 1 : 25 to explain the structural and building physics concept. The presentation should include the following contents and statements on the choice of materials and colors as well as dimensions:
› At least one detailed section of a sun-exposed façade (east or west facing) at full building height and with at least 1.0 m room depth
› Details of the wall and roof structure (including construction, roof connection, differentiation of opaque and transparent surfaces, designation of facade elements to be opened and fixed)
› Information on energy and building physics aspects (material types and thicknesses including insulation and storage mass concept and explanation of glare and sun protection) as well as presentation of energy-relevant facade elements (e.g., facade-integrated solar technology surfaces)

Layout specifications
› **Number and format of the plans:** The amount and format of the sheets to be submitted should be specified uniformly for all participants. When developing the specification, on the one hand the space required to present the required content at the required scale should be taken into consideration, and on the other hand the jury meeting and the exhibition of the competition work should be taken into account in advance so that it is ensured that all plans can be presented and evaluated in an appropriate manner (room size, light, etc.).
› **Paper quality:** We recommend not to use plans mounted on boards so as to reduce production and shipping costs and the use of boards containing plastic. Instead, we recommend to request the presentation plans in rolled form with paper of a quality of about 140g/sqm.
› **Orientation:** indicating north orientation of all site plans and floor plans is recommended (in the southern hemisphere south orientation).
› **Measurement unit:** a unit of measurement to be applied to all submitted plan documents should be specified (usually meters).

Completion and marking of the documents to be submitted.
The following specifications are recommended:
› **Marking:** In most competitions, anonymity is one of the important basic principles. The designs are to be presented to the jury without any indication of authorship. In support of this requirement, it is common for projects to be submitted anonymously. All documents are to be marked with a code chosen by the participants themselves, such as a six-digit code consisting of capital letters and Arabic numerals). Especially since even this code could allow a conclusion, and to facilitate the discussion in the jury, it is helpful to replace the codes of the participants with a continuous camouflage number and to paste over the codes accordingly. The reference of the code number to the names of the authors takes place via a declaration of authorship, which must be submitted in a sealed envelope.
› **Submission of files:** When submitting digital documents, compliance with anonymity must be ensured by choosing neutral file and layer names and deleting hidden information in the files. In terms of file formats to be submitted, specifications are recommended.
› **Cross-references:** Cross-references by QR codes or similar are to be excluded.
› **Number of copies:** Typically, two full sets of the plan sheets are requested – one set in high print quality for the presentation to the jury and a second in simple print quality for the preliminary examination.
› **Number of entries:** For clarity of assessment, it should be made clear that only one design may be submitted per participating office and that variants will be excluded.

Model
The following specifications are recommended:
› If there is a model of the surroundings: Reference to the standardized insert plate provided physically or digitally to all participants.
› If there is no model of the surroundings: Reference to the desired section and the maximum dimensions of the model.
› If relevant, indication that working models are sufficient.
› Scale
› Explanation of the representation of the topography. If necessary, the participants will be provided with model building material that corresponds to the area model
› In the case of existing buildings in the competition site, it may be useful to provide the participants with the existing buildings to be preserved as a model building blocks
› If relevant, color (white) and type of representation of trees to correspond to the area model
› Suggestion to use stable and safe packaging

Explanatory texts and forms

With an explanatory report, the participants are expected to provide a brief description of the design idea in relation to the expectation and goal of the competition task. If necessary, separate texts on the technical and/or sustainability concept may be also requested in addition to the description of the design idea. With the help of several forms, which are also provided as blank for technical information about the project, the participants complete the statements for the presentation plans (for more details see Chapter 10.1).

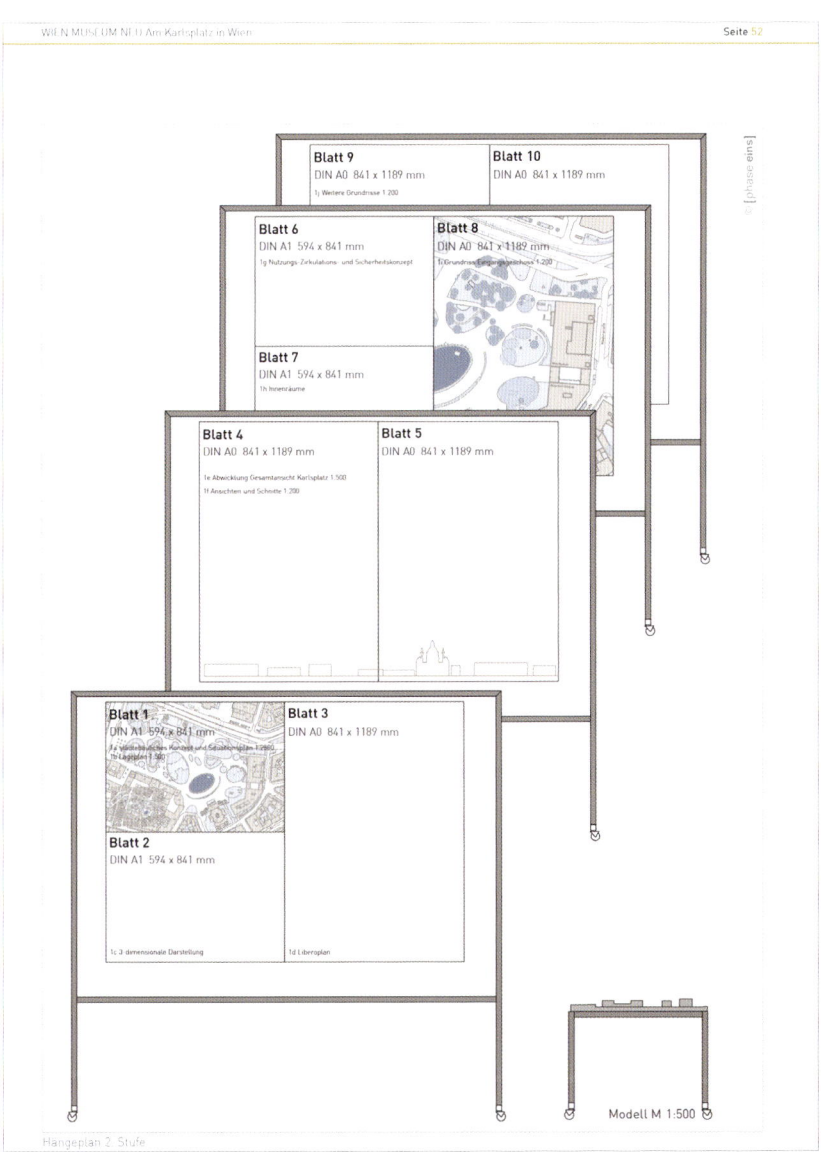

Suspension plan explaining the specifications for the presentation of the competition entries in the "Wien Museum Neu" competition

Tatiana Bilbao
Architect, Mexico City

" What is important for me as a competitor, when taking part in a competition, is to be sure that the promoter, the jury, and the participants are talking the 'same language'. Meaning that everyone is working around the same principles and/or is open to being challenged by different approaches. We are often confronted with the fact that our thinking is too progressive, or too conservative, or too distant from the jury, and even from the promoter. Therefore, I expect the competition organization to achieve a far-reaching coordination of the specifications between the stakeholders in advance, in order to ultimately achieve a 'good' match between the participants, the jury and the awarding authority and thus wonderful, suitable and yet progressive results.

9 COMMUNICATION DURING THE COMPETITION

9.1 Communication despite anonymity?

An intensive and direct dialogue between the client and the design team is essential in all design processes in order to achieve mutual understanding and reach possible solutions. This cooperative atmosphere, which includes authorities, experts, the neighborhood, is interrupted during design competitions. Direct personal communication between the client and the designer – which otherwise takes place in regular personal meetings, when sketching together on a napkin, or through argumentation with gestures and verbosity – is taboo in favor of the participation of many with different ideas and thus the need to define and adhere to "rules of the game." The concept of anonymity, i.e., not knowing which design team is behind which proposal, is essential for the trust in a process with many unknown parties involved. Nevertheless, what means are available to share information to the necessary extent?

9.2 Jury colloquium

Communication among the jury members is the basis for a successful decision at the end of the competition, ideally supported unanimously by all parties involved. The jury colloquium is the kick-off meeting of this process. This is where the jury members get to know each other and begin the necessary process of building trust. The core of the colloquium is initially the visit of the competition site followed by the discussion of the correct formulation of the task and, if necessary, the optimization of the details of the procedure. However, it should not be underestimated that it is also an opportunity for the jury members to bond as a group, which is why it is advisable to organize an accompanying program that will provide additional opportunities to get to know each other and start working together.

9.3 Significance and distribution of the competition materials

The most important medium through which the sponsor of a competition communicates the objectives of their project are the competition materials, here in particular the competition brief with texts, illustrations, tables, etc. The obvious importance of this aspect is in practice too often underestimated, and can happen in incomplete, misleading, or even contradictory documents. Investing in careful, well-structured, and attractively designed documents is the most important means of compensating for the above-mentioned "disruption" of "normal" communication. The great advantage of this circumstance is the need to make unambiguous statements about the project at a very early stage, coordinated with all parties involved (for more details, see Chapter 10).

9.4 Written queries and colloquia

As in any tender procedure, competitors have the opportunity to ask questions about the competition documents and the process. These questions can be submitted in writing, potentially trough an online portal or a project homepage, which ensures that all participants receive the questions and answers anonymously and at the same time. In addition, it is usually possible to clarify questions during a colloquium, where the competitors are also given the opportunity to visit the site.

In addition, participants' colloquia offer the sponsor and the jury the opportunity for a personal, oral explanation of the project objectives. In particular, the communication of strategic goals and their significance (e.g., on economic efficiency, sustainability, and innovation) is often only possible to a limited extent in the written form of the competition announcement. The importance of such topics can be authentically explained through a personal presentation by the sponsor or a specialized lecture. To ensure the same level of information for all participants, such lectures can be shown online or recorded in the case of hybrid events and made available afterwards.

Prof. Dietmar Eberle
Architect, Lustenau

!! The quality of a result of a competition is determined by the understanding of the objectives of sponsor and jurors.
This is the real challenge.

Scenes from colloquia with participants, **1**: ThyssenKrupp Quarter, Essen, **2**: KFAS Head Office and Conference Center in Kuwait, **3**: Wien Museum Neu, **4**: University of Manitoba in Winnipeg, **5**: Parliamentary Precinct Redevelopment Ottawa, **6**: European Parliament Brussels, **7**: BMW FIZ Future Munich, **8**: Babyn Yar Holocaust Memorial Center in Kiyv

9 Communication during the competition

9.5 Personal presentations by the competitors and dialogue

In some projects, lifting anonymity in favor of a direct dialogue between the competitors, the jury and the sponsor is more important for the project than the anonymous evaluation of the designs. This approach is permissible according to many rules and regulations. Mutual understanding of the task and thus also of the design approaches can be better achieved in this way in the case of complex tasks. Often, final specifications for relevant individual aspects of the task can only be formulated after a discussion of the design approaches in an intermediate meeting.

Formats

In practice, these processes, known as "cooperative procedures", or "study commissions" in Switzerland, can only be implemented in procedures with a small number of competitors (or in the second phase of a two-stage competition). They are equally suitable for urban development tasks (if necessary, also in connection with participation of the citizens) as for architectural projects with very complex functional requirements or e.g., projects with interventions in listed buildings, where the direct dialog is helpful in the context of weighing up the appropriate extent of an intervention.

A useful and texted format for this dialogue is an interim colloquium with individual appointments with each team, for which 45–75 minutes is appropriate – usually introduced by a 15–20-minute presentation by the participants and then a joint discussion with the jury of relevant topics.

In the case of single-stage competitions, the appropriate time for this interim colloquium is after approximately one third of the working period; in the case of two-stage competitions, such a colloquium may be appropriate immediately at the beginning of Stage 2, then on the basis of the findings from the jury session of Stage 1. On the other hand, a final presentation during the final jury meeting is less advisable. It is replaced by the presentation by a professional competition organizer – on the one hand in order not to increase the effort for the competitors by a new presentation (possibly including travelling), on the other hand to clearly focus on the design solution and not on the rhetorical qualities of the presentation or the presenters when deciding on the competition.

There are also procedures, especially regarding urban design or landscape design, where the process is designed in the form of a "workshop" with all participants working together to develop the best solution. Here, it is often not a matter of selecting one design and commissioning one team, but rather of jointly developing a concept on which the subsequent design process is to be based.

Challenge

Meeting the designers in person during the the process and having a dynamic dialogue entail a considerable responsibility for the competition organizer, the sponsor, and the jury. It is important to deal carefully and fairly with the knowledge and experience gained during the process, to give all teams equal opportunities, and to share the insights gained from the dialogue with all participants afterwards.

Deliverables

In a cooperative competition, the presentation file is an additional deliverable. Here too (see Chapter 8.5), precise requirements should be formulated: no company presentations should be given, a note on the extent to which films are accepted as part of the presentation (if so, with a specification of the maximum length), specification of permissible file formats. It may also be allowed for participants to use sheets of paper with sketches or working models as part of the interim colloquium to communicate with the sponsor and the jury. Overall, the goal should be to manage the effort for all competitors in such a way that the time required for each participating team remains reasonable and a workload is defined for the competitors that corresponds to the fees paid in the competition.

Scenes from colloquia with interim presentations by participants, **1:** BMW FIZ Future Munich (Volkwin Marg), **2:** i-Campus Munich (Erasmus Eller), **3:** BMW Plant Munich – urban production (Ursina Fausch), **4:** Parliamentary Quarter Ottawa (Donald Schmitt), Daimler (Bjarke Ingels)

Ian Ritchie
Architect, London

❝ Lord Bardolph Henry VI Pt2, Act 1 Scene 3: Bardolph:
 'When we mean to build, We first survey the plot, then draw the model, And when we see the figure of the house, Then must we rate the cost of the erection, Which if we find outweighs ability, What do we then but draw anew the model In fewer offices, or at last desist To build at all?' 'But, by your leave, it never yet did hurt To lay down likelihoods and forms of hope.'

Modern translation: 'When we decide to build something, first we look at the land and then we draw up the plans. When we know what the house will look like, we work out how much it is going to cost. If we find that the cost is more than we can afford, we change the plans so that the house has fewer rooms, or we decide to cancel the building project completely. But, forgive me, it's doesn't hurt to think about possible outcomes of the battle and hopeful strategies that we could use.'

The context of the quote is whether to engage in another competition or not (the English considering yet another battle with the French). For the initiator, the client, plan ahead carefully, assess the risks of it going awry, and to avoid disappointment, consult the best competition manager! Same for the architects considering entering a competition.

Or, you may prefer this recommendation to a private client envisaging an architectural competition: 'meet the potential architects you are considering inviting to compete before you invite them! You will spend a lot of time with them and a good chemistry between you and the architect will be vital'. And, to a public client, 'have a face to face live pre-competition seminar where the limits of architecture & design acceptability can be explained in the context of the political and economic framework'.

What is important for me as a Juror, is to know the fundamental needs and desires of the client, and that these are extremely well articulated in the competition brief. When assessing competition submissions, it is vital to be able to read and understand the client's true motivations, and the ideal scenario is one where the jury members can interrogate the client live while the assessment of the submissions is taking place.

9.6 "Virtual competition"

In the wake of the 2021-2023 pandemic, many sectors of society received a forced development boost. Home offices and video conferencing were the means of choice to keep processes running to some extent. Some of the lessons learned in this context will remain permanently valid, especially as they serve efficiency and sustainability: less travel, more flexible working hours, faster decision-making, and more digitization in communication. What did this development mean for competitions? Due to the industry's already extensive digitization and the majority of those involved having a strong comfort with it, the barriers to use more and more online conferencing, especially during the pandemic, were relatively minimal. The implementation of design competitions, however, posed challenges in terms of technical organization and procurement law. When deciding on the right event format (personal, hybrid, or online) or, alternatively, rescheduling events, the importance and necessity of face-to-face interpersonal communication was often a key-factor in the decision-making process. Below, we discuss the implications of this experience for the conduct of competitions, rather than the specific case of the pandemic itself.

Online distribution of competition documents

The distribution of printed competition documents to competitors and thus the (mass) mailing of brochures and plan rolls is steadily decreasing anyway: the distribution of competition documents via download is standard and makes sense for cost reasons alone. The printout of competition brochures is usually only a service for the jury members, as the paper form suits the reading and archiving habits of many. The competitors, on the other hand, find the digital form convenient for their work processes.

Online submission of projects

The issue of digital submission of designs is more complex. Particularly in the case of international projects, it can reduce the cost of transport. However, the printing effort may only be shifted to the sponsor, since the jury usually works with printed paper plans to be able to make direct comparisons and discuss them together.

The guarantee of anonymity during data upload can be ensured by appropriate programming of the online portals. Plan documents, forms and reports can thus be transferred easily - corresponding systems are available on the market. A greater challenge is the encrypted submission of the declaration of authorship, which traditionally takes place in a sealed envelope. Here, the digital system must offer parallel folder structures with encrypted files to ensure anonymity in a legally secure manner. Of course, it is not possible to send physical models in this way, but the submission of digital 3D models is still an exception, and it remains to be seen to what extent these models can establish themselves as the standard in competitions.

Colloquia and jury meetings

During the pandemic, it was difficult or even impossible to hold the jury and participants' colloquia as well as the jury meetings in person. Bringing people together in one space and traveling were prohibited in phases, traveling abroad anyway. Against this background and the concern that competitions would have to be postponed or even cancelled due to the pandemic, an optimistic legal assessment was quickly available and communicated by several architectural associations in Germany: colloquia and jury sessions were also permissible via videoconferencing, physical attendance was not mandatory under German regulations, and so was the change to a purely digital submission of materials. The methods of online submission of competition entries were either developed quickly or many a blind eye was turned during this time. The extent to which these optimistic assessments will have an impact after the pandemic is only beginning to be seen in practice.

During the pandemic, for example, there were colloquia organized entirely online and even occasional jury meetings. Does this mean that everything will be better, and that competition will receive a boost in innovation as a result of the crisis? Perhaps. In any case, after these sessions, one first noted with joy that the CO_2 footprint of the colloquium conducted by video remained smaller and that one had to spend less time traveling.

However, it also became clear that there are limits in communicating via video. Focusing on the screen for several hours is an enormous strain, which often proves detrimental to concentration on the subject. In addition, the quality of perception, including gestures and body language, is limited, side conversations during coffee breaks are not possible, and debates immediately in front of plans and models are limited to the section of the screen. The discussion of designs in presence allows an exchange that is indispensable for clarifying content and building mutual understanding as a basis for joint decisions. Architecture is not a legal text, and jury meetings not only serve to make technical decisions but are also a platform for building social consensus.

In this respect, it is advisable to include the options practiced in the pandemic period as an option in the consideration of organizational forms, but to critically examine their application. In particular, hybrid implementation can develop advantages in practice if individual jury members are enabled to participate in a colloquium in this way, or if, for example, part of each design team participates in a participant colloquium in presence on site, while another part participates online, so that travel can be saved and a larger part of the project teams can nevertheless experience the statements in the colloquium live. However, the quality of communication remains limited, which is why we generally advise against colloquia conducted purely online.

We would also largely rule out purely online solutions for design competitions, not only because of the restrictions on technical discussions, but also because of the restriction of the possibility, relevant for the implementation of a project, of building up a mutual understanding between the participants in such a meeting, who will also later accompany the project together in the realization phase. This kind of consensus and trust building can hardly take place online (see Chapter 13). Even hybrid solutions with the online participation of individual members of the jury should be an exception. In suitable individual cases, however, and if necessary, the online participation of experts, who have familiarized themselves with the projects during the preliminary examination and can save travel time through online participation without this being detrimental to the described trust-building of those who would also continue to accompany the project, is conceivable.

In summary, it can be stated that in principle all events within the framework of a competition procedure can be handled with the help of technical solutions such as video conferencing, but that this is not advisable in all cases. Both the participation of all or individual jury members in colloquia via video and the online participation of individuals in participant colloquia are instruments that will continue to simplify many procedures in the future. They also contribute to climate protection and should be implemented accordingly in practice and anchored in the updating of the rules and regulations. In our opinion, however, jury meetings conducted via video must remain a rare exception in order not to accept the loss of important qualities of discourse in the context of competitions and thus risk a deterioration of the results.

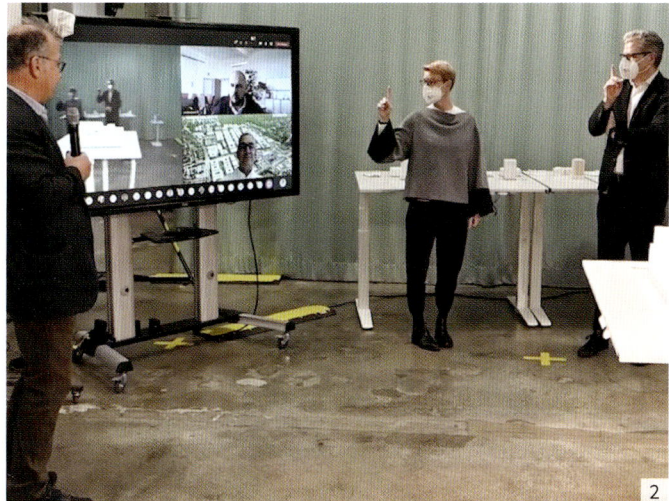

Jury meeting under Covid 19 pandemic measures: **1:** "Holcim Awards for Sustainable Construction" in June 2020 (right: Prof. Marilyne Andersen), **2:** "1st construction phase Siemensstadt 2.0" in November 2020, **3:** "Urban drainage and environmental analysis Nuremberg" in October 2020, **4:** "European Parliament in Brussels" in February 2021

VII MASTER PLANS FOR INDUSTRY AND RESEARCH

The development of master plans for industry and research is a special topic of urban design, being an independent field of activity. In addition to the classical issues of building structure, outdoor space design and traffic planning, there are sometimes complex technical and functional requirements for building use, equipment and logistics; there are also high demands for long-term flexibility to be able to cope with changes in the research requirements and/or the production focus; and there are usually high safety requirements regarding accident prevention and confidentiality. Some of these dimensions are less familiar to the design teams involved and may need to be communicated by the sponsor and the competition organizer. The dimension of designing attractive workplaces and an identity-creating environment is among the challenges, as are the requirements of climate protection as well as energy and resource planning. Because of to the unique dimension of the tasks, the project-specific requirements should be communicated clearly. As a result of these constraints, collaborative, multi-stage processes are recommended for this type of task.

Diagram explaining the existing distribution of functions in the competition "Water Sewage Facilities in Nuremberg"

BMW Group FIZ Future, Munich

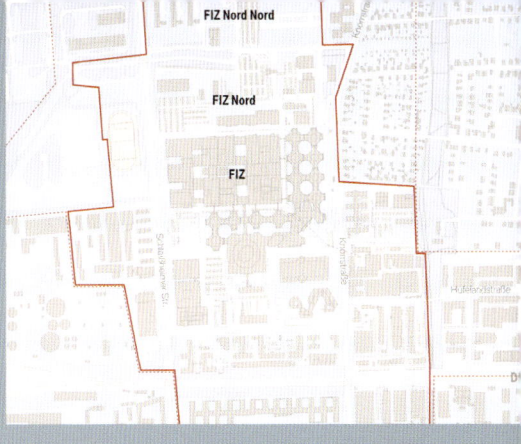

BMW GROUP RESEARCH AND INNOVATION CENTER
The Research and Innovation Center (Forschungs- und Innovationszentrum – FIZ) is considered one of the most modern large-scale technology centers worldwide and is the heart of the BMW Group's research and development activities. In the long-term the BMW Group wants to bolster and expand the facility (currently accommodating 26,000 company jobs) with a total of approximately 1 million sqm IJFA and around 5,000 further jobs for suppliers and partner companies, thus optimizing its spatial-functional structure. To this end, around 20 ha of property bordering the northern edge of the current facilities was acquired. The FIZ is located in the north of Munich, close to Frankfurter Ring, part of Munich's ring road. The location is of strategic importance due to its proximity to the BMW Group headquarters and main production facility. At the same time, FIZ is an integral part of the urban structure of Munich North.

COMPETITION TASK The goal was to find an interdisciplinary design for mid- and long-term expansion and restructuring of the FIZ and its surrounding areas. Following the competition, the design was reworked into a masterplan as a cooperation between the BMW Group, the city of Munich, its citizens and other property owners. The masterplan should draft relevant determinants and remain flexible for future growth. Apart from the development structure, green-space planning and traffic and parking alternatives for the distribution of operations and development scenarios should be considered within expansion stages in 2025 and 2050. By 2025, approximately 500,000 sqm of new floor area could be constructed. Due to the size, location and importance of the development, the 100-ha competition area was defined beyond the FIZ borders and divided into a primary core area and a secondary interconnected area.

PROCEDURE In order to work through the complex task in close cooperation with all relevant stakeholders from the outset, the competition was carried out as an interdisciplinary and "cooperative" procedure, i.e., with direct dialogue with the planners, and was embedded in a number of early town meetings or "neighborhood dialogues."

Location: Munich, Germany **Client:** BMW Group in cooperation with the city of Munich **Year:** 2013 – 2014 **Project size:** approx. 100 ha **Type of competition:** Two-stage design competition preceded by an open application procedure **Participants:** 1st stage: 12; 2nd stage: 6

PRIZEWINNERS:
(01) **1st prize** Henn Architekten, Munich (D), with Topotek 1, Berlin (D); **2nd prize** ernst niklaus fausch architekten, Zurich (CH), with Müller Illien Landschaftsarchitekten, Zurich (CH), and Rapp Infra, Basel (CH); **3rd prize** West 8 Urban design & Landscape Architecture, with Atelier Kempe Thill – Architects and Planners, Rotterdam (NL), and Transver, Munich (D)

VII Master plans for industry and research

BMW Group FIZ Future, Munich 107

Lühn Bau Company Headquarters in Lingen

LÜHN BAU The Gerhard Lühn GmbH & Co. KG is one of the long-established construction companies in the Emsland region and today operates throughout northern and western Germany with approximately 150 employees. Originally founded as a craftsman's business in 1710, the company expanded under the leadership of Gerhard Lühn in the mid-19th century to become a construction company that played an increasingly important role in shaping the public urban landscape. It was Lühn Bau, for example, that built the Lingen water tower in 1909. With the steady growth in the past years and the positive outlook for the future, there is increasing demand for additional space at the central location in Lingen for administration and production preparation.

LINGEN TECHNOLOGY AND BUSINESS PARK

In order to accommodate this demand and to provide attractive workplaces and good conditions for productivity in the long term, the company is developing a technology and industrial park on a site of approx. 10 hectares. The land, which was previously used for agriculture, is located in the south of the city of Lingen, where the development of further industrial sites is predicted. The site will be connected to the B 70 by two traffic junctions and has a slight slope. Part of the task was the master planning for the entire area. Approximately 30 % of the site is earmarked for the buildings and facilities of Gerhard Lühn GmbH & Co. KG are envisaged. The remaining areas are to be used by other innovation companies and start-ups. High-quality commercial and office buildings, central community facilities (day-care center, gastronomy, etc.) as well as open spaces with amenity quality are to be created. Architecture should have a clear communicative significance for the technology and business park and become part of its identity.

COMPANY HEADQUARTERS The buildings of Gerhard Lühn GmbH & Co. KG are to be both a central and integral part of the entire technology and industrial park, including an administrative building for 40–65 employees, a workshop and open spaces for storage.

Location: Lingen, Germany **Client:** Gerhard Lühn GmbH & Co. KG **Year:** 2017 – 2018 **Project size:** approx. 12 ha competition site, approx. 10,000 ha UFA **Type of competition:** Interdisciplinary design competition in two stages **Participants:** Stage 1: 9; Stage 2: 4 **Competition budget:** EUR 140,000 (prizes: EUR 40,000; Compensation stage 1: EUR 50,000; Compensation stage 2: EUR 50,000)

PRIZEWINNERS:
(01) **1st prize** LAVA Laboratory for Visionary Architecture, Berlin (D), with A24 Landschaft GmbH, Berlin (D); **3rd prize** PFP Planungs GmbH, Hamburg (D), with Rainer Schmidt Landschaftsarchitekten GmbH, Munich (D); **3rd prize** EM2N Mathias Müller Daniel Niggli Architekten AG, Zurich (CH), with Studio Vulkan Landschaftsarchitektur GmbH, Zurich (CH); **3rd prize** eins:eins Architekten, Hamburg (D), with HAHN HERTLING VON HANTELMANN Landschaftsarchitekten GmbH, Hamburg (D)

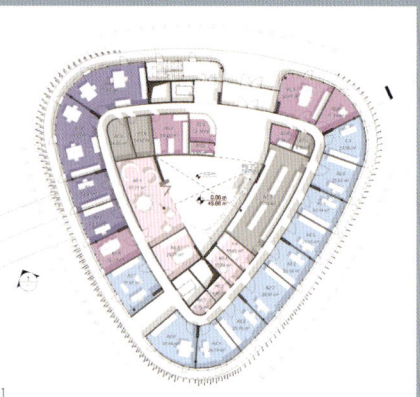
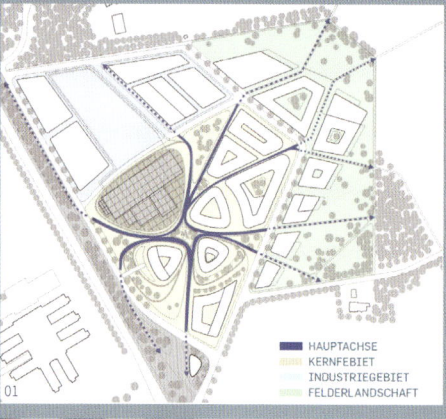
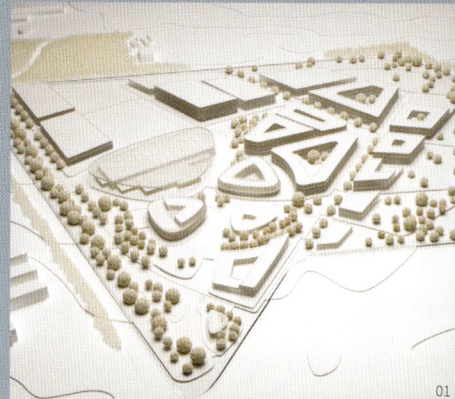

Water Sewage Facilities, Nuremberg

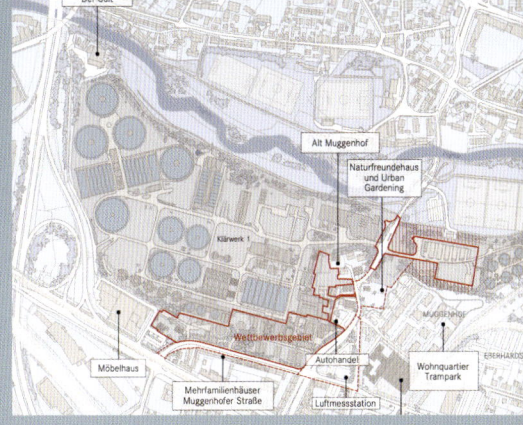

CITY SEWAGE MANAGEMENT AND ENVIRONMENTAL ANALYSIS The Wastewater Treatment Plant 1 is located in the Muggenhof district of Nuremberg. It is the larger one of the two large sewage treatment plants in Nuremberg and is designed to serve a population equivalent of 1.4 million. It was put into operation in 1931, and since 1956 there have been continuous additions and modifications to increase the treatment capacity. Today, the Wastewater Treatment Plant 1 is a two-stage biological treatment plant with a downstream wastewater filter. Parts of the site are occupied by the administration buildings, the sewer depot with the tasks of sewer maintenance, sewer cleaning, sewer inspection, vehicle parking and discharge control in the sewer network, as well as the laboratories of the environmental analysis department. In the laboratories, all cleaning processes in the sewage treatment plant are monitored and external water samples are analyzed. There are also two vacant listed buildings located on the site.

TASK The subject of the competition was the design of the new and reconstruction of the current operating, laboratory, and administrative buildings with the aim of restructuring and updating the building substance and improving the operating processes. An integral part of the design was the outdoor facilities inside and partly outside the plant premises in order to achieve a better integration into the landscape and urban context. Thus, the project is also part of the urban renewal plan "Weststadt" for the development of the neighborhood. Building during ongoing operations was a particular challenge for the design of the complex.

PROGRAM The program comprises a total of approx. 11,500 sqm net area, including 3,200 sqm for laboratories, 3,500 sqm for the sewage depot (incl. workshops and garages for special vehicles), 1,300 sqm for wastewater treatment workshops and 3,000 sqm of offices for various departments.

Location: Nuremberg, Germany **Client:** Nuremberg City **Year:** 2019 – 2021 **Project size:** approx. 72,800 sqm competition area, approx. 13,000 sqm UFA **Type of competition:** Architectural design competition in two stages **Participants:** Stage 1: 18; Stage 1: 7 **Competition budget:** EUR 452,000 (prizes: EUR 150,000; Compensation stage 1: EUR 120,000; Compensation stage 2: EUR 182,000)

PRIZEWINNERS:
(01) **1st Prize (commissioned)** CODE UNIQUE Architekten GmbH, Dresden (D), RSP Freiraum GmbH, Dresden (D); (02) **1st Prize** Nickl Architekten Deutschland GmbH, Munich (D), Latz+Partner mbB, Kranzberg (D); **3rd Prize** blauraum Architekten GmbH, Hamburg (D), KRAFT.RAUM. Landschaftsarchitektur Dusseldorf (D); **4th Prize** Behles & Jochimsen Gesellschaft von Architekten mbH, Berlin (D), Grosser-Seeger & Partner mbB, Nuremberg (D)

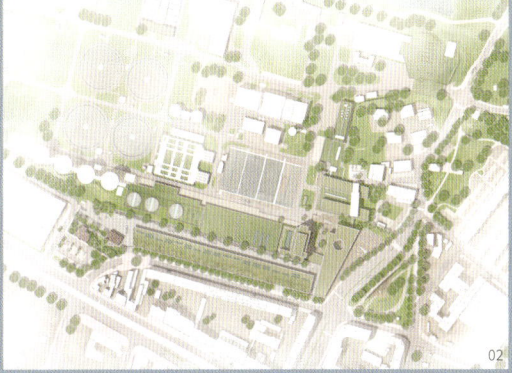

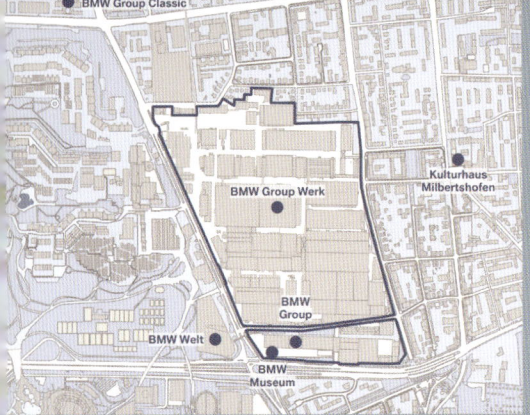

BMW Group Plant Munich – Urban Production

BMW GROUP PLANT MUNICH The Munich plant is the company's principal plant – this is where the history of the BMW Group began 100 years ago. Until today, the plant is a key element in the BMW Group's international network of production sites. Currently, about 800 vehicles are produced daily and about 8,400 employees from more than 50 countries are employed here. Once located on the outskirts of Munich, the urban fabric has grown around the plant over the years and, with the Olympic Park, the Olympic Village, the residential quarters of the Milbertshofen district and, last but not least, the BMW Group headquarters, forms an urban neighborhood that is unique worldwide for an automobile plant of this dimension.

MASTER PLAN
"BMW MUNICH – URBAN PRODUCTION"

In the context of an ambitious overriding sustainability strategy and the safeguarding of the plant's productivity, the special feature of the task lies in the overlapping of classic urban planning and the design for a hitherto hermetically sealed, highly efficient production site. The master plan is intended to define a vision for the development structure, traffic, and logistics areas for the constantly changing requirements of production. At the same time, qualities are to be developed for the people employed at the plant and for a new coexistence with the neighborhood. The gradual opening of the factory grounds and their passage for the public as well as the creation of insights are declared goals.

PROCESS The competition, which was carried out in coordination with the city of Munich, included intermediate workshops with the design teams to provide a better understanding of the requirements and give advice for solutions. At the end of the competition, the jury selected two equal winning projects, whose authors, OMA and 3XN, were jointly commissioned to merge their designs into a common master plan. The result of the joint revision was confirmed by the jury.

Location: Munich, Germany **Client:** BMW Group **Year:** 2021 – 2022 **Project size:** approx. 44 ha competition site **Type of competition:** Design competition **Participants:** Office for Metropolitan Architecture (O.M.A.), Rotterdam; 3XN AS, Copenhagen; HENN GmbH, Munich; Allmann Sattler Wappner . Architekten GmbH, Munich; SPACECOUNCIL, Zurich; Ernst Niklaus Fausch Partner AG, Zurich

PRIZEWINNERS:
(01) **Joint revision into a common overall plan** Office for Metropolitan Architecture (O.M.A.) & 3XN AS; **1st prize** Office for Metropolitan Architecture (O.M.A.) Stedebouw B.V., Rotterdam (NL), Vogt Landschaft GmbH, Berlin (D), Systematica Srl, Milan (I), Transsolar Energietechnik GmbH, Munich (D); **1st prize** 3XN AS, Copenhagen (DK), Latz + Partner, Kranzberg (D), WSP, Taastrup (DK), GXN, Copenhagen (DK)

adidas World of Sports, Herzogenaurauch

adidas-SALOMON AG In 1998, adidas-Salomon AG decided to restructure its global headquarters at the international home of adidas in the city of Herzogenaurach, Franconia, and to continue development there. The area of the former US military base ("Herzo Base") was to be redeveloped, forming a new district of Herzogenaurach, the basic structure of which was to be planned in this competition. This site was to serve as the location of the "World of Sports", the primary and largest element of the development area. It was also to include a new housing area and further commercial areas, along with the integration of the landscape.

WORLD OF SPORTS The "World of Sports" was to be developed on approx. 40 hectares of land. In addition, this area was to provide a unique combination of functions such the corporation's HQ and Administration, Global Marketing, Global Sourcing & Logistics, Research & Development as well as various sports facilities, in a campus-like setting. This complex was to be complemented by a boarding house and an international school. In coordination with the city of Herzogenaurach, the plan was to offer 2,800 residents (among whom employees of adidas-Salomon AG) with the approx. 163-ha competition area, as well as provide commercial and recreation areas. The housing development was to embody the idea of "the eco-friendly city of short distances". Required was a mix of different building types grouped in varying density and extending the urban space toward Haundorf, as well as a transition toward the landscape space.

COMPETITION AREA The competition area, then, was to bridge between denser urban structures and an open landscape. Planning of the outside areas needed to reflect this, offer a maximum of open space and passageway and at the same time create areas with a wide variety of appeal. To sum up, the desired solution was to possess the potential to transform this area, hitherto isolated from Herzogenaurach, into an attractive, lively place for work, living and leisure within the confines of the city.

Location: Herzogenaurauch, Germany **Client:** GEV Grundstücksgesellschaft, on behalf of adidas-Salomon AG and the city of Herzogenaurach **Year:** 1989 – 1999 **Project size:** approx. 163 ha **Type of competition:** Restricted urban design project competition preceded by an open application procedure **Participants:** 266 applicants, 47 competitors **Competition budget:** EUR 123,700

PRIZEWINNERS:
(01) **1st prize** Angélil/Graham/Pfenninger/Scholl, Zurich/L.A.; (02) **2nd prize** AS&P – Albert Speer & Partner, Frankfurt a. M., and Kamel Louafi, Berlin; (03) **3rd prize** Auer + Weber, Munich/Stuttgart, and Gesswein Henkel + Partner, Ostfildern; **4th prize** Fink + Jocher, Munich, and Burger + Tischer, Munich; **5th prize** Massimiliano Fuksas, Rome; **purchase award** Morphosis, Santa Monica and Bernd Lederle, Ditzingen; **purchase award** ASTOC, Cologne, and Juurlink en Geluk, Rotterdam; **purchase award** MVRDV, Rotterdam

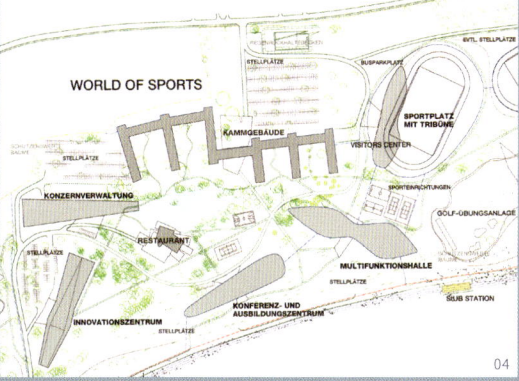

10 COMPETITION MATERIALS

10.1 Structure

In design, the "program" of a project includes the design objectives specified by the sponsor, particularly the technical spatial and functional requirements. In competitions, the term "program", or "competition program" or "competition brief", has a broader meaning. Here, the "program" not only includes the description of the task, but also all the conditions relevant to the procedure, necessary to understand the task, such as the background information on the site, the project, and the sponsor. The quality of the competition materials is therefore important to the overall success of the project.

As explained in Chapter 5.3 (Tasks of the competition organization), the compiling the competition materials is one of the main tasks in the preparation of a competition. They are gathered in close cooperation between the sponsor and the competition organizer and with the involvement of the relevant authorities and experts. The division of work in the preparation of these documents can be organized in different ways, but the formulation and final compilation of the documents should ultimately be the responsibility of the competition organizer. The final draft of the materials should be discussed with and confirmed by the jury members during the jury colloquium.

The materials, which will be made available to all participants, include:

› **Competition brief:** A brochure with textual and graphic description of the aim and objective of the project, procedural conditions, information on the situation and planning guidelines as well as the task, supplemented by illustrations on the location (including site plans explaining the boundaries of the competition site, traffic situation and topography) and the objectives of the task (including spatial and functional program but also strategic objectives). The competition brief forms the basis for the work of all those involved in the competition and, regarding the conditions of the process, also in the sense of a contract between the sponsor and the competition participants. It is also used to document and agree on the status of coordination between those involved in the project Thus, the document has a relevance that goes beyond its significance in the competition. Since a competition brief contains a complex variety of information, a comprehensible structure and the overall layout of the document are important.
› **Plan documents:** files (CAD, pdf).
› **Forms:** Blank forms to indicate authorship, building description (table with information on essential components), characteristic values (FAR, SOR, GV, GFA, NFA, envelope area, etc.), cost characteristics, etc.
› **Studies:** Additional documents provided to the participants (such as soil reports, zoning plan, tree list, wind reports, traffic reports).
› **Insert plate for area of the surroundings:** Base plate with precise dimensions to fit the opening in the model of the surrounding.

10.2 Situation and planning guidelines

The result of the fact collection includes all information on the current and sometimes also future situation that is relevant as a basis for design and background information, usually divided into the following topics:

› Location and size of the competition site
› History of the site
› Urban environment
› Buildings in the surrounding area
› Buildings within the competition site
› Current planning in the surrounding area
› Existing planning law
› Traffic situation
› Landscape, vegetation, and fauna
› Trade and social infrastructure
› Subsoil
› Supply and disposal/technical infrastructure
› Topography
› Climatic conditions

10.3 Task and program

Decisive for the quality of the task description are:

› Comprehensible and unambiguous formulations
› Precision of the specifications
› Completeness of the specifications
› Unambiguity in the differentiation between obligatory components of the task as well as the leeway for the solution
› Openness to unforeseen solution proposals
› Inclusion of all relevant disciplines and parties in the coordination process

Outline

For many reasons, it is advisable to have a clear structure of the texts of the competition brief and especially the task. The brief is a working document for many parties with different interests, who are involved in its creation and of the competition itself. Thus, the chapter structure, the findability of text modules and the accompanying illustrations are just as important as the clarity of the text wording itself.

When compiling the contents, it should be carefully considered how comprehensive and detailed they should be. On the one hand, it is desirable to have a summary in short concise statements, also because this ensures that all contents will be noticed by all participants. On the other hand, shortening in the form of summarizing may also mean omitting content, which can mean excluding specific topics and thus particular interest groups. Shortening can thus result in a lack of unambiguity. Especially since the competition brief often has a significance as a consensus document beyond the competition, it is advisable to often integrate content that is not relevant for the competition at first glance. As the size of the document and the complexity of the content increase, the structure of the brief becomes even more important.

In the case of extended competition briefs, it is therefore advisable to summarize the main content in an introductory chapter (= executive summary) as well as provide a detailed table of contents.

Binding specifications

Mandatory requirements should be clearly stated as such in the procedure rules of the competition brief if a violation of these requirements is to result in immediate disqualification. Since such a regulation has serious consequences, we recommend great caution in formulating such binding specifications. The necessary exclusion from further proceedings, which for formal reasons must consequently take place without the jury, usually represents an unnecessary hardship. Often it is advisable to allow special solutions and to point them out to the jury so that it can deal with them and to advise the sponsor about the effects on the further design.

In general, however, it is better to have an appropriate degree of openness in the terms of reference is generally a better approach, as otherwise creative solutions that are feasible in principle may have to be excluded for formal reasons. In addition, the discussion of such solutions may also lead to a re-evaluation of the specification "in the light of the unexpected proposal".

In this respect, binding specifications should be limited to formal aspects such as late submission or violation of anonymity.

10.4 Sustainability in competition

Almost every project strives for uniqueness of design as well as optimal functionality, respectful consideration of the context, economical use of resources and economic efficiency. The diversity and possibly contradictory nature of expectations with respect to these and other aspects of the solution is inherent in the nature of things, and not every demand can be satisfied to the same degree. The formulation of the challenge should begin with a consensus that recognizes the need to balance the many requirements – no single aspect alone can define the quality of a project.

"Sustainability" is not a separate issue here; rather, the above-mentioned holistic consideration of all criteria represents the description of the requirements for the sustainability of the project and the subsequent evaluation of the proposals.

The details of the requirements for the individual aspects (design quality, ecology, functionality, economy, etc.) are as diverse as the projects themselves are. Various systems are offered worldwide to assess and certify the sustainability of realized projects – more or less comprehensively and clearly: LEED, DGNB, BREEAM, BNB, HQE, Valideo, CASBEE, Green Star, BCA Green Mark, HK-BEAM, Verde, Green globes and many more. The evaluation of the projects takes place after their completion and is sometimes continues during the operational phase. In addition, many of the certification systems require that the project be documented with respect to sustainability criteria in the conception and design phase so as to receive a higher rating. As the understanding of the importance of sustainable design and construction is now well established, the question of future sustainability certification of projects submitted to competitions is becoming increasingly important.

Few systems have addressed the question of the extent to which the design proposals in the competition design phase already demonstrate the potential for special sustainability, which criteria are relevant in this phase, and which documents can be requested from the participants in this regard. The German SNAP tool is an attempt to describe and evaluate such aspects at an early stage (see also Chapter 12). Regardless of the evaluation system, it is important for the clarity of the task to formulate the requirements for the sustainability of the project at a central point in the text. The standard formulations often used here are not wrong in principle, but should be supplemented by concrete, project-related requirements - and it makes sense to explain these additionally in the participants' colloquium.

Prof. Marc Angélil
Architect, Los Angeles / Zurich

The One-Page Brief

❚❚ Making a case in support of the design brief itself, I would like to ask: How brief should a brief be? The short answer would be, the shorter the better. Over the last few decades, competition briefs or programs have tended to be more and more elaborate, in effect, drowning participants in a slew of unnecessary information. Case in point is a recent competition that included, in addition to a 100-page brief, more than 1,500 pages of attachments. Though we won the competition, I am arguing that the jury missed the opportunity to fully meet its obligations. For it goes without saying that the design of the design brief itself has since time immemorial been the most important first step in any competition. As a document that will be read and reread by designers, the brief establishes the grounds for any design propositions that will follow. Consider the brief as a proto-design exercise, for which no expense should be spared. Rather than being taken for granted and treated as an incontestable given, the brief cannot be outside the jury's purview. On the contrary! Herein lies the first task of any jury, namely, to scrutinize a brief's underlying assumptions, its vision, desires, contradictions, requirements, and fair or unfair practices, while contributing to its construction as a design project in and of itself, one – as the term implies – that must be 'brief' and hence to the point. Thus, the shorter the better, maybe even just a single page long.

Torben Østergaard
Architect, 3XN, Copenhagen

❚❚ As frequent competition participants, we know that access to solid and streamlined information is crucial for us to get an immediate understanding of the task ahead. When starting new competitions, we should be focused on our approach and not spend too much time understanding the structure of information in the brief. Two things stand out: the briefing needs to establish a hierarchy of information and should remain stable throughout the duration of the competition. Now imagine if there was a standard for all this … well, that's probably not going to happen, however, working with [phase eins]. it does appear they have a steady hand on the wheel.

Monika Jauch-Stolz
President of the Competition Commission SIA 142/143, Zurich

❚❚ The program should be as precise as possible. It is not the task of architects to solve political or social problems. An optimal comparability of the projects is only given with an accurate program. This in turn makes a significant contribution to the fact that the solutions are easily comparable and that the best project can be selected by a competent jury.

10 Competition materials

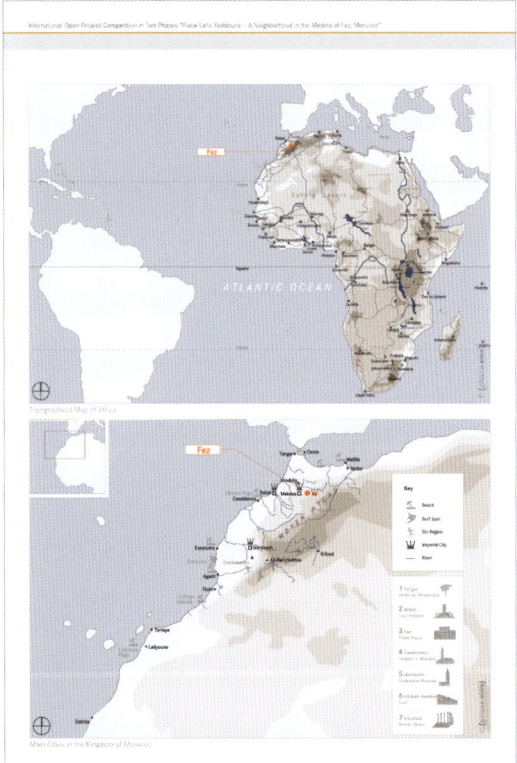

Excerpts from the competition brief for the "Revitalisation of the old town of Fez": illustrations for the introduction of the site

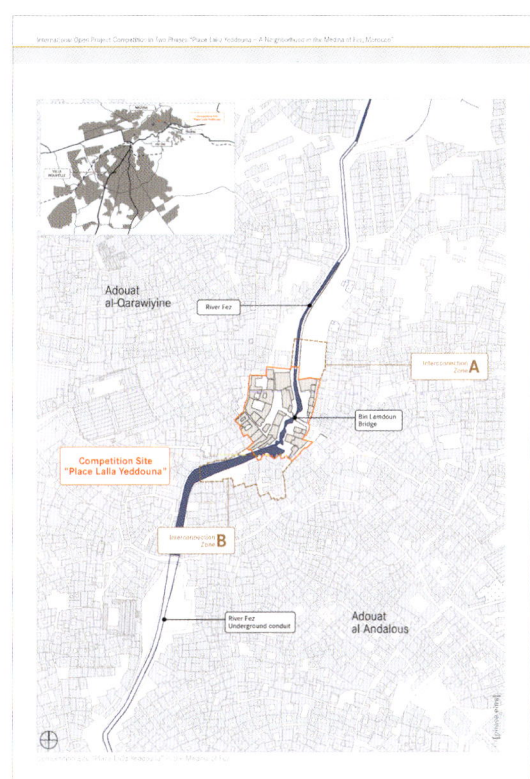

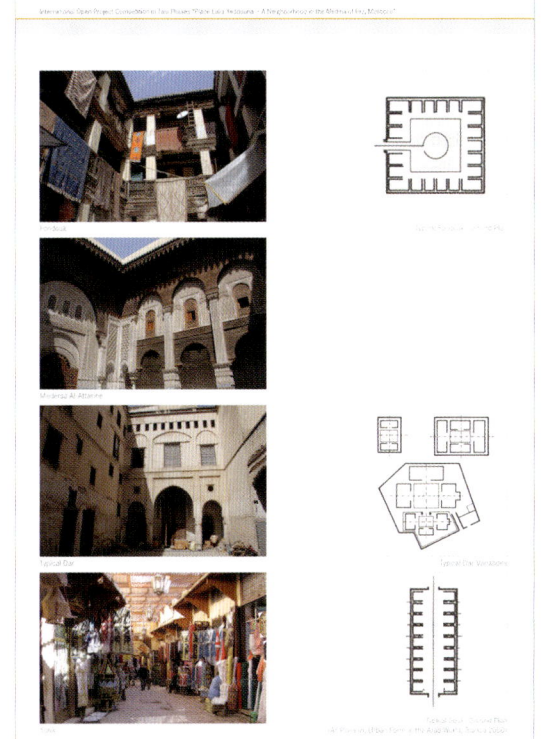

10 Competition materials

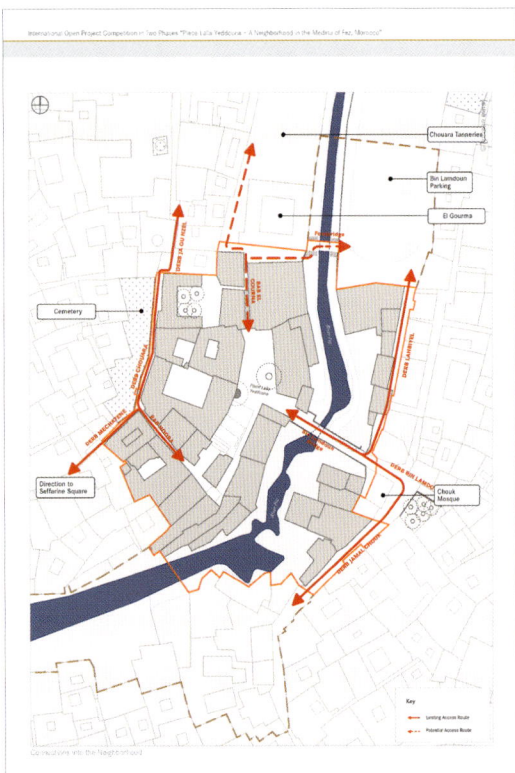
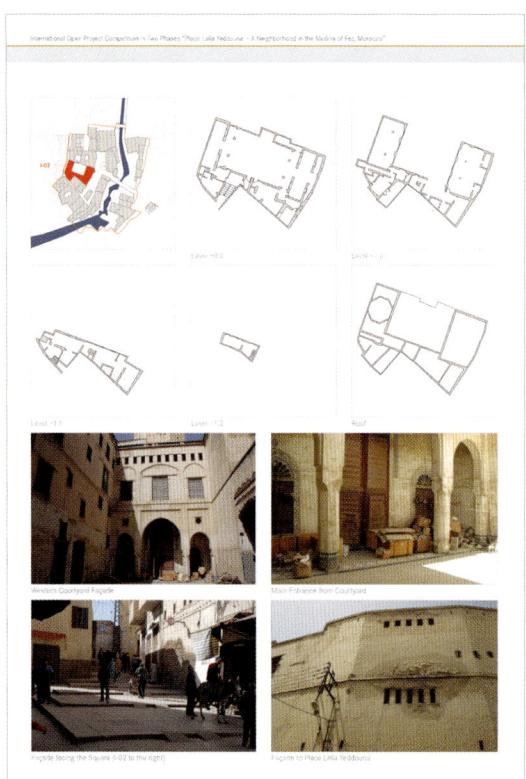

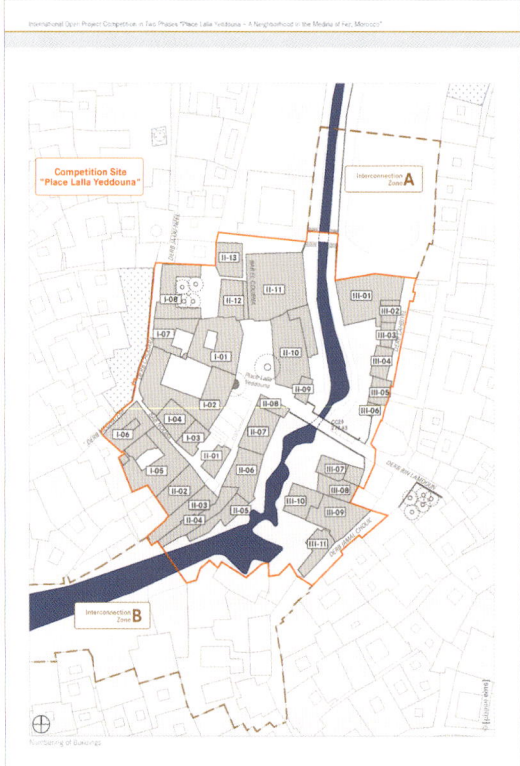

Excerpts from the competition brief for the "Revitalisation of the old town of Fez": Illustrations explaining the existing buildings

10 Competition materials

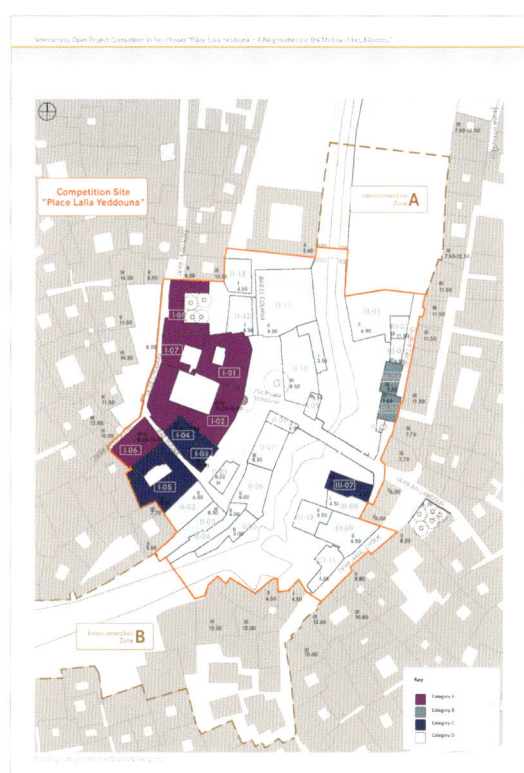
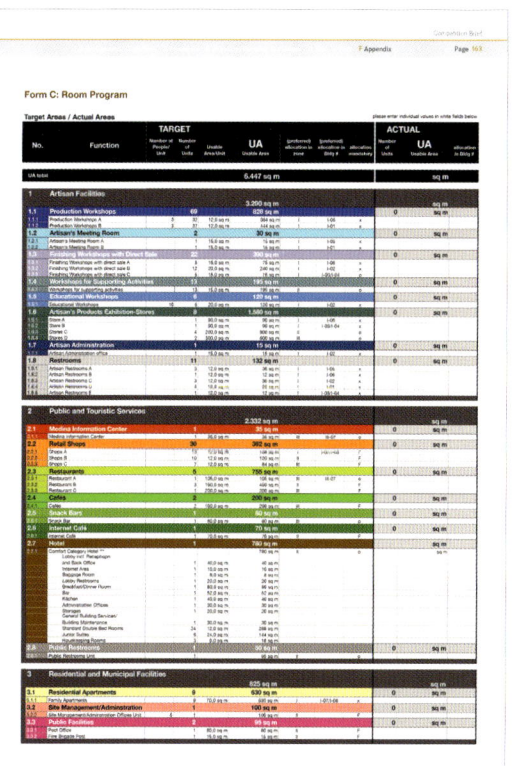
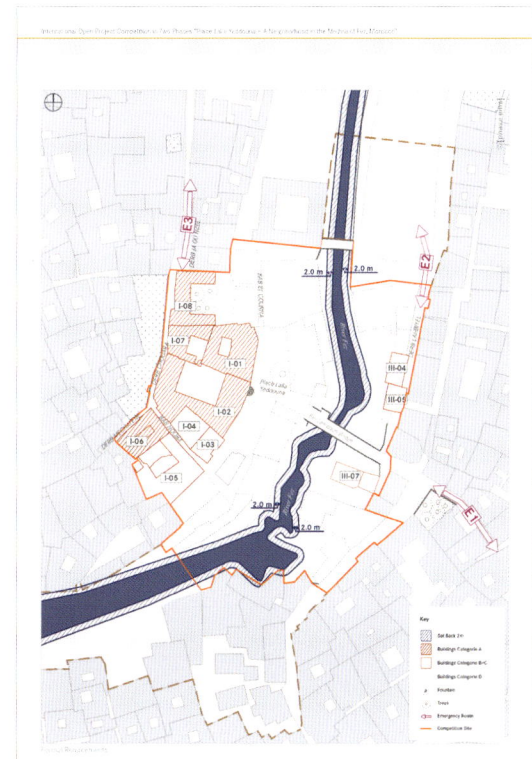
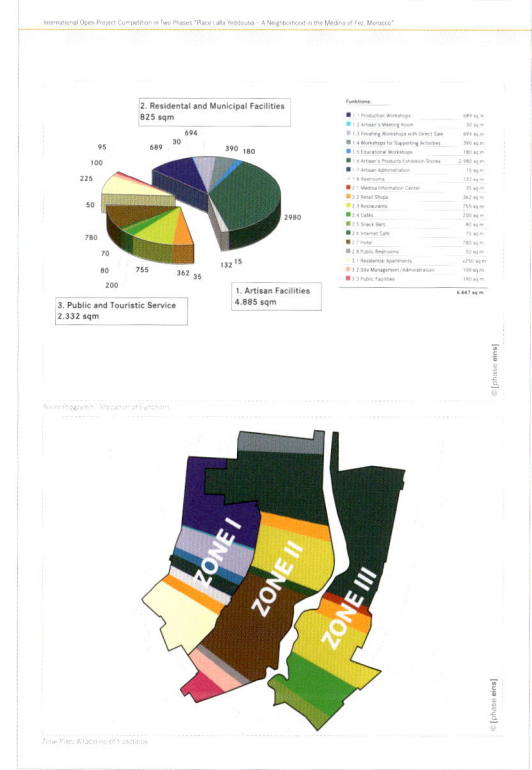

Excerpts from the competition brief for the "Revitalisation of the old town of Fez": Illustrations explaining the brief

10 Competition materials

10.5 Illustrations

Layout
The layout of the competition brochure should not be an end in itself. However, it should also not be underestimated that a competition brief is not just a sober, technical document, but a document that must be able to convey the sponsor's idea of the project. Depending on the project, the sponsor may have corporate identity specifications that must be considered, but above all they may have ideas that cannot be captured in text alone. Also, the complexity of the task in terms of use may have dimensions that cannot be described purely textually.
Beyond the actual text, the overall quality of the materials, the brilliance and expressiveness of illustrations, the atmospheres conveyed by illustrations, the appreciation for the process expressed by the care taken, in other words, the overall quality of the provided competition materials, is of great importance

Illustrations
Illustrations required depending on location and task:
› Map with location of site in a larger context
› Plan of the competition site with its surroundings
› Plans explaining the situation of traffic, greenery, topography, utility lines
› Historical plans and images of the site
› Images of the site (from different perspectives, possibly in different seasons)
› Aerial photos
› Images explaining the use
› Diagrams to explain functional relationships and processes
› Diagrams for the explanation of partial requirements of the task
› Spatial or utilization program in form of a table

Film
Creating a film, possibly a drone film, to show the site can be a valuable addition, especially if visiting the site would be too inconvenient for the design teams.

10.6 Plan Documents

Information plans
A set of plans (CAD, pdf) with all relevant information on the existing situation, usually divided into:
› Site plan (basic plan with all information on boundaries, existing buildings, roads and paths, vegetation, and topography)
› Views, sections, and floor plans of existing buildings on the competition site, which are to be considered during design
› Views of the buildings in the immediate vicinity
› Piping plan (technical infrastructure)
› If applicable, excerpts from master planning, zoning plans or comparable documents

Working plans
If desired, working plans (editable basic plans) can be used to define specifications for the required representations to support the comparability of the designs in the jury meeting. As a rule, these are working plans for the site plan and the first-floor plan where the scale, the north orientation and the section are defined. Other working plans can concern the specification of a certain view, a section, or the eye point for a 3-dimensional representation.

Left page: Excerpt from a drone film showing the competition area in the "Burchardplatz and Kontorhausviertel in Hamburg" competition, **Right page:** Information drawings from the competition "Wien Museum Neu" (top) and "Neues Wohnen in der Gartenstadt Falkenberg in Berlin" (bottom)

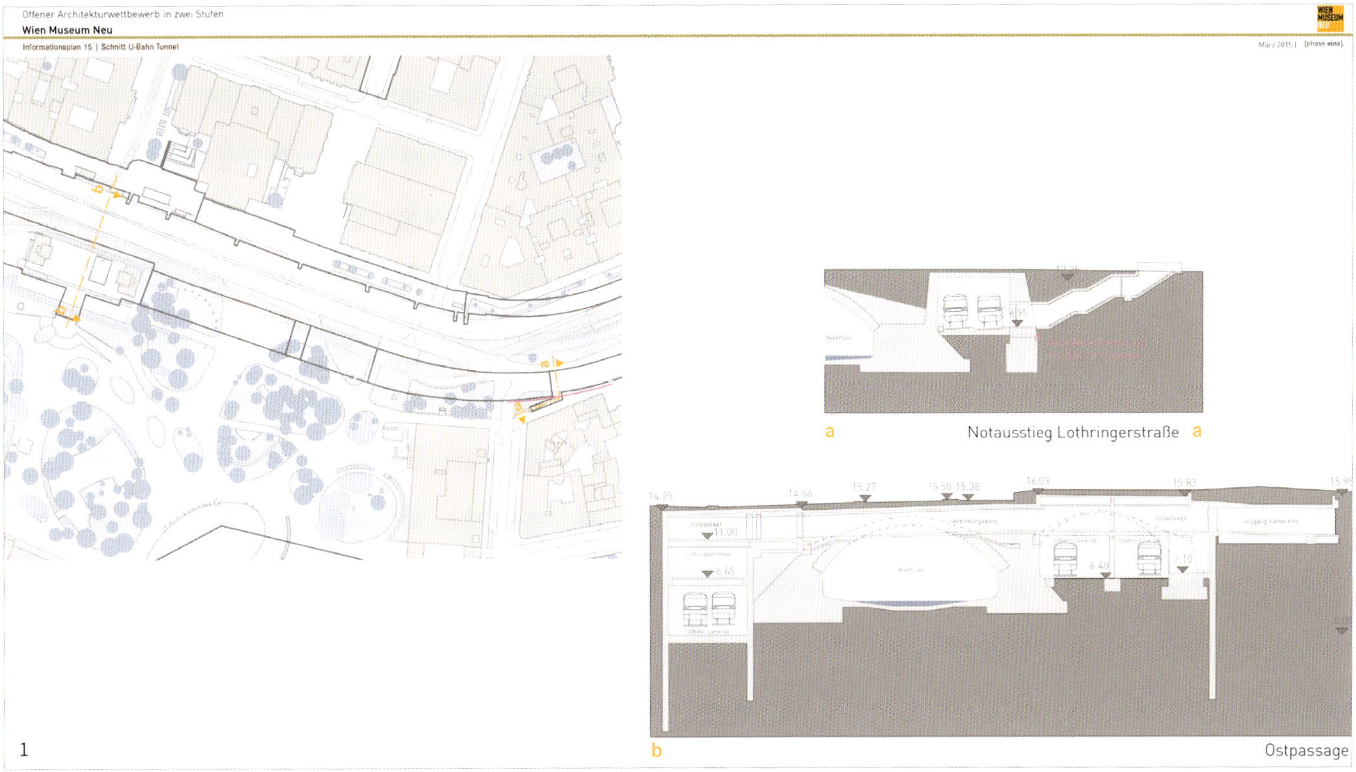

Offener Architekturwettbewerb in zwei Stufen
Wien Museum Neu
Informationsplan 15 | Schnitt U-Bahn Tunnel

Notausstieg Lothringerstraße

Ostpassage

1

Realisierungswettbewerb
Neues Wohnen in der Gartenstadt Falkenberg
Informationsplan 2 | Ansichten

A1 Ansicht Nord

A2 Gartenstadtweg
Straßenabwicklung West

A3 Gartenstadtweg
Straßenabwicklung Ost

2

10 Competition materials

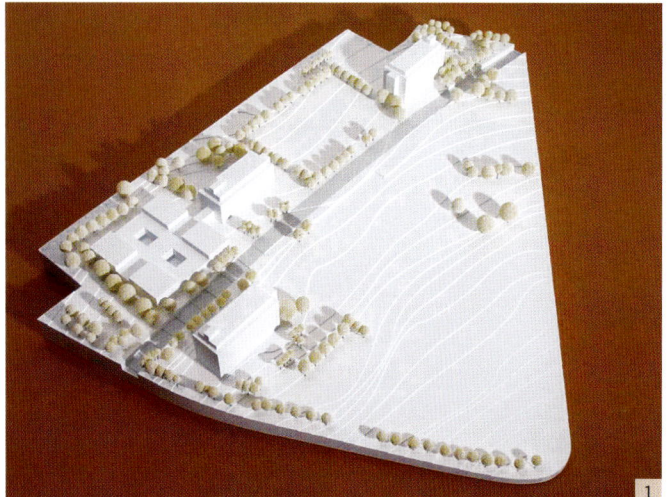

10.7 Model of the surroundings

Models on a suitable scale are an important instrument for presenting the design ideas in the competition – in architectural competitions usually on a scale of 1:500, if necessary, also 1:200, in urban design competitions are common models on a scale of 1:1,000 and 1:500. The models enable the jury to best evaluate the spatial impact of the designs. To include the spatial context in this evaluation, i.e., the built environment and the immediate surroundings of the site, it is customary to create a model of the surroundings. This is used to represent the topography and adjacent buildings; an opening is left in the model for the competition plot, into which the models submitted by the participants (inset models) are inserted to fit exactly. In addition to its function in the jury meeting, the area model with the inserted model of the winning design serves in communicating the project to the public, especially in the exhibition of the competition proposals or in the context of a press conference.

Working basics for model making

As a rule, model construction is carried out by a professional model-maker. However, the specifications for model building are developed while creating the information plans to ensure the compatibility of the information. The 3-D data of the environment model then created by the model maker on this basis can in turn be made available to the participants, so that on the one hand they can more easily create a working model of the area themselves and on the other hand their insert model can be produced to fit exactly.

Model size and cutting

The area model should at least represent all prominent elements of the immediate surroundings of the competition site. A larger section also allows the representation of more distant reference points. A larger model with side lengths of 1.2 m to 1.8 m has the added value that a larger number of people can group around the model both in the jury meeting and in later presentation situations. On the other hand, in addition to the higher production costs, the question of transport and storage must also be considered.

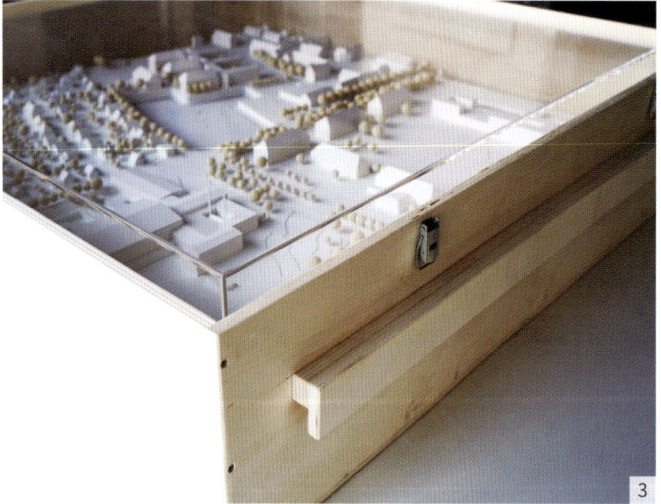

1: Insert plate, **2:** Repairs to damaged models, **3:** Shipping container for environment model, **4:** Jury inserting the model into the surroundings model in the "Volksbank Raiffeisenbank in Bargteheide" competition, **5:** Cover of the surroundings model in the "Siemensstadt 2.0" competition

Size of the opening for insert models

The cutout in the area model for the participants' insert models usually corresponds to the size of the competition site. However, depending on the situation, it is advisable to simplify the basic shape of this cutout to make it easier to insert and remove the models. Similarly, the insert plate should not end directly at the boundary of the competition area if it is possible to build up to this boundary. Increasing the size by 0.5 cm to 1.0 cm will avoid damaging the insert models at these edges.

The cutout in the surrounding model should be constructed so that the top edge of the raw inset plates provided to the participants is 1 or 2 mm below the top edge of the area model, allowing the participants to build their individual elevation.

Should the competition site have a more distinct topography, or should it be expected that participants propose significant excavations, this option must be taken into consideration when creating the area model by providing a corresponding depth in the area of the cutout.

Detail degree

Especially relevant is the correct conversion of the site plan into the third dimension – dimensions and location of plots and streets/roads as well as topography. A detailed representation of details of existing buildings is usually less relevant than the representation of reality by means of a reduction to the essential statements about building dimensions and roof forms. Only in the case of special buildings in the immediate vicinity of the competition area or prominent landmarks is a more precise representation desirable.

Construction

The area model initially rests on a solid frame that achieves the necessary stability through stiffening. On the one hand, the outer frame serves as decoration; on the other hand, a rail or upstand accommodates the covering hood. The base plate rests on the frame. For large models, dividing the model into segments is helpful for transport and storage. A mechanism for lifting the insert models is advisable for removal, as the sensitive insert models should not be used as a "handle".

Other items regarding model making include the production of a solid shipping box for the model of the surroundings, as well as the insert plates for the participants and potentially shipping boxes for these insert plates, if necessary.

Regula Lüscher
Architect, former Senate Building Director of Berlin

‖ The most important thing for me is the competition coordination to recognize the contradictions in content, triggered by conflicting interests of property owners, different administrative representatives, or users, and brings everyone together at one table to resolve them BEFORE the competition is launched. These should not be "delegated" to the participating offices.

Prof. Volker Staab
Architect, Berlin

‖ The best briefing documents for design competitions describe the task and the client's preferences as precisely as possible and at the same time contain as few exclusion criteria as possible. Such competitions enable the competitors to develop a solution from a new perspective that, in the best case, exceeds the expectations of the sponsor.

Heribert Fruhauf
Wien Museum

‖ What is important for me as a competition promoter: To organize the competition as purposefully as possible. Particularly with the complex framework conditions for the project "Wien Museum Neu" it was important to prepare this multitude of requirements as comprehensibly as possible to give the participating architects enough freedom of thought on the one hand and on the other hand to produce a result that in the end can be implemented. To achieve this, the competition brief (with all its appendices) and the jury (in its diversity) must work together perfectly. And in the end, as so often, it is the interpersonal component that decides between success and failure. It is important to establish a trusting relationship with all those involved in the project right from the start.

Manuel Scholl
Architect and Urban Planner, Zurich

‖ A good competition clearly formulates the intentions, prescribes only what is necessary, and leaves space for creative suggestions. If, in addition, good people come together, it is also fun.

VIII REDEVELOPMENT AND RECONSTRUCTION

The tasks for the renovation and conversion of existing buildings can relate to any of the typologies presented in the other chapters, even to urban design issues. In the context of the need to preserve the existing substance, or at least to ensure a careful use of resources, more and more projects are expected in the future that will require a design and planning approach to an existing building, in whole or in part. In the future, this will increasingly affect not only historic and/or listed buildings, but almost all regular buildings. The ability to organize design competitions for such tasks is not as well established as it is for new buildings, so the profession will be challenged in the coming years to communicate the many advantages of qualitatively renovated and, if necessary, converted, or repurposed buildings. On the one hand, the challenge for the competition organizers lies in providing the design documents, information on existing statics, materials, pollutants, and other, and in determining the extent to which certain components must be preserved or are available for disposal. On the other hand, the designs should be analyzed during the preliminary examination with regard to these questions, so as to present the jury with a precise basis for decisions making. Since the specifications for preservation often cannot be formulated conclusively in advance and complex considerations have to be made – especially in the case of listed buildings, ensembles and green spaces – multi-phase competitions and those with a cooperative dialogue are particularly suitable procedures.

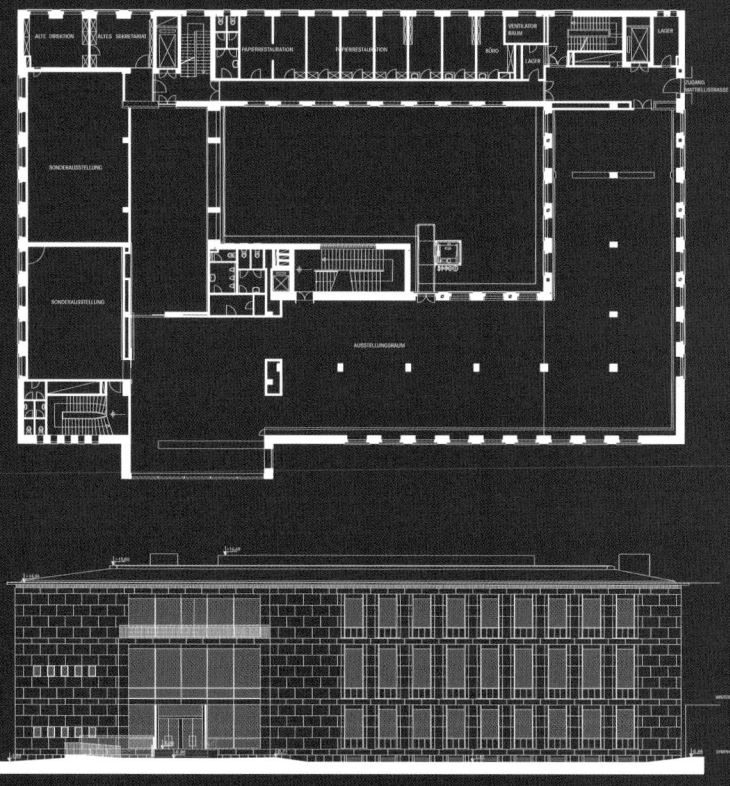

Diagram of the floor plans of the existing building of the Wien Museum explaining the listed individual components

Wien Museum Neu at Karlsplatz

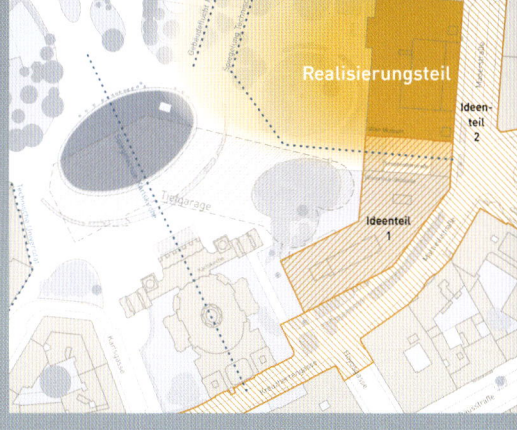

WIEN MUSEUM The changes in the cityscape, the emergence of critical historical studies and the rise of the middle class were the main reasons for the foundation of the Historical Museum of the City of Vienna. From 1888 onwards, city collections, including weapons from the armory, architectural remains (such as from St. Stephen's Cathedral and the demolished city walls), Franz Grillparzer's flat, coins, sculptures, etc., were exhibited in the mezzanine of the City Hall. Due to the lack of space there and the constant growth of the collection, the decision was made in 1900 to build a new building. The realization of the results of two competitions, on Karlsplatz and the former parade ground on Schmelz, failed due to debates in the community and the outbreak of the First World War. It was not until 1953, after another failed competition, that the new building was completed according to the design of Josef Hoffmann's student Oswald Haerdtl, who had been directly commissioned, and it became the first and, until the construction of the MuseumsQuartier, the only new museum building of the Second Republic.

However, the constriction of space caused problems from the very beginning, as large-format objects could not be exhibited and the collection continued to grow: it comprises around one million objects, from everyday objects to world-famous works of art. The renowned fashion collection alone numbers around 20,000 objects. Only a fraction of these can be exhibited.

TASK For the necessary extension to house the 11,000 sqm (net area) program, precise specifications were made by monument protection, urban planning, building regulations and functional requirements; nevertheless, no specifications were made for the spatial orientation of the extension.

PROCEDURE The diversity of possible solutions was correspondingly great in the open competition with 274 entries, whose evaluation by the jury was made possible by sufficient time and careful organization and preparation in the preliminary examination with respect for the commitment of the participants.

Location: Vienna, Austria **Client:** Wien Museum Projekt GmbH **Year:** 2014 – 2015 **Project size:** approx. 11,000 sqm UFA **Type of competition:** Architectural design competition in two stages **Participants:** Stage 1. 274, Stage 2. 14 **Competition budget:** EUR 154,000 (prizes and mentions; EUR 42,000; Compensation per participant stage 2: EUR 8,000

PRIZEWINNERS:
(01) **1st prize** winkler + ruck architekten, Klagenfurt am Woerthersee (A), Architekt Ferdinand Certov, Graz (A), Winkler Landschaftsarchitektur, Seeboden am Millstättersee (A); (02) **2nd prize** Kim Nalleweg Architekten GbR, Berlin (D), TDB Landschaftsarchitektur Thomanek Duquesnoy Boemans, Berlin (D); (03) **3rd prize** Ilg Santer Architekten, Zurich (CH), Hager Partner AG, Zurich (CH); (04) **Mention** Juri Troy Architects, Vienna (A), YEWO Landscapes e.U., Vienna (A); (05) **Mention** Fiechter & Salzmann Architekten GmbH, Zurich (CH), Andreas Geser Landschaftarchitekten, Zurich (CH); (06) **Mention** querkraft architekten zt gmbh, Vienna (A), Doris Haidvogl, Vienna (A)

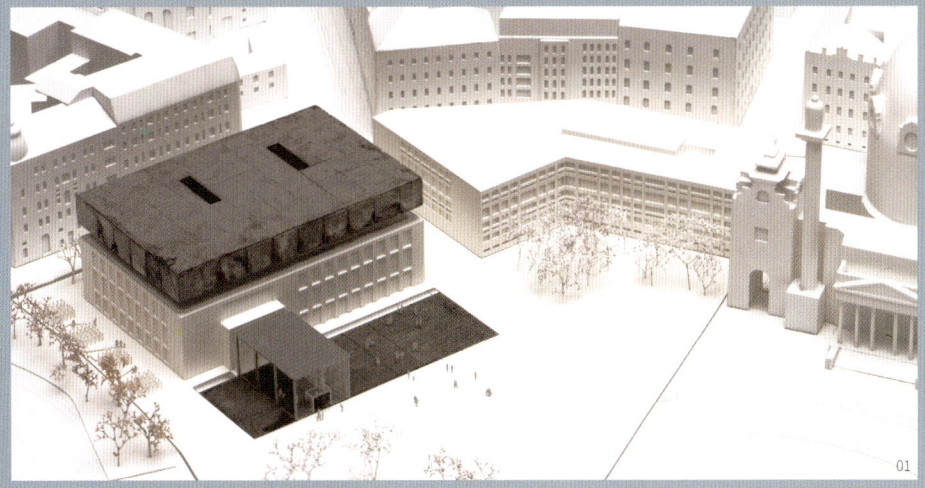

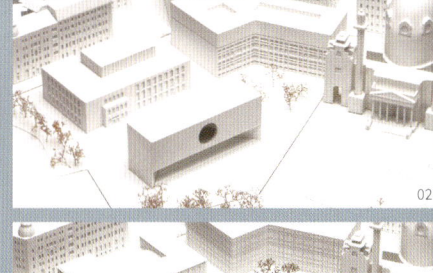

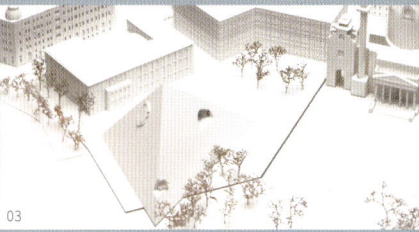

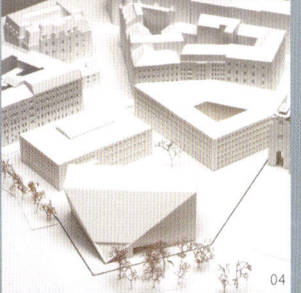

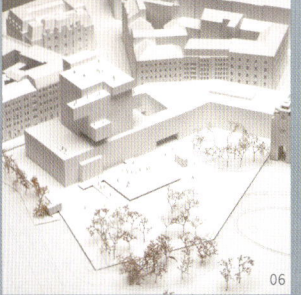

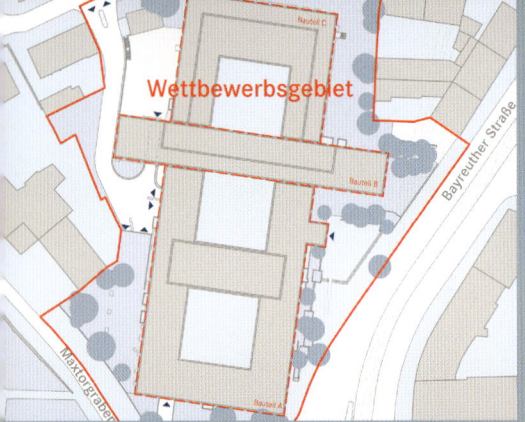

Location: Nuremberg, Germany **Client:** ELKB Nuremberg Bayreuther Straße 1 Vermögensverwaltungs GmbH & Co. KG **Year:** 2019 **Project size:** approx. 27,000 sqm UFA **Type of competition:** Design competition **Participants:** 12 **Competition budget:** EUR 420,000 (Prizes: EUR 90,000; Compensation: EUR 330,000)

PRIZEWINNERS:
(01) **1st prize** Carmody Groarke Ltd., London (UK), and Riehle + Assoziierte GmbH + Co. KG, Stuttgart (D), with Jonathan Cook Landscape Architects, London (UK); **2nd prize** Franz and Sue ZT GmbH and EGKK Landschaftsarchitektur, Vienna (A); **3rd prize** Bär, Stadelmann, Stöcker Architekten + Stadtplaner Part GmbB, Nuremberg (D), with club L94 Landschaftsarchitekten GmbH, Cologne (D); **Mention** Bruther, Paris (F), with Vogt Landschaftsarchitekten AG, Zurich (CH)

Reconstruction and New Building for Lutheran University of Applied Sciences, Nuremberg

EVANGELICAL LUTHERAN CHURCH IN BAVARIA (ELKB) The Bavarian state church has 2.3 million parishioners in 1,537 parishes and is Germany's third-largest state church by membership. In addition to the Protestant life in the parishes, there are ministries, regional associations, interest groups, initiatives, and Protestant associations. The spectrum is wide: from helping others to church music, work with children and young people, art, education, families, the environment, work with the elderly, and aid for people in foreign countries. Many institutions and services of the Bavarian regional church are located in Nuremberg and the surrounding area.

SITE AND THE PROJECT For the project, the ELKB acquired the building complex of the former Oberpostdirektion from 1972, an up to 9-story commercial and office building with 45,000 sqm GFA in a central location on the northeastern edge of Nuremberg's old town. The subject of the competition was its utilization and addition to the "Evangelical Campus Nuremberg", which includes educational institutions (Nuremberg Protestant University, vocational school or academies of the Rummelsberger Diakonie e. V., Christliches Jugenddorfwerk, Johanniter-Unfall-Hilfe e. V); spaces for offices and administration, common areas (e.g., hostel, conference center), day care center and nursery as well as culinary offers for the users of the building.

IDEA The architecture should embody the key values, goals, and self-image of the Protestant community both externally and internally and strengthen the sense of "we" amongst all users of the future campus. In particular, the fact that approximately 2,000 primarily younger people will learn and work in this building should be reflected in the building's design.

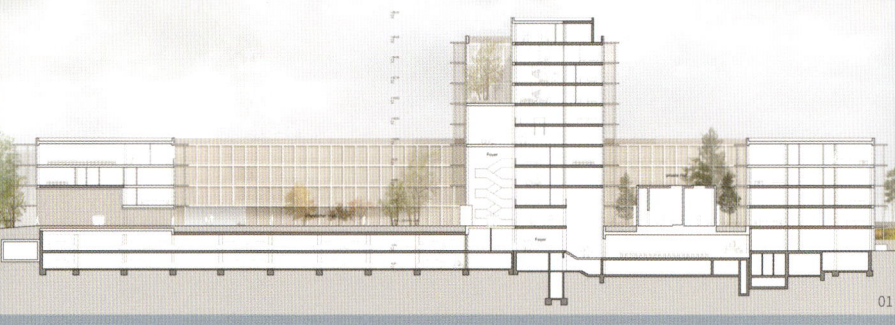

Mönchengladbach City Hall

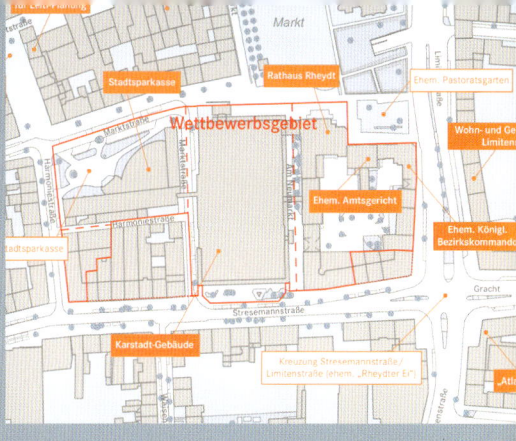

MÖNCHENGLADBACH The city of Mönchengladbach is located west of the Rhine River in the administrative district of Düsseldorf and is part of the Rhine-Ruhr region. Founded in the 10th century, the city developed during the industrialization of the 19th century into one of the most important locations of the textile industry and the textile-oriented machine industry. Since World War II, a comprehensive structural change has taken place, characterized by the decline of the textile industry and the rise of a diversified economic structure.

TASK One of the central construction projects of the current urban development strategy is the "City Hall of the Future mg+". The aim of the project is to consolidate most the City Council's administrative offices, currently scattered over 26 locations, in one central location, thus enabling synergies, optimized administrative processes, better citizen service and contemporary, attractive workplaces. The project is located at the main square "Markt" in the Rheydt district. In three adjoining city blocks, the historic city hall and several adjacent buildings are to be organized into a new complex through conversion and new construction. In addition to workplaces for the approximately 1,900 employees of 20 administrative departments, the complex is to include a meeting place for the city council, a branch of the Stadtsparkasse, a district library, and retail space for a Karstadt department store. The project is also expected to revitalize Rheydt's city center.

PROCEDURE A two-stage competition was held to select the best project and architectural design team, followed by a negotiation process with the prizewinners. At the time of publication of this book, the project was suspended after the winner had completed the services up to the design planning.

Location: Mönchengladbach, Germany **Client:** City of Mönchengladbach **Year:** 2019 **Project size:** approx. 30,000 sqm UA **Type of competition:** Restricted design competition in two stages **Participants:** Stage 1: 16; Stage 2: 8 **Competition budget:** EUR 625,000 EUR (prizes: EUR 210,000; compensation stage 1: EUR 240,000; compensation stage 2: EUR 175,000)

PRIZEWINNERS:
(01) **1st prize** sop architekten, Dusseldorf (D); (02) **2nd prize** HPP Architekten, Dusseldorf (D); (03) **3rd prize** RKW Architektur + Rhode Kellermann Wawrowsky, Dusseldorf (D); (04) **4th prize** Schmidt Hammer Lassen Architects, Copenhagen (DK)

New Art Archive, Beeskow

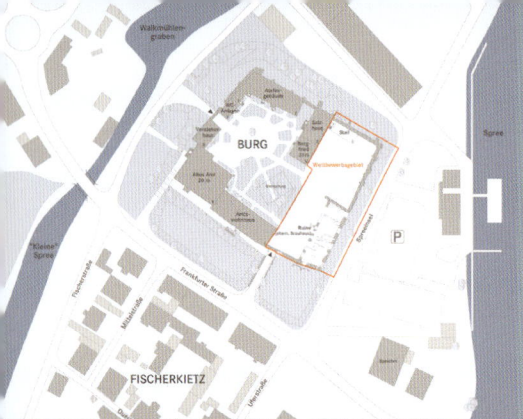

Location: Beeskow, Germany **Client:** City of Beeskow in collaboration with the Oder-Spree administrative district **Year:** 2009 – 2010 **Project size:** 3,000 sqm UFA **Type of competition:** Project competition preceded by an open application procedure **Participants:** 15 **Competition budget:** EUR 27,000 (prizes: EUR 22,000; honorable mentions: EUR 5,000)

PRIZEWINNERS:
(01) **1st prize** Max Dudler Architekten, Berlin (D); **2nd prize** Marte.Marte Architekten, Weiler (D); **3rd prize** CO A. Architektenkooperative, Berlin (D); **4th prize** Staab Architekten, Berlin (D); **Honorable mention** Peter Kulka Architektur, Dresden (D); **Honorable mention** Stephan Braunfels Architekten, Berlin (D); **Honorable mention** Nieto Sobejano Arquitectos, Madrid (E); **Honorable mention** Kraaijvanger . Urbis, Rotterdam (NL)

BEESKOW ART ARCHIVE The purpose of the project is to merge the Beeskow Art Archive with the Artothek holdings of the Soziale Künstlerförderung Berlin (Social Advancement of Artists Berlin) and to permanently secure both collections. The Beeskow Art Archive is a documentation center of the visual arts from the GDR. The 23,000 largely commissioned artworks from the estates of GDR political parties and mass organizations were moved to the public domain after dissolution of the GDR. The approximately 14,000 works of art in Artothek's holdings document the results of government arts funding in West Berlin and in reunified Berlin from 1950 to 2003. Together the collections document Germany's cultural-historical development after 1945. The guiding principle was to keep the new Beeskow Art Archive alive as a learning and research center for art history. Furthermore, the project should contribute to the cultural landscape and become a tourist attraction in the Oder-Spree district.

BEESKOW CASTLE The competition area is located in the eastern section of the listed medieval Beeskow castle. The site is situated between two arms of the Spree River on the edge of Beeskow's historic town center in eastern Brandenburg. The castle originates from the 13th century and today serves as the district educational and cultural center and music school. The regional museum, a medieval cellar and other exhibition spaces are housed in the center. The new building is to integrate remnants of the former brewery and the eastern castle wall.

COMPETITION TASK Over 3,000 sqm UFA space was to be created for the archives, adjoining rooms and a small public exhibition area meant to complement the other programs offered at the castle. The new areas should also support development of a communication center for the public about art and science. In addition, the task involved designing a proposal that has a respectful relationship towards the built context and uses that context as a reference for materiality and color while still emphasizing an independent architectural accent.

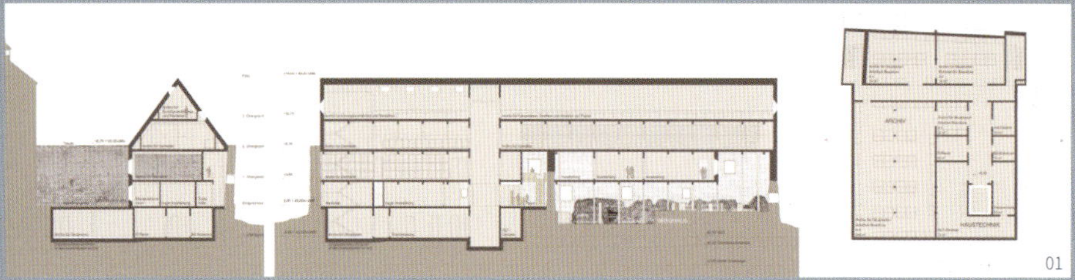

Revitalizing the Old City of Fez, Place Lalla Yeddouna

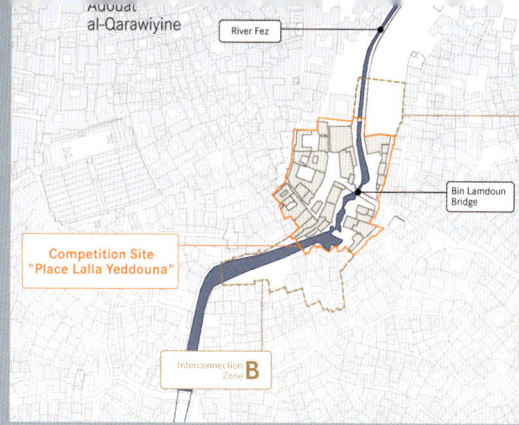

THE ARTISAN AND FEZ MEDINA PROJECT
The joint project organized by the Moroccan government and the US-funded Millennium Challenge Corporation (MCC) is meant to revitalize five locations that are particularly important to tourism and the local economy in the old town (medina) of Fez. The promotion of economic growth should reduce poverty among the medina's residents and improve the working and environmental conditions in the area. In sum, the medina should become established as a sustainable place to live and work. The project's five locations (Lalla Yeddouna Square and the Chemmayine, Sbitriyine, Staouniyine and El Barka fonduks) and the structural maintenance of their cultural and architectural treasures are thereby indirectly secured.

LALLA YEDDOUNA SQUARE
The 7,400-sqm competition area is located in the medina of Fez, the third largest city in Morocco and the oldest of the country's four imperial cities. As an archetypal oriental city, the medina has been on the list of UNESCO World Heritage Sites since 1981. The mosaic of small, sand-colored houses and maze of narrow streets has perpetuated a traditional way of life within its walls as a living museum. The neighborhood surrounding Lalla Yeddouna Square is close to the 8th century Andalusian quarter, which is the oldest part of the medina, and is known for its traditional artisanry, tanneries and brass and copper smithies. Appropriately enough the quarter is representative for the project because of the interlinkage of working and living in the medina.

COMPETITION TASK
An urban-architectural strategy was sought to strengthen in an exemplary manner the socio-economic structure of the neighborhood around the square and along a section of the river. Without imposing concrete parameters about areas and density, the design concept should present a model of how valuable substance can be restored, maintained and extended with new small-scale buildings in a very confined area creating a lasting vital structure.

Location: Fez, Morocco **Client:** The Government of the Kingdom of Morocco **Year:** 2010 – 2011 **Project size:** approx. 7,400 sqm **Type of competition:** Open two-phase project competition **Participants:** Stage 1: 176; Stage 2: 8 **Competition budget:** USD 440,000 (prizes Stage 2: USD 120,000; fees per participant Stage 2: USD 40,000)

PRIZEWINNERS:
(01) **1st prize** mossessian & partners architecture, London (UK), with Yassir Khalil Studio, Casablanca (MA); **2nd prize** Studio Ferretti-Marcelloni, Rome (I), with Bahia Nouh, Fez (MA); **3rd prize** Moxon Architects, London (UK), with Aime Kakon, Casablanca (MA)

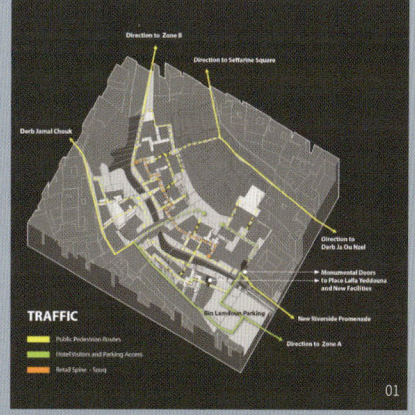

Revitalizing the Old City Fez, Place Lalla Yeddouna

11 EVENTS

11.1 Event formats

An integral part of each competition are the various events. On the one hand, these are project meetings with the sponsor and, for example, the approval authorities to discuss and concretize various partial aspects before, and sometimes during, the competition. These meetings concern the usual project discussions and do not normally require any further organization apart from agendas, submittals, and minutes. The main design competition events are, however, different. These have very specific formats, some with very special requirements, and therefore need early and extensive planning:

Jury colloquium
- **Persons participating:** all members of the jury, including experts, i.e., approx. 20 up to 80 persons.
- **Online meeting or participation:** for selected individuals, in exceptional cases for the whole jury panel.
- **Aim:** to discuss the competition brief before its finalization at the end of the preparatory phase of the competition (see Chapters 6 and 9.2).
- **Duration:** 3–5 hours for the meeting plus time for visiting the competition site.
- **Procedure:** following the joint visit to the competition site and welcome greeting, all components of the competition brief are discussed based on a draft text sent out in advance (competition brief draft). Moderation and documentation are undertaken by the competition organizer.
- **Seating arrangement:** the persons involved, at least the voting members of the jury, should sit "together at the table" and be able to see each other. Experts and guests may also be seated "in the second row", if necessary.

Participants' Colloquia
- **Persons participating:** all offices participating in the competition are invited, along to sufficient jury representatives and key experts. In the case of invited and restricted competitions, it is generally possible to count on 1 to 2 persons per participating office. In the case of open competitions, it is advisable to conduct an open survey among the unknown offices to determine their attendance at the colloquium. The number of participants can range from 40 to 200.
- **Online meeting or participation:** for selected individuals, if necessary, or in exceptional cases, for the whole jury panel during the entire meeting.
- **Aim:** to discuss and clarify participants' questions, sometimes including project-related presentations to explain the framework conditions and strategic goals of the competition as well as the task (see Chapter 9.4).
- **Duration:** 3–5 hours for the meeting plus time for visiting the competition site.
- **Procedure:** following the joint visit to the competition site and welcome greeting, all components of the competition brief are discussed based on a draft text sent out in advance (competition brief draft). Moderation and writing of the minutes are undertaken by the competition organizer.
- Seating arrangement: sponsor's representatives and jury members should sit together on a podium with the moderating person of the competition organization.

Jury meetings
- **Persons participating:** all members of the jury, including the experts and the preliminary examiners, i.e., approx. 20 up to 80 persons.
- **Online meeting or participation:** not recommended.
- **Aim:** to decide on the competition result, in the case of two-phase competitions in Stage 1 as an interim result, and also formulate recommendations for further work or forther course in the project.
- **Duration:** usually an extensive one-day meeting, if necessary "open end", often one and a half days with a total of 12-15 hours meeting duration, if necessary up to 3 days (see Chapter 6.3).
- **Procedure:** the meeting usually takes place first at a meeting table and then in front of the plans and models. The exact procedure depends on the number of projects as well as the methodology for presenting the projects. Basically, two methods are recommended: presentation of the plans in front of the sitting panel, i.e., the plans are brought in front of the jury panel or projected, or the jury panel moves along the boards through the exhibition of the plans ("tour"), for more details see Chapter 13.
- **Seating arrangement:** The persons involved, at least the voting members of the jury, should sit "together at the table" and be able to see each other. Experts and guests may also be seated "in the second row", if necessary.

Exhibition
- **Number of persons:** depending on the importance of the project, the exhibition of a competition may attract very few or thousands of guests. Here, a valid assessment should be made in advance so as to plan the exhibition accordingly in terms of duration, premises, and information material.
- **Online presence:** an online exhibition is advisable in parallel.
- **Aim:** to inform the competition participants about the result and inform the public, especially the expert public, about the project and the result of the competition (see Chapter 14).
- **Duration:** usually 10–14 days with locally usual opening hours (see Chapter 6.3), possibly shorter if an online exhibition is also held.
- **Procedure:** at the beginning, there may be an opening event and/or press conference.

Jury meetings: **1:** Parliamentary Precinct Redevelopment Ottawa, **2:** BMW FIZ Future in Munich and **3:** Museum of the Maidan Revolution in Kyiv

---

Shigeru Ban
Architect, Tokyo

" In my view, the key to a successful competition is to have a kick-off meeting on site, and the brief should present a clear vision and objectives, but without too many detailed requirements. It is also important to disclose the list of jury members as well as the competition report when announcing the result. This point is still missed by many competitions. Furthermore, I believe that competitions should keep their doors open to young architects without a significant track record. I have the impression that the competitions organized by [phase eins]. are well balanced in many of these respects.

10 Events

11.2 Venues

Finding and reserving/renting suitable venue should not be underestimated when organizing a competition. Colloquia do not have complex meeting space requirements but are held at short notice after the start of the process, so timely booking can be an issue. Due to the required size of the premises for the meeting(s) of the jury and their technical equipment, the supply of suitable premises is often limited, so that here, too, evaluating the suitability and reserving suitable rooms should be carried out early on as part of the preparation. The following requirements must also be met for the jury meetings:

› **Size:** on the one hand, sufficient space is needed for the meeting table, which ideally sit all members of the jury. On the other hand, space is needed for the exhibition of the projects. This should be spatially related to the meeting room but does not necessarily have to be housed together in one room. However, floor changes are not advisable. There should be adequate space in front of the plans and models on display for the jury panel, especially if the panel's discussions are to take place in front of the plans and the projects are not to be moved in front of the panel seated at the meeting table.
› **Side rooms and storage:** space should be provided for, if necessary confidential, discussions during breaks and for the storage of packaging material for the models, etc.
› **Flooring:** if the plans are presented on rollable boards, threshold-free rooms with smooth floor coverings are of advantage.
› **Acoustics, room quality, and safety:** room acoustics, as well as appropriate temperature control and air exchange, should be considered in the selection of space. Since the meetings are confidential, it must be possible to ensure that unauthorized persons cannot enter the room or see in from outside.

11.3 Furnishing

All events in a competition require concentrated work by all participating members, so it makes sense to plan every detail to support good visibility, acoustics, air quality, seating comfort, and efficient operations:

› **Seating arrangement:** not only ensure they that those with decision-making authority are given central seats, but also, for example, mixed seating arrangements for members of a heterogeneous panel support interaction among participants during the meeting. It is important that all participants have the best possible view of the plans and models, but also of the other members of the panel.
› **Furniture:** to reduce fatigue during possibly long sessions, comfortable chairs are advantageous, as is planning the sequence of the jury session to allow sitting for long periods of the session. At the very least, the members of the jury should be provided with tables for meeting materials, name tags, notepads, and beverages.
› **Display of the projects to the jury:** All projects should be displayed in a clearly visible and well-lit manner so that they can be included in the discussions at any time. In a central position, space should be provided for an "arena" in which the model of the surroundings is positioned, and, in addition, one or more projects find space to allow the discussions to take place there, standing in front of the plans and the model.

If a press conference and/or exhibition opening is planned immediately after the jury meeting, this must be considered when planning the furnishings.

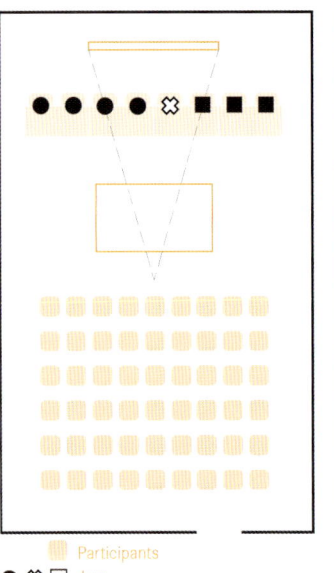
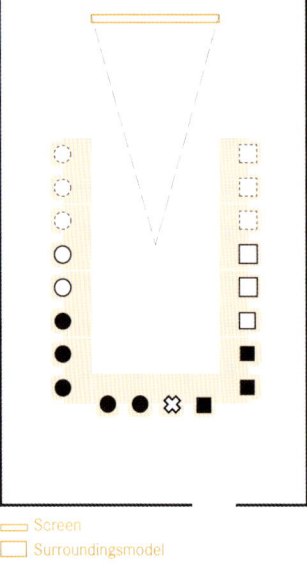
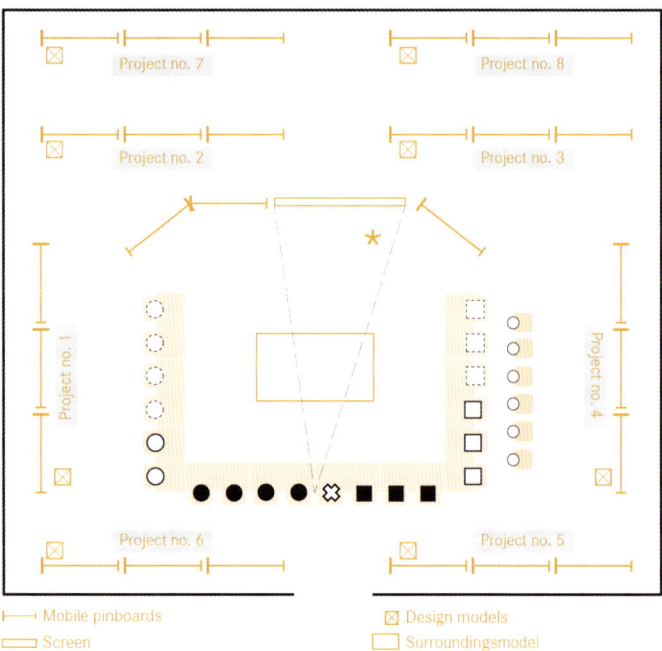

Typical seating arrangements for colloquia and jury meetings

11.4 Event planning

The success of any event depends also on the "invisible" details, the relevance of which is often not recognized until they have been adequately addressed:

› Meeting documents
› Table and name tags
› Paper, pens
› Lighting, sound, and presentation equipment
› Catering
› Translation services
› Security

Event organisation: **1:** Meeting table "BMW FIZ Future in Munich", **2:** Translator "Babyn Yar Holocaust Memorial Center in Kiyv", **3:** Seating arrangement for the participants' colloquium "Wien Museum Neu", **4:** Event technology "Parliamentary Precinct Redevelopment Ottawa"

IX HEALTH AND RESEARCH BUILDINGS

The projects of this use typology are strongly characterized by their purpose and are among the most complex projects in terms of costs and approval processes. The requirements for functionality, hygiene, accessibility, and safety have the highest priority and must be precisely described in the competition brief, and carefully evaluated in the preliminary examination to ensure that the concepts structurally meet the various requirements. The users are usually already known and should be closely involved in the procedure, both in the preparation of the content and in the selection process. They can identify the very specific requirements with a high degree of competence. The competition organizer structures and controls this process to achieve the right degree of precision in the formulation of requirements and openness to further input from the designers. Questions of load-bearing capacity and special requirements for the introduction of new equipment, and ventilation requirements, must already be included in the competition. In addition to these technical dimensions, it is important to remember that these buildings are also workplaces. They must provide space for communication among employees and be attractive to highly paid medical, research, and scientific professionals. In the case of healthcare buildings, the "human factor" must be considered in a special way, a dimension that must be included in the concept phase of the competition, regardless of all the technical constraints mentioned above.

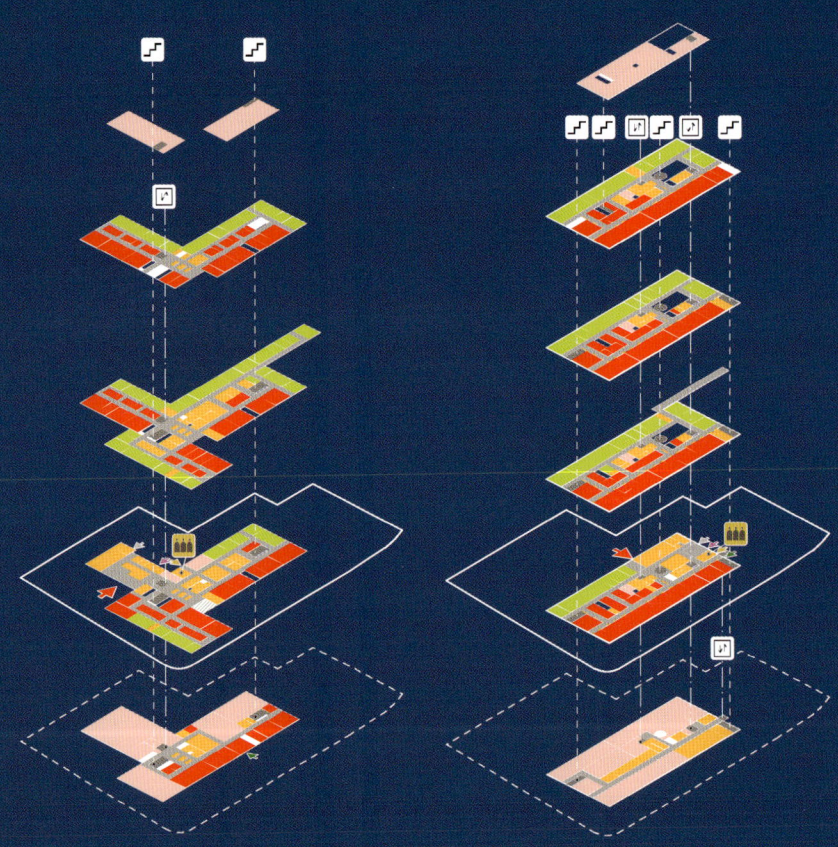

Analysis graphics of the preliminary examination in the competition "BiologieCampus, Forschungszentrum Jülich" to explain the distribution of functions, in particular the spatial relationship of laboratories to offices

University Hospital Pediatric Clinic and Clinic for Nuclear Medicine, Essen

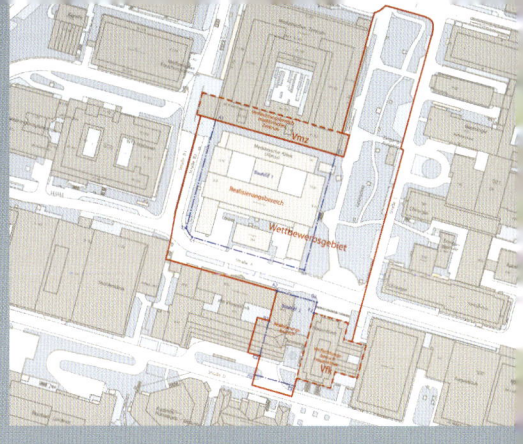

ESSEN UNIVERSITY HOSPITAL Essen University Hospital (UKE) is a university maximum-care provider and pacesetter in cutting-edge medicine in the metropolitan Ruhr region. At the UKE, 150,00 outpatients and 50,000 inpatients are treated per year. To a great extent the specialist departments are strewn throughout individual buildings over the campus resulting in functional and organizational disadvantages. Internal strategic planning in 2000 and 2010 foresees a structurally and functionally centralized campus, the heart of which is the new Medizinisches Zentrum (MZ) constructed in 2011 as part of the first planning phase. The MZ is to be complemented by a new building for pediatric medicine and a clinic for nuclear medicine.

COMPETITION SITE The new building will be centrally situated on the campus along the main north-south axis, a pedestrian access route. It abuts directly onto the new Medizinisches Zentrum. Some of the floor area is to be housed within the existing pediatric clinic and women's health clinic on the other side of an internal road. Overall, the site is characterized by the striking hillside topography and high building density and is dominated by the very technical and functional appearance of many buildings.

COMPETITION TASK The Pediatric Clinic and Clinic for Nuclear Medicine with Radiochemistry is to be provided with 11,500 sqm UFA. The building should fulfill all the requirements of modern clinic management with respect to communication, education and research. In addition, the design of the new building and the green axis on the western and southern side of the site is expected to lend order and provide orientation on campus. The complexity of housing pediatric and nuclear medicine in the same building is further increased by requirements of providing connections to bed tunnels and other departments in neighboring buildings, maintenance of hospital operations during construction and a nearby helicopter landing pad.

Location: Essen, Germany **Client:** Essen University Hospital **Year:** 2013 – 2014 **Project size:** approx. 11,500 sqm UFA **Type of competition:** Two-phase design competition preceded by an open application procedure **Participants:** Stage 1: 16; Stage 2: 6 **Competition budget:** EUR 340,000 (prizes Stage 2: EUR 156,000; fees per participant Stage 1: EUR 7,000; Stage 2: EUR 12,000)

PRIZEWINNERS:
(01) **1st prize** Heinle, Wischer Gesellschaft für Generalplanung, Berlin (D); **2nd prize** Ludes Generalplaner, Berlin (D); **3rd prize** Nickl & Partner Architekten, Munich (D); **4th prize** Brunet Saunier Architecture, Paris (F), with Kemper Steiner & Partner Architekten + Stadtplaner, Bochum (D)

01

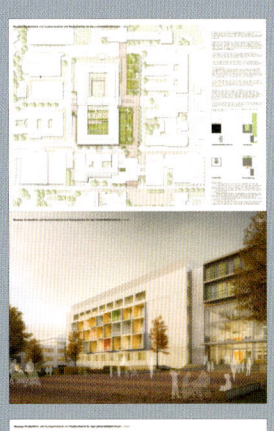

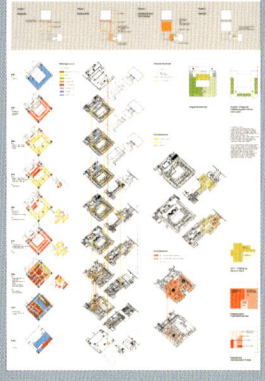
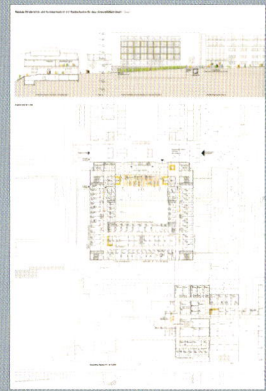
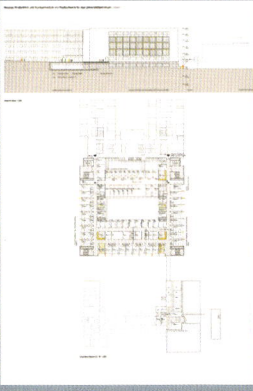
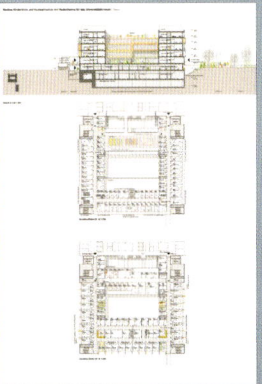
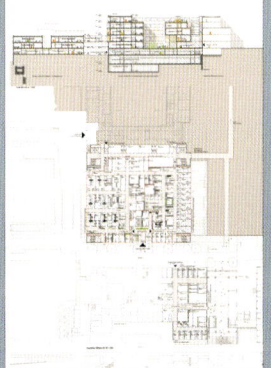
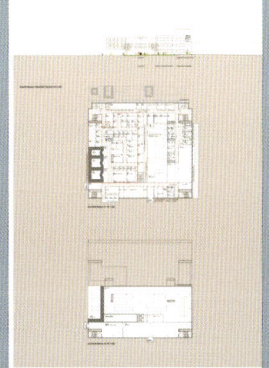
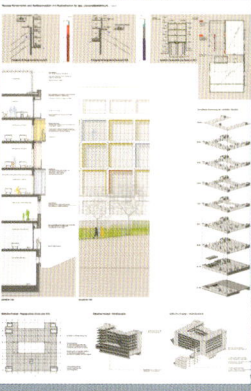

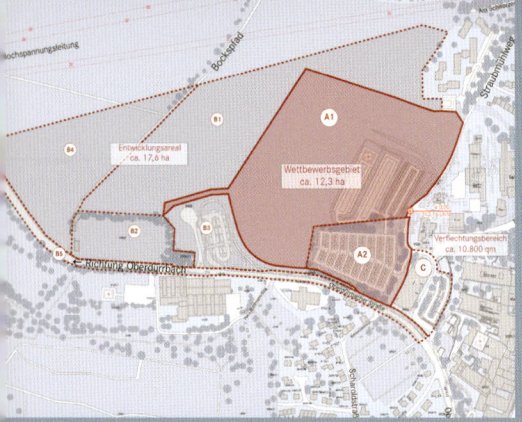

Location: Würzburg, Germany **Client:** The State of Bavaria **Year:** 2021
Project size: approx. 12 ha competition site, approx. 70,000 sqm UFA
Type of competition: Design competition in two stages **Participants:** Stage 1: 15; Stage 2: 7 **Competition budget:** EUR 2,220,000 (prizes: EUR 1,145,000; Compensation per participant Stage 1: EUR 25,000; Compensation per participant Stage 2: EUR 100,000)

University Hospital Würzburg, Head Clinic and Women & Children's Center

UNIVERSITY HOSPITAL WÜRZBURG (UKW) Together with the medical faculty of the Julius Maximilians University of Würzburg (JMU), the UKW is responsible for the "University Medicine Würzburg". It was founded at the end of the 16th century as a result of the affiliation between the Medical Faculty and the Juliusspital Hospital, making it one of the oldest university hospitals in Germany. In 1850, the first children's clinic of a university hospital in the world was opened at the UKW. The UKW is a full-service hospital and has an important care function for the region and beyond. Every year, approximately 260,000 outpatients and 73,000 full and partial inpatients are treated in the hospital's approximately 1,500 planned beds. The UKW comprises 19 clinics and three clinical institutes. The UKW employs about 6,800 people. 2,500 medical students are enrolled at the UKW and JMU.

NORTH EXPANSION In order to meet the significant space requirements of the UKW and to permanently satisfy the demand for cutting-edge medicine and research at the highest level, a comprehensive expansion of the historically grown clinic campus on the eastern slope of the main riverbank on a 27-ha site north of the existing location was decided, which is to be implemented in several construction phases.

COMPETITION TASK As a first building step, the construction of the head clinics and the center for women, mothers, and children, as well as the necessary infrastructure measures including the construction of an energy center are planned on an area of approx. 12.2 ha in two construction phases. A medium-term planned supply/administration center (VVZ) was an integral part of the task. It was to be shown that the structure would be excellent in terms of urban development and climate-sensitive, that it would fit into the local and countryside character and that it would create an overall positive new image. The aim is to erect future-oriented new buildings which, in an innovative and at the same time economical manner, optimally provide space for the requirements of the most modern hospital operations, for communication, teaching and research.

01

01

PRIZEWINNERS:
(01) **1st prize** Hascher Jehle Objektplanung GmbH, Berlin (D), Architektengruppe Schweitzer GmbH, Brunswick (D), wh-p GmbH Beratende Ingenieure, Stuttgart (D), Planungsbüro Waidhas GmbH, Chemnitz (D), ibb Burrer & Deuring Ingenieurbüro GmbH, Leipzig (D), Gänßle + Hehr Landschaftsarchitekten PartGmbB, Esslingen (D); **2nd prize** gmp International GmbH, Aachen (D), Kempen Krause Ingenieure GmbH, Aachen (D), ZWP Ingenieur-AG, Cologne (D), WES GmbH LandschaftsArchitektur, Hamburg (D); **3rd prize** Nickl Architekten Deutschland GmbH, Munich (D), Leonhardt, Andrä und Partner Beratende Ing. VBi AG, Munich (D), Planungsgruppe VA GmbH, Nuremberg (D), Rainer Schmidt Landschaftsarchitekten GmbH, Munich (D)

Helmholtz Institute for RNA-based Infection Research, Würzburg

HIRI The Helmholtz Institute for RNA-based Infection Research is the first institute worldwide to combine infection research with RNA-based technologies. As a member of Germany's largest scientific organization, the Helmholtz Association, HIRI will be part of the Helmholtz Center for Infection Research Braunschweig.

SITE Located in the historical campus of the University Hospital Würzburg and the facilities of the Julius-Maximilians-University, the HIRI is the first non-university research institute in the complex. Like the entire campus, the building site is characterized by its hillside location above the main river, which is both a challenge due to its topography and attractive due to the distant view over the valley. The site for the new building has limited space between an existing research building in the south and the historic women's hospital building in the north.

TASK The program (approximately 4,500 sqm net) includes primarily laboratories and offices, including S2 laboratories, as well as large areas required for technology in laboratory buildings. HIRI wants the building structure to promote communication between the research areas in HIRI and between all users and visitors of the building. Spatial organization, design, and lighting should support an atmosphere for formal and informal exchange in both central and decentralized areas. Proposals that promote the concept of a laboratory and workplace landscape within the specifications for S2 laboratories, including elements such as balconies, (roof) terraces, seating in circulation zones, stimulating visual relationships, coffee bars, integrated art, etc. were explicitly welcomed.

Location: Würzburg, Germany **Client** Helmholtz-Zentrum für Infektionsforschung (HZI) **Year:** 2018 **Project size:** approx. 6,000 sqm UFA **Type of competition:** Design competition **Participants:** 11 **Competition budget:** EUR 155,000 (prizes: EUR 62,000; Compensation per participant: EUR 6,200)

PRIZEWINNERS:
(01) **1st prize** doranth post architekten GmbH, Munich (D); **2nd prize** Birk Heilmeyer und Frenzel Gesellschaft von Architekten mbH, Stuttgart (D); **4th prize** Auer Weber Assoziierte GmbH, Stuttgart (D); **4th prize** ATELIER 30 Architekten GmbH Fischer/Creutzig, Kassel (D)

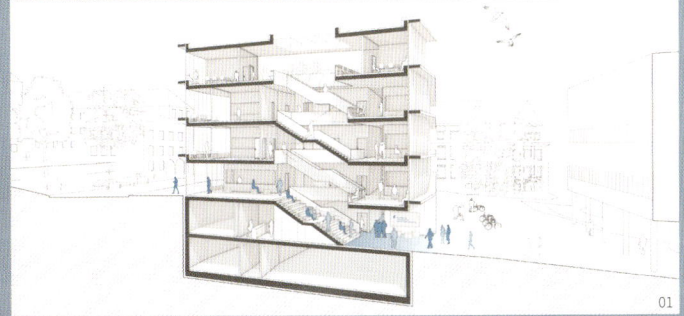

Helmholtz Institute for RNA-based Infection Research, Würzburg

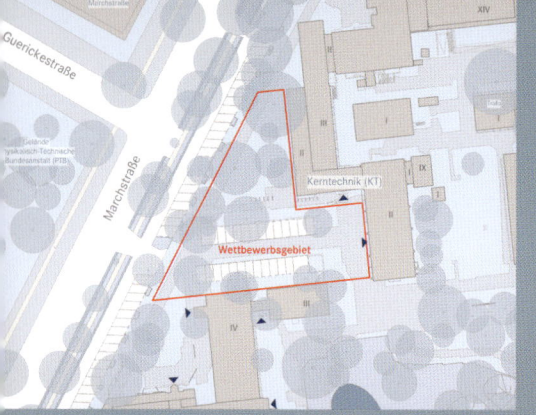

Chemical Invention Factory, Berlin

Ort: Berlin, Germany **Client:** Technische Universität Berlin **Year:** 2020 **Project size:** approx. 1,100 sqm UFA **Type of competition:** Restricted competition for general planner **Participants:** 14 **Competition budget:** EUR 86,000 (prizes)

PRIZEWINNERS:
(01) **1st prize** SWAP Architekten ZT GmbH, Vienna (A); (02) **1st prize** SEHW Architektur GmbH, Berlin (D); **3rd prize** erchinger wurfbaum I wenzel + wenzel, Berlin (D)

TECHNICAL UNIVERSITY OF BERLIN CAMPUS With approximately 33,000 students, 100 study programs and 40 institutes, the TU Berlin is one of Germany's large, internationally renowned and traditional technical universities. The competition area is located amidst the campus of TU in Charlottenburg, directly on the Ernst Reuter Square and not far from the station Zoological Garden and Kurfürstendamm. Most of the TU Berlin institutes are located here, as well as the main building with the Auditorium Maximum.

CHEMICAL INVENTION FACTORY The aim of this project is to build a pre-start-up center for green chemistry, the "John Warner Center for Start-ups in Green Chemistry Chemical Invention Factory – CIF", on Marchstrasse. A laboratory building is to be built that will offer start-up teams in the field of green chemistry qualified space in the form of 12 laboratory units to advance research and development, enable cooperation both among various start-up teams and with partners from academia and the private sector. Spin-offs are part of the TU Berlin's strategy. So far, this could only be implemented insufficiently in the field of chemistry, because the future companies need appropriate laboratories. The Chemical Invention Factory is intended to close this gap and further strengthen this outstanding field of research in Berlin.

INTEGRATED PLANNING In order to achieve the building's high standards of sustainability and efficiency, a planning and construction process is required that will benefit from close interdisciplinary collaboration. Accordingly, the competition was already open to teams from the disciplines of architecture, landscape architecture, structural engineering and building services.

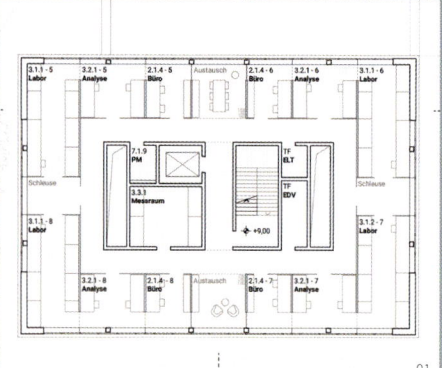

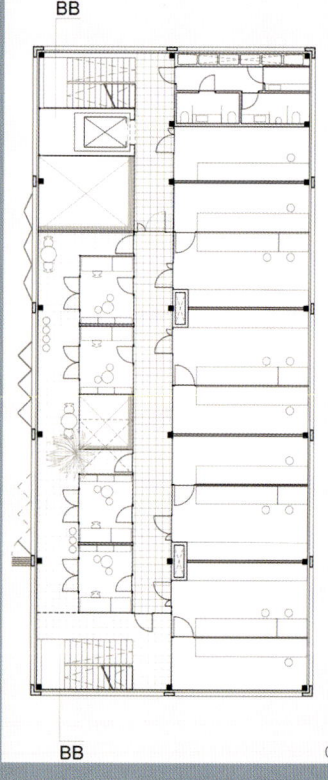

German Center for Neurodegenerative Diseases, Bonn

GERMAN CENTER FOR NEURODEGENERATIVE DISEASES Even today the causes and mechanisms of neurodegenerative diseases are largely unknown. The main focus of the German Center for Neurodegenerative Diseases (DZNE) is the promotion of a comprehensive approach to research and development in the field of neurodegeneration. Focus is on the transfer of findings from basic research into clinical practice and return feedback from observations in the clinical setting back to basic research. In addition, the DZNE should help promote international visibility of German research in this field.

BONN AS A LOCATION The largest facility and center of the DZNE has been located in the city of Bonn since 2009. Partner institutions are located in Dresden, Göttingen, Magdeburg, Munich and Tübingen among other cities. The property for the new building is situated on the southern edge of the University Hospital Bonn Venusberg (UKB) campus. Its structural and functional development by 2020 is defined in a masterplan updated annually. Content of the masterplan includes: restructuring the southern areas (the "Neuro-Zentrum") of the campus through construction of a new building for neurology, psychiatry and palliative care; establishment of an Emergency Center South; renovation and replacement of the clinic for psychiatry; and a connection to the new DZNE.

COMPETITION TASK The scope of the procedure was the general planning of the new DZNE. The new building should encompass 16,000 sqm UFA and provide an international research team with ideal conditions for extraordinary scientific work. The program included biomedical laboratories, a clinical research area and space for MRI imaging and population studies. Centralized research facilities and the DZNE administration were to be accommodated in the new building. With space for expansion on the property, the planners were to also consider the DZNE's long-term growth potential on the site.

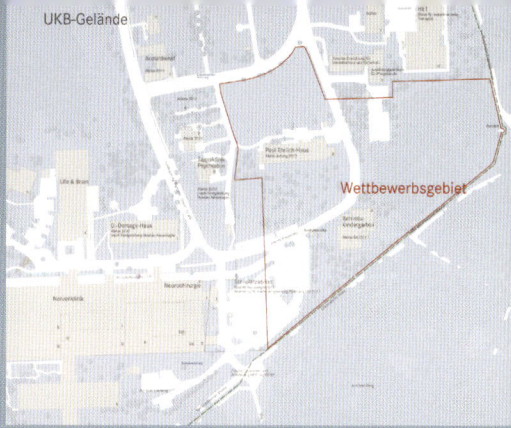

Location: Bonn, Germany **Client:** Deutsches Zentrum für Neurodegenerative Erkrankungen e.V. (DZNE) **Year:** 2011 **Project size:** 15,400 sqm UFA **Type of competition:** Project competition preceded by an open application procedure **Participants:** 12 **Competition budget:** EUR 580,000 (prizes: EUR 280,000; fees per participant: EUR 25,000)

PRIZEWINNERS:
(01) **1st prize** wulf & ass. Architekten, Stuttgart (D); (02) **2nd prize** hammeskrause architekten, Stuttgart (D); (03) **3rd prize** SOW Planungsgruppe, Berlin (D)

German Center for Neurodegenerative Diseases, Bonn

12 PRELIMINARY EXAMINATION

12.1 Significance of the preliminary examination

A competition is concluded with the jury's decision on the submitted designs. This step marks one of the most strategically important decisions in the entire project. Accordingly, the responsibility of all parties involved in this step of the project is great; responsibility towards the project, as well as towards the participating offices, to ensure a careful handling of their creative performance and their investment, that a competition entails in any case. However, the duration of the jury meeting will never be long enough for it to be able to examine all aspects of the proposed solutions with sufficient precision.

In order to counter this circumstance, the preliminary examination takes place prior to the jury meeting. Important tasks are delegated to the preliminary examination team, the results of which then form the basis for the work in the jury. The preliminary examination team is given sufficient time (see Chapter 6) to carry out a precise examination of the submitted competition entries in cooperation with experts. The aim of the preliminary examination is to check neutrally and with the necessary intensity whether or how and to what extent the specifications of the project required by the sponsor have been implemented. All test results are summarized in a report of the preliminary examination, which is presented to the jury. To meet the high level of responsibility for technical and professional precision in the preliminary review, the level of all steps in the preliminary review must correspond to the complexity and importance of the decision to be made as well as to the sponsor's demand for quality in the decision-making processes. Consequently, conducting the preliminary review requires technically competent and experienced personnel, careful procedures, time, and creativity.

12.2 Tasks, team and process planning

The competition organizer is responsible for conducting the preliminary examination and either in-house or by outsourcing it, if necessary. In addition to the selection of the procedure type and the participants (jury members, participants, and experts) as well as the precise description of the task, the preliminary examination is the fourth decisive element for a successful competition. This service includes a wide range of activities, from logistics and formally sensitive evaluation processes to the coordination of model repair and photography, as well as a high level of technical understanding of the designs. In addition to the preparation of the competition documents, the preliminary examination is a significant part of the competition management mission and requires the largest staff effort in the process over a short period of time. Depending on the number of designs submitted and the complexity of the task, the project team at this phase can comprise up to 10, in exceptional cases up to 20 members and consists of:

› **Preliminary examination manager(s):** responsible for the concept and management in terms of content and organization
› **Preliminary examiner(s):** they have the same qualifications as the competition participants, carry out the technical examination and present the projects neutrally within the framework of the jury meeting
› **Assistant(s):** a team for logistics, formal examination as well as, in interaction with the preliminary examiners, the execution of the quantitative examination and the preparation of analyses
› **Graphic designer(s):** Responsible for the preparation of the preliminary examination report

In practice, the preliminary examination consists of the following sub-processes, for which scheduling and capacity planning must take place at an early stage:

› Receipt and formal examination
› Quantitative examination
› Analysis of design concepts
› Involvement of experts
› Preparation of the preliminary examination report

Typically, the preliminary examination is scheduled to last three to five weeks. Many factors must be considered when planning, including the possible delayed arrival of shipments with the projects due to longer transportation times or customs inspection, possible translation of texts, production of the report, transportation of the documents from the place of the preliminary examination to the place of the jury meeting.

12.3 Receipt and formal examination

At the end of the working period, the participants send the required documents by courier or mail to the collection office, usually to the office of the competition manager, or hand them in personally there. First of all, it is important to have the necessary personnel in the collection point as well as appropriate storage capacities. In the case of larger competitions, the number of rolled plans and model boxes can reach a considerable volume.

The first task of the preliminary examination is the formal examination, immediately after the receipt of the documents, verifying:

› compliance with the submission deadlines
› completeness of the documents
› observance of anonymity in the documents

Jan Musikowski, Christoph Richter
Architects, Berlin

❝ A good jury finds the best design – a good competition finds the best jury. In addition, there are some other things that we think are important:
› uncomplicated pre-qualification procedures (if necessary, at all),
› inspiring, motivating, incentivizing, well-researched competition briefs with a clearly formulated task,
› clear structure of the competition documents,
› possibility to visit the site, to hear the competition sponsor's opinion and transparent possibilities to ask questions,
› sufficient time for processing,
› transparent evaluation and follow-up of the results (digital and/or analog exhibition).

CAD-based precise checking of quantities as part of preliminary tests: **above** on an urban planning scale, **below** on a building construction scale

12 Preliminary examination

The results of the formal examination must be carefully documented. As regards the compliance to the **submission deadline**, it is usually agreed that the time of document dispatch is the decisive time for the deadline, not the actual arrival of the documents at the delivery office. This is because the time of dispatch of the documents is not always immediately apparent, as courier services, for example, often do not record the date of dispatch, but rather the date stamps of intermediate warehouses. In such cases of doubt, after the competition has been completed, the participants are required to provide concrete proof that the documents were sent in time. In the case of digital submissions, the relevant log files must be archived. The completeness check is based on the list of required services stated in the competition brief (plans, models, forms, texts as well as files, see Chapter 8.5). As a rule, the principle of anonymity applies in competitions, i.e., the jury members are not aware of the assignment of the designs to the participants (see Chapter 3.2 "Communication" and 8.5). In order to achieve this, the submission of the competition entries is also generally anonymous, i.e., each submitted document, including the packaging, bears a code number, but not the name of the submitting office. All code numbers are "anonymized" by the preliminary examination employees, i.e., by being overlayed with a new cover number. Should there nevertheless be references to the collection office on the packages or shipping documents, e.g., for reasons of shipping specifications with international courier services, these are blacked out by preliminary examination staff and the circumstance itself is documented. The envelopes containing the declarations of authorship ("authors' declarations") are kept under lock and key and are not opened until the final decision on the competition result has been made.

In addition, the organizational part of the preliminary examination also includes, if necessary, the repair of the models submitted by the participants, possibly damaged during transport, as well as the photographing of the models.

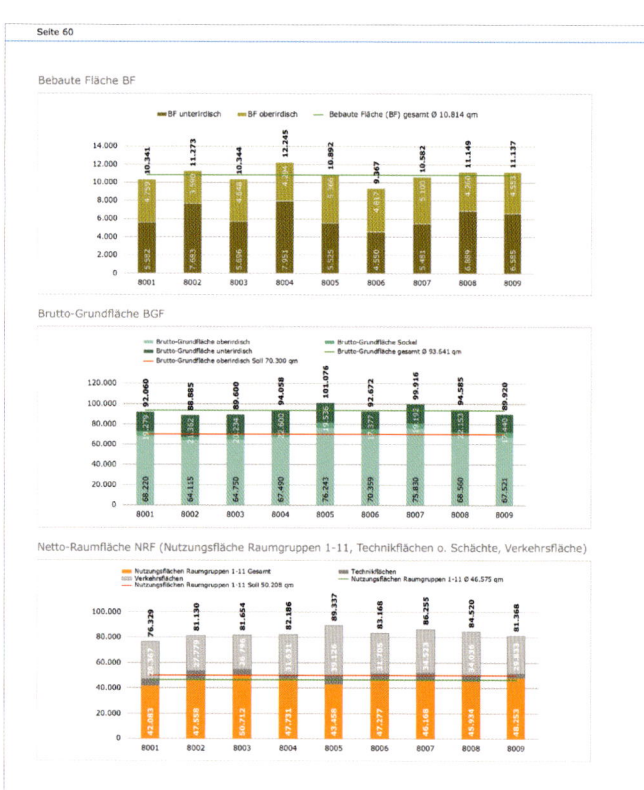

12.4 Quantitative testing

Part of the technical preliminary examination concerns quantifiable and objectifiable criteria, i.e., the "measurable" components of the designs. First of all, these are measurable dimensions of the design proposals, expressed in terms of area and volume parameters (e.g., gross floor area, usable floor area, floor area ratio, floor area ratio, etc.), volumes (gross volume ratio, BRI), surfaces (enveloping surfaces), number of rooms, etc.).

The extent to which these are in accordance with any specifications and how they compare with other designs is determined.

For this purpose, the plans and forms submitted by the participants are at least checked for plausibility and verified in random samples by measurements. The resulting characteristic values are an essential part of the evaluation of core aspects of the task, e.g., with regard to space efficiency or required urban development characteristic values. However, in order to generate a reliable basis for comparison, it is advisable not only to check random samples, but to have all relevant areas and volumes remeasured by the preliminary examination team. For this purpose, [phase eins]. has developed a CAD-based system that has been tried and tested for many years and produces precise results with a reasonable amount of effort.

The results of this part of the preliminary examination are summarized in tables and diagrams.

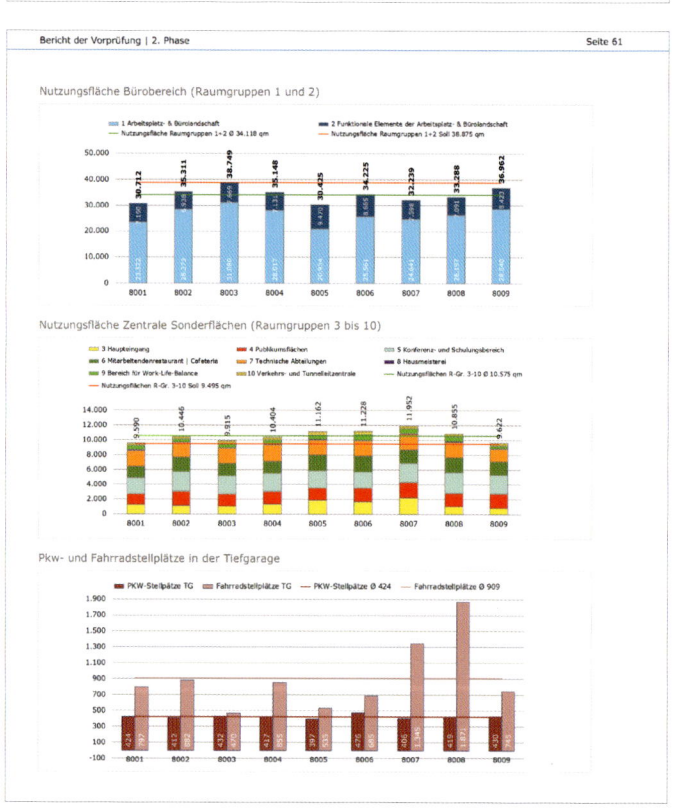

Left page: Overview of the results of the quantitative assessment in the preliminary examination report
Right page: Presentation of the surface area analysis in the preliminary examination report for precise information on the compliance with the spatial programme and description of the allocation of functions

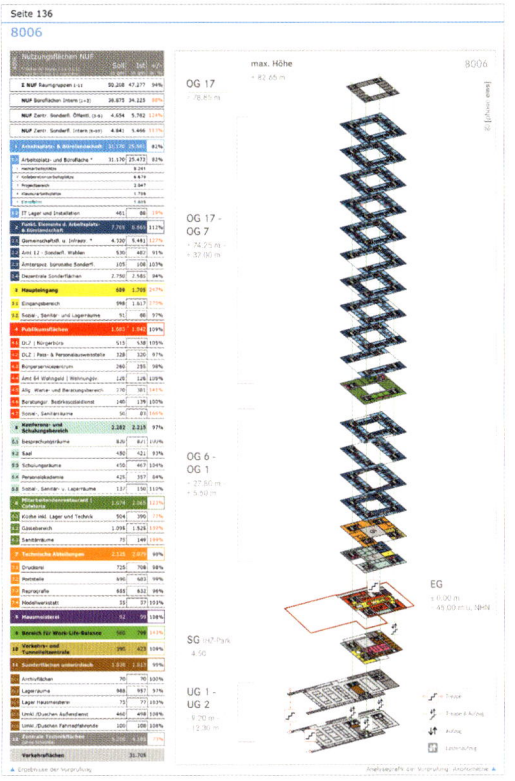
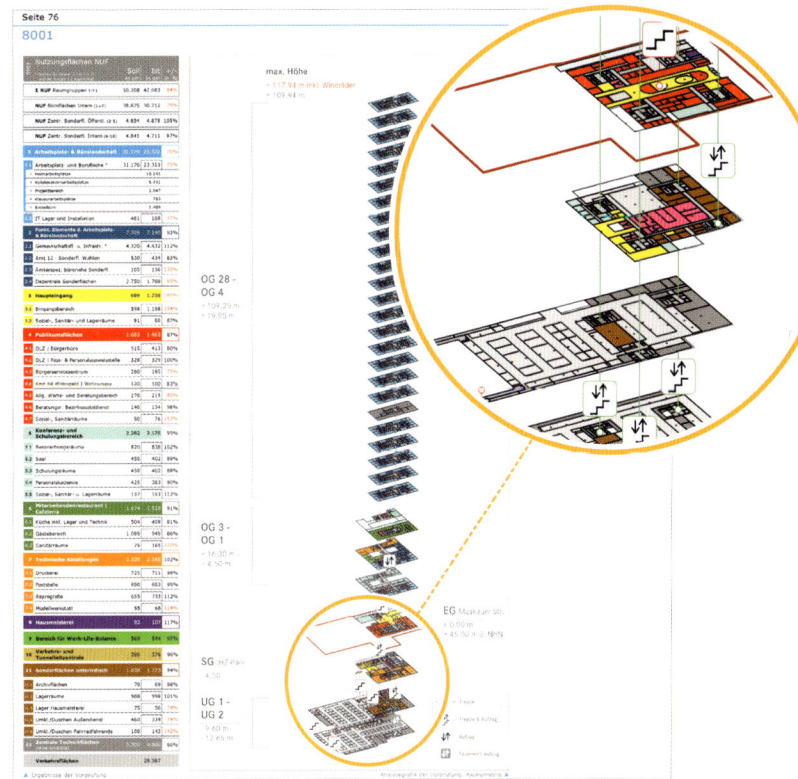
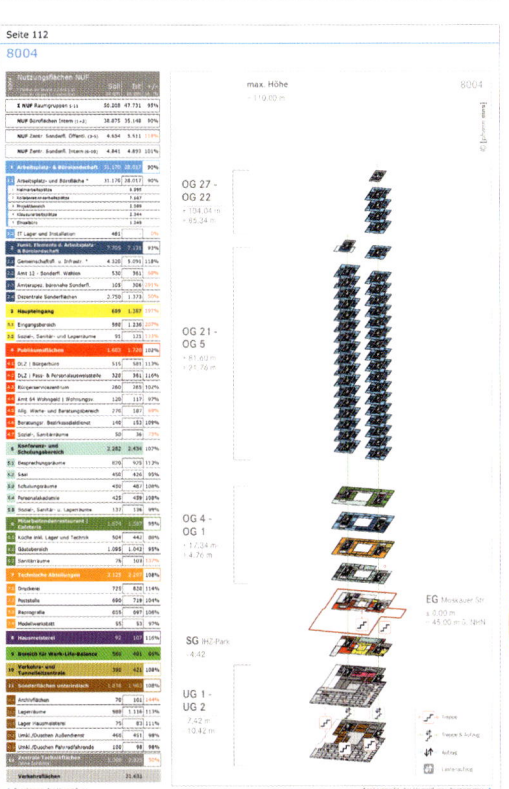
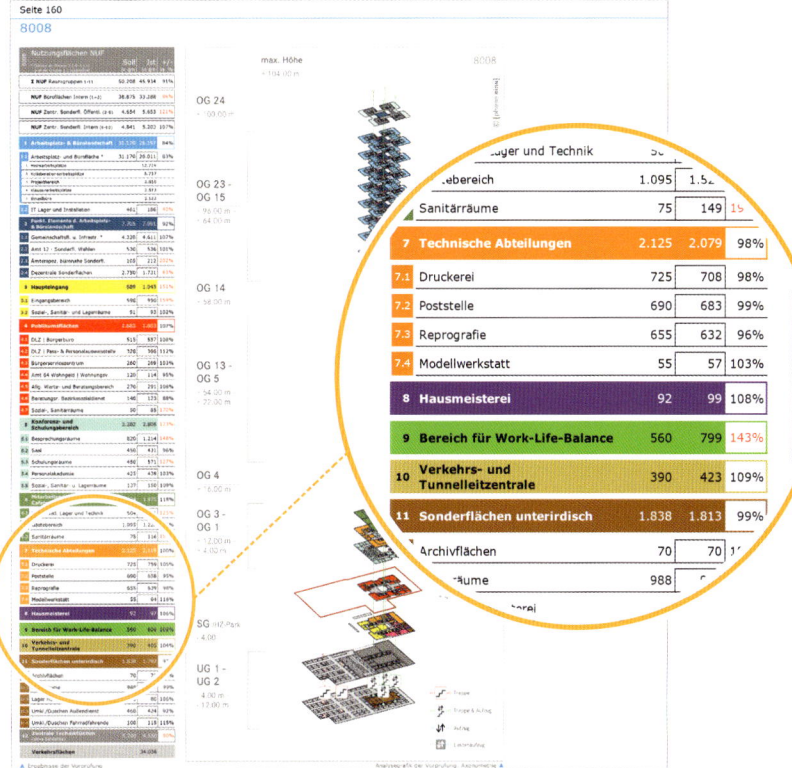

12 Preliminary examination

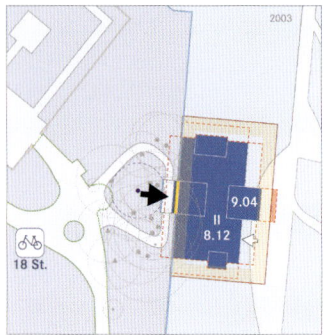 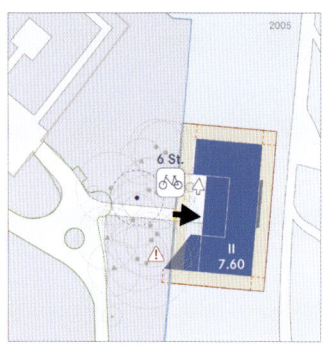
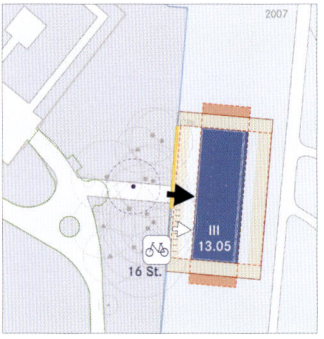 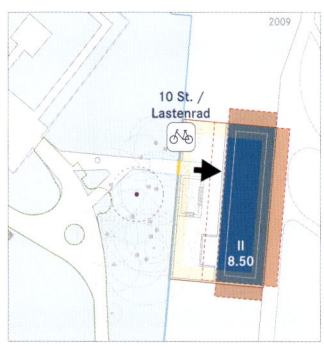

Left page: Analysis diagrams in the preliminary examination report to illustrate the location, proportions and utilisation of designs in comparison. **Right page:** Presentation of the results of the experts' review as part of the preliminary examination

12.6 Involvement of technical experts

The task of technical experts is to advise sponsor and the jury on partial aspects of the task, usually technical and planning law issues (building construction, ecology, energy, traffic, fire protection, approval, monument protection, costs, etc.). This consultation is relevant both in the context of the preparation of the competition, and especially in the context of the decision. To be able to provide a well-founded assessment of the above-mentioned aspects during the jury meeting and thus in the decision-making process, it is useful to also involve the experts appointed for the procedure in the preliminary examination for the analysis and assessment of these topic groups.

In a compact experts' meeting held as part of the preliminary examination, they assess all submitted projects according to criteria of their respective expertise and prepare a report. These statements (reports), sometimes in the form of a matrix, become part of the preliminary examination report. The result is then incorporated into the evaluation of the jury. If there are questions on behalf of the jury members, the experts are generally personally available to elaborate on their assessments.

Assessing the quality of the designs in terms of their sustainability and potential for eventual certification is an integral part of the expert examination. Ideally, either the examiners or an expert or auditor for subsequent certification will bring together the findings of the experts for the relevant technical topics (quality of working places, energy, rainwater management, building physics, circular economy, wind, etc.).

12.5 Design concept analysis

The second part of the technical preliminary examination concerns the qualitative examination and analysis of the submitted proposals. Depending on the task, this concerns, for example, checking the fulfillment of required functional relationships and compliance with building and planning regulations. Furthermore, this test step includes the recording and description of the concepts and ideas on which the design is based with regard to, for example, urban design, building or outdoor spaces design, spatial formation, choice of materials, etc. The results of this test are then presented in text form, in the form of a report, and in the form of a report.

The results of this examination are summarized textually, or better also graphically, in the preliminary examination report and presented to the jury at its meeting by the preliminary examiners.

Other preliminary examination tasks could possibly be performed by representatives of other disciplines, businesspeople, lawyers and graphic designers. However, in terms of understanding and summarizing the design concepts for design projects with their inherent complexity, an appropriate handling of the available information can only be achieved if the persons involved in the preliminary examination are professionally capable of processing this complexity, which requires the same qualification as that required of the participants – i.e., as a rule, licensed and practicing architect, urban designer or landscape architect with experience in the analysis and description of concepts and designs that goes beyond the usual scope of services.

EINSCHÄTZUNG DER SACHVERSTÄNDIGEN: ÜBERSICHT

		3001	3002	3003	3004	3005	3006	3007	3008	3009	3010	3011	3012	3013	3014
Nutzung/Funktion															
	Résumé	+0,3	-0,7	+0,7	0,0	-0,3	0,0	0,0	+0,3	+0,7	-0,7	-0,7	-0,3	-0,3	-0,3
1	Adressbildung	+1	-1	+1	0	-1	0	+1	+1	+1	-1	-1	0	0	0
2	Publikumsführung	+1	0	+1	0	0	-1	0	0	+1	0	0	0	0	-1
3	Interne Abläufe	-1	-1	0	0	0	+1	-1	0	0	-1	-1	-1	-1	0
Realisierung															
	Résumé	0,0	-0,3	+0,8	+0,3	+0,8	-0,3	-0,5	+0,8	+0,8	-0,3	0,0	-0,3	-0,3	-0,5
1	Baulicher Aufwand	-1	-1	+2	0	+2	0	-2	+2	+2	-1	-1	-1	-1	-1
2	U-Bahn-Trasse	+1	+1	0	+1	0	+1	+1	+1	+1	+1	+1	+1	+1	+1
3	Baumbestand	+1	0	+1	0	+1	0	+1	0	0	0	0	0	0	0
4	Wirtschaftlichkeit	-1	-1	+1	0	+1	-1	-2	0	0	-1	0	-1	-1	-2
Tragwerk															
	Résumé	-0,2	+0,1	+0,6	+0,3	+0,5	0	-0,4	+0,6	+0,3	0,0	+0,3	+0,2	-0,2	
1	Gründung	-1	0	+1	+1	+1	-1	-2	+1	+1	0	+1	0	0	
2	Deckensystem	0	-1	+1	+1	+1	-1	0	+1	+1	0	+1	+1	0	
3	Lastabtrag gesamt	-1	+1	+1	+1	+1	-1	-1	+1	+1	+1	+1	+1	0	
4	Aussteifung	0	0	+1	+1	+1	-1	-1	+1	0	+1	+1	+1	0	
5	Anschluss an Bestand	0	0	+1	0	0	0	+1	0	0	0	0	0	0	
6	Eingriffe in Bestand	0	0	0	0	0	0	-1	0	0	0	0	0	0	
7	Sonderkonstruktionen	0	0	0	0	0	+1	0	0	0	0	0	0	0	
8	Hochwertige UG Nutzung	0	0	0	0	0	0	0	0	0	0	0	0	0	
9	Wirtschaftlichkeit	0	0	+1	0	+1	0	-2	+1	0	0	0	0	-1	
10	Nachhaltigkeit - konstruktiv	0	0	0	0	0	+1	0	0	0	0	0	0	0	
Technische Ausrüstung															
	Résumé	-2,0	-1,0	-0,3	0,0	-0,3	-1,0	0,0	+0,3	-0,5	-0,8	0,0	-0,3	-0,5	-1,8
1	Ausrüstung - Konzeption	-2	-1	-1	+1	0	-2	-1	0	0	-1	0	0	0	-1
2	Technische Funktionsflächen	-2	-2	0	0	0	0	+1	+1	0	-2	0	-2	-2	-2
3	Medienführung	-2	-1	0	0	-2	+1	-1	0	-1	0	0	+1	+1	-2
4	Energieeffizienz / Nachhaltigkeit	-2	0	0	+1	-2	-2	+1	0	-1	0	0	+1	0	-2
Winterthur-Gebäude (WT)															
	Résumé	0,0	-2,0	-2,0	0,0	-2,0	-1,5	+2,0	-1,5	-2,0	-1,0	+1,0	+2,0	-2,0	+2,0
1	Kompensationsflächen	-2	-	-	-1	-	-1	+2	-1	-2	-1	+1	+2	-2	+2
2	Adressbildung	+2	-2	-2	+1	-2	-2	+2	-2	-2	-1	+1	+2	-2	+2

Bewertung: 2 bis -2

EINSCHÄTZUNG DER SACHVERSTÄNDIGEN: REALISIERUNG

SACHVERSTÄNDIGER: HERIBERT FRUHAUF

Bewertung: -2 bis +2

Aus Sicht der Realisierung werden die Erweiterungsflächen in einem kompakten Solitär bevorzugt.
Bei Erweiterungsflächen in architektonisch aufwendigen Neubauten ist auf die Kosten verursacht durch die Tragwerke zu achten.
Bei Aufstockungen auf den Bestand ist auf die Lastabtragung zu achten.

12 Preliminary examination

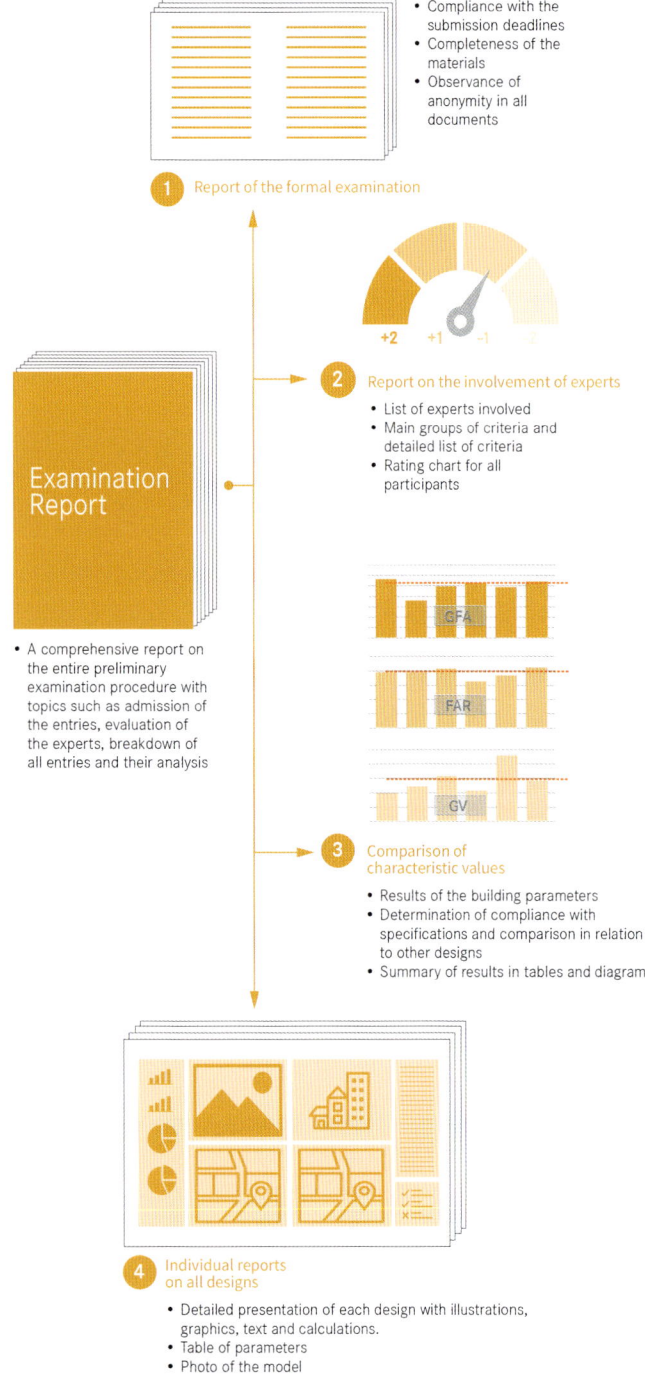

12.7 Preparing the preliminary examination report

The preliminary examination report is presented to all members of the jury in printed form at the beginning of the jury meeting. It contains all the results of the preliminary examination and serves on the one hand as a basis for the jury's evaluation and on the other hand as documentation of the submitted designs. Components of the preliminary examination report are:

› Report of the formal examination
› Report on the involvement of experts
› Comparison of characteristic values
› Individual reports on all designs

The question of content, structure, and level of detail of the individual reports is handled in practice with very different effort and measure. The effort should always be oriented to the needs of the jury - how many designs must be reviewed and evaluated in how much time? What are the main aspects to be considered? The scope of these reports is wide. It ranges from very simple reports with the reproduction of a few key data and, if necessary, a model photo, summarized on half a page per design in black-and-white print, to 12-page multi-color reports per design, with a comprehensive explanation of the respective design, quotations from the texts of the participants and reproduction of the relevant illustrations, model photos as well as results of the quantitative examination and analysis graphics of the preliminary examination.

12.8 BIM in competitions

The authors have carried out an initial pilot project on the use of BIM in competitions; Switzerland and Scandinavia also have initial experience in this area. The extent to which the use of BIM in competitions will become established as a standard procedure cannot yet be assessed conclusively. The finding so far is that the very narrow specifications for the creation of BIM data required for this, which are necessary for comparability, are too restrictive for the diverse design and working methods of the participants in the early design phase of the competition and that CAD-based testing based on 2D data remains therefore an appropriate method.

Right page: Contents of preliminary examination reports

12 Preliminary examination

X EDUCATIONAL BUILDINGS

Probably the most important task of the competition organizer when preparing competitions for educational buildings is to comprehend the intended teaching and learning concept in order to summarize it in the competition brief and communicate it to the participants. During the preliminary examination, it is then necessary to examine to what extent the educational concept has been successfully implemented in terms of spatial qualities, usage contexts, color, and material concepts, etc., and is to support the pedagogical work. This applies equally to kindergartens, schools as well as college and university buildings. Designers often have extensive experience with all these types of uses from previous projects, but the teaching and learning concepts can be fundamentally different, which is why the careful communication, and if necessary, also the preparation of these concepts, is particularly important. Another characteristic of educational buildings is that few types of use have such detailed regulatory requirements for spatial programs and equipment features. Unfortunately, these specifications are not always up to date, or the project was approved so long ago that the specifications have become obsolete. Such a problem must be identified and solved in the conception phase of the project, i.e., when preparing the design competition, at the latest by entering into an open dialogue of the general jury members, representing the client, with the members of the technical jury and the users, so as to then be able to implement contemporary – if not future-oriented – teaching and learning concepts in the building.

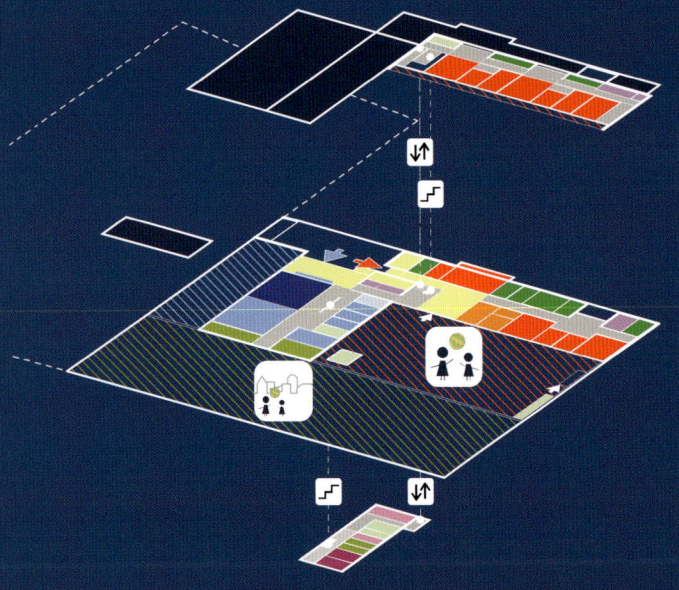
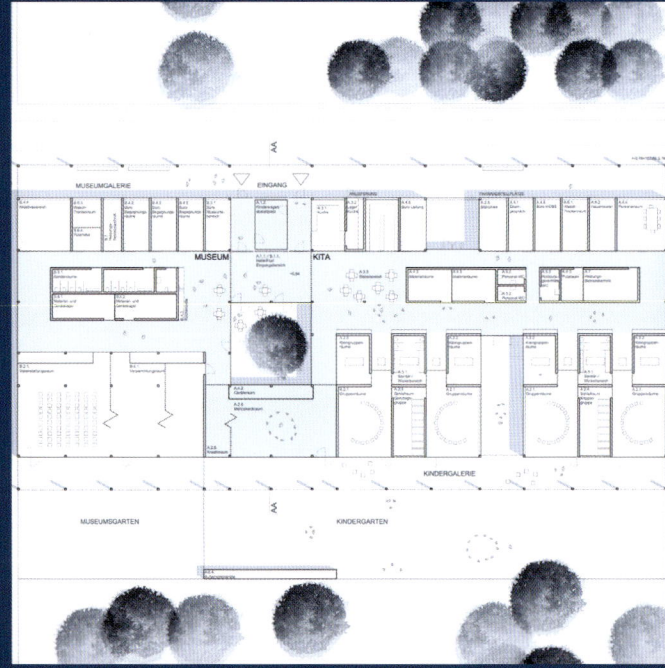

Site plan and corresponding analysis graphic of the preliminary examination for explaining the distribution of functions in the competition "Day Care in Bürgerpark in Lahr", 1st prize (se)arch Architekten, Stuttgart

Elementary and Special School, Eutin

EUTIN The city is located in the east of Schleswig-Holstein between Hamburg, Kiel and Lübeck and has about 17,000 inhabitants. It is surrounded by the nature park Holsteinische Schweiz between Großer Eutiner See, Kleiner Eutiner See, Kellersee and Ukleisee. Eutin has a well-preserved old town and Eutin Castle is known far beyond the city limits.

PROJECT The competition is intended to establish the unique location by the lake as a visible flagship for school development in the entire Ostholstein district. The new school building on the site of an existing school is intended to bring together a total of 320 students from several schools and school-related institutions: an elementary school, a mental development support center, the learning support center, and an open all-day school. The three schools are not only to be combined at one location or in one building; rather, further integration of the three schools is to take place by combining the educational spaces of the three schools in four clusters, grade by grade. In this way, a structure of four clusters is to be formed, each containing pedagogical spaces of the three schools.

PROGRAM Planned are rooms with a total usable area of almost 5,000 sqm UFA, in it, in addition to the teaching rooms of the four clusters, by additional rooms of the two support centers, specialized rooms, rooms of the open all-day school with canteen and all-day areas, teaching staff areas of all three schools and the administration. The program also included a three-field gymnasium, outdoor sports facilities, and a traffic training area. The aim is to create a sustainable building with a focus on climate protection, whereby one of the challenges is the structural implementation during ongoing school operations

Location: Eutin, Germany **Client:** City of Eutin **Year:** 2021 – 2022 **Project size:** approx. 7,200 sqm UFA **Type of competition:** Restricted design competition **Participants:** 12 **Competition budget:** EUR 190,000 (prizes: EUR 100,000; Compensation: EUR 90,000)

PRIZEWINNERS:
(01) **1st prize** Staab Architekten and Atelier Loidl Landschaftsarchitekten Berlin (D); **2nd prize** Schulz und Schulz Architekten and rossa rossa-banthien Landschaftsarchitekten, Leipzig and Dresden (D); **3rd prize** Hess/Talhof/Kusmierz Architekten und Stadtplaner BDA and NUWELA Büro für Städtebau und Landschaftsarchitektur, Munich and Unterhaching (D)

01

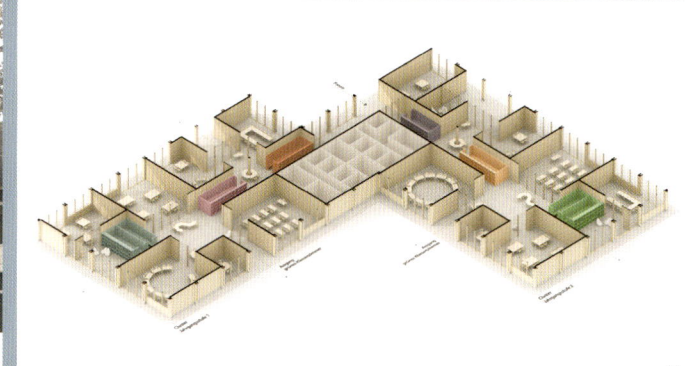
01

01

01

Elementary and Special School, Eutin

High School, Dallgow-Döberitz

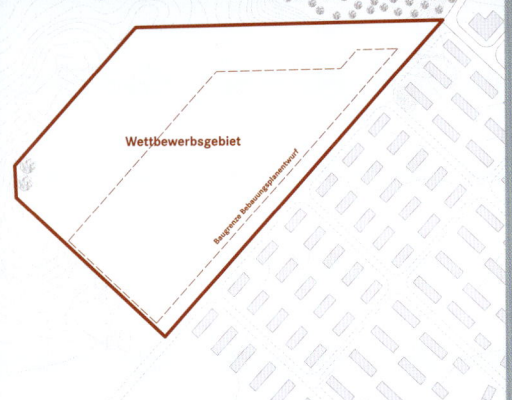

Location: Dallgow-Döberitz, Germany **Client:** Havelland district **Year:** 2001 **Project size:** approx. 6,000 sqm UFA **Type of competition:** restricted design competition with open pre-qualification **Participants:** 22 **Competition budget:** EUR 67,000 (prizes and mentions)

PRIZEWINNERS:
(01) **1st prize** Grüntuch Ernst Architekten BDA, Berlin (D); (02) **3rd prize** CHG Architekten – Gramlich, Stuttgart (D); (03) **4th prize** Backmann, Schieber, Kohler, Berlin (D); (04) **5th prize** Elz, Rothkegel, Potsdam (D); (05) **5th prize** J. Böge + Lindner Böge, Hamburg (D); **Acquisition** Bloss + Keinath Architekten + Stadtplaner, Winterbach (D); **Acquisition** Zwink Architekten, Munich (D)

DALLGOW-DÖBERITZ Together with the town of Falkensee, the municipality of Dallgow-Döberitz forms the eastern edge of the Havelland district in Brandenburg, in the transition to the Berlin city limits. It is located on federal highway B5, the historical connection between Berlin and Hamburg. Due to the attractive location and quality of life as well as the good educational opportunities, the community has grown significantly since the 1990s. Since 1990, the population has increased from about 2,900 to about 9,200 in 2015 and is expected to continue to grow.

PROJECT This was accompanied by a need for high school spots in the Havelland district. The district chose the Dallgow-Döberitz location from several options, particularly because of its proximity to the train station and Berlin. The municipality of Dallgow-Döberitz provided a plot of land in the "Neu Döberitz" residential area for this purpose. Its location between settlement and landscape is to be used through an optically perceptible opening to the landscape.

PROGRAM The new building was based on a mixed-use concept with a technical and scientific character. In addition to just meeting the needs in Osthavelland, it had to represent an attractive offer for promotion of gifted pupils, which also had to offer the option of a European high school through the integration of a boarding school. The project had to be able to be realized in two construction phases. In the 1st phase, a 3-grade high school with a triple-field sports hall and outdoor facilities for 560 pupils was built, including the central facilities for the 2nd phase (sports facilities etc.). In the 2nd construction phase, depending on the decision on the further differentiation, the expansion of subject classrooms or the expansion into a 5-grade high school for 935 students. In the 1st construction phase, 24 classrooms and group classrooms with a size of 40-60 sqm as well as four teaching material rooms, each with 20 sqm, belonged to the program. After the 2nd construction phase, the boarding school was to be realized under independent sponsorship, depending on demand.

University and State Library, Darmstadt

DARMSTADT In 1997, the Hessian ministry of the interior awarded Darmstadt the title "City of Science" in recognition of the importance of its scientific and research institutions. Also, Darmstadt's Technical University (TUD) became Germany's first ever "autonomous model university" in 2005, as part of a five-year experiment. This status affords TUD a more independent and pro-active role, particularly in planning and executing its building program. The key project within this program is the construction of a new university and state library (ULB), primarily to support research and education at TUD. It sees itself as a modern hybrid library: As its first function, it will be an academic service center for information retrieval, a place for study and work, for communication and human encounter. The second, more public function is that of a state library whose importance, in view of its highly valued historic collection, surpasses regional boundaries.

LOCATION The project site is located at TUD's long-established premises, adjacent to the palace and Darmstadt's city center. It is framed around an inner courtyard which is listed as a heritage site and borders on the "old suburb", likewise a listed site. The area lies in between the TUD's historic main building, the former army barracks, various 20th-century industrial buildings, and the university commons which dates from the 1970s and is dominated by an administrative block some 30 meters high.

TASK The main task set to the architects was to find sensitive and original ways to integrate the new structure into the context of a highly eclectic group of buildings, some of them are listed, and thus create a new overall architectural scenario. The new building is to house some 1.15 million media materials in the open access section, 1.5 million more in the magazines and 560 public workplaces, on approx. 19,000 sqm of main effective area. The program of spaces includes various reading rooms, administrative areas, event venues, magazines, and workshops.

Location: Darmstadt, Germany **Client:** TU Darmstadt **Year:** 2005 **Project size:** 19,000 sqm **Type of competition:** Restricted two-stage project competition preceded by an application procedure **Participants:** 1st stage: 55; 2nd stage: 14 **Competition budget:** EUR 172,000

PRIZEWINNERS:
(01) **1st prize** Bär, Stadelmann, Stöcker Architekten, Nuremberg; (02) **2nd prize** netzwerkarchitekten, Darmstadt; (03) **3rd prize** Burger Rudacs Architekten, Munich; **3rd prize** Thomas Müller Ivan Reimann, Berlin; **5th prize** Gerber Architekten, Dortmund; **1st acquisition** agps, Zurich; **Acquisition** SCHULTES FRANK ARCHITEKTEN, Berlin; **Acquisition** Plasma Studio, London

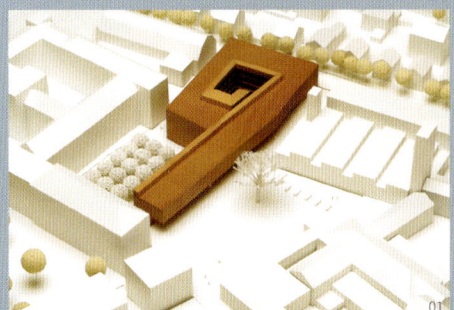
01

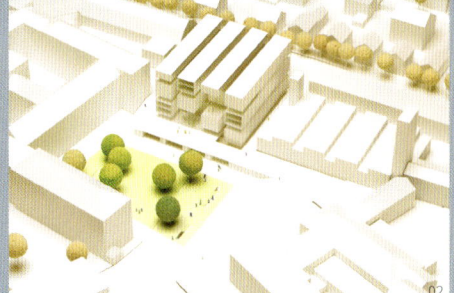
02

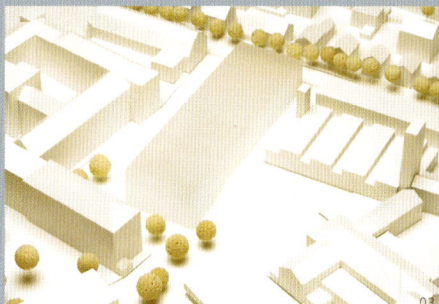
03

© Thomas Ott
01 - built

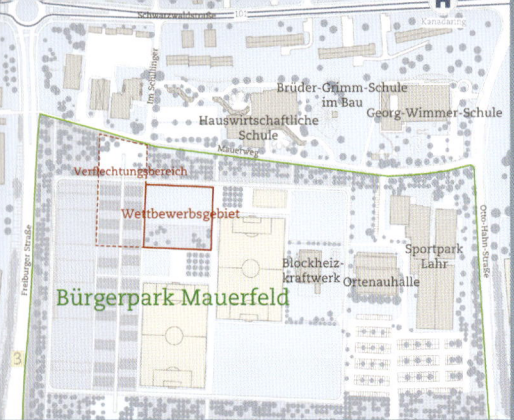

Location: Lahr, Germany **Client:** City of Lahr **Year:** 2014 **Project size:** 1,500 sqm GFA **Type of competition:** Design competition preceded by an open application procedure **Participants:** 11 **Competition budget:** 22,000 EUR in prizes

Kita+, Lahr

LANDESGARTENSCHAU 2018 The city of Lahr is hosting Baden Württemberg's 2018 Landesgartenschau (State Horticultural Show). For Lahr, located 50 km north of Freiburg im Breisgau, the horticultural show marks the occasion to initiate several measures for long-term urban development in certain districts. Besides creating and designing a large public park, the development plans generate an effective long-term infrastructure program including: the "Kita+" (Day Care+); a generous playground and athletics grounds; and a three-court gym with multi-purpose hall named "Sporthalle+". Furthermore, approximately 47.5 ha around the city's main entrance are to be redesigned and upgraded within these measures.

THE PUBLIC PARK AND VIA CERAMICA The concept for the state horticultural show was designed by club L94 landscape architects from Cologne, Germany, and is composed of three sub-areas connected by a bridge. One of these sub-areas is the public park with space for people to meet and socialize, and facilities for sports and games. Kita+ is located in the northwest section of the park. An archaeological site revealing historical traces from the Roman period is also located in the park and is an integral part of the Horticultural Show. To preserve evidence of the ancient Roman "Via Ceramica" settlement, a Gallo-Roman half-timber house is being reconstructed and the form of the settlement along the former Roman road will be delineated through plants and other landscape elements.

KITA+ The program calls for approx. 1,250 sqm UFA accommodating three main functions: daycare facilities for four groups of children; museum spaces; and small meeting rooms for local residents. The three functions are connected by shared spaces (the foyer, cafe and kitchen). The building is scheduled for completion before the horticultural show opens. The new exhibition spaces will be dedicated to a special purpose during the show, and should be identifiable in the long term in conjunction with the public park and the reconstructed ancient Roman house. The new building's architecture must be both child-friendly as well as meet the requirements of the other two areas.

PRIZEWINNERS:
(01) **1st prize** (se)arch – Freie Architekten, Stuttgart (D); (02) **2nd prize** harris + kurrle architekten, Stuttgart (D); (03) **3rd prize** L/A Liebel/Architekten, Aalen (D); **Finalist** Walter Huber Architekten, Stuttgart (D)

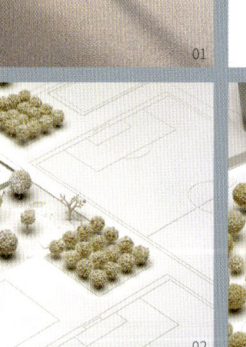

Paulus Community Center, Berlin-Tempelhof

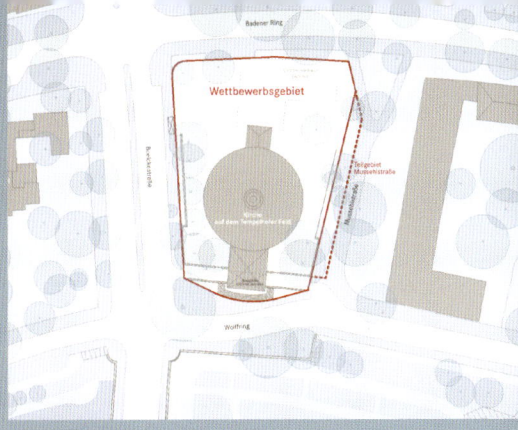

EVANGELICAL PAULUS CHURCH CONGREGATION
The congregation is located in the northeastern part of the Tempelhof-Schöneberg district in Berlin, west of the former Tempelhof Airport, one of the city's potential development areas. It was formed in 2006 from the merger of three smaller parishes. On the occasion of this merger, as well as from the constantly evolving space requirements, strategic goals for the municipality's properties were developed. The most important measure in this context is the restructuring of the Neu-Tempelhof site. In addition to the congregation's most important church building, the site is now home to the congregation's former parish hall and, on a neighboring property, a daycare center for the congregation's children.

LOCATION The site is dominated by the prominent round church, which is a listed building and can be seen from afar. It was built in 1928 according to plans by architect Fritz Bräuning. The two-story parish hall was added to the church building in 1959 according to plans by architect Gottfried Römer. Due to the energetically uneconomical building fabric and functional deficiencies, it was decided to abandon the existing parish hall and to erect a new building in its place, which would also integrate the kindergarten that was previously located on the opposite side.

PROGRAM The new building was to combine the functions of the parish hall and the daycare center with 105 places under one roof and in the immediate vicinity of the church building – a "children's and family center" with offerings for all generations. The challenge to be solved was the reduced space available on the site, the spatial-functional requirements for the new planning, including the requirements for open spaces for the daycare center, and the requirements of historic preservation. One planning option was the joint use of parts of the church building.

Location: Berlin, Germany **Client:** Evangelical Paulus Church Congregation Tempelhof **Year:** 2009 – 2010 **Project size:** approx. 1,130 sqm UFA **Type of competition:** Restricted design competition **Participants:** 6 **Competition budget:** EUR 28,000 (prizes: EUR 13,000; Compensation: EUR 15,000)

PRIZEWINNERS:
(01) **1st prize** Kersten + Kopp Architekten, Berlin (D); **2nd prize** Klaus Block Architekten, Berlin (D); **3rd prize** Burchard Architekten and Clarke und Kuhn freie Architekten Berlin (D)

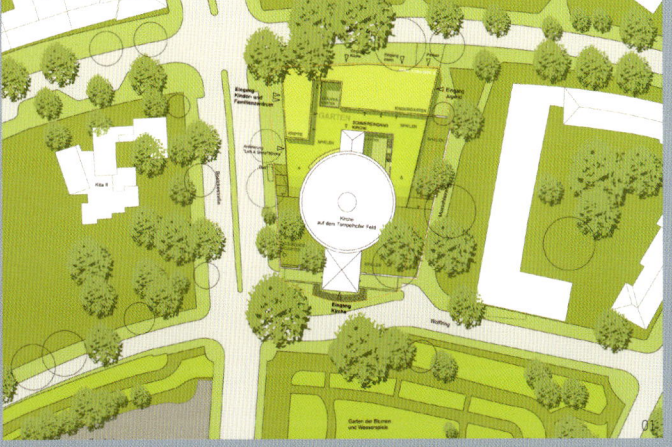

13 JURORS' EVALUATION

13.1 Importance of the jury meeting for the project and the competition

In many ways, jury meetings are a special moment in the entire project – for the client and everyone else involved in the project, but especially for the firms participating in the design competition. The jury meeting offers the excitement – if not the drama – of a sports tournament or a court hearing. Viewed soberly, it marks the moment when the design of the project and its commission are decided. Emotionally, it sets the stage for a special "moment of creation" shared by all present. In contrast to a direct commission or a design contract commissioned through a negotiation process, in a competition the moment of transition from abstract, theoretical concept discussion to a concrete design solution takes place precisely in this joint jury meeting. The decision thus has a high identification potential for the entire project that should not be underestimated or neglected.

All relevant participants of a project are involved in a competition procedure and ideally united in the interest of an optimal solution for the project: designers, sometimes from different disciplines, people from politics, administration, users and possibly also citizens' representatives, works councils, and other interest groups. During the competition, these people, as jury members or advisors, got to know each other through discussions about the project, built trust among themselves and formed a group to prepare and then make the decision on this common basis.

Up to the moment of the jury meeting, the discussion may take place over months based on rather abstract principles: textual and graphical descriptions of the framework conditions and project objectives and perhaps initial general preliminary studies. Typically, everyone involved in this phase of the project has a personal idea and expectation of the solution in mind.

On the day of the jury meeting, the anticipation comes to an end: the individual expectations meet concrete statements, proposed solutions, and images for the first time at this meeting. For some of the people involved, including members of the jury panel, there is a moment of disappointment at first, as the proposed solutions always have their own shape, which differs from one's own perception. Getting acquainted with and discussing the projects together, exchanging ideas and listening to each other offers the chance to experience an act of appropriation and to grasp the best idea in the meeting.

All those who know these processes will confirm that in many projects the competition phase and especially the jury meeting are remembered as important moments; moments in which solutions are found and possibly first recognized and accepted, which otherwise would not have been possible.

The organizational and content-related preparation of this moment is therefore a special challenge of great responsibility in every competition. Not only does everything have to be organized correctly – from the invitation letter to the name tag, from the hotel reservation to the catering – even more important is the choreography of the discourse, which encompasses all technical matters and ensures that every area of expertise and every perspective on the project is taken into consideration. The deciding factor is the atmosphere and the joy of doing things together, which gives the group the confidence to make the right decision and to be able to defend it.

The jury meetings in two-stage competitions are a special case. The meeting at the end of the first stage of a competition marks the same "eureka" moment as described above, but at its end there is initially only an interim result regarding the selection of the projects. Added to this is then the special significance of composing the jury's comments, since these form the basis for the further development of the projects qualified for the second stage. The discourse in the meeting of the second stage then has less potential for surprise but builds on the discussions already held and the trust formed in the first stage and thus often continues these in greater depth.

13.2 Preparation

› **Strategic planning:** In addition to organizational planning, coordination of the strategic process also takes place prior to the meeting. The competition organizer and the sponsor are involved, as is the technical juror who is to chair the meeting. The aim is to reach a consensus on the course of the meeting, the time required for the procedural steps, the methodology for presenting the projects, and the objectives of the meeting, which influence subsequent steps of the project and may require organizational interlinking (e.g., press conference, exhibition, negotiated procedure).

› **Scheduling, invitations, attendance, representation:** The presence of all nominated jury members is of great importance, which is why the scheduling and individual invitations to the meeting including details on date, time, duration, and venue should be sent well in advance. The representation of institutions in the general jury is usually of strategic importance, so that at least the continuous presence of a deputy should be guaranteed. Attendance confirmation some days prior to the meeting helps to avoid the possibility of spontaneous rescheduling.

› **Venue and equipment:** The selection and reservation of the venues as well as the planning, booking, or renting the necessary transport, furniture, technical equipment (sound, lighting, presentation technology), catering and, if necessary, security measures form the backbone of a successful meeting and must be taken into account early on in the preparation (see Chapter 11).

› **Staff:** Depending on the number of participants, the number of designs submitted, technical requirements, translation, and catering requirements, service providers and personnel must be secured at an early stage to support the competition organization team on site.

Jury meetings **1:** Siemensstadt 2.0 in Berlin (center: Stefan Behnisch), **2** and **4:** Parliamentary Precinct Redevelopment Ottawa (**2:** David Fortin, **4:** Anne Bordeleau), **3:** Wien Museum Neu (Emanuel Christ), **5:** Khandama Project in Makkah, **6** and **8:** Babyn Yar Holocaust Memorial Center in Kyiv (**8:** left David Adjaye, right Anna Kyrii), **7:** Revitalisation of the Old Town of Fez, **9:** Concert Hall Munich

13 Jurors' evaluation

13.3 Venue layout, boards for project display

Suitable rooms and the venue layout are decisive for the course and success of the meeting. The room layout outlined in Chapter 11.2 ideally also takes into account the dynamics during the meeting, as do the notes on furnishing in Chapter 11.3: Parts of the meeting take place at the meeting table, but the discussion in the evaluation rounds is better held in front of the plans and models, with an increasingly reduced number of projects as the meeting progresses. Flexibility in the presentation of the plans and models helps to present the projects optimally to the jury, to allow maximum time for discussion, and to minimize changeover time to move between projects. Lighting and sound must be just as flexible in creating optimal conditions as any requirements for translation or video transmission.

Experience shows that mobile systems for presenting plans and models are well suited for gathering the panel in a well-lit central location and moving the projects into that location ("arena") where they are discussed separately or in comparison to each other. Mobility is achieved either by lightweight boards that can be carried back and forth by support staff during the meeting, or (better) by boards that can be wheeled. The arena is also the appropriate place for the model of the surroundings into which participants' insert models can be placed.

13.4 Process

The process of a jury meeting, which is described in detail in individual competition rules, usually includes the following steps (rule sequence, general details):

› Opening and welcome (10–20 min.)
› Composition of the jury by establishing attendance and quorum, moderated by the competition organizer (5 min.)
› Admission of persons not previously involved, e.g., additional experts
› Election of the chairperson and discussion moderator (10 min.)
› Assurance of each person present that they have not had any conversation with competitors about the competition task and its solution outside of colloquia, will not have such an exchange during the jury meeting, do not have any knowledge of the competition projects until the jury meeting, unless they have participated in the preliminary examination, that the confidentiality of advice will be maintained, that the anonymity of all works will be preserved, and that they will refrain from making assumptions about the authorship of the works
› Obligation of the jury members to make an objective assessment based solely on the competition brief
› Explanation and discussion of the planned course of the meeting and the process of voting and decision making (10 min.)

- Report of the preliminary examination on the result of the formal examination as well as decision on the admission of the works (20–30 min.)
- Presentation of the submitted projects by the examiner(s) without evaluation, usually in front of the original plans and models. Sufficient time must be allowed for the relevant statements – usually 5 to 15 minutes per project. In total, the presentation requires 2 to 3 hours, in the case of open competitions with a large number of participants, possibly even a complete meeting day. In the case of more than 100 proposals, special solutions must be found for the procedure in order to achieve the best possible appreciation of all designs.
- Statement of the experts on the results of their involvement in the preliminary examination (15–60 min.)

- Discussion and evaluation rounds, usually organized as elimination rounds, in which all projects still remaining in the procedure are discussed and at the end votes are taken on whether they will remain in the competition (see Chapter 13.7)
- Formulation of the jury's comments (60 min.)
- Decisions on the ranking and allocation of prizes (60 min.)
- Decision on the recommendation of the jury to the sponsor (15 min.)
- Finally, discharge of the examiner(s) from their responsibility (10 min.)
- Return of the chair to the sponsor

Deviations from the regular procedure are necessary in the following cases:
- Particularly large number of submitted proposals
- Personal presentation by the competition participants
- Meeting of the first stage of a two-stage competition
- Partial participation of the public in the meeting

13.5 Completeness, chairmanship, approval of the work

Completeness

The competition brief should include the names of the jurors and their deputies, and thus also the planned number of voting members of the jury. If a voting member is not present, a nominated deputy takes over the voting right. Many rules and regulations stipulate that members of the technical jury do not regain their voting rights after an absence, even temporary absence, whereas this is possible for members of the general jury, provided that the temporarily absent person is adequately informed of the progress of the session upon their return. Therefore, a sufficient number of deputies must be appointed, especially in the case of two-stage competitions.

If there are not enough persons present to represent absent members of the technical jury, one member of the general jury may have to relinquish the right to vote so that the jury regains the usually required odd number of persons with voting right with a majority of technical jurors.

Chair

The chair is elected among the technical jurors at the beginning of the first jury meeting (i.e., usually not already during the jury colloquium). In the case of larger jury panels and two-stage competitions, it is advisable to elect a deputy chair. The chair moderates the jury meetings and is also often involved in other voting or press meetings as a representative of the technical jury. In addition, the chair is co-responsible for the release of the minutes.

Jafar Tukan
Architect, Amman (1938–2014),
in memory of one of the most established figures on the Jordanian architecture scene

" Since my graduation from the school of architecture and starting to train in a well-established firm in Lebanon, I became aware of the importance and the challenges of architectural competitions. Early in my training period I was involved, as part of the design team, in a competition for a prison project in Lebanon. During the process, I started feeling the difference between working on a project on which a contract was signed with the client and one in which you have to hopefully get through competition with another architect. In the former there is an open dialogue with the client, there is the comfort of working on a secured project. In the latter, communication with the client is very restricted, there is always the challenge of having to come up with a new idea that could increase the probability of winning, or sometimes losing, the competition.

In the Middle East and until only a few years ago, awareness of organizing competitions was still unfamiliar. The idea of the prospective client was, in most cases, that a competition is like window shopping for a commodity. Clients were not aware of the cultural as well as the economic implications that the creative process of designing a building involves. They were not also aware of the significance of the evaluation process and criteria. There were many disappointing experiences that I personally was exposed to, as well as, I am sure, many other colleagues of mine, where our effort was not compensated, where the evaluating team was appointed only after the submission of the competition deliverables, and where such a team was grossly unqualified. In many other cases we were requested to submit a design fee to be applied if we won the competition, which frequently resulted in selecting the project of the lowest bidder and plagiarize some of the better ideas of the better, but higher bidding projects.

For all the above reasons I took the decision not to participate in any competition where the international rules of competitions are not strictly applied, implemented, and followed through.

A few years ago, I was invited by [phase eins]. to be a member of the Jury for a competition they were organizing for a project in Abu Dhabi. That experience, to me, was very impressive. It took care of all the anxieties that used to discourage me from participating in competitions. There, you find a team dedicated to the organizing process from day one, meticulously preparing a detailed and thorough brief, assigning fair compensation for all competitors, selecting the jury members very meticulously, defining very clear milestones for meetings, questions and answers, and submissions, with complete transparency.

In this way [phase eins]. represented to me, the full solution to the chronic problem of competitions in the Middle East and, I am sure, in many other places in the world. To me, they were the first office that specializes in organizing architectural competitions as I have not heard of such specialized offices before. A very important feature of their service is that, because of their professionalism, organization, and transparency they could attract the top names in the field of architecture to offer their services to [phase eins]. clients.

Gulzar Haider and Jafar Tukan at the jury meeting for the Amman Concert Hall and Theatre, 2008

13 Jurors' evaluation

Admission of the works

At the beginning of the session, the chairperson decides on the admission to the procedure and approves for evaluation all competition works that:

› Comply with the formal conditions of the competition brief
› Meet the sponsor's specifications designated as binding (see Chapter 10.3)
› Correspond in essential parts to the required scope of services (see Chapter 8.5)
› Have been received in due time
› Which, if agreed in advance, do not reveal any breach of anonymity

Projects that clearly violate any of the requirements stated above should be excluded from the evaluation. Likewise, as a rule, partial services that exceed the required level in terms of type and scope are excluded to ensure fair competition and thus keep the workload for the participants at a reasonable level. Since the reasons for a possible exclusion are usually determined during the preliminary examination, the decision is largely based on the respective report and the confidence in the diligence required for such a momentous decision.

13.6 Presentation of the designs and report of the experts

The presentation of the submitted designs is carried out by the examiner(s) – an important task of the competition organizer or any examiners involved in the organization of the competition. Only in exceptional cases, and only in the case of invited competitions, the presentation is made by the design authors themselves. In this case, too, the presentation is still followed by the neutral report of the examiner(s) on the results of the examination.

The presentation should include the following topics:
› Explaining the concept, as well as functional and technical features
› Naming relevant facts, especially related to the main dimensions and spatial program
› Mentioning violations of relevant specifications (e.g., exceeding limits, heights, etc.)
› Integrating the results of the examination, unless the technical experts present them themselves

Thereby challenges and requirements arise such as:
› The summary of all aspects (in a few minutes!)
› Presentations of all proposals in the same structure and duration
› A neutral, unambiguous form of speech
› Presentation skills to a larger panel (voice, volume, gestures)

In connection with the presentation of the proposals by the examiner(s), the experts should also be given an initial opportunity to present the results of their review. It makes sense to structure this presentation thematically (see Chapter 12.6). In the case of a small number of proposals, the first report can be project-related; in the case of a larger number, it makes sense to first present the approach and relevant, generally valid findings of the expert examination. In this case, the experts' comments on individual projects are then made during the subsequent discussion rounds.

Jury meetings **1**, **7** and **8**: Babyn Yar Holocaust Memorial Center in Kyiv (Volodymyr Klytschko), **2**: Beirut Museum of Art (middle: Richard Rogers and Rem Koolhaas), **3** and **5**: Revitalisation of the old town of Fez (**3**: Marc Angelil, Fouad Serrhini, Matthias Sauerbruch), **4**: Jewish Museum in Albania, **6**: Urban Drainage and Environmental Analysis Nuremberg, **9**: Technical City Hall Düsseldorf

Jan Kleihues
Architect, Berlin

❞ Both as a competition participant and as a juror, I have noticed again and again that, just like in architecture – where a house/a project can only ever be as good as the cooperation and mutual respect between architect and client dictates – the result is a competition is particularly convincing when good and well-prepared architects and jurors form the basis of the process.

13.7 Decision-making process in rounds, voting methodology

With the presentation of all designs in their essential outlines and the first statement of the experts, the jury has an overview of the range of solution approaches, basic principles of the solutions, conspicuous features within the spectrum, as well as topics that are solved not so well or particularly well according to the assessment of the experts.

1st round

On this basis, a general discussion of the jury can take place about what has been observed and about the application of the decision criteria, which then leads into a first evaluation round in which all proposals are discussed one after the other.
For the start of the discussion, it is helpful if projects are assigned at the beginning of the meeting, if necessary, already with the agenda, i.e., an assignment of proposals to each technical juror. In this scenario, the jurors responsible should make a well-founded statement at the beginning of the discussion of the works assigned to them in the first round.
The early assignment allows these jury members to prepare well so that an intensive introduction to the discussion of the individual projects can take place without delay. In any case, the jury should have an open discussion in which all relevant criteria are addressed. In this way, an overall picture of the evaluation emerges. The concrete vote in the 1st round can take place either immediately after discussion of the respective work or in a voting block after all works have been discussed. Some rules and regulations stipulate that projects can only be eliminated in this round with unanimity, since the design proposals could not yet be discussed in depth to this point.
If the entire jury panel is unanimous, it is assumed that the works to be eliminated have too low qualities or several serious weaknesses in comparison with all projects.

2nd round and further rounds

The proposals remaining in the competition after the 1st round are subjected to increasingly intensive examination and discussion in further rounds.
All panel members, including the experts, should be involved in these rounds.
At this stage, it may be helpful to directly compare typologically similar projects, or, for example, several or all projects with a focus on resolving individual sub-issues. There is no one way to go about the process at this stage of the meeting, and no binding requirements in the rules and regulations.
Rather, it requires the moderation skills of the chair, the experience of the jury panel, the advice of the competition organizer if necessary, and an eye on the time budget of the meeting to make a selection that is supported by all members of the panel quickly and yet with adequate time for discussion of all contributions. This does not always happen unanimously in these rounds, which is why decisions are usually made here with a simple majority.

Recall-motion

At the end of each round, the procedure allows for a revision of a possible exclusion by means of a recall motion. This can be submitted by any voting member of the jury who is of the opinion that particular qualities of a project that was initially excluded were overlooked or incorrectly assessed. Often this concerns projects that were voted on at the beginning of a round and whose quality only became apparent after other work was discussed later in the round. Provided the motion is supported by a majority, the design in question is reinstated in the procedure.

Shortlist/prize group

Once the decision process has resulted in several design proposals that largely correspond to the scheduled number of prizes and metnions, this is referred to as the "shortlist" or "prize group." At this point, it is helpful to pause the meeting to write the jury comments, or at least to collect key ideas for a later writing of these comments. This break allows all participants to sum up individually or to talk in smaller groups, which ensures that, if necessary, further details of the task or the solutions can be included in the decision-making process or that topics already discussed can be re-evaluated.

Ranking and allocation of the prizes

A final discussion follows with the voting on the ranking of the projects and then the allocation of the prizes. Since it is not only about the honor to win, but also about an – often lucrative – design contract, the experience of the chair as a moderator, as a diplomat and last but not least as a trustee of the interests of the sponsor, but also of the colleagues participating in the jury, is required at the latest in this phase of the competition. Here, too, the leader of the competition organization can play an important role as co-moderator and as a further person of trust for the sponsor.

Voting methods

Apart from the specifications on absolute or simple majorities for resolutions, there are no specifications in rules and regulations for competitions on the methodology of voting. These are usually proposed by the chair and may vary. In practice, open votes by hand raising are common, and secret ballots are rare. In some situations, straw polls are helpful. There is the option of anonymous or non-anonymous list voting, in which all voting jurors write down the cover numbers of their favored projects and the result can be used to establish a trend or prepare a decision. There are other methods, including those used in the case of online organized jury meeting, especially in price competitions.

13.8 Comments of the jury, minutes of the meeting

Written comments and recommendations of the jury

The formulation of written comments and the decision on the jury's recommendation on how to proceed in the further design process are two of the jury's main tasks. They are important in order to make the decision comprehensible for the public and the competitors. In addition, they may be significant in a subsequent negotiation procedure (see Chapter 15.1) as well as in the subsequent design steps, especially since comments and recommendations sometimes describe necessary significant changes to the competition design.

The comments should express the jury's assessment of the respective project and describe the qualities and shortcomings which, in the jury's discussion, led to the decision to award the prize.

In the case of competitions with a small number of proposals, it is advisable to write comments also on the designs that were not awarded.

The decision on the recommendation of the jury can be formulated as follows: "The jury unanimously recommends the sponsor to commission the authors of the design awarded with the 1st prize to continue working on the project in accordance with the competition brief. In the further development of the project, particular attention should be paid to the points explained in detail in the jury's written assessment".

Stefan Behnisch
Architect, Stuttgart

" For us architects – at least for a large part of the profession – competitions are of paramount importance. They were established early in the new republic and, I believe, have ensured a demand for quality. We are in competition, not only directly but also in the broadest sense, through the publication of the results. For the clients, the design competition is of advantage, because they receive an objectively evaluated, large selection of proposed solutions for relatively little money. For the architects, it is important because it has created a fair and sophisticated tendering system that is not dependent on social influence, money, and corruption. Of course, the competition system has changed over time and in some cases has become problematic, especially in the pre-qualification procedures. Young, new architects no longer have much chance of being selected to participate in competitions because they do not have the required experience. Taken to its logical conclusion, this means that those who have done a task many times before will be allowed to do the same tasks again in the future. This is, of course, counterproductive, because it stifles innovation per se. Experience tempts us to repeat what we have already thought. When we, as architects, participate in competitions, we depend on a fair procedure that adheres to promises made: that the statements mentioned in competition briefs and agreements will be indeed fulfilled. The first important step is very good preparation for the competition, a precise and well-coordinated competition brief, appropriate advice to the potential sponsor on how such a fair procedure should work and what the sponsor can expect from the contributing parties and vice versa. Once you have taken part in the competition and submitted the deliverables, you are "at the mercy" of the preliminary examiners and jury members. One relies on a fair examination and fair, as well as objective, presentation at the jury meeting, and the fact that the effort and expense on behalf of the participants are also recognized accordingly. However, as jury members, we often experience that, despite a well-prepared and objective preliminary examination, some members of the committee try to deviate from the statements of the competition in the evaluation; from objectivity to a "I like it, I don't like it". This must not happen. The content must be discussed argumentatively. And, so, the most important contribution of the preliminary examination is usually the objective fair preparation, the objective fair consultation, and the ensuring of an organized procedure.

Jury meetings **1** and **3**: Parliamentary Precinct Redevelopment Ottawa, **2**: Babyn Yar Holocaust Memorial Center in Kyiv (Kjetil Thorsen and Dieter Bogner), **4**: Technical City Hall Düsseldorf, **7**: Day care center in Lahr (front left: Tobias Wulf), **8**: ThyssenKrupp Quarter, Essen, **9**: KFAS Headquarters and Conference Center in Kuwait (left: Markus Allmann)

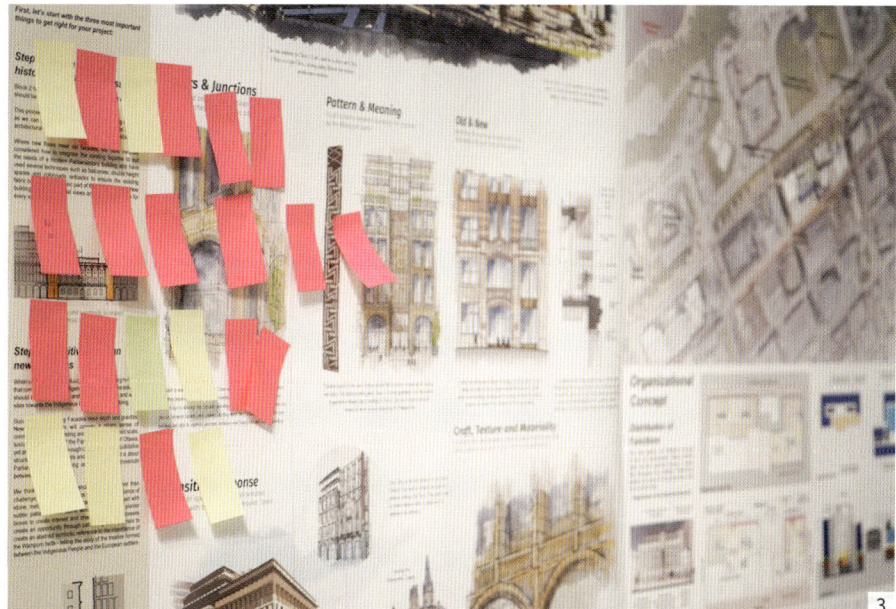

13 Jurors' evaluation

Meeting minutes

A record of the results of the entire meeting is prepared. It summarizes the main points of the discussion, all decision-making steps and resolutions with the results of the votes, as well as the written comments of the jury and the recommendation for further commissioning. It also includes the names of all parties present as well as the venue, date, and duration of the meeting. The minutes are usually prepared by the competition organizer and confirmed by the chair. In formally demanding situations, the minutes are written during the meeting, read out, decided upon, and signed by all jurors. The minutes are made available to all participants after the meeting. In addition, there is often a documentation of all submitted design proposals, which is also provided to all participants. This is done against the background of making the decision as transparent and comprehensible as possible to all participants to increase the acceptance of the decision made.

13.9 Envelope opening, notifying the prizewinners

After all decisions have been made and the preliminary examiners have been discharged, the anonymity of the participants is lifted by opening the envelopes with the declarations of authorship, which have been sealed until then, and reading out the names of the design teams or authors mentioned there. With this step and the closing words of the sponsor, the jury meeting is concluded. All participants should then be informed of the results immediately – the prizewinners by telephone and directly after the meeting.

Right page: Excerpt from the minutes of a jury meeting with the jury's formulation for further commissioning

Prof. em. Kees Christiaanse
Architect and urban planner, Zurich/Rotterdam

❝ Urban planning and architectural competitions are vital components of building culture and significantly contribute to its advancement. These competitions allow for various, innovative design approaches and concepts to be put to the test, examined, and compared. Such measures are essential for the sustainable use of our precious and limited buildable area and cultural landscape. The tendering process for public contracts must serve as a tool for social-democratic culture of construction, where a diverse array of professional perspectives from the industry are evaluated on their respective merits by an unbiased panel.

In over four decades of professional experience, I have participated in numerous competitions and served on several juries. The Parc de la Vilette competition in Paris in 1983, where the OMA team, of which I was a member, secured second prize, stands out as one of the most significant competitions for me. Our submission was a fascinating and original work in the field of urban planning and landscape research, which subsequently set a precedent for flexible, scenario-based design in the worldwide professional arena. The competition comprised of two stages: an initial open phase, followed by a closed stage featuring only ten chosen designs. As per the jury's account, our design was originally consigned to the scrapyard during the initial phase until Roberto Burle Marx intervened at the eleventh hour and salvaged it. I am unsure of the veracity of this anecdote, but it demonstrates the element of chance in competitions and highlights the significance of a fair and neutral jury. Speaking of the importance of a balanced jury, our office supposedly won the Holzhafen competition in Hamburg due to the inability of two factions on the panel to come to an agreement, ultimately settling on our proposal as a compromise. However, I cannot confirm the accuracy of this information.

Finally, this also demonstrates the refinement of an open competition that welcomes many, even inexperienced participants, combined with a closed second phase for select projects. This approach ensures both opportunities for budding talent and an ultimately professional standard. Throughout my competition and jury career, I have disliked competitions with excessive requirements for building experience in specific building types and minimal business turnover. Further, I have found competitions with inadequate compensation or prize money and preselected participants to be unsatisfactory. Additionally, "test planning," a Swiss invention, whereby several offices produce designs with no claim to a follow-up contract, and a completely new office collages together the "advantages" from the designs as a "Cadavre Exquis" or a "Cadavre Manqué," is also disagreeable.

Competition remains imperative for establishing a high-quality construction culture in the free world within a balanced milieu of the aforementioned factors.

Design Competition for the National Memorial for the Heavenly Hundred Heroes
and Revolution of Dignity Museum in Kyiv

	Jury Meeting Stage 2	Minutes	
Page 6/10	Wednesday, June 27, 2018	Drafted 09.07.2018, Ho	[phase eins].
#	Topic		

I — Decision on Prizes

At 5.40 p.m., the jury unanimously confirmed to distribute the prize money as stated in the competition brief. In addition, the jury unanimously decided to attribute, according to the opinion formed in the discussion and the outcome of the ballots, the following prizes:

1st prize	21,000,- Euro	1002
2nd prize	13,000,- Euro	1003
3rd prize	8,500,- Euro	1001

J — Suggestions of the Jury as to Further Project Development

Afterwards, the jury unanimously agreed on the following recommendation:

"The jury unanimously recommends that the promoter of the competition shall commission the team of authors of the winning project with the services as stated in the competition brief. Further, the jury recommended that the promoter and the authors consider during the further development of the design, the statements made by the jury in its remarks on the project."

K — Remarks by the Jury

From 5.45 p.m. to 6.30 p.m. the jurors drafted assessments of each entry and, after further discussion unanimously confirmed the drafts at 7.00 p.m. It was unanimously decided that, subsequent to the meeting, these texts should be finalized for inclusion in the minutes.

1001

The jury appreciates the idea of a museum that looks and works like a mountain. The design invites the visitor onto a spiraling rooftop path to the very top of the building thus offering a natural continuation to the Alley of the Heavenly Hundred Heroes in a simple and positive way. The roof terraces allow the visitors to literally take possession of the building and allow for interaction between visitors and neighbours before and after the museum visit. They also provide space for outdoor installations in addition to or as part of the museum exhibitions. Even though the scale and the routing developed from the Avenue of Heavenly Hundred seems appropriate, the jury doesn't believe the integration of the building into its context is not completely convincing.

Further, the idea of a roof park is doubtful as the extensive planting of these areas (that is shown on the renderings) will probably reach technical limits very quickly. There was also a passionate discussion about the appropriateness of a café on the top floor of a memorial museum. It was felt that some aspects of this design have an aura of entertainment and seem to miss the necessary respect for the fallen heroes. Thus, also the perforated metal screens symbolizing bullet holes were considered Kitsch and definitely not acceptable.

The grand gesture of the spiral (which doesn't lead to the interior) overshadows the main entrance and hence complicates orientation for visitors both from Maidan and the Metro Station. The entrance hall is not very inviting with the low ceiling and the views oriented to the interior of the block. Similarly, internal circulation is not easy, particularly for groups and handicapped visitors. There is a big variety of exhibition spaces in size and height but the language of these spaces is unsuitably reminiscent of an art gallery. There are also too many spaces below entrance level. However, the House of Freedom is well integrated into the complex.

The jury appreciates the serious work that was undertaken between stages 1 and 2 to optimize the idea of a participatory museum building. However, ultimately, it also feels that this concept has led to a project which lacks iconic character and won't be able to present a strong image when seen from afar.

Overall, the jury judges this proposal as a bold and consistent concept of outstanding quality but is ultimately not convinced about its presence in the city.

1002

This project is a simple, spiritual and characteristic piece of architecture, well integrated into its urban context, with a high degree of functionality. It is continuing the legacy of European Classical architecture in an interesting and modern way while responding to the complex and partially contradictory requirements of the site and the whole context. The solution offers a

14 PUBLICITY

14.1 Participation

From a technical point of view, the objective of a design competition is primarily to find the best solution to a design task, usually followed by signing a design contract. However, every competition also marks the beginning of a design process, which in most cases concerns the (re)design of the built environment. Every building, urban development, or outdoor space design project addresses issues of social relevance, appealing not only to those directly involved in the project, but also to the general public. For example, the design of the habitat is shaped by the architectural quality of the building, whereas usability is influenced by functional quality, organizational solutions have an impact on traffic, and holistic design has a significant impact on ecological aspects and the climate.

Those affected by design and construction can be divided into the internal public (e.g., staff), the immediate neighbors and the general public. The degree to which people are affected and interested in being involved in participatory processes varies not only according to the location, size, and use of the project, but has also rational and emotional aspects. The consideration of both dimensions is crucial for the broad acceptance and success of a project.

Public participation in design is a complex issue. The organization of such processes is a separate activity field and is only partially elaborated here. In this context, design competitions are an important instrument, established as a framework for participation on several levels since their beginning in the 19th century: the involvement of the professional public in decision-making and the provision of information to the public.

Both components have always been part of competitions and have thus always contributed to public discourse and the overall objective of the competition: to strengthen the acceptance of the design.

With the general development of democratic and participatory processes, the public's interest in participating in design has also developed in recent decades. The new (technical) possibilities of communication support this development. Discourse is no longer limited to expert circles but has found its way into Web 2.0 and social media.

Crucial to the success of participation and competition is the mutual respect of those involved and the appropriate integration of the various tools. As explained in Chapter 3.1 with reference to the choice of the competition type, there is also no generally applicable solution with regard to the linking of participation and competition, but rather the need for specific solutions tailored to each project. Competitions offer great potential for making design processes transparent and comprehensible. With the variety of type of procedures, they offer different possibilities for participatory elements, which are already established instruments in many places:

› **Before the competition:** in the form of informational events, thematic workshops, walks to the site with the stakeholders, or online surveys to integrate their opinions and knowledge in the project specifications.
› **During the competition:** involvement stakeholders' representatives as guests or, if necessary, as voting jury members.
› **After the competition:** information and discussion events, e.g., as part of the public exhibition of the competition results.

Although participation is intensified in specific parts of the design process, it is recognized and justified that the process must be largely closed during the ongoing competition to achieve the desired design quality in a short period of time with focus on the technical discussion and, ultimately, to ensure the fairness and legal certainty of the process and any that may follow the competition.

14.2 Press

The specialist press and the regional daily press should be informed about the competition announcement and later about the result, in the case of significant projects also the feature sections of the national press. If participatory components are integrated into the process, the relevant portals and the scheduled events should also be announced.

The press release announcing a competition must contain the essential facts that could be of interest to the public, but also to design offices interested in participating. The reference to a project homepage is a practical solution here.

For the announcement of the competition result in the form of a press release or in a press conference, a press text is usually prepared, the quality of which must be suitable for complete reproduction and should contain all facts about the project that are relevant for the public (sponsor, objective, location, size, costs, construction period, result, excerpt from the recommendation of the jury for the further design steps, reference to a public exhibition and, if relevant, an online exhibition). Visual material is expected to be attached to the prizewinning projects with information on the image rights.

For the specialist press, the package is usually extended to include all essential plans, model photos and explanatory texts of the prizewinning projects, as well as an excerpt from the minutes of the jury meeting with the comments of the jury.

1: Participation event as part of the "BMW FIZ Future in Munich" competition.

14.3 Project homepage

Most design competitions are presented on an online platform. The creation of this project homepage lies in the responsibilities of the competition organizer and is handled either by their own system, a tender platform, or a private provider of corresponding standard pages. The internet presence serves the communication with three groups:

› **Public:** information about the project and potential proposals for participation
› **Professional public:** possibility to apply for participation in the competition
› **Competition participants:** communication and exchange of information and data

Depending on the type of procedure, the following components are usually mentioned:

› **Project:** general information in the form of texts, photos, maps, and plans
› **Procedure:** relevant details; in the case of public projects, identical in content to the announcement in the official journal
› **Members involved:** sponsor and jury members
› **Registration:** possibility to register in case of an open competition
› **Application:** possibility to submit an application for participation in case of an open competition
› **Online forum:** platform to submit questions anonymously during the application process and later during the competition, offering the possibility to read all questions and answers
› **Material:** download area with different hierarchy levels of access: public files (press release, public announcement, etc.), non-public files (for competition participants) and internal files (e.g., for exchange between the competition organizer and the sponsor)
› **Online exhibition:** presentation of all submitted entries with plans, photos of models, explanatory texts, comments from the jury and the names of the designers or design teams

2 and 3: Press conferences as part of the "Museum for the Maidan Revolution in Kyiv" and **4:** "Exhibition redesign and extension in the old tower of the Kaiser Wilhelm Memorial Church in Berlin" competitions.

14.4 Exhibition

The public presentation of the competition signals the conclusion of a competition and can be an integral part of public relations and a participatory process, promoting professional discourse, inspiring student education and professional training and, finally, offering the sponsor an opportunity to present themselves and the project. In addition to the organizational requirements mentioned in Chapter 11, the first strategic question to be clarified in the design process is the objective of the exhibition: is it a "compulsory exercise" or should the opportunities be seized? With these questions answered, the timing, duration, scope, and cost of the exhibition can be determined. However, the availability of space and people is often also critical to the decisions to be made.

In general, the exhibition should include a presentation of all designs, in the case of two-stage competitions also of the designs from Stage 1 of the competition. This inspires respect for the work of all participants in the competition, on the other hand. The presentation of the entire spectrum also serves the project itself since the transparency and the participation in this often very impressive final result supports the comprehensibility of the decision.

The main part of the exhibition is formed by the presentation plans and models, usually the originals submitted in the competition. In case of lack of space in the exhibition venue, the plans can also be reprinted in a reduced format. All works should be complimented by the information on the authorship, including at least the authorship should information, the explanatory texts of the participants and, if necessary, the jury's comments on the respective work.

For a better introduction of the visitors of the exhibition to the project and the competition, it is recommended to create informative boards to present information on the task, the procedure, and an overview of all submitted projects. Furthermore, the competition announcement and the minutes of the jury meeting should be available, at least upon request.

Kristiaan Borret
Architect, Bouwmeester-Maître Architecte of the Brussels Capital Region

» It is the role of the Bouwmeester/Maître-Architecte to stimulate the quality of urban development projects in Brussels Capital Region, on behalf of the government but in an independent position. I have been working on that since 2015, and supporting architecture competitions is an important part of the job because they mean absolutely the best way to drive ambition in any project. So, it was very useful when it turned out that [phase eins]. would be in charge of managing two important competitions for the European Commission and Parliament in Brussels. The preparation was done very professionally and brings reliability both for the public authority and for the participating architects. After all, a competition only runs smoothly if the brief is clearly and fully formulated. If the question is asked well, the architects will be able to answer well too. Flimsy questions result in fuzzy designs. In addition, I personally think an open competition climate is very important: oral explanation by the candidates themselves, public attendance of the presentations, a participation process before the competition starts … These are the methods we are exploring in Brussels to evolve the competitions even more into a public, interactive and outreaching event.

Exhibition poster with details of the brief and procedure for the "Revitalisation of the old town of Fez" competition

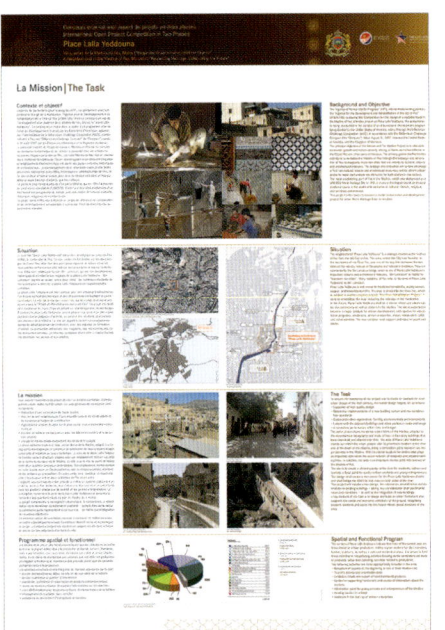

Exhibitions as part of the competitions **1:** Jewish Museum in Albania, **2:** Wien Museum Neu, **3:** Siemensstadt 2.0 Berlin, **4:** ThyssenKrupp Quarter, Essen, **5:** Mönchengladbach Town Hall

XI UNIVERSITY CAMPUSES

The term campus, often used also in other contexts, is particularly associated with universities through their history – the prestigious universities of Great Britain, Harvard University, the Jordan University of Science and Technology, the American University of Beirut and Mexico City are some of the world's best-known examples. The structure of the building and the outdoor spaces represents academic life – the unity of research and teaching – is represented in a unique way. They are also well known because the many alumni have spent an important part of their lives there and therefore this place remains "in their hearts" in later life.

The establishment of new universities, as well as the further development of existing universities, and the corresponding campus design competitions, involve both the urban design dimension of a building ensemble and its development, as well as the design of many individual buildings with very different usage requirements as well as the design of outdoor spaces. Even if the design of these buildings in a campus design competition may not reach the same level of detail as in a competition for a single institute or library building due to the larger number of buildings, a competition for a campus must take into account both the special requirements of the use in terms of building depths, floor heights, development, orientation, location on the campus, etc., and the design context between the buildings: the design of a campus creates the context for the individual building plans, the buildings in turn define the context. In the formulation of the task, in the definition of the competition requirements, and in the context of the preliminary examination, the user requirements as well as questions of the definition of the construction phases and the integration of the outdoor facilities are to be considered. In contrast to many urban design competitions, in this case the users and therefore the requirements for the building are usually known. Therefore, the involvement of the users in the competition process plays a special role.

In the case of design competitions for the densification and further development of an existing campus or for the use of existing buildings that have previously been used for other purposes, the requirements are extended to also include components for dealing with existing buildings that may be listed, and questions of relocation management for implementation during ongoing operations, which must be reflected in the competition itself due to the strategic importance of these issues.

Consideration must be given to the possibility of long implementation periods, for which responsibility is likely to be in the hands of others than those responsible for launching the project and the competition. The contents of the competition must therefore be valid in the long term and the result must be sufficiently flexible ("robust") for constantly changing requirements.

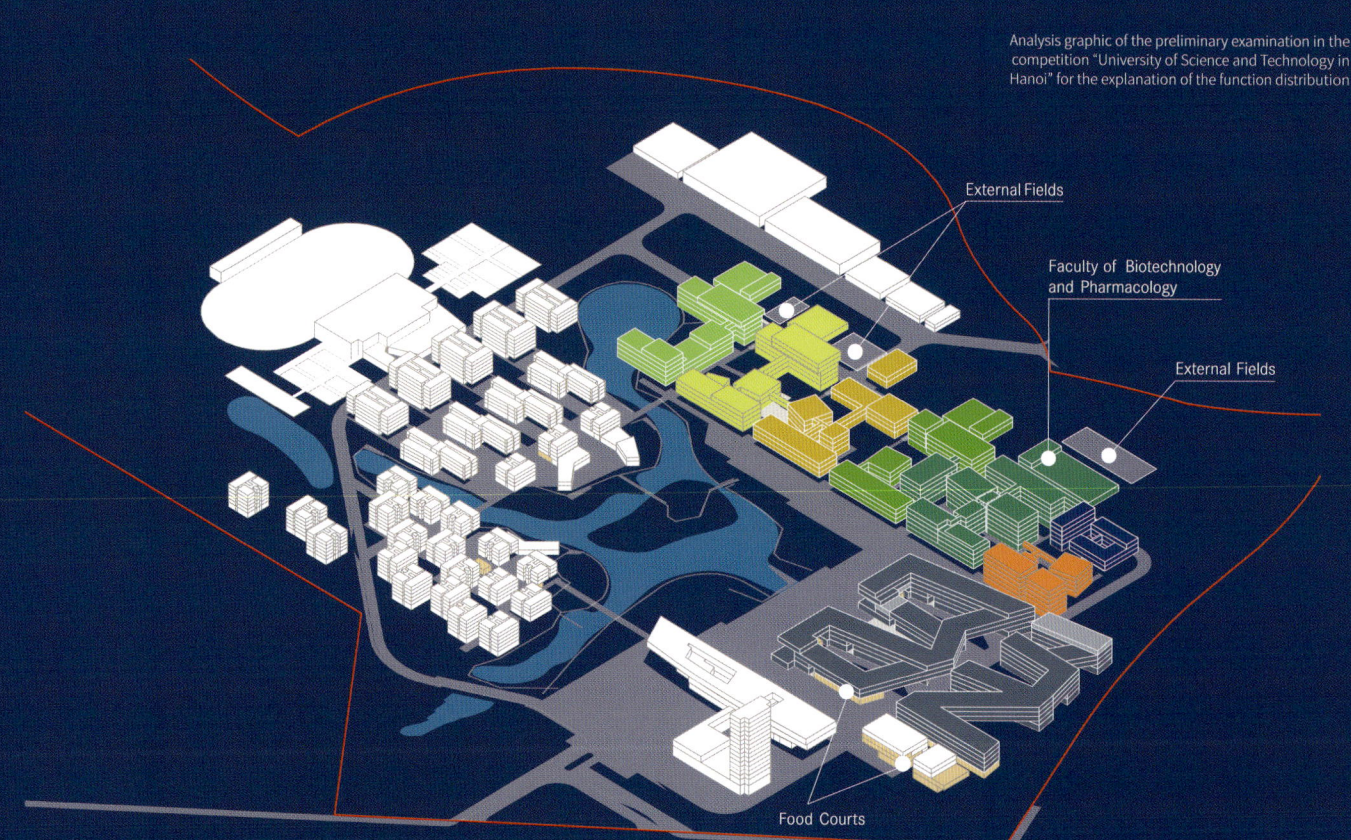

Analysis graphic of the preliminary examination in the competition "University of Science and Technology in Hanoi" for the explanation of the function distribution

Vietnamese-German University, Ho Chi Minh City

VIETNAMESE-GERMAN UNIVERSITY To ensure sustainable national development, the Vietnamese government has created a program for higher education reform. Among other things, the program provides for the construction of a number of new universities. The universities should enable the young population to train under specialists matching international standards. In an initial step of the reform program, four "Model Universities" were established – each university teamed with a partner country. One of these Model Universities is the Vietnamese-German University VGU. The partner countries support Vietnam in curriculum development, provide teaching staff in the development phase and consult in issues related to the design and implementation of structural facilities, among other areas. The VGU is supported by Germany's Federal Ministry of Education and Research, the State of Hesse, and a number of German universities. Primary funding is provided through World Bank loans.

THE SITE The competition site is located approximately 50 km northwest of Ho Chi Minh City in the northern part of Binh Duong Province. The province is one of the most rapidly developing regions in the country with industrial complexes, research and science institutions and large residential projects. The 51-hectare competition site is situated on National Highway 13 (one of HCMC's primary arterial roads) and bordered by Ring Road 4 to the north. Existing rural residential developments border the site in the south. A drainage canal runs through the site.

THE COMPETITION TASK The university should be built in two phases. In the first phase (up to 2017) construction of approximately 135,000 sqm GFA for 5,000 students is planned; in the second phase an additional 190,000 sqm GFA is to be built for 12,000 students in total. The task includes general planning of the entire new campus. In addition to new facilities for teaching, research and a science park, the campus will house sports complexes and technical facilities, in addition to housing and accommodation for students and teachers. Planners should take the geographic, climatic, and cultural contexts into consideration in their proposals.

Location: Ho Chi Minh City, Vietnam **Client:** Socialist Republic of Vietnam represented by the Ministry of Education and Training (MoET) and in cooperation with the World Bank **Year:** 2012 – 2013 **Project size:** 50.5 ha **Type of competition:** Design-bid-build competition for general contractors preceded by an open application procedure in accordance with World Bank guidelines **Participants:** 5 **Competition budget:** 150,000 USD in prizes

PRIZEWINNERS:
(01) **1st prize** Machado and Silvetti Associates, Boston (USA); **2nd prize** KSP Jürgen Engel Architekten, Frankfurt a. M. (D); **3rd prize** Itsuko Hasegawa Atelier, Tokyo (J); **4th prize** Riegler Riewe Architekten, Graz (A); **5th prize** Henn Architekten, Munich (D)

University of Science and Technology Campus, Hanoi

Location: Hanoi, Vietnam **Client:** Socialist Republic of Vietnam represented by the Ministry of Education and Training (MoET) and co-ordinated with the Asian Development Bank **Year:** 2013 – 2014 **Project size:** 65 ha, 143.000 sqm GFA **Type of competition:** Design-bid-build competition for general contractors preceded by an open application procedure in accordance with Asian Development Bank guidelines **Participants:** 6 **Competition budget:** not specified

PRIZEWINNERS:
(01) **1st prize** AS. Architecture Studio, Paris (F); (02) **2nd prize** Coelacanth and Associates (C+A), Nagoya (J); (03) **3rd prize** Auer + Weber + Assoziierte, Munich (D); (04) **4th prize** AREP Ville, Paris (F); **5th prize** CPG Consultants, Singapore (SGP); **6th prize** D'Appolonia, Genoa (I)

UNIVERSITY OF SCIENCE AND TECHNOLOGY HANOI (USTH) Similar to the Vietnamese-German University (VGU) also presented in this book, the USTH is also one of the four "Model Universities" in Vietnam set up together with partner countries in order to establish international standards of higher education. In the case of the USTH founded in 2009, France is the partner country. The university will be operated by the Vietnamese Ministry of Education and Training in cooperation with the French Ministry of Research and Education. A French consortium of 40 universities is another strategic partner involved. The project was financed primarily through credit from the Asian Development Bank (ADB), therefore ADB procurement rules were applicable.

LOCATION IN THE HOA LAC HIGH-TECH PARK The USTH is located within the Hoa Lac High-Tech Park, 37 km west of Hanoi. The high-tech park is to become a center of science and technology with research and education institutions and high-tech industries that are to be located here. For Vietnam, the location should have a stature similar to Silicon Valley for the United States or Bangalore within India. Until now the approximately 65 ha of property was used for military and agricultural use and is characterized by a hilly topography and large areas of surface water. The property borders National Road Nr. 21 to the west, Road E in the southeast and Road Nr. 1 in the northeast.

COMPETITION TASK The object of the competition was development of an urban masterplan and general planning of the entire campus that is to be constructed in two phases. Approximately 250,000 sqm GFA should be constructed by 2020 for around 5,000 students: a total of approximately 400,000 sqm GFA by 2030 for 15,000 students and 2,200 faculty members. The program includes teaching facilities for six departments, centralized buildings like a library and cafeteria, as well as administrative offices, sports facilities and student housing.

Helmut Schmidt University, University of the Federal Armed Forces, Hamburg

HELMUT SCHMIDT UNIVERSITY (HSU) In 1972, the "Hochschule der Bundeswehr Hamburg" (University of the Federal Armed Forces Hamburg) was founded on the initiative of the then Minister of Defense, Helmut Schmidt. Its main purpose is the academic training of Bundeswehr officers, but it is also used as a science center for civilian students. 2,500 students are enrolled in the fields of natural sciences and engineering as well as economics, humanities, and social sciences. In addition, research of a high technical standard takes place; HSU is involved in two of Hamburg's four clusters of excellence.

CAMPUS The HSU campus was established in the 1970s on the site of the Douaumont barracks in Hamburg-Jenfeld according to a design by the office of Heinle, Wischer und Partner. Preserved barracks buildings from the 1930s, primarily serving as accommodation for students, were supplemented by an ensemble of educational buildings, connected by green spaces characterized by openness and soft forms. The ensemble is considered a successful architectural interpretation of the development towards a Bundeswehr of citizens in uniform. The educational buildings, with their significant suspended steel truss structure, together with the open spaces were listed in 2017 and form monument ensemble of national significance.

TASK The project was prompted by the need for an additional approx. 60,000 sqm of usable space for the HSU and the urgent need to renovate the educational buildings from the 1970s, whose structure has proven to be less than suitable for many academic uses. The subject of the competition was the development of a master plan for the overall structural development, which considers both the monument situation, safety requirements and an implementation in the ongoing university operations. It should define guidelines for an identity-defining building structure, open space design and traffic routing, ensure sustainability goals of a climate-neutral campus and guarantee implementation in stages with realistic relocation scenarios.

Location: Hamburg, Germany **Client:** Federal Republik of Germany, represented through Bundesbauabteilung Hamburg (BBA) **Year:** 2022 – 2023 **Project size:** 26 ha **Type of competition:** Restricted, interdisciplinary two-stage design competition **Participants:** Stage 1: 14; Stage 2: 7 **Competition budget:** EUR 246,000 (prizes: EUR 66,000; compensation Stage 1: EUR 100,000; compensation Stage 2: EUR 80,000)

PRIZEWINNERS:
(01) **1st prize** h4a Gessert + Randecker Architekten with Glück Landschaftsarchitektur and Wick + Partner Architekten Stadtplaner, all Stuttgart (D); **2nd prize** bizer architekten with koeber Landschaftsarchitektur, both Stuttgart (D); **3rd prize** Kuehn Malvezzi Architekten with bbz landschaftsarchitekten, both Berlin (D), and ASTOC Architecs and Planners, Cologne (D)

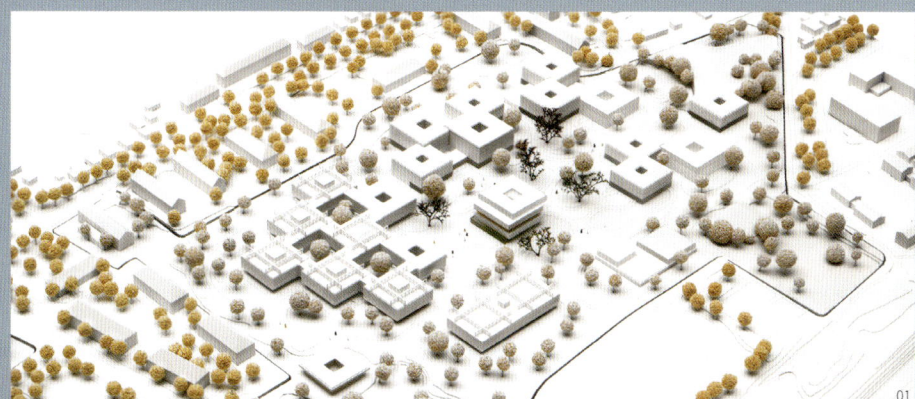

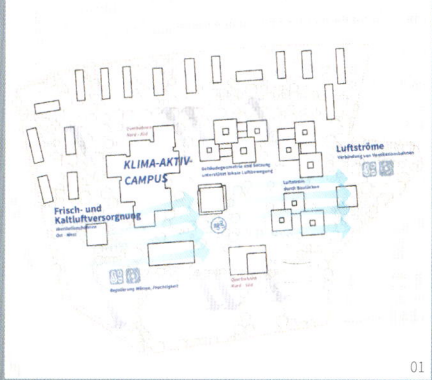

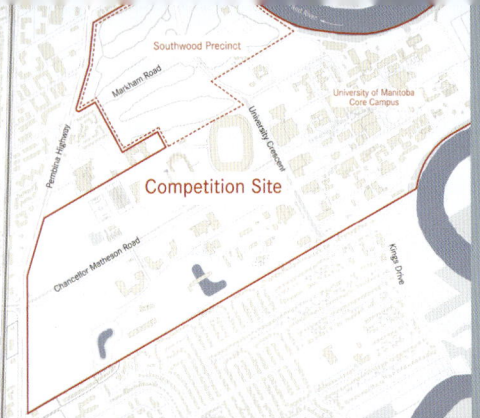

Location: Winnipeg, Canada **Client:** University of Manitoba **Year:** 2012 – 2013 **Project size:** 279 ha **Type of competition:** International, open design competition in two stages **Participants:** Stage 1: 45; Stage 2: 6 **Competition budget:** CAD 60,000; fees 2nd phase: CAD 30,000)

PRIZEWINNERS:
(01) **1st prize** Janet Rosenberg & Studio, Toronto (CDN); **2nd prize** Perkins+Will, Vancouver (CDN); **3rd prize** DTAH, Toronto (CDN); **4th prize** IAD Independent Architectural Diplomacy, Madrid (E)

University of Manitoba Campus and Neighborhood, Winnipeg

UNIVERSITY OF MANITOBA The University of Manitoba (UofM) is one of the state universities in Winnipeg, Manitoba, the capital of the province. UofM was founded in 1877 and has two campuses: the downtown Bannatyne Campus with the medical school and the Fort Garry campus just outside of the city. Twenty university departments, three colleges, dormitories and other student facilities are housed on the Fort Garry campus. Twenty-six thousand students are enrolled, and 6,000 teachers are employed at the university.

FORT GARRY CAMPUS The campus is located about 13 km south of the city center. The Red River borders the campus on the east and the Pembina Highway, an important transportation route and location for trade and commerce, on the west. The Fort Garry campus, like all of Winnipeg, is located in traditional territory of the Anishinaabe tribe and in the Métis settlement area. The 280-ha competition area encompasses the entire existing university campus including the former Southwood Golf Course adjacent to the university in the northwest. The golf course alone is 49 ha in size. The need for a new residential area close to campus with access to a new downtown express busline and acquisition of the golf course property triggered the project.

COMPETITION TASK The point of the competition is to establish a masterplan for the future development of the entire campus to ensure an integrated complete development. Within a superordinate concept, proposals should suggest individual solutions for seven subareas with partly diverging character and needs addressing issues of density, public infrastructure, building form and landscape. A convincing landscape concept, efficient mixed-use urban areas and access to public transportation were desired. Four-thousand two-hundred residential units and 21,000 sqm of space for retail and gastronomy were to be planned on parts of the former golf course; a partial area of the new development was to be presented in greater detail as a pilot project.

Johann Wolfgang Goethe University – Westend Campus, Frankfurt a. M.

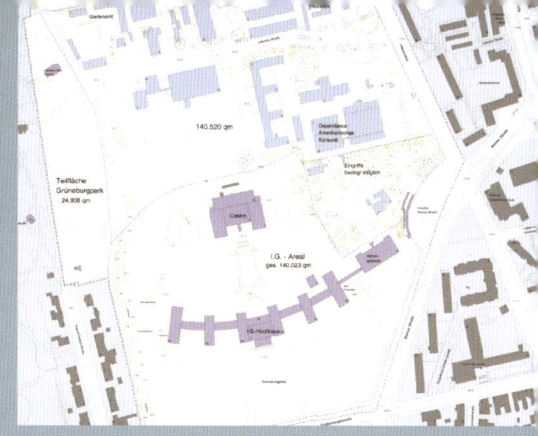

J. W. GOETHE UNIVERSITY The intent of the sponsor, the German state of Hesse, was to make the Johann Wolfgang Goethe University one of the most advanced institutions of education in Germany. The university was founded in 1914 at the initiative of Frankfurt citizens and is named Johann Wolfgang Goethe University since 1932. In 1953, the state of Hesse replaced the former state of Prussia as the funding authority. In 1967, the status of the university changed from endowment-funded to a state-funded one.

LOCATION The creation of a seminar working and study environment in research and education was seen as the basis for an outstanding level of efficiency and competitiveness, at a par with quality standards. The new Westend Campus includes the premises of the former headquarters of IG Farben, a site bordering Frankfurt's inner city on the northwest. Situated on the south part of the area, the former administrative seat of IG Farben was built from 1928 to 1930 to a design by Hans Poelzig. These buildings are among the most important works of German expressionist architecture and along with the surrounding park, are a listed heritage site. Undamaged during World War II, they served for a period of 50 years as the headquarters of the US military forces in Germany. In 1996, the state of Hesse purchased the premises in order to extend the university.

TASK To transform the site into a university campus, an overall town-planning concept was required. This concept had to answer the university's aspiration to promote outstanding scientific achievement with optimum working conditions and to provide an architectural environment commensurate with the institution's top-quality standards. As a university campus, the overall facilities were to represent the academic culture of living and studying through a holistic design concept with marked spatial and architectural dimensions and qualities. The Westend Campus town-planning competition aimed at obtaining an outstanding town-planning design for the development of this new university site.

Location: Frankfurt a. M., Germany **Client:** State of Hesse **Year:** 2002 – 2003 **Project size:** 38,000 sqm **Type of competition:** Open two-stage integrated town-planning project competition for architects, town planners and landscape architects **Participants:** Stage 1: 197; Stage 2: 25 **Competition budget:** EUR 80,000

PRIZEWINNERS:
(01) **1st prize** Ferdinand Heide Architekt, Frankfurt a. M. and TOPOS, Berlin (D); **2nd prize** SIAT, Munich with Kraus_Milkovich, Frankfurt a. M. (D), and Planungsbüro EGL, Landshut (D); **3rd prize** pmp – Architekten, Munich (D), and Atelier Bernburg, Bernburg (D); **4th prize** de+ Architekten, Berlin (D), and Mauro Hagel, Berlin (D); **5th prize** Braun & Voigt, Frankfurt a. M. (D), and Sommerland Haase Kuhli, Gießen (D)

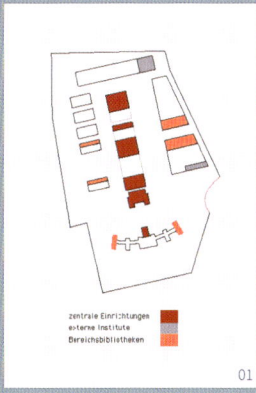

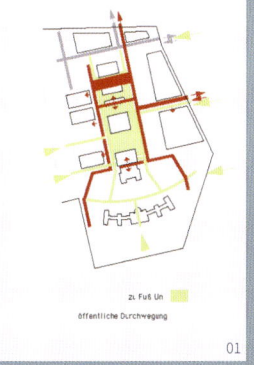

XI URBAN DESIGN AND HOUSING

Urban design and residential design are probably the most challenging tasks because it affects the living environment of the entire population and the development of entire districts, including their density, atmosphere, climatic conditions, and thus the cohesion and the basis for sustainable development. Urban design competitions are often more flexible in terms of program than design competitions for a building, where the focus is usually on a specific investment with defined spatial and financial conditions. Urban design competitions are therefore often launched as idea competitions, the results of which are then used as a starting point for land-use planning, for example. Because of their broad significance for a large part of the population, it is particularly useful to introduce participatory elements in urban design competitions. If the aim is to implement urban planning objectives, urban design competitions should also be launched as project competitions, where the contract promise usually includes the further development of the urban design into a master plan. This includes defining the mix of uses (residential, work, social, commercial, production, sports, etc.), transportation (roads, paths, parking), as well as the framework for outdoor space design, rainwater management, and more.

Depending on the complexity of the task, it is advisable for urban design competitions to have an interdisciplinary jury with experts in urban design, transport, landscape architecture, architecture, and nature conservation, so that the participating teams are also interdisciplinary.

When it comes to residential construction, depending on the project location and size, the client, and regional traditions, it is important to define in the competition brief clear and completely individual requirements of housing guidelines, funding programs, market requirements and expected housing types. The various life models should be reflected in the housing proposals, although the specific users are rarely known; rather, a very heterogeneous and possibly changing population must be considered to create a correspondingly flexible and robust design. All of this should be expressed by the competition organizers in the competition specifications and taken into consideration during the pre-examination so as to be presented to the jury.

Thorsten Schmitt
Berliner Bau- und Wohnungsgenossenschaft von 1892 eG

❞ The competition for a new cooperative development project offers the opportunity to combine innovative residential construction with economic, ecological, and socio-cultural qualities to form a synthesis. Bruno Taut, World Heritage architect and one of the important protagonists of the 1920's, emphasized this identity-creating design task: 'The basis of the cooperative system and thus also the spiritual content of the cooperatives is the community spirit. One of the architect's most beautiful tasks, because something supra-individual must be embodied here accordingly.'

Analysis graphics of the preliminary examination in the competition "New Housing in Gartenstadt Falkenberg" explaining the distribution of buildings

New Housing in Gartenstadt Falkenberg, Berlin

BERLINER BAU- UND WOHNUNGSGENOSSEN-SCHAFT VON 1892 EG After completing the competition for the extension to the Schiller Park settlement (see p. 174) the "1892" housing cooperative published two more competitions for the extension of another housing estate, which was added to the list of UNESCO World Heritage sites in 2008 along with five other classical modernist apartment buildings in Berlin: the Gartenstadt Falkenberg (nicknamed the "paintbox settlement").

GARTENSTADT FALKENBERG The Gartenstadt Falkenberg ("garden city") is located in southeast Berlin in the Treptow-Koepenick district. The settlement was planned from 1913 to 1916 by Bruno Taut and Ludwig Lesser and has been expanded since 2002 in three building phases. By the end of 2014, it consisted of a total of 53 houses with 342 apartments. The competition site is located in the buffer zone of the World Heritage site. Proximity to the Gartenstadt, highway 96a and the parallel embankment with a height difference of up to 7 m down to the street are the main influential factors in the area. A park bordering the area to the south is to be developed as a central recreational space for several residential complexes in the neighborhood.

COMPETITION TASK The object of the competition is to design an ensemble of buildings of various typologies with at least 28,000 sqm living space based on a preliminary draft of an urban masterplan. The task included both optimization of the urban configuration and the design of buildings and outdoor facilities. The housing should be intergenerational and practical for use as shared apartments with an average net rent below EUR 10 per sqm. The special character of the housing should be represented in the differentiation of structure and quality of the floorplans and outdoor spaces. Following the idea of the Gartenstadt, an important part of the task was an integrated design of outdoor space. Beyond that, an appropriate structure of public and private areas should be taken into consideration.

Location: Berlin, Germany **Client:** Berliner Bau- und Wohnungsgenossenschaft von 1892 eG **Year:** 2014 **Project size:** approx. 300 units **Type of competition:** Cooperative design competition **Participants:** 8 **Competition budget:** EUR 83,000 (prizes: EUR 31,000; fees per participant: EUR 6,500)

PRIZEWINNERS:
(01) **1st prize** zanderroth architekten, Berlin (D); (02) **2nd prize** ROBERTNEUN™ Architekten, Berlin (D); (03) **2nd prize** Heidenreich & Springer Architekten, Berlin (D)

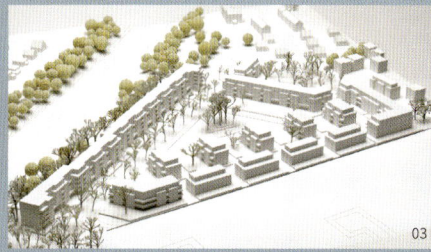

Schillerpark Housing Estate Development, Berlin

Location: Berlin, Germany **Client:** Berliner Bau- und Wohnungsgenossenschaft von 1892 eG **Year:** 2012 **Project size:** approx. 90 units **Type of competition:** Design competition **Participants:** 10 **Competition budget:** EUR 54,400 (prizes: EUR 12,400; fees per participant: EUR 3,500)

PRIZEWINNERS:
(01) **1st prize** Bruno Fioretti Marquez Architekten, Berlin (D); **2nd prize** HAAS Architekten, Berlin (D); **3rd prize** blauraum architekten, Hamburg (D)

BERLINER BAU- UND WOHNUNGSGENOSSENSCHAFT VON 1892 EG The "1892" is the second-oldest housing cooperative in Berlin. Established in times of housing shortages and squalid conditions in Berlin tenements, the cooperative was from the outset a place for reformist ideas affecting not only architecture, but social and cultural issues as well. Around 20 settlements have been built over the years on behalf of "1892" by architects like Alfred Messel, Bruno Taut and Hans Hoffmann. The settlements are all united by the idea of giving an appropriate built framework to cooperative living and sustainable high-quality structures. The competition took place during the 120-year anniversary of the cooperative's founding, a year the United Nations also proclaimed as the "International Year of Cooperatives."

SCHILLERPARK SETTLEMENT The property is located on Schwyzer Strasse at the corner of Barfusstrasse in the Berlin-Wedding district. Important landmarks in the area include Schiller Park located to the south and the listed Church of St. Aloysius built in 1956. The Schillerpark settlement towards the northwest was built in three building phases as the first residential social building project after World War I beginning in 1924. From 1954 to 1959 the settlement was expanded and now includes approximately 600 apartments. In July 2008, along with five other classical modernist apartment buildings in Berlin, the settlement was added to the UNESCO World Heritage list.

COMPETITION TASK Based on a development plan adopted in 2010, an ensemble of residential buildings should be built with underground parking and at least 5,200 sqm of rentable area. An essential part of the task was to address the existing Schillerpark settlement urbanistically and architecturally and to transfer the original expectation of contemporary innovative forms of housing to the floorplans, exterior and green spaces. In addition to one-, two- and three or four-bedroom apartments, the program also included a shared apartment for seniors with space for 10 residents.

Landscape and Urban Planning Competition
Bruno-Taut-Strasse, Berlin

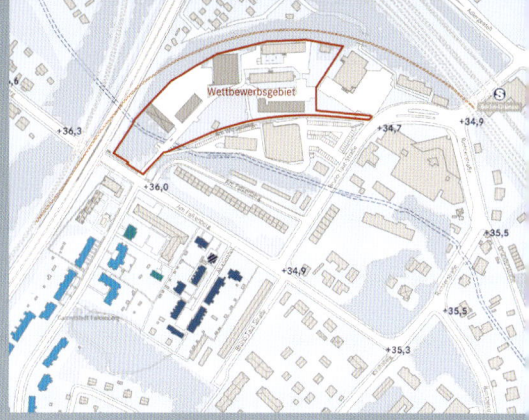

LOCATION The 21,500-sqm competition site is located at Bruno-Taut-Strasse 4–6 in the southwest of Berlin's Treptow-Köpenick district, near the Grünau S-Bahn station. It is located in the buffer zone of the "Falkenberg Garden City", which was inscribed on the UNESCO World Heritage List in 2008 as one of the six "Berlin Modernist Housing Estates". In addition to its proximity to Bruno Taut's Falkenberg Garden City, the site is also characterized by its location on the B 96a federal highway and the two S-Bahn lines that run parallel or orthogonally to it. To the north, the site is bordered by a disused, arched railway embankment.

PROJECT The sponsor plans to construct residential buildings, selectively designate commercial space compatible with residential use, as well as the renovate and integrate two existing 5-story buildings for use as lodging establishments. Among other issues to be considered were the historic preservation requirements for the buffer zone of the World Heritage Site, the tree population, and a small stream on the site, as well as the topographical and landscape situation of the railroad embankment bordering the site to the north, the public pedestrian and bicycle path at the southern edge of the site, and the noise pollution from the neighboring discounter.

TASK The goal was to reach a joint decision between the investor and the district administration on a suitable urban and landscape architecture structure, which would become the basis for securing the sustainable urban development of the area under planning law. Part of the planning was the traffic development. The planning specifications were the usual density (site occupancy ratio SOR 0.4, floor area ration FAR 1.2) as well as a housing key: 15 % 1.5–2 room apartments (40–55 sqm), 47 % 2.5 room apartments (60–65 sqm), 15 % 3–3.5 room apartments (65–80 sqm), 20 % 4–4.5 room apartments (100–120 sqm) and 3 % 5 room apartments (115–125 sqm). A suitable location for a day care center with appropriate outdoor facilities was to be identified.

Location: Berlin, Germany **Client:** S6. Bärlin Invest Immobilien GmbH **Year:** 2015 – 2016 **Project size:** approx. 21,500 sqm **Type of competition:** Urban and landscape design competition **Participants:** 8 **Competition budget:** EUR 31,500 (prizes: EUR 7,500; compensation per participant EUR 3,000)

PRIZEWINNERS:
(01) **1st prize** wiechers beck gesellschaft von architekten mbh with Rudolf Kaufmann, Landschaftsarchitekt, Berlin (D); **2nd prize** Jan Wiese Architekten with POLA Landschaftsarchitekten, Berlin (D)

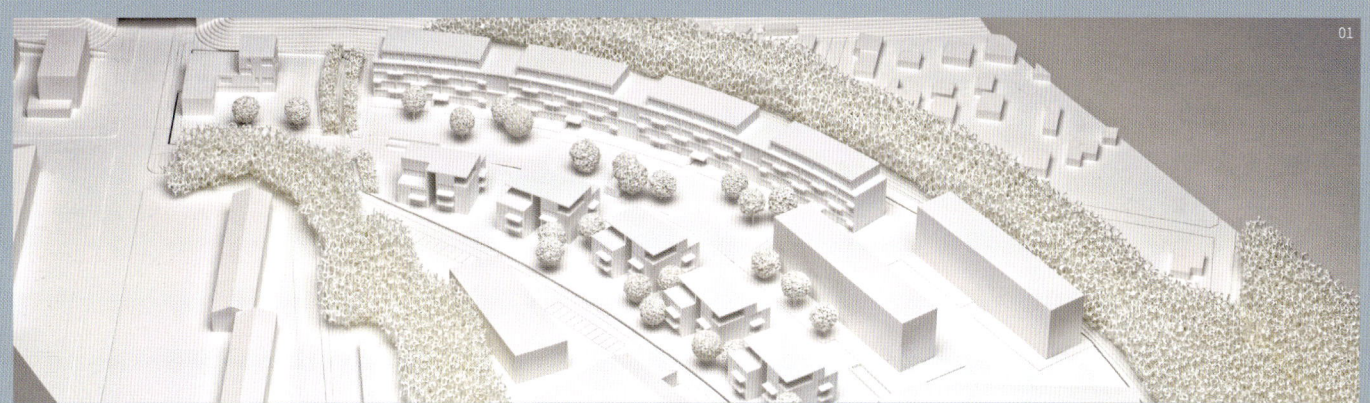

Southbank Project, Stellenbosch

AFRICA CENTRE STELLENBOSCH Until now, Africa has no single institution representing the culture of the entire continent under one roof. When the sponsors of this competition, old-established winemakers in South Africa's western cape province, decided to build "Southbank", a new residential development, they also set themselves the ambitious goal of making the "Africa Centre" its centerpiece.

PROCEDURE Accordingly, there was a period of several years spent elaborating the concept and program, involving many African and Afro-American artists who were also invited to participate in the subsequent urban-design and architecture competition. The obvious plan was to run the procedure for this project as an open competition; the management was entrusted to [phase eins]. and the University of Witwatersrand, Johannesburg. The ensuing collaboration resulted in an exciting two-way transfer of know-how and produced creative answers to numerous issues. In stage one of this competition, entries were submitted online, thereby reducing costs for both competitors and jury.

Stage two, with a substantially reduced field, was conducted as a "classical" competition.

TASK The plan called for a usable area of 150,000 sqm, mainly for various forms of residential uses, on an 80-ha site embedded in a valley landscape. The Africa Centre proper was to cover approx. 11,000 sqm of the usable area. Furthermore, there would be a guesthouse, retail, sports facilities, school, nursery school, etc. The project committed itself to a high standard: A vibrant blend of residential, artistic, and cultural functions, a meeting place for traditional and contemporary art and culture, an amalgam of museum and culture center set in a community where artists can reside temporarily or permanently.

Location: Stellenbosch, South Africa **Client:** Spier Holdings **Year:** 2006 **Project size:** 100 ha **Type of competition:** Open, two-stage project competition **Participants:** 1st stage: 96; 2nd stage: 6 **Competition budget:** USD 225,000

PRIZEWINNERS:
01) **1st prize** thread collective & normaldesign, Brooklyn (USA); (02) **2nd prize** LOVE architecture and urbanism, Graz (A); (03) **Honorable mention** Martin Mechs with Architekturbüro Uli Tischler, Graz (A)

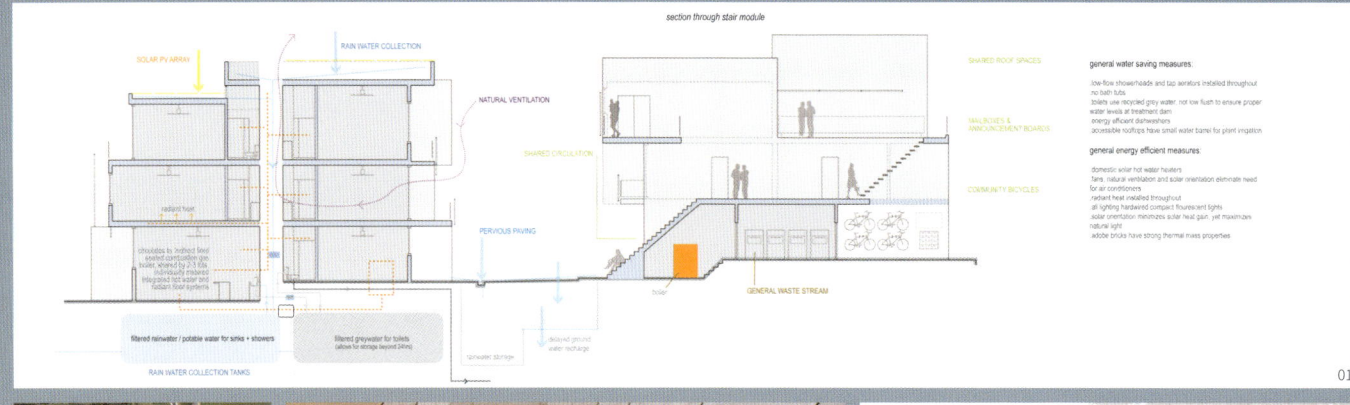

Housing and Working in Vienna-Heiligenstadt

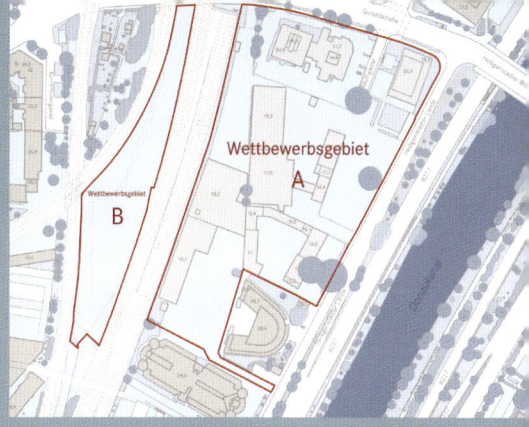

HEILIGENSTADT Vienna's 19th district "Döbling", located about 5 km northeast of the city center, is one of Vienna's most preferred residential areas. The district includes both highly priced villa areas as well as social housing, including important examples such as the Karl-Marx-Hof. An exception within this residential dominated structure of the district is a previously commercial neighborhood in the eastern part, in the Heiligenstadt area. The area between a railroad track and the Danube Canal, located on both sides of Muthgasse and south of Gunoldstrasse, is characterized by buildings of various scales. For some years now, the commercial use has been steadily displaced by other uses such as office, retail, service and educational facilities.

TASK The aim of the project is the reorganization of the approx. 30 ha large area, the development of which has been a challenge so far due to complex topography, property layouts and ownership despite the advantageous public transport connection to the city center. The project was jointly supported by the five owners at the time, with the aim of realizing a dense, multi-functional neighborhood with approx. 110,000 sqm GFA (residential, hotel, office, retail).

PROCEDURE The competition built on the result of a cooperative planning procedure by the City of Vienna completed in 2016. In the first stage of the competition, all participants developed the urban planning concept for the site, and the concept of Behnisch Architekten, Stuttgart, was selected as the interim result and became the basis for the second stage. In this stage, four parallel competitions were held in five sub-areas in an overall procedure with different fields of participants.

Location: Vienna, Austria **Client:** Property Owners' Association **Year:** 2017 – 2018 **Project size:** ca. 110,000 sqm GFA **Type of competition:** Design competition in two stages **Participants:** 12 **Competition budget:** EUR 300,000 (Prizes: EUR 60,000; Compensation per participant Stage 1: EUR 10,000, Compensation pro participant Stage 2: EUR 8,000)

PRIZEWINNERS:
Building site 1
(01) **1st prize** AllesWirdGut Architekten ZT GmbH, Vienna (A), with Atelier an der Wien, Vienna(A); **2nd prize** Zechner & Zechner ZT GmbH, Vienna (D)
Building site 2
(02) **1st prize** Eller + Eller Architekten GmbH, Berlin (D); **2nd prize** Sauerbruch Hutton gva, Berlin (D)
Building site 3
1st prize AllesWirdGut Architekten ZT GmbH, Vienna (A), with Atelier an der Wien, Vienna (A); **2nd prize** Eller + Eller Architekten GmbH, Berlin (D)
Building site 4
(03) **1st prizes** Sauerbruch Hutton gva, Berlin (D); **3rd prize** HNP architects ZT GmbH, Vienna (A); **3rd prize** COBE Berlin GmbH, Berlin (D)

15 AFTER THE COMPETITION

15.1 Commissioning

One of the main goals of any project competition is the subsequent commissioning of one of the design teams whose design has been awarded a prize. In many respects, the commissioning and contract negotiation is no different from tendering a contract without a prior design competition.

The following is required:

› A schedule for the procedure
› Clarification of the parties involved
› A draft contract describing the scope of services and any further terms and conditions of the assignment
› Clarification of the commissioning criteria (e.g., implementation concept, capacity planning, experience of project team members, financial proposal)

This is followed by a request for proposal and contract negotiations.
The basic framework conditions for the commissioning after a design competition is usually already defined in the competition announcement and the information about the procedural conditions (as part of the competition brief):

› Which services of which disciplines are to be commissioned?
› Should there be (initially) negotiations only with the authors of the 1st prize or with all prizewinners? If negotiations are to be held with all prizewinners in parallel, how will the results of the competition be weighted in the criteria for the contract decision? Assuming a total of 100 points, the competition result should be weighted with at least 40 to 45 points so as to ensure the priority of the 1st prizewinner. Accordingly, the 1st prize could receive the 40 to 45 points, the last prize 0 points, and the prizes in between the interpolated value.
› Are there fee standards that can be used as a basis for the fee and possibly also for the definition of a service profile?
› How are the aspects of copyright and utilization rights regulated?

If these terms and conditions are not already known, they must be provided with the request for fee proposal.
As a further component of the commissioning decision, the assessment of solution competence can be applied.
For this purpose, it is possible to ask the prizewinners, afterwards bidders, to comment on the jury's remarks on their design and to point out corresponding possible solutions during the negotiation talks through a presentation in which they also present their planning methodology and their project team.
This gives the award of the contract following a competition a second dimension that is important for the overall success of the project and which a negotiated procedure without a competition could not offer.

Martin Steiner
Specialist attorney for public procurement law as well as specialist attorney for construction and architectural law, Berlin

❚❚ Experience has shown that in design competitions, lawyers are not consulted to the same extent as in other major procedures awarding design services, such as in tenders with a prequalification procedure. This is in line with the fact that competition participants very rarely complain about procedural rules and decisions taken during the procedure. This seems to correspond to a general ethos of design offices not to challenge the jury's decision.
Nevertheless, it is advisable to ensure legal support for the preparation and organization of competitions. On the one hand, this is to secure compliance with the requirements of public procurement law. Even if these are often regarded by bidders as a necessary evil, they do serve to guarantee transparency, equal treatment, and fairness in the competition, which should be in the interests of all those involved in the process. Moreover, special attention must be paid to the implementation of a correct competition type when the contract to be awarded after the competition is (partly) financed with subsidies.
This is because, if the body examining the subsidies finds a formal violation of contract, there is a risk that the subsidies will be denied, irrespective of whether the result of the competition is excellent and good from an economic point of view. On the other hand, the requirements for contract drafting and negotiation should not be underestimated. The design competition ends with the signing of a contract. Often, the subject of a design competition is an economically significant and complex project with numerous participants. Accordingly, the contract must be carefully drafted as the basis for further cooperation with the competition winner. In addition, the winning office usually acts very confidently in the final contract negotiations knowing that they will be awarded the contract. A high degree of negotiating skills and experience is therefore often required to assert the interests of the sponsor.
When lawyers are called in to advise on competitions – arguably one of the most enjoyable tasks a procurement lawyer can be entrusted with – they are particularly dependent on close and cooperative collaboration not only with the sponsor, but also with the competition organizer. Without their experience and input on the one hand, and smooth cooperation on the other, it is not possible for a legal advisor to always provide the sponsor with timely and substantive legal support in their interests. In this respect, it is advisable for the sponsor to rely on a well-coordinated team of competition organizers and lawyers.

15.2 Project archiving and return

Each design competition and its organization have special significance not only for the sponsor and the project itself, but possibly also beyond that, e.g., for public debates, architectural history and education, and possibly also subjects to be preserved for cultural reasons.

The plans and models submitted by the participants should therefore be permanently saved after the end of the exhibition. This applies to the prizewinning designs as well as to all other designs, which may be re-evaluated in the long term. The time, space and financial resources required for appropriate archiving should be planned for at an early stage. In some cases, this is complicated by the question of ownership rights to the physical documents, which, depending on the competition rules, may have to be returned to the participants. Digital archiving of all documents and high-quality photographic documentation of the models are therefore even more important.

The basic principles developed in the first project phase are generally of great importance for the subsequent project steps and should therefore be carefully compiled and made available to the design teams that are commissioned with the further design steps.

Rainer Hascher
Architect, Berlin

❞ What is important for me as a participant in a competition?

If a ceiling for construction costs is demanded in advance in a design competition, which I fundamentally consider to be completely premature at this time point, these should at least be defined according to current and correctly indexed comparative figures, for example from the Chamber of Architects, and not according to arbitrary wishes of the client.

Pre-signatures on pre-predetermined, non-negotiated contract provisions should not be a prerequisite for admission to a design competition, as a contract should in principle be negotiated by both sides and not dictated unilaterally.

Left: Archiving of competition documents.
Above: Return of models.

Brinda Somaya
Architect, Founder and Principal of Somaya & Kalappa Consultants, Mumbai

❞ When a client decides on organizing a competition, it is to get as many different ideas as possible from the competitors. The jury often likes various thoughts of different proposals from more than one participant. However, for the development of the project, it is advisable that the client adopts and builds the solutions proposed by the winner only. As a juror for the competition which involves an online judging process, I would suggest that it is planned to be held in two-stages. If it is an in-person jury then a single stage is possible, and of course a good briefing document is crucial.

APPENDIX

Appendix

SERVICES PROVIDED BY THE COMPETITION MANAGER

Based on our experience in managing more than 200 competitions, we have developed the service catalog presented below, which describes the services required to manage all common types of competitions.

CUSTOMIZATION OF THE CATALOG

Depending on the competition type (open/restricted, single/two-stage, architecture/urban design/landscape architecture/general planning/exhibition architecture, etc.), the requirements for competition management vary, and the catalog should be adapted accordingly. In some cases, this customization affects essential components, while in others, only details are changed.

Furthermore, it should be considered whether some services should be provided by the sponsor themselves or are desired at all (marked as "optional services"). For example, whether:
› the competition manager should also be involved in the contract negotiations or the negotiation process after the competition
› an exhibition should be organized after the competition

1. UNDERSTANDING THE REQUIREMENTS AND OBJECTIVES OF THE COMPETITION

1.1 General preparation and communication

Understand the objectives of the sponsor and other parties involved (through meetings and assessment of project goals etc.)
› Validate objectives, clarify, and establish cooperative relation Review information, identify additional information needs
› Provide ongoing briefing to all members of the process, managing the necessary written correspondence
› Continuously archive all relevant documents (see also Chapter 9.2)
› Set up the "Download" online tool on the competition management website as an web-based data space for internal, password-protected document exchange (with multiple hierarchies) of project-related files (minutes, schedules, address lists, templates)
› Act as a project liaison office during the preparation, ecution, and evaluation phases of the competition
› Maintain an address list of all participants

+ Optional services:
› Organize the translation into a second language of all relevant technical documentation (online forum, participant colloquia, jury meetings), and documents (competition brief)
› Coordinate the work of translators and transfer their texts into the layout of the original language
› Communicate with jury members and participants in the second language, if required
› Possibly create a bilingual project webpage
↑ Can be deleted, if necessary

1.2 Internal workshops with the sponsor
› Advise on the overall scope of services and required studies
› Provide continuous general and specific advice to the sponsor on project development and organization
› Participate in the organization, scheduling, and preparation of an internal kickoff meeting (Workshop 1) to define responsibilities, general project objectives, the formation of a project team, and the handover of initial documents

› Participate and lead the organization, scheduling, and preparation of three additional internal project team meetings (Workshops 2, 3, 4)
› Attend all four face-to-face workshops, each with a duration of up to one session day
› Take minutes during the workshops
↑ Determine the appropriate number of workshops and whether they should be half-day or full-day

› Prepare and distribute preliminary copies of project documents (spatial program, functional program, competition brief) for coordination with those involved in the preparation (in the case of the competition brief, up to 5 concept drafts and a final version), as well as the necessary submittals for the discussion and finalization of organizational topics
› Obtain board approval of interim results (procedure, program, competition brief, etc.)

+ Optional services:
› Schedule, prepare, and participate in further workshops and meetings, take minutes
↑ This optional service creates a mode (fee) for the case of exceeding the previously agreed number of voting dates.

1.3 Schedule management
› Plan and coordinate the schedule: define key milestones, prepare, and coordinate a project schedule for the duration of the project
› Define dates of (meetings, colloquia, jury meetings etc.) with the relevant parties
› Maintain/update the schedule in consultation with the sponsor

1.4 Determination of procedure type and the parties involved
› Provide advice on the selection of a suitable competition procedure
› Create presentation materials to illustrate alternative procedure formats
› Formulate decision criteria for the selection of other professionally involved parties in the process
› Provide guidance on the composition of the jury and the involvement of experts
› Invite members of the jury to participate in the procedure, clarify their compensation and terms of participation - if necessary, sign contracts
› Create profiles (CVs, portrait photo) of potential jury members and experts

› Advise and assist in the composition of the selection committee
↑ For public sponsors and procedures with a competitive bidding process

1.5 Travel management
› Support nonlocal jury members (technical jurors and technical experts) their necessary travel arrangements and, if required, hotel reservations in connection with the competition events
› Coordinate cost-effective and timely travel connections

1.6 Cost estimation and budget management
› Estimate the procedure costs (participants, jury members and experts, event costs, printing and model construction costs, travel costs, etc.) and update the total cost overview
› Calculate the award sum (prizes and honoraria)
› Check the invoices of third parties involved in the process (jury members, experts, and service providers)
› Prepare and update of a payment schedule

2. PROGRAM

2.1 Analysis
› Clarify the task on the base of specifications or the sponsor's requirements
› Site visit
› Prepare step-by-step the competition documents and integrate the services of other parties involved in the project
› Obtain all project-relevant documents, information, and elaborations, as well as analyze, prepare, and clarify information related to:
  – urban context and goals
  – site-specific factors, such as urban or architectural history
  – urban planning legal context and conditions
  – relevant heritage conservation requirements and goals, if relevant
  – safety-related requirements and goals
  – economic requirements and goals
  – traffic/accessibility requirements
  – ecological and open space situation and goals
  – existing buildings, requirements for their integration
  – ongoing construction activities in the vicinity
  – neighboring development and connection conditions, as well as planning directives in the surroundings

› Formulate the general conditions/requirements and the textual description of the task:
  – type and extent of building use
  – urban development
  – safety concept
  – economic efficiency
  – protection of historical monuments, if relevant
  – relevant legal regulations
› Supervise a photographic survey

2.2 Program, function, and equipment planning
› Collaborate on the completion of a spatial, and functional program of the project based on a largely completed space requirement planning, in the level of detail required for the competition
↑ Adjust if necessary, if no building construction

› Classify and describe individual functional and usage areas by size, dimensioning, area qualities, density, general requirements, and allocation requirements
› Describe qualitative standards for each usage unit
› Describe guidelines for the location of usage areas
› Provide area allocation and coding

› Create diagrammatic representations to explain necessary functional relations
↑ Optional service if necessary

3. COORDINATION WITH AUTHORITIES AND OTHER EXTERNAL PARTIES

3.1 Erarbeitung der formalen Bedingungen des Verfahrens
› Draft, discuss, and finalize the competition announcement, particularly with regard to the formal requirements of the prequalification procedure in accordance with the national procurement law, including the specification of eligibility and selection criteria as well as examination and award criteria
↑ Only in case of a pre-qualification procedurer

› Draft formal requirements of the design competition in accordance with RPW 2013, including the presentation of required competition services and evaluation criteria
› If necessary: discuss the draft with a procurement law specialist appointed by the sponsor
› As part of the competition announcement: conduct preliminary coordination of the composition of the jury, calculation of the competition amount, and other parameters of the procedure with the relevant Chamber of Architects, possibly in an individual meeting

› Concretize the procedure in its final version with the relevant Chamber of Architects
› Obtain the registration number from the Chamber of Architects
↑ If necessary also chamber of engineers

3.2 Coordination with authorities
› Participate in the planning and preparation of meetings with (external) authorities involved in the procedure
› Participate in up to two meeting sessions for negotiations and coordination with the authorities and other parties involved in the procedure
↑ Depending on whether the awarding authority is a public sponsor

- Prepare the required meeting minutes for coordination meetings
- Discuss the competition documents with the authorities involved, possibly during the jury colloquium

+ Optional services:
- Participate in additional meeting sessions for negotiations and coordination with the authorities and other parties involved in the procedure, take minutes

3.3 Coordination of experts
- Coordinate the involvement of experts in the process to clarify the project's constraints
- Coordinate the participation of experts in workshops (1.2)
- Incorporate the statements of experts into the preparation of the competition brief

4. PREPARATION OF THE COMPETITION BRIEF MATERIALS

4.1 Preparation of the competition brief
- Summarize the results of the previous phases
- Compile the competition documents, including:
  - Preparing a table of contents
  - Drafting the formal competition brief/competition conditions according to the RPW 2013
  - Describing and illustrating the competition task
  - Preparing plans as drawing templates for the participants
  - Summarizing the competition program
  - Formulating general and specific requirements
  - Writing presentation notes
  - Referencing relevant regulation for design services
  - Creating forms for calculating data derived from plans and characteristic values
  - Drafting the declaration of authorship
- Incorporate the results of the jury colloquium
- Design the cover page and the inside pages, if necessary, based on the sponsor's CI specifications
- Formulate presentation guidelines
- Prepare graphics to explain specific technical, traffic, and/or planning constraints
- Produce sets of forms to calculate design data, characteristic values, program compliance, and declaration of authorship
- Coordinate the reproduction of the final version (digital copy, ring binding) by an external service provider

4.2 Preparation of the plan documents
- Obtain the necessary plan and map materials from the sponsor and, if necessary, from authorities and other sources (e.g., planners from previous studies)
- Prepare various plan documents as optimized CAD templates for the competition participants and, if necessary, compiling additional information materials
- Format the CAD-generated plan documents
- Prepare a hanging plan as a template for the participants

4.3 Model making services
- Advise on the selection of an appropriate scale and section for a model of the surroundings
- Obtain additional plan documents required for the construction of the model of surroundings, and prepare them as specifications for the model maker
- Participate in the planning of the model of surroundings
- Prepare and participate in the bidding process for the model makers
- Coordinate, supervise, and accept the deliverables from the model maker

4.4 Compiling files and sending the documents
- Convert the plan files into various common file formats and program versions
- Prepare the competition documents as downloadable files on the competition website
- Distribute the competition documents to the jury members and participants

5. PARTICIPANT SELECTION

5.1 Participation in the selection process
- Design the procedure

> - Participate in the selection of suitable candidates
> - Organize appropriate presentation materials introducing the candidates
> ↑ Variant for simple invited competitions

- Participate in the selection of participants
- Notify candidates

5.2 Preparation of the registration procedure
- Design the online registration procedure

> - Prepare application specifications and content requirements
> - Coordinate the establishment of a database with online registration/form on the bidder's internet domain to collect contact details of interested companies (e-mail, company name, city, country)
> ↑ Variant for open competitions

- Conduct the necessary correspondence with interested parties

5.3 Design and preparation of the selection procedure
- Design the procedures

> - Prepare application specifications, forms, and content requirements
> - If relevant: participate in the selection of suitable participants
> ↑ In case of open prequalification procedures

- Coordinate the creation of an applicant database with online registration and forms, securely stored in accordance with e-tendering on the bidder's web domain including archive, search and analysis functions. This database is used for entering applicants' personal information and details of references, including image files.
- Alternatively: use a tendering platform provided by the sponsor

5.4 Online forum application phase
- Establish an online forum on the domain of the competition management for the entry of feedback questions by the applicants on the Internet and for the administration and presentation of their answers.
- Enter the answers in the online forum

5.5 Answering queries during the prequalification phase
- Act as a project liaison, handling all questions regarding the competition or the application/selection process
- Receive written questions
- Participate in answering questions
- Coordinate/agree on the response to the queries with all parties involved
- Draft, finalize, and dispatch minutes

5.6 Receiving applications
› Receive applications
› Compile a general list
› Archive applications

5.7 Processing / evaluating prequalification submissions
› Check the completeness of the submitted documents, especially with regard to proof of qualification, and other formal requirements
› If necessary: request missing or additional information from the applicants
› Conduct preliminary evaluation of the applications based on the criteria defined in the announcement
› Perform rough classification based on the pre-assessment of applications
› Prepare a report on the result of the formal examination and preliminary evaluation of all applications with a systematic, tabular presentation of the content of the applications and the evaluation

5.8 Preparation of the meeting of the selection committee
› Advise the sponsor on the selection of a suitable venue
› Provide advice on the organization of the catering and the preparation of the event venue
› Write and, if requested, dispatch invitation letters
› Prepare the agenda
› Organize necessary aids, such as computers, etc.

5.9 Meeting of selection committee
› Participate in the meeting of the selection committee (project leader and project manager)
› Present the applications, moderate
› Participate in the selection/evaluating/drawing lots
› Take minutes of the meeting

5.10 Conclusion of the application phase
› Notify applicants about the design
› Archive the application documents

6. EVENTS OF THE COMPETITION PROCEDURE

6.1 Preparing / organizing the jury colloquium

› Support the sponsor in the selection and reservation of a suitable venue
› Coordinate scheduling
› Write and, if requested, dispatch invitation letters
› Prepare the agenda
› Support the sponsor in organizing the catering and preparing the venue (e.g., drafting a furniture plan and, if requested, the sitting arrangement)
› Organize a site visit (if required)

6.2 Jury colloquium (preliminary meeting of the jurors)
› Participate in the jury colloquium (project leader and project manager)
› Participate in a site visit to the competition area
› Moderate the meeting (project leader)
› Prepare/confirm and dispatch minutes

6.3 Answering questions
› Receive written questions

› Participate in answering the questions
› Coordinate/agree with the parties involved on the answers to the questions

› Compilee the queries and answers in minutes

↑ For 2-stage competitions for both stages

6.4 Online forum (forums)
› Coordinate the creation of an online forum on the competition manager's domain for the anonymous submission of questions by participants via the web and for the management and presentation of their answers

› Enter the answers in the online forum

↑ For 2-stages competitions for both stages

6.5 Organizing / preparing the participants' colloquium
› Assist the sponsor in the selection and reservation of a suitable venue
› Coordinate scheduling
› Write and, if requested, dispatch invitation letters
› Prepare the agenda
› Support the sponsor in organizing the catering and preparing the venue (e.g., drafting a furniture plan and, if desired, seating arrangement)
› Provide all required information
› Organize technical support

6.6 Participants' colloquium
› Participate in the colloquium (project leader and project manager/s)
› Participate in the visit to the competition site
› Moderate the meeting (project leader)
› Prepare/confirm and dispatch minutes

6.7 Organizing / preparing participants' colloquium Stage 2
› Assist the sponsor in the selection and reservation of a suitable venue

› Coordinate scheduling
› Writing and, if requested, dispatching invitation letters

↑ Only for 2-stage competitions

› Prepare the agenda
› Support the sponsor in organizing the catering and preparing the venue (including drafting a furniture plan and, if desired, seating arrangement)
› Provide all required information
› Organize technical support

6.8 Participant colloquium Stage 2
› Participate in the colloquium (project leader and project manager/s)

› Moderate the meeting (project leader)
› Prepare/confirm and dispatch minutes

↑ Only for 2-stage competitions

6.9 Organizing a citizens' forum before / after the competition
› Advise on the concept of the citizens' forum with regard to program and participants
› Assist the sponsor in the selection and reservation of a suitable venue
› Coordinate the participation of jury members and/or prizewinner(s)
› Coordinate scheduling
› Write and, if requested, dispatch invitation letters
› Prepare the agenda
› Support the sponsor in organizing the catering and preparing the venue (including drafting a furniture plan and, if desired, seating arrangement)
› Provide all required information
› Organize technical support

› Announce the event in the press
↑ If applicable, as an optional service

6.10 Citizens' forum before / after the competition
› Participate in the citizens' forum (project leader)
› Moderate the meeting (project leader)
› Prepariy/confirm and dispatch documentation
↑ If applicable, as optional service

7. PRELIMINARY EXAMINATION

7.1 Preparing the preliminary examination
› Select and coordinate the preliminary examiners and assistants

› Brief the preliminary examination team, determining the leader or the person responsible for the preliminary examination
› Clarify the scope of the preliminary examination together with the specifications of the competition services in the competition brief
› Prepare a concept for the technical and organizational process of the preliminary examination and set up the required basic databases and files
↑ In the case of two-stage competitions, the services apply to both stages, whereby the testing effort can be requested in a differentiated manner, if necessary

› Provide premises for the preliminary examination in the office of the competition manager and technical equipment
› Prepare a pre-check list, proofs of submission, and a material submission list
› Receive the submitted competition materials/deliverables

7.2 Conducting the preliminary examination

7.2.1 Administrative part of the preliminary examination
› Receive the submitted competition projects and anonymize them
› Set up the "Receipt" online tool that allows the competitors, upon entry of their ID number, to check whether their competition entry has been received
› Safekeep of the competitors' sealed envelopes
› Safekeep of packaging materials
› Coordinate any required model construction work for the repair of insert models or adaptation of the insert models to the model of surroundings by a professional model maker
› Coordinate the photographing of the models and of reproduction work for the preparation of the preliminary examination report

7.2.2 Checking the adherence to stated formal requirements
› In particular, the following are to be verified:
  – violations of anonymity (if relevant)
  – completeness of the submitted documents
  – missing services
  – services not required (to be covered)
  – violations in presentation or presentation against competition regulations
  – check of all entered documents and plans for mutual consistency

7.2.3 Preliminary examination of technical parts of the entries
› Examine the urban planning quantities (gross floor area GFA and gross volume GV) on the basis of the program return copy, the plans submitted and possibly on the basis of the calculation documents supplied by the participants
  – Recalculation and comparison of target/actual areas for plausibility
  – CAD-supported area and volume calculation, if necessary subdivided
  – according to location (above-ground/underground)

↑ Requirements are to be adapted according to the task (e.g. urban development or open space planning).

› Check of the program fulfillment (usable area UA) on the basis of the program return copy, the submitted plans and, if necessary, on the basis of supplied calculation documents of the participants
  – Recalculation and comparison of target/actual areas for plausibility
  – CAD-supported area calculation, structured according to functional groups and location (floor)
↑ In the case of 2-stage competitions, only in Stage 2

› Examination of the building envelope (subdivided according to above-ground/underground, closed/transparent, vertical/horizontal) on the basis of the program return copy, the plans submitted and possibly on the basis of calculation documents supplied by the participants
  – Recalculation and comparison of target/actual areas for plausibility
  – CAD-supported area calculation
↑ In the case of 2-stage competitions, if necessary, only in Stage 2

› Check and recalculation of the urban planning parameters:
  – Built-up area, BCR and FAR
› Checking and recalculation of further quantifiable requirements according to the specifications in the tender:
  – Number of parking spaces
  – Area of outdoor facilities
› Check the legal building regulations/parameters such as building lines, building boundaries, border distances and height specifications (if necessary, in cooperation with experts appointed/commissioned by the sponsor)
› Check the provisions of the building code, e.g., the state building code (in particular with regard to escape routes; if necessary, in cooperation with experts appointed/commissioned by the sponsor)
› Check other requirements of the invitation to tender, e.g.
  – Urban design qualities
  – Open space/outdoor facilities
  – Design features and spatial qualities
  – Access concept/Safety concept
  – Functional fulfillment/functionality
  – Ecological qualities
  – Economic efficiency features (by determining characteristic values)

7.2.4 Creating tables and diagrams
› Create comparative tables and diagrams with the results of the computational determination of characteristic values
› Create comparative analysis graphics for the presentation of project-relevant single topics. For each design, an urban planning and traffic analysis, a functional analysis graphic for the 3-dimensional representation of the distribution of functions and, if required, a further graphic for the representation of solutions to other relevant topics of the task should be prepared

7.3 Involvement of experts in the preliminary examination
› Coordinate the involvement of experts in the preliminary examination; for each preliminary examination and, if applicable, competition stage, one appointment of up to two days each
› Writing and, if required, dispatching invitation letters
› Moderate and document the expert meeting
› Support the experts during their participation in the preliminary examination and during the preparation of their criteria catalogs
↑ In 2-stage competitions, the services apply to both stages

- Participate in the preparation of the experts' evaluation matrix
- Summarize and evaluate the experts' statements for the preliminary examination report

7.4 Preparing the preliminary examination report
- Summarize the results of the administrative part as well as the technical examination, conduct documentation
- Structure a clear, uniform preliminary examination layout for a presentation of all contributions in three double pages each (approx. DIN A4)
- Organize the duplication of the preliminary examination report

↑ To be adapted according to the forecast on the number of participants (>100 participants: 1 page, 30-100 participants: 2pages, 12-30 participants: 3 pages etc.)

8. JURY MEETING

8.1 Preparing / organizing the jury meeting
- Assist the sponsor in the selection and reservation of a suitable venue
- Coordinate scheduling
- Write and, if requested, dispatch invitation letters
- Prepare the agenda
- Prepare a furniture plan and, if desired, seating arrangement
- Plan the partition system including hanging order plan
- Prepare and support the installation of the movable wall system
- Coordinate, monitor and oversee the installation of movable partition walls and prepare the event venue
- Assist in organizing catering
- Hang up the submitted proposals
- Label/signage
- Organize technical support

↑ In 2-stage competitions, the services apply to both stages

8.2 Participation in the jury meeting(s)
- Attend the meeting with at least 3 pers.: project leader, project manager, assistant
- Coordinate the participation of the external preliminary examiner(s) (who do not receive a fee for attending the meeting)
- Moderate the meeting, if required
- Summarize an oral report of the formal preliminary examination
- Prepare and deliver a beamer-based presentation to explain the pre-examination report
- Prepare and deliver a beamer-supported presentation of the competition entries
- Coordinate the preliminary examiners' presentation of the competition entries and their further participation in the meeting
- Provide continuous consulting to the sponsor during the meeting and answer the inquiries of the jury
- Assisting the jurors in the formulation of the jury's comments and recommendations
- Participate in the orientation tour and the evaluation of all proposals
- Provide the submittal list and the envelopes with the declarations of authorship after the ranking has been determined
- Mark the non-selected works
- Run a secretariat during the jury meeting
- Prepare/conform the minutes, organizing their dispatch
- Notify the prizewinners and qualified participants
- Organize/supervise the dismantling work of the presented entries

↑ In 2-stage competitions, the services apply to both stages

9. COMPETITION DOCUMENTATION

9.1 Illustrated documentation brochure
- Prepare an illustrated final documentation of the procedure: brochure with excerpts from the competition brief, the minutes of the jury meeting(s) and the preliminary examination report(s). The extracts from the preliminary examination report present all the designs in detail and explain the analysis of the preliminary examination and experts. Other elements include photos of the competition events and screenshots of the project website.
- Organize the reproduction and dispatch of the brochure

9.2 Brief competition documentation folder
- Create a folder for the documentation of the procedure for the sponsor, with complete and sorted presentation of the most important competition documents (minutes, address lists, schedules, brochures, etc.)
- Compile of the relevant files (pdf soft copies of the brochures, model photos, press report, etc.) on a suitable data carrier (DVD, USB) for further availability to the sponsor

10. PRESENTATION TO THE PUBLIC

10.1 Announcement of the competition
- Advise on the decision to publish the competition in specialized journals and, if necessary, in official journals
- Organize the publication of the competition brief in professional journals
- Organize the publication in the relevant official journals

10.2 Presentation on the internet – competition website
- Organize the creation of a competition website on the competition manager's domain with an individual address for direct and exclusive communication with the participants and the public (if required)
- Design a layout for the competition website within the framework of a standard layout of the bidder
- Design and implement a security concept to protect the relevant data stored online
- Organize the implementation of the web modules:
  - General information on the project (texts, site plan, image gallery)
  - Information on the procedure
  - Illustrations (plans and picture gallery)
  - Application/registration
  - Questions and answers section (online forum)
  - Downloads
  - Press release
  - Online exhibition (of the competition results)
  - Aktualisierung der Wettbewerbshomepage
- Update of the competition homepage
- If required: compile the documents for the presentation of the process on the sponsor's website

10.3 Services rendered to the press
- Prepare and dispatch press materials for the announcement of the competition results in selected specialized journals (data of the prizewinning projects, excerpt from the minutes of the jury meeting)
- Participate in the organization of a press conference (preparing the agenda, coordinating the participation of the jury chairperson, if required, the first prizewinner)
- Invite the specialized press to the press conference, informing them about the dates of the exhibition
- Collaborate in the formulation of a press release

› Collaborate in the preparation of a press kit for the visitors of the press conference (e.g., press release, model photos) or, if required, provide the files on the project homepage
› Cooperate/participate in the press conference, including moderation (if required)

10.4 Organizing the exhibition
› Participate in designing the exhibition with regard to time, location, scope, exhibition layout
› Draft a furnishing plan for the preparation of the exhibition rooms
› Advise the allocation of the exhibition/guarding services
› Organize/supervise the installation of movable walls and the preparation of the exhibition venue
› Send invitation letters to the participants of the competition
› Create signage for the exhibition premises
› Prepare and participate in the opening of the exhibition (advice on catering, scheduling)
› Remove and return the non-awarded entries
› Organize/supervise dismantling work

10.5 Exhibition posters and flags
› Create a poster to announce the exhibition with information on location, time, etc.
› Create up to three information posters to present general information about the competition (procedure/participants, task, result) in the exhibition
› Create "flags" that provide information about the author and result for each work, as well as possibly including further content (explanatory report, comments of the jury, etc.)

10.6 Invitation card and exhibition flyer
› Create an invitation card (DIN A 6) with information on the exhibition and its opening
› Create brief information about the procedure (excerpts from competition brief, result)
› Organize reproduction and/or printing

11. CONCLUSION OF THE COMPETITION

11.1 Formal Note on the Awarding procedure
› Summarize, explain and document the results of the first phase
› Compilation of the formal note for the duration of the commission (communication with candidates/participants/bidders, minute of meetings addresses, time schedules, brochures etc.) for further use by the Client
↑ Only for public sposor, and if completely necessary, as option

11.2 Negotiation talks
11.2.1 Content preparation
› Content preparation
  – Negotiation procedure: preparation, coordination, and form preparation
  – Collaborate in formulating the contract's scope of services
  – Participate in the creation of additional components of the proposal documents
› Create a detailed evaluation matrix for the negotiation procedure, based on the announcement

11.2.2 Organizational preparation
› Draft the invitation to submit offers (compiling documents, drafting a proposal, and finalize the text)
› Coordinate and obtain approval for the invitation
› Send the invitation for offer submission

11.2.3 Questions
› Act as liaison for bidders
› Receive bidder questions, develop response proposals, confirm and send responses

11.2.4 Examination and evaluation
› Conduct technical examination and evaluation of up to 4 offers
› Conduct a preliminary assessment of offers based on formal requirements
› Conduct a preliminary assessment of offers based on price adequacy

11.2.5 Negotiation meeting
› Prepare the negotiation meeting including scheduling and invitations
› Participate in negotiation meetings for up to 2 session days (including recording)
› Request submission of a final binding offer
› Finalize the evaluation of offers after negotiation talks and submission of a final binding offer
› If necessary: moderate, or comoderate, if the sponsor or an external legal expert is moderating

11.2.6 Rejections
› Draft the information letter according to § 134 GWB
› Coordinate and obtain approval for the information letter
› Send the information letter (3 minus 1 bidders)

11.2.7 Communication on award of contract
› Draft the letter for the award
› Coordinate and obtain approval for the letter of award
› Send the letter of award

11.2.8 Publication
› Draft / confirm / send the publication of contract award in the EU Official Journal

11.3 Project handover
› Participate in a meeting with the commissioned designers to hand over documents and information
↑ Optional

Appendix

RECOMMENDED LITERATURE

In addition to a substantial number of publications from professional associations (including the UIA, BDA, RIBA, SIA) detailing the benefits and traits of competitions and recommendations for their organisation, and various guidelines from government institutions and funding banks (including the World Bank, ADB, MCC, BMVBS), we recommend the following books on the subject.

Andersson, Jonas E., Gerd Bloxham Zettersten, and Magnus Rönn (eds)
Architectural Competitions – Histories and Practice.
Stockholm, The Royal Institute of Technology and Rio Kulturkooperativ, 2013.

Becker, Heidede
Geschichte der Architektur- und Städtebauwettbewerbe.
Schriften des Deutschen Instituts für Urbanistik. Stuttgart, Berlin, Cologne, Verlag W. Kohlhammer/Deutscher Gemeindeverlag, 1992.

Becker, Heidede
Stadtbaukultur – Modelle, Workshops, Wettbewerbe – Verfahren der Verständigung über die Gestaltung der Stadt, Vol. 1 & 2
Schriften des Deutschen Instituts für Urbanistik. Stuttgart, Berlin, Cologne, Verlag W. Kohlhammer/Deutscher Gemeindeverlag, 2002.

Bondar, Hanna
Architektur- und Gebietsentwicklungswettbewerbe: Demokratie in Aktion.
Kyiv, ТОВ Art Kniga, 2017 (Бондар Ганна: Архітектурні конкурси та конкурси розвитку територій: демократія в дії, ТОВ Київ Арт Книга, 2017).

Chupin, Jean-Pierre, Carmela Cucuzzella, and Bechera Helal (eds)
Architecture Competitions and the Production of Culture, Quality and Knowledge: an international inquiry.
Montreal, Quebec, Potential architecture books, 2015.

Collyer, Stanley
Competing Globally in Architecture Competitions.
West Sussex, Academy Press, Wiley Academy, Chichester, 2004.

Franke, Ulrich and Karsten Kümmerle
Thema Architektenwettbewerbe, Strategien, Wirtschaftlichkeit, Erfolg.
Basel, Birkhäuser Verlag, 2006.

Müller-Herbers, Sabine
Methoden zur Beurteilung von Varianten.
Universität Stuttgart, Fakultät Architektur und Stadtplanung, Institut für Grundlagen der Planung, 2007.

Stefan, Günther, et al.
Wettbewerbe – Abschluss der Projektentwicklung und Beginn der Planung.
Vienna, TU Graz, Institut für Baubetrieb, Bauwirtschaft, Projektentwicklung und Projektmanagement, 2010.

Weinbrenner, Eberhard, and Rudolf Jochem
Der Architektenwettbewerb.
Wiesbaden and Berlin, Bauverlag, 1988.

Witzling, Laurence, and Jeffrey Ollswang
The Planning and Administration of Design Ccompetitions.
Milwaukee, Wisconsin, Midwest Institute for Design Research, 1986.

IMPRINT

[phase eins].
Benjamin Hossbach, Christian Lehmhaus
Dipl. Ing. Architekten BDA VBI

D – 10555 Berlin
www.phase1.de
office @ phase1.de

Editorial team
Benjamin Hossbach, Elif Demiroglu, and Ronny Kutter

Overall concept and texts
Benjamin Hossbach

Proofreading
Christine Eichelmann and Christian Lehmhaus

Graphic design
Olrik Neubert with Susanne Mocka and Angela Salzburg

Illustrations
Nour Aldeen Alradif, Elif Demiroglu, and Reela Nentwich

Translation
English version: Elif Demiroglu, Xenia Pasternak
Ukrainian version: Olena Tsymbaliuk, Xenia Pasternak
with literary editing by Liudmyla Lobozets and Kateryna Sozanska
and the assistance of the translation company Awatera

Printing
Printing house "From A to Z", Kyiv, Ukraine, https://fromatoz.ua

Illustration
Unless otherwise stated below, all photos, drawings, images and texts shown here are the copyright of [phase eins]. The images of competition designs reproduced in the chapters "Sample Projects I–XII" were kindly provided by the competition sponsors or the authors of the designs. The copyright for the model photos is held by Hans-Joachim Wuthenow, except for p. 32 by PSPC.
Aerial photographs: p. 23: City of Essen, p. 53: Jülich Research Center.
Further illustrations: Max Cramer: p. 163 (bottom), M. Didichenko: p. 7 (4), p. 13 (top), p. 69, p. 131 (2), p. 153 (6, 8), p. 156 (7, 8), p. 159 (2, 5), p. 163 (top and center), Christine Fenzl: p. 9, p. 51 (bottom left), A. Mikhaylov: p. 129 (bottom), Thomas Ott: p. 149 (bottom left), Juryj Sefanyak: p. 7 (3), p. 61 (1), BMW: p. 7 (5), p. 24, p. 57 (6), p. 58 (2), p. 101 (7), p. 102 (1), p. 129 (2), p. 131 (1), Holcim Foundation for Sustainable Construction: p. 105 (1), Maidan Museum: p. 18 (bottom right), Wien Museum: p. 7 (7), p. 101 (3), p. 131 (3),
Sources and copyright holders are named to the best of our knowledge.
If any information is incorrect or missing, please let us know.

Copyright
All publications, including excerpts, require approval from [phase eins]. Excerpts taken from the text must be clearly marked. Before publication, please send an advance copy to [phase eins] for correction or approval.

© Copyright 2024 DOM publishers
www.dom-publishers.com

© Copyright for photos and drawings held by the respective companies, architects and photographers.

This work is protected by copyright law. Any use beyond the limits of copyright law requires written consent from the publisher and is punishable by law. This includes reproductions, translations, microfilming, and storage and processing in electronic systems.

ISBN 978-3-86922-316-2 (English)
ISBN 978-3-86922-240-0 (German)
ISBN 978-3-86922-881-5 (Ukrainian)

This publication is listed in the German National Bibliography by the German Library. For detailed bibliographic information, please visit:
http://dnb.d-nb.de

A DOM publishers